The Life of George Washington

THE LIFE

OF

GEORGE WASHINGTON,

WRITTEN FOR

THE USE OF SCHOOLS,

BY

JOHN MARSHALL,

LATE CHIEF JUSTICE OF THE SUPREME COURT
OF THE UNITED STATES.

NINTH EDITION.

PHILADELPHIA:
JAMES CRISSY, No. 4, MINOR STREET.
THOMAS, COWPERTHWAIT & CO.
....
1839.

STEREOTYPED BY J. FAGAN.......PHILADELPHIA
PRINTED BY J. CRISSY.

(2)

ADVERTISEMENT.

they owe them   Where in the annals of Greece or Rome will they find more true and steadfast patriotism, more courage and fortitude, more devoted and enduring service, amidst perplexities, defeat, disasters and wants of every kind? How full of sublime interest is the final success, which gave liberty, not only to our own country, but imparted an irresistible impulse to her principles and lessons, which is improving the condition of mankind every where! Should an American boy be able promptly to answer who was Julius Cæsar, and to narrate the leading incidents of his life, and be at fault when the same question is asked of George Washington? Shall he talk fluently of Marathon and Philippi, and know nothing of Saratoga and Yorktown? Shall he have a competent knowledge of the old governments and civil institutions, and be shamefully ignorant of his own?

The little volume you have published affords an excellent beginning of these studies, and I think you cannot fail in your design of introducing it into our schools.

When I was a boy, we were taught to connect the name of Washington with every thing that was great and good in the human character, and time has proved, and will long continue to prove, that it was a lesson of truth.

Most respectfully yours,

JOS HOPKINSON.

Letter from Chief Justice Taney.

BALTIMORE, MARCH 29, 1839

SIR—When I received the copy of Marshall's Life of Washington, which you were good enough to send me, I was too ill to write to you, and am not yet sufficiently recovered to resume my business pursuits   But I take the earliest moment in my power to return you my thanks for the volume, and to express the pleasure I feel in seeing the work so handsomely executed, and to find that it has already reached the fourth edition

No American ought to be considered as properly educated, who is not familiar with the Life of Washington—and no one was so worthy of being the writer of that life, as Chief Justice Marshall   The book is, I presume, used in every respectable school, and is well calculated to create the best impressions on the minds of its youthful readers   It is most happily adapted by its distinguished author to the use of schools

With much respect, I am, your obedient servant,

R B. TANEY.

Letter from Horace Binney, Esq.

DEAR SIR—I have read with great satisfaction, "The Life of Washington written for the use of Schools," by the late Chief Justice Marshall.

It is quite remarkable that the Chief Justice, who enjoyed with the keenest relish, the most abstruse investigations of legal and political science, should have given a portion of his busiest days to the preparation of an abridgment, in which he was not required to exercise, to any considerable extent, the powers of his remarkable understanding   The fact must be explained, I think, by his cordial attachment to the men and principles of the Revolution, by his conscientious approval of the measures of General Washington's administration, both as a system of public policy, and as an exposition of the Constitution,—and by his paternal solicitude for the youth of our country, upon whom he desired to impress his own feelings and convictions on all these subjects   The work was designed

ADVERTISEMENT.

by him to attain this end, rather than to add to his reputation; and we may therefore see its motives in his affections, which every one knows to have been of the purest kind.

As a condensed Life of Washington, which is also a history of the Revolutionary War, of the Constitution, and of the past years of the Federal Government, it could not, in my judgment, have been better done. It contains in substance the whole of the original work,—the structure, much of the language, and most of the sentiments and reflections. Such parts only appear to have been retrenched, as were unnecessary for young persons in the course of education; but I have not found that it omits any fact material to the story, or to the exhibition of its immortal subject in all his relations to his country. I may add, that the author has not expressed a sentiment in it, that as a father, I should not wish to be remembered and adopted by my children. I hope it will be universally diffused through our schools.

I remain, very respectfully, your obedient servant,

HOR. BINNEY.

Mr. James Crissy.

Extract of a Letter from the Rev. E. Cheever, of Newark, (N. J.)

I have examined the Life of Washington by Chief Justice Marshall, and do not hesitate to give it the preference, in nearly every particular, to any volume on this subject which I have seen. It will answer the double purpose, in our higher schools, of a reading book, and a text book, on American history. I hope and I am almost sure that its appearance will be hailed as a good omen, and that it will have a rapid and extensive sale.

E. CHEEVER.

Newark, Dec. 3, 1838.

As means have been adopted for supplying the work extensively, orders for any number will be received and promptly attended to, by

JAMES CRISSY,

No. 4, Minor St, Philadelphia.

ADVERTISEMENT.

MARSHALL'S LIFE OF WASHINGTON,

PREPARED FOR SCHOOLS.

The unprecedented demand for this excellent work calling for a seventh edition within six months, is a convincing proof of the interest which the community take in the life and character of their country's father, and the entire adaptation of Marshall's Biography to the purposes for which it was intended.

The publisher deems it proper to state, that this work, though only a duodecimo, is not a mere abridgment by an inferior hand, but was *written entirely* by the late venerable Chief Justice Marshall, for the purpose of a School Book, that the youth of our country might have an early knowledge of Washington, and the great events of our national history with which his name and character are connected. To complete the adaptation of the volume to the uses of a school as a class book, questions have been prepared for each page, which relate to the important facts set forth in the text, and will serve to aid both teacher and pupil. The work has been adopted as a class book in the public schools of Philadelphia, and has also been introduced into many private schools.

It is deemed proper here to append a few of the letters which have been received from distinguished citizens, expressive of their sense of the importance of the work to the young, and especially of the propriety of its introduction into schools.

Letter from Judge Hopkinson.

PHILADELPHIA, FEB. 22, 1839.

SIR—I have read the "Life of Washington," written for the use of Schools, by the late Chief Justice Marshall. The character of the author, as well as the subject of the book, entitles it to the confidence and patronage of the American public. We think it a necessary part of the education of our youth, to make them acquainted with the celebrated men of antiquity, and the great events which affected the destinies of nations. The "Lives of Plutarch" are read by every body, and the young are directed to look there for examples of the virtues they should strive to imitate. Ought we, then, to suffer them to neglect our own history, and to be ignorant of our own great men, and the noble deeds by which they achieved the independence of our country?—Let our children know the struggles, dangers and sufferings by which the prosperity and happiness they enjoy were obtained, that they may estimate their value and the deep debt of gratitude

(1)

ADVERTISEMENT

OF THE PUBLISHER.

THE valuable School Book, now presented to the public, was written by the late JOHN MARSHALL, Chief Justice of the Supreme Court of the United States, not long before his lamented death. It is adapted to the instruction of the rising generation, and contains, in a condensed form, the substance of the author's larger work. Its appearance has been hitherto delayed by circumstances connected with the publication of the revised edition of that great work.

The character of Chief Justice Marshall as a historian for research, truth, and impartiality, is equal, if not superior, to that of any other uninspired writer. As illustrative of that character, the following extract is made from the Honorable Horace Binney's Eulogy:—

"He composed and published, in the year 1804, a copious biography of Washington, surpassing in authenticity and minute accuracy, any public history with which we are acquainted. He found time also to revise it, and to publish a second edition, separating the history of the American Colonies from the biography, *and to prepare, with his own pen, an edition of the latter for the use of schools.* Every part of it is marked with the scrupulous veracity of a judicial exposition; and it shows, moreover, how deeply the writer was imbued with that spirit which will live after all the compositions of men shall be forgotten,— the spirit of charity, which could indite a history of the revolution and of parties, in which he was a conspicuous actor, without discoloring his pages with the slightest infusion of gall. It could not be written with more candor an hundred years hence."

3

ADVERTISEMENT.

The life of WASHINGTON is an indispensable study for American youth, because it forms an integral and most important part of the history of the foundation of our great Republic, and offers to their susceptible minds the most brilliant example of human virtue in the conduct of the founder; whether he be viewed as a statesman, a soldier or a man.

It must be considered, therefore, as a most fortunate circumstance for our country, that so bright an intellect, and so pure a heart, as those of John Marshall, were faithfully devoted to recording the important events of the life of her greatest man; and it is not doubted that she will receive this history as a precious bequest, to be perpetually preserved; and to be studied by her youth to the end of time.

The text has been carefully and faithfully printed from the author's own manuscript: the questions under the line at the bottom of each page, have been added by another hand, to aid the memory of those engaged in studying the history.

CONTENTS.

1*

CHAPTER VII.

CHAPTER VIII.

CHAPTER IX.

CHAPTER X.

CHAPTER XI.

CHAPTER XII.

CHAPTER XIX.

CHAPTER XX.

CHAPTER XXI.

CHAPTER XXII.

CHAPTER XXIII.

CHAPTER XXIV.

CHAPTER XXV.

CHAPTER XXVI

CHAPTER XXVII.

CHAPTER XXVIII.

CHAPTER XXIX.

CHAPTER XXX.

CHAPTER XXXI.

CHAPTER XXXII.

CHAPTER XXXIII.

MARSHALL'S

LIFE OF WASHINGTON.

CHAPTER I.

Birth of George Washington.—His mission to the French General of Ohio.—Is appointed Lieutenant of a Colonial regiment.—Surprises Monsieur Junonville.—Capitulation of fort Necessity.—Appointed Aid-de-camp to General Braddock.—Defeat and death of that General.—Appointed to the command of a Colonial regiment.—Distress of the frontiers.—Expedition against fort Du Quêsne.—Defeat of Major Grant.—Fort Du Quêsne evacuated.—Colonel Washington resigns.—His marriage.

GEORGE WASHINGTON, the third son of Augustine Washington, was born on the 22d of February, 1732, near the banks of the Potomac, in the county of Westmoreland, in Virginia. His father married Miss Butler, who died in 1728; leaving two sons, Lawrence and Augustine. In 1730, he intermarried with Miss Mary Ball, by whom he had four sons, George, John, Samuel, and Charles; and one daughter, Betty, who intermarried with Colonel Fielding Lewis, of Fredericksburg.

His great-grand-father, John Washington, had emigrated from the north of England, about the year 1657, and settled on the place where Mr. Washington was born.

At the age of ten years, he lost his father. An affectionate mother continued to impress those principles of religion and virtue on his tender mind, which constituted the solid basis of a character that was maintained throughout all the trying vicissitudes of an eventful life. But his education was limited to subjects strictly useful, not even extending to foreign languages.

At the age of eighteen, he was appointed a surveyor in the western part of the northern neck of Virginia; and, in that office, acquired such information respecting vacant lands, and formed those opinions concerning their future value, which afterwards contributed greatly to the increase of his fortune.

Those powerful attractions, which the profession of arms presents to young and ardent minds, possessed their full influence

Mention the date and place of Washington's birth. What was his parentage? Relate the course of his early life.

11

over Mr. Washington. Stimulated by the enthusiasm of military genius, to take part in the war in which Great Britain was then engaged, he pressed earnestly to enter into the navy, and, at the age of fifteen, a midshipman's warrant was obtained for him. The interference of a timid and affectionate mother deferred the commencement, and changed the course, of his military career. Four years afterwards, when the militia were to be trained for actual service, he was appointed one of the Adjutants-General of Virginia, with the rank of Major. The duties annexed to this office soon yielded to others of a more interesting character.

France was beginning to develop the vast plan of connecting her extensive dominions in America, by uniting Canada to Louisiana. The troops of that nation had taken possession of a tract of country claimed by Virginia, and had commenced a line of posts, to be extended from the Lakes to the Ohio. The attention of Mr. Dinwiddie, Lieutenant-Governor of that province, was attracted to these supposed encroachments, and he deemed it his duty to demand in the name of the King, his master, that they should be suspended.

This mission was toilsome and hazardous. The Envoy would be under the necessity of passing through an extensive and almost unexplored wilderness, inhabited by fierce savages, who were either hostile to the English or of doubtful attachment. While the dangers and fatigues of this service deterred others from undertaking it, they seem to have possessed attractions for Mr. Washington, and he engaged in it with alacrity.

On receiving his commission, he proceeded to Wills' creek, then the extreme frontier settlement of the English, where guides were engaged to conduct him over the Alleghany mountains. At the mouth of Turtle creek he was informed that the French general was dead, and that the army had retired into winter quarters. Pursuing his route, he examined the country through which he passed, with a military eye, and selected the confluence of the Monongahela and Alleghany rivers, the place where fort Du Quèsne was afterwards erected by the French, as a position which it would be advisable to seize and fortify immediately.

After employing a few days in securing the fidelity of the Indians in that neighborhood, he ascended the Alleghany to a French fort where he was received by the commanding officer on the Ohio, to whom he delivered the letter of Mr. Dinwiddie, and from whom he received an answer with which he returned to Williamsburg. The exertions made by Mr. Washington on this mission, the perseverance with which he surmounted the difficulties he en-

---

What was the commencement of Washington's military career? Mention the designs of France in North America. What mission was deputed to George Washington? How did he execute it?

countered, and the judgment displayed in his conduct toward the Indians, raised him in the public opinion as well as in that of the Lieutenant-Governor. His journal, drawn up for the inspection of Mr. Davidson, was published, and impressed his countrymen with very favorable sentiments of his understanding and fortitude.

As the answer from the commandant of the French forces on the Ohio indicated no disposition to withdraw from that country, it was deemed necessary to make some preparations to maintain the rights asserted over it by the British crown; and the Assembly of Virginia authorized the Executive to raise a regiment for that purpose, to consist of three hundred men. The command of this regiment was given to Mr. Fry, and Major Washington was appointed Lieutenant-Colonel. Anxious to be engaged in active service, he obtained permission, about the beginning of April, to advance with two companies to the Great Meadows, in the Alleghany Mountains. Soon after his arrival at that place, he was informed by some friendly Indians that the French, having dispersed a party of workmen employed by the Ohio Company to erect a fort on the south-eastern branch of the Ohio, were engaged in completing a fortification at the confluence of the Alleghany and Monongahela rivers; a detachment from which place was then on its march towards his camp. Though open hostilities had not yet commenced, the country was considered as invaded; and several circumstances were related, confirming the opinion that this party was approaching with hostile views. Confident of this, Lieutenant-Colonel Washington resolved to anticipate them. Proceeding under the guidance of Indians, through a dark and rainy night, to the French encampment, he completely surrounded it; and, at daybreak, his troops fired and rushed upon the party, which immediately surrendered. One man only escaped capture; and Monsieur Junonville alone, the commanding officer, was killed.

While the regiment was on its march to join the detachment advanced in front, the command devolved on Lieutenant-Colonel Washington by the death of Colonel Fry. Soon after its arrival, it was reinforced by two independent companies of regulars. After erecting a small stockade at the Great Meadows, Colonel Washington commenced his march towards fort Du Quêsne, with the intention of dislodging the French from that place. He had not proceeded more than thirty miles, when he was informed by some friendly Indians, that the French, "as numerous as the pigeons in the wood," were advancing rapidly to meet him. Among those who brought this information was a trusty chief, only two days

What expedition was now raised to oppose the designs of the French, and what station was assigned to Washington? Whither did the troops proceed, and who finally had the chief command?

2

from the post on the Ohio, who had observed the arrival of a considerable reinforcement at that place, and had heard them express the intention of marching immediately to attack the English, with a corps composed of eight hundred French and four hundred Indians.

The ground occupied by Colonel Washington was not adapted to military purposes. A road leading through other defiles in the mountains, would enable the French to pass into his rear, intercept his supplies, and starve him into a surrender, or fight him with a superiority of three to one.

In this hazardous situation, a council of war unanimously advised a retreat to the fort at the Great Meadows, now termed fort Necessity; where the two roads united, and where the face of the country was such as not to permit an enemy to pass him unperceived. At that place he intended to await the arrival of reinforcements.

In pursuance of this advice, Colonel Washington returned to fort Necessity, and began a ditch around the stockade. Before it was completed, the French and Indians, computed at fifteen hundred men, commanded by Monsieur de Villier, appeared before the fort, and commenced a furious attack upon it. They were received with great intrepidity by the Americans, who fought partly within the stockade, and partly in the surrounding ditch, which was nearly filled with mud and water. Colonel Washington continued the whole day on the outside of the fort, encouraging the soldiers by his countenance and example. The assailants fought under cover of the trees and high grass with which the country abounds. The action continued from ten in the morning until dark, when Monsieur de Villier demanded a parley, and offered terms of capitulation. These were rejected, but, in the course of the night, articles were signed, by which the fort was surrendered on condition that the garrison should be allowed the honors of war—should be permitted to retain their arms and baggage, and be suffered to march unmolested into the inhabited parts of Virginia.

The loss of the Americans in this affair is not ascertained. A return made after arriving at Wills' creek, states the killed and wounded of the Virginia regiment at fifty-eight. The loss sustained by the two independent companies was not reported. That of the assailants was supposed to be more considerable.

Great credit was given to Colonel Washington by his countrymen, for the courage displayed in this engagement. The legislature evinced its satisfaction with the conduct of the whole party, by passing a vote of thanks to him and the officers under his com-

What were the disadvantageous circumstances under which Washington was attacked at fort Necessity? What was the result? Did this unfortunate issue impair the confidence reposed in Washington?

mand; and by giving three hundred pistoles to be distributed among the soldiers engaged in the action.

The regiment returned to Winchester to be recruited; soon after which it was joined by a few companies from North Carolina and Maryland. On the arrival of this reinforcement, the Lieutenant-Governor, with the advice of council, unmindful of the condition and number of the troops, ordered them to march immediately over the Alleghany mountains; and to expel the French from fort Du Quêsne, or to build one in its vicinity.

The little army in Virginia, now under the command of Colonel Innes of North Carolina, did not exceed half the number of the enemy, and was neither provided with the means of moving, nor with supplies for a winter campaign. With as little consideration, directions had been given for the immediate completion of the regiment, without furnishing a shilling for the recruiting service—Colonel Washington remonstrated against these orders, but prepared to execute them. The assembly however, having risen without making any provision for the farther prosecution of the war, this wild expedition was abandoned, and the Virginia regiment was reduced to independent companies.

In the course of the winter, orders were received " for settling the rank of his majesty's forces then serving with the provincials in North America." These orders directed " that all officers commissioned by the king, or by his general in North America, should take rank of all officers commissioned by the governors of the respective provinces : and further, that the general and field officers of the provincial troops should have no rank when serving with the general and field officers commissioned by the crown; but that all captains, and other inferior officers of the royal troops, should take rank over provincial officers of the same grade, having senior commissions."—

Still professing his attachment to a military life, Colonel Washington could not submit to hold the station assigned to him, and retired indignantly from a service in which he was degraded by loss of rank.

His eldest brother had lately died and left him Mount Vernon,—a considerable estate on the Potomac. To this delightful spot he withdrew, resolving to devote his future life to private pursuits This resolution was not long maintained.

General Braddock, being informed of his merit, and his knowledge of the country which was to become the theatre of action, gratified his desire to make one campaign under an officer sup-

What was now determined by the Lieutenant-Governor? Why was the plan abandoned? What orders in respect to military rank were received from England? What was the consequence? Did Washington resume his martial pursuits?

posed to possess some knowledge of war, by inviting him to enter his family as a volunteer aid-de-camp.

Having accepted this invitation, he joined the commander-in-chief on his march from Alexandria to Wills' creek. The army was detained at that place until the 12th of June, by the difficulty of procuring wagons, horses, and provisions. Colonel Washington, impatient under these delays, suggested the propriety of using pack-horses instead of wagons: though the commander-in-chief at first rejected this advice, its propriety, soon after the commencement of the march, became too obvious to be longer neglected.

On the third day after the army had moved from Wills' creek, Colonel Washington was seized with a violent fever which disabled him from riding on horseback, and was conveyed in a covered wagon. Being still privately consulted by the commander-in-chief, he urged that officer strenuously to leave his heavy artillery and baggage with the rear division, and with a chosen body of troops, and some pieces of light artillery, to press forward to fort Du Quêsne. In support of this advice, he stated that the French were then weak on the Ohio, but daily expected reinforcements. These could not arrive during the drought existing at that time, because the river Le Bœuf, on which their supplies must be brought to Virginia, was too low for the purpose. A rapid movement might enable him to carry the place before the arrival of the expected aid. But should the army remain united, the delays attending its march were such, that rain sufficient to raise the waters might be expected, and the whole force of the French might be collected for their reception;—a circumstance which would render the success of the expedition doubtful.

This advice according with the temper of the commander-in-chief, it was determined in a council of war that twelve hundred select men, to be commanded by the General in person, should advance with the utmost expedition against fort Du Quêsne. Colonel Dunbar was to remain with the residue of the regular troops and all the heavy baggage.

Colonel Washington was obliged to stop at the Great Crossings of the Yohogany—the physician having declared that his life would be endangered by continuing with the army. He obeyed the positive orders of the General to remain at this place; having first received a promise that means should be used to bring him up with the army before it reached fort Du Quêsne.

The day before the action of the Monongahela, he joined the General in a covered wagon; and, though weak, entered on the duties of his station.

In what capacity did Washington join the army of General Braddock? What was his advice to that commander? What detained Washington at the Great Crossings? When did he join the army again?

In a short time after the action had commenced, Colonel Washington was the only aid remaining alive and unwounded. The whole duty of carrying the orders of the commander-in-chief, in an engagement with marksmen who selected officers, especially those on horseback, devolved on him. Two horses were killed under him, and four balls passed through his coat. To the astonishment of all he escaped unhurt, while every other officer on horseback was killed or wounded. "I expected every moment," says an eye-witness, "to see him fall. His duty and situation exposed him to every danger. Nothing but the superintending care of Providence could have saved him from the fate of all around him."

At length, after an action of nearly three hours, General Braddock, under whom three horses had been killed, received a mortal wound, and his troops fled in great disorder. Every effort to rally them was ineffectual until they had crossed the Monongahela. The General was brought off in a tumbril, by Colonel Washington, Captain Stewart of the guards, and his servant. The defeated detachment retreated to the rear division of the army, where General Braddock expired. The military stores not necessary for immediate use were destroyed, and Colonel Dunbar marched the remaining European troops to Philadelphia.

Colonel Washington, who was much dissatisfied with the conduct of the regular soldiers in this action, bestowed great praise on the provincials. "The Virginia companies," he said in a letter to the Lieutenant-Governor, "fought like men and died like soldiers. Captain Peronny and all his officers, down to a corporal, were killed. Captain Poulson had almost as hard a fate, for only one of his escaped."

Colonel Washington had long been the favorite soldier of Virginia, and his reputation grew with every occasion for exertion. His conduct in this battle had been universally extolled, and the common opinion of his countrymen was, that, had his advice been pursued, the disaster had been avoided.

The Assembly, which was in session when intelligence of this defeat and of the abandonment of the province by Colonel Dunbar was received, immediately determined to raise a regiment for the defence of the colony, the command of which was given to Colonel Washington, who was also designated in his commission as the commander-in-chief of all the forces raised and to be raised in Virginia. The uncommon privilege of naming his field officers was added to this honorable manifestation of public confidence.

After making the necessary arrangements for the recruiting ser-

Give an account of the battle wherein Braddock was defeated. What was the conduct of Washington throughout that affair? What appointment was soon afterwards conferred upon him?

2 *

vice, and visiting the posts on the frontier, he set out for the seat of government; but was overtaken by an express carrying the intelligence that a large number of French and Indians, divided into several parties, had broken up the frontier settlements; were murdering and capturing men, women, and children; burning their houses, and destroying their crops. The troops stationed among them for their protection were unequal to that duty, and instead of affording aid to the inhabitants, were blocked up in their forts.

Colonel Washington hastened back to Winchester, but his efforts to raise the militia were unavailing. Instead of assembling in arms and obtaining safety by meeting their invaders, the inhabitants fled into the lower country, and increased the general terror. He endeavored to collect and arm the men who had abandoned their houses, and to remove their wives and children from this scene of desolation and carnage. Pressing orders were despatched to the newly appointed officers to forward their recruits, and to the county lieutenants east of the Blue Ridge to hasten their militia to Winchester. Before these orders could be executed, the invading enemy had recrossed the Alleghany Mountains.

Early in the following spring another irruption, spreading death and desolation around, was made into the inhabited country. The number of troops on the regular establishment was unequal to the protection of the frontier, and effective service from the militia was found to be unattainable. The people either abandoned the country, or attempted to secure themselves in small stockade forts, where they were in great distress for provisions, arms, and ammunition, were often surrounded, and sometimes cut off. The letters of Colonel Washington at the time show the deep impression made on his mind by this afflicting and irremediable state of things.

The incompetency of the military force to the defence of the country having become obvious, the assembly determined to augment the regiment to fifteen hundred men. Colonel Washington urged the necessity of increasing it still further, and demonstrated the total incompetency of the number proposed to the protection of the extensive frontier of Virginia. His representations did not succeed, and the distress of the country increased. As had been foreseen, Winchester became almost the only settlement west of the Blue Ridge on the northern frontier; and fears were entertained that the enemy would pass even that barrier, and ravage the country below it. Express after express was sent to hasten the militia, but sent in vain. At length, about the last of April, the French and

---

What misfortune assailed the western frontier of Virginia? What increase of defensive means was proposed by Washington? Were the measures of the Assembly adequate to the urgency of the danger?

their savage allies, laden with plunder, prisoners, and scalps, returned to fort Du Quêsne.

Some short time after their retreat, the militia appeared, and were employed in searching the country for small lingering parties of Indians, and in making dispositions to repel another invasion. A fort was commenced at Winchester, which, in honor of the General then commanding the British forces in America, was called fort Loudoun; and the perpetual remonstrances of Colonel Washington at length effected some improvement in the military code.

Successive incursions continued to be made by the French and Indians, who kept up a perpetual alarm, and murdered the defenceless wherever found. In Pennsylvania, the inhabitants were driven as far as Carlisle; and, in Maryland, Fredericktown, on the eastern side of the Blue Ridge, became a frontier. With less than one thousand men, aided occasionally by militia, Colonel Washington was required to defend a frontier nearly four hundred miles in extent, and to complete a chain of forts.

This campaign furnishes no event which can interest the reader; yet the duties of the officer, though minute, were arduous; and the suffering of the people beyond measure afflicting. It adds to the many instances history records of the miseries always to be expected by those who defer preparing the means of defence, until the moment when they ought to be used, and then rely on a force neither adequate to the danger, nor of equal continuance with it.

As soon as the main body of the enemy had withdrawn from the settlements, a tour was made by Colonel Washington to the south-western frontier. There, as in the North, repeated incursions had been made; and there too, the principal defence of the country was entrusted to our ill-regulated militia.

After returning to Winchester, he gave the Lieutenant-Governor, in curious detail, a statement of the situation in which he found the country, urging, but urging in vain, arguments which will always be suggested by experience, against relying chiefly on militia for defence.

Sensible of the impracticability of defending such an extensive frontier, Colonel Washington continued to press the policy of enabling him to act on the offensive. The people of Virginia, he thought, could be protected only by entering the country of the enemy; giving him employment at home, and removing the source of all their calamities by taking possession of fort Du Quêsne.

What was the condition of the frontiers, and with what amount of force was Washington required to defend them from French and Indian ravage? What measure was recommended by him to secure the frontier?

His inability to act offensively was not the only distressing and vexatious circumstance to which he was exposed. The Lieutenant-Governor, who seems to have been unequal to the difficulties of his station, frequently deranged his system by orders which could not be executed, and sometimes could not be well understood. He seems, too, to have occasionally manifested unreasonable dissatisfaction with the conduct of the commander-in-chief.

In the midst of these embarrassments, Lord Loudoun, in whose person the offices of Governor and commander-in-chief were united, arrived in Virginia. A comprehensive statement of the situation of the Colony in a military point of view, and of the regiment in particular, was drawn up and submitted to him by Colonel Washington. In this, he enumerated the errors which had prevented the completion of his regiment, showed the insufficiency of militia for military purposes, and demonstrated the advantages of an offensive system.

This statement was probably presented by Colonel Washington in person, in the winter when permitted to visit Lord Loudoun in Philadelphia, when that nobleman met the Governors of Pennsylvania, Maryland, and North Carolina, and the Lieutenant-Governor of Virginia, in order to consult with them on the measures to be taken in their respective provinces, for the ensuing campaign. He was, however, disappointed in his favorite hope of being able to act offensively against the French on the Ohio. Lord Loudoun had determined to make a grand effort against Canada, and to leave only twelve hundred men in the middle and southern colonies; yet his anxious wishes continued to be directed towards fort Du Quêsne. In a letter written in May to Colonel Stanwix, who commanded in the middle colonies, he observed, "You will excuse me, sir, for saying that I think there never was, and perhaps never again will be, so favorable an opportunity as the present for reducing fort Du Quêsne. Several prisoners have made their escape from the Ohio this spring, and agree in their accounts that there are but three hundred men left in the garrison. Surely then, this is too precious an opportunity to be lost."

But Mr. Pitt did not yet direct the councils of Britain, and a spirit of enterprise and heroism did not yet animate her generals. The campaign to the North was inglorious; and nothing was even attempted towards the West which might relieve the middle colonies.

Large bodies of savages in the service of France once more spread desolation and murder over the whole country west of the Blue Ridge. The regular troops were inadequate to the

What statement was drawn up by Washington, and laid before the assembled Governors and Lord Loudoun? Were the suggestions therein contained complied with? What were the consequences?

defence of the inhabitants, and the incompetence of the defensive system to their security became every day more apparent. He continued to urge on the Lieutenant-Governor, and on the Assembly, in his letters to the Speaker, the necessity of vigorous exertions. Without them he predicted that there would not be found an individual west of the Blue Ridge the ensuing autumn, except the troops in garrison, and a few in Winchester under the protection of the fort.

It was impossible that Colonel Washington, zealous in the service of his country, and ambitious of military fame, could observe the errors committed in the conduct of the war without censuring them. These errors were extended to Indian affairs. The Cherokees and Catawbas had hitherto remained faithful to the English, and it was very desirable to engage the warriors 1757. of those tribes heartily in their service; but so badly was the intercourse with them conducted, that, though considerable expense was incurred, not much aid was obtained, and great disgust was excited among them. The freedom with which his censures were uttered gave offence to the Lieutenant-Governor, who considered them as manifesting a want of respect for himself. Sometimes he coarsely termed them *impertinent ;* at others, charged him with looseness in his information, and inattention to his duty. On one of these occasions, Colonel Washington thus concluded a letter of detail : " I must beg leave before I conclude, to observe in justification of my own conduct, that it is with Aug. 27. pleasure I receive reproof when reproof is due, because no person can be readier to accuse me than I am to acknowledge an error when I have committed it, nor more desirous of atoning for a crime when I am sensible of being guilty of one. But on the other hand, it is with concern I remark that my best endeavors lose their reward; and that my conduct, although I have uniformly studied to make it as unexceptionable as I could, does not appear to you in a favorable point of light ; otherwise your honor would not have accused me of *loose* behavior, and *remissness* of duty, in matters where I think I have rather exceeded than fell short of it. This I think is evidently the case in speaking of Indian affairs at all, after being instructed in express terms not to have any concern with or management of Indian affairs."

Not long after this he received a letter informing him of some coarse calumny, reflecting on his veracity and honor, which had been reported to the Lieutenant-Governor. He inclosed a copy of this letter to Mr. Dinwiddie, and thus addressed him : " I should take it infinitely kind if your honor would please to inform me

In regard to the errors respecting the defence of the country, did Washington express his opinion freely ? Whose ill-will did he draw upon himself by his frankness on this subject ?

whether a report of this kind was ever made to you; and, in that case, who was the author of it.

"It is evident from a variety of circumstances, and especially from the change in your honor's conduct towards me, that some person as well inclined to detract, but better skilled in the art of detraction than the author of the above stupid scandal, has made free with my character!

"If it be possible that * * * *, for my belief is staggered, no being conscious of having given the least cause to any one, much less to that gentleman, to reflect so grossly; I say if it be possible that * * * * could descend so low as to be the propagator of this story, he must either be vastly ignorant of the state of affairs in this country *at that time*, or else he must suppose that the whole body of the inhabitants had combined with me in executing the deceitful fraud.

"It is uncertain in what light my services may have appeared to your honour; but this I know, and it is the highest consolation I am capable of feeling, that no man that ever was employed in a public capacity, has endeavored to discharge the trust in him with greater honesty, and more zeal for the country's interest than I have done."

In a letter some short time after this to the Lieutenant-Governor, he said, "I do not know that I ever gave your honor cause to suspect me of ingratitude; a crime I detest, and would most carefully avoid. If an open disinterested behavior carries offence, I may have offended, for I have all along laid it down as a maxim to represent facts freely and impartially, but not more so to others than to you, sir. If instances of my ungrateful behavior had been particularized, I would have answered them. But I have been long convinced that my actions and their motives have been maliciously aggravated."

Mr. Dinwiddie soon afterwards took leave of Virginia, and the government devolved on Mr. Blair, the president of the council. Between him and the commander of the colonial troops the utmost cordiality existed.

After the close of the campaign of 1757, Loudoun returned to England, and General Abercrombie succeeded to the command of the army. The department of the middle and southern provinces was committed to General Forbes, who, to the inexpressible gratification of Colonel Washington, determined to undertake an expedition against fort Du Quêsne.

1758.   He urged an early campaign, but he urged it ineffectually; and before the troops were assembled, a large body of

State the substance of a letter from Washington to Mr. Dinwiddie. Who succeeded this latter gentleman as Governor of Virginia? What two officers had now the chief military commands?

French and Indians broke into the country, and renewed the horrors of the tomahawk and scalping-knife. The attempts made to intercept these savages were unsuccessful; and they recrossed the Alleghany with their plunder, prisoners, and scalps.

Among other motives for an early campaign, Colonel Washington had urged the impracticability of retaining the Indians. His fears were well founded. Before a junction of the troops had been made, these savages became impatient, and finding that the expedition would yet be delayed a considerable time, they left the army, promising to rejoin it at the proper season.

In pursuance of orders, the Virginia troops moved in detachments from Winchester to fort Cumberland, where they assembled early in July; after which they were employed in opening a road to Raystown, where Colonel Bouquet was stationed.

Colonel Washington had expected that the army would march by Braddock's road; but, late in July, he had the mortification to receive a letter from Colonel Bouquet, asking an interview, in order to consult on opening a new road from Raystown, and requesting his opinion on that route. "I shall," says he, in answer to this letter, "most cheerfully work on any road, pursue any route, or enter upon any service, that the General or yourself may think me usefully employed in or qualified for; and shall never have a will of my own when a duty is required of me. But since you desire me to speak my sentiments freely, permit me to observe that, after having conversed with all the guides, and having been informed by others acquainted with the country, I am convinced that a road to be compared with General Braddock's, or indeed that will be fit for transportation even by pack-horses, can not be made."

A few days after writing this letter he had an interview with Colonel Bouquet, whom he found decided in favour of opening the new road. After their separation, Colonel Washington addressed to him a letter to be laid before General Forbes, in which he stated his reasons against this measure. He concluded his arguments against it (arguments which appear to be conclusive) by declaring his fears that, should the attempt be made, nothing more could be done than to fortify some post west of the Alleghany, and prepare for another campaign. This he prayed heaven to avert.

In a letter to Major Halket, aid-de-camp to General Forbes, he thus expressed his forebodings of the mischiefs to be apprehended from the adoption of the new route. "I am just returned from a conference held with Colonel Bouquet. I find him fixed—I think I may say unalterably fixed—to lead you a new way to the Ohio

For what important expedition were the Virginia troops now assembled? What new project interfered with the early opening of the campaign? What was Washington's opinion respecting it?

through a road, every inch of which is to be cut at this advanced
season, when we have scarcely time left to tread the beaten track,
universally confessed to be the best passage through the mountains.

"If Colonel Bouquet succeeds in this point with the General,
all is lost! all is lost indeed! our enterprise is ruined; and we
shall be stopped at the Laurel Hill this winter; but not to gather
laurels, except of the kind which cover the mountains. The
southern Indians will turn against us, and these colonies will be
desolated by such an accession to the enemy's strength. These
must be the consequences of a miscarriage; and a miscarriage
the almost necessary consequence of an attempt to march the
army by this route."

Colonel Washington's remonstrances and arguments were unavailing; and the new route was adopted. His extreme chagrin
at this measure, and at the delays resulting from it, was expressed
in anxious letters to Mr. Fauquier, then governor of Virginia, and
to the Speaker of the House of Burgesses.

Sept. 21. He was soon afterwards ordered to Raystown. Major
Grant had been previously detached from the advanced
post at Loyal Hanna, with a select corps of eight hundred men, to
reconnoitre the country about fort Du Quêsne. The morning after
his arrival in the vicinity of the fort, he detached Major Lewis of
Colonel Washington's regiment, with a baggage-guard, two miles
in his rear; and sent an engineer with a covering party, in full
view of the fort, to take a plan of the works. An action soon
commenced, on which Major Lewis, leaving Captain Bullett with
about fifty Virginians to guard the baggage, advanced with the
utmost celerity to support Major Grant. The English were defeated with considerable loss; and both Major Grant and Major
Lewis were taken prisoners. In this action the Virginians manifested the spirit with which they had been trained. Of eight officers, five were killed, a sixth wounded, and seventh taken prisoner.
Captain Bullett, who defended the baggage with great resolution,
and contributed to save the remnant of the detachment, was the
only officer who escaped unhurt. Of one hundred and sixty-two
men, sixty-two were killed on the spot, and forty-two wounded.

Oct. 11. It was at length determined that the army should move
from Raystown, and the colonels of regiments were required to submit severally to the consideration of the General, a
plan for his march. That proposed by Colonel Washington has
been preserved, and appears to have been judiciously formed.

They reached the camp at Loyal Hanna, through a road inde-
scribably bad, about the fifth of November. At this place, as had

---

Relate the incidents connected with the defeat of Major Grant. When
was the army directed to take up its march, and at what time did it reach
Loyal Hanna?

been predicted, a council of war determined that it was unadvisable to proceed farther this campaign. It would have been almost impossible to winter an army in that position. They must have retreated from the cold inhospitable wilderness into which they had penetrated, or have suffered immensely, perhaps have perished. Fortunately, some prisoners were taken who informed them of the extreme distress of the fort. Receiving no support from Canada, the garrison was weak, in great want of provisions, and deserted by the Indians. This encouraging intelligence changed the resolution which had been taken, and determined the General to prosecute the expedition.

Colonel Washington was advanced in front, and, with immense labor, opened a way for the main body of the army. The troops moved forward with slow and painful steps until they reached fort Du Quêsne, of which they took possession on the 25th of November; the garrison having on the preceding night, after evacuating and setting it on fire, proceeded down the Ohio in boats.

To other causes than the vigor of the officer who conducted the enterprise, is the capture of this important place to be ascribed. The naval armaments of Great Britain had intercepted the reinforcements designed by France for her colonies; and the pressure on Canada had disabled the Governor of that province from detaching troops to fort Du Quêsne. Without the aid of these causes, the extraordinary and unaccountable delays of the campaign must have defeated its object.

The works were repaired, and the new fort received the name of the great minister who, with unparalleled vigor and talents, then governed the British nation.

After furnishing two hundred men from his regiment as a garrison for fort Pitt, Colonel Washington marched back to Winchester, whence he proceeded to Williamsburg to take his seat in the General Assembly, of which he had been elected a member by the county of Frederick, while at fort Cumberland.

A cessation of Indian hostility being the consequence of the removal of the French from the Ohio, Virginia was relieved from immediate danger; and the object for which alone he had continued in service, after finding that he could not be placed on the permanent establishment, was accomplished. His health was much impaired, and his private affairs required his attention. Impelled by these and other motives of a private nature, he determined to withdraw from a service which he might now quit without dishonor; and, about the close of the year, resigned his commission as colonel of the first Virginia regiment, and commander-in-chief of all the troops raised in the colony.

To what causes may we attribute the easy capture of fort Du Quêsne? Why did Washington wish to retire from the army?

The officers whom he had commanded were strongly attached to him, and manifested their regret at parting with him, by an affectionate address, expressing the high opinion they entertained both of his military and private character.

This opinion was not confined to the officers of his regiment. It was common to Virginia; and had been adopted by the British officers with whom he served. The duties he performed, though not splendid, were arduous; and were executed with zeal and with judgment. The exact discipline he established in his regiment, when the temper of Virginia was hostile to discipline, does credit to his military character; and the gallantry the troops displayed when they were called into action, manifests the spirit infused into them by their commander.

The difficulties of his situation while unable to cover the frontier from the French and Indians, who were spreading death and desolation in every quarter, were incalculably great; and no better evidence of his exertions under these distressing circumstances can be given, than the undiminished confidence still placed in him by those he was unable to protect.

The efforts to which he incessantly stimulated his country for the purpose of obtaining possession of the Ohio; the wise system for the conduct of the war which he continually recommended; the vigorous and active measures always urged upon those by whom he was commanded; manifest an ardent and enterprising mind, tempered by judgment, and quickly improved by experience.

Not long after his resignation he was married to Mrs. Custis, a young lady to whom he had been for some time attached; and who, to a large fortune, and fine person, added those amiable accomplishments which ensure domestic happiness, and fill with silent but unceasing felicity the quiet scenes of private life.

CHAPTER II.

Colonel Washington appointed commander-in-chief of the American forces.—Arrives at Cambridge.—Strength and disposition of the army,—Deficiency in arms and ammunition.—Falmouth burnt.—Measures to form a continental army.—Difficulty of re-enlisting the troops.—General Lee detached to New York.—Possession taken of the heights of Dorchester.—Boston evacuated.—Correspondence respecting prisoners

COLONEL WASHINGTON took a decided part against the claims of supremacy asserted by the British parliament; and was elected a member of the first congress. He was soon distinguished as the soldier of America, and placed on all those committees whose duty it was to make arrangements for defence. When it became

---

What character had Washington acquired by his military services? Whom did he marry? What part did he take in the approaching difficulties with the mother country?

necessary to appoint a commander-in-chief, his military character, the solidity of his judgment, the steady firmness of his temper, the dignity of his person and deportment, the confidence inspired by his patriotism and industry, and the independence of his fortune, combined to designate him in the opinion of all for that important station. Local jealousy was suppressed by the enthusiasm of the moment, and, on the 14th of June, 1775, he was unanimously chosen "general and commander-in-chief of the armies of the united colonies, and all the forces now raised or to be raised by them."

On the succeeding day, when this appointment was communicated to him, he modestly expressed his high sense of the honor conferred upon him, and his firm determination to exert every power he possessed in the service of his country and of her "glorious cause." Declining all compensation for his services, he avowed an intention to keep an exact account of his expenses, which he should rely on Congress to discharge.

He hastened to the American army, which was encamped around Boston, in which place the British troops commanded by General Gage were besieged. It consisted of fourteen thousand five hundred men, but several circumstances combined to render it less effective than its numbers would indicate.

In the hope of avoiding open hostilities, the time for preparing to meet them had passed away unemployed, and this neglect could not be remedied. In the essential article of ammunition, it was discovered, soon after the arrival of the General in camp, that the magazines would furnish only nine cartridges for each man. Powder was to be obtained, not from officers under the control of Congress, but from committees and other local powers, who had collected small parcels for local defence. Arms, too, were deficient in number, and inferior in quality. The troops were almost destitute of clothing, and without tents. A siege was to be carried on without engineers, and almost without intrenching tools. In addition to these defects, many were discontented with the general officers appointed by Congress : and the mode of appointing regimental officers, in some of the colonies, where they were elected by the soldiers, was extremely unfavorable to discipline. Yet, under all these disadvantages, the General observed with pleasure, "the materials of a good army." There were "a great number of men, able-bodied, active, zealous in the cause, and of unquestionable courage." Possessed of these materials, he employed himself indefatigably in their organization.

The commander-in-chief felt the full importance of destroying

What high appointment was conferred upon Washington by the American Congress? What were the force and condition of the army besieging Boston?

the army in Boston, before it should be reinforced in the spring. The result of his assiduous inquiries into the situation of the enemy, seems to have been a strong inclination to the opinion that, to carry their works by storm, though hazardous, was not impracticable; but, a council of general officers being unanimous against making the attempt, it was abandoned.

To relieve the wants of his army, produced by the rigorous blockade of Boston, the British general frequently detached small parties by water, in quest of fresh provisions. The task of repelling their incursions became so burdensome to the inhabitants of the sea-coast, that the several governors pressed for detachments from the main army, for their protection; and the manifest danger of granting the request did not appease the irritation excited by refusal. Congress was at length induced to pass a resolution, declaring that the army before Boston was designed solely to oppose the enemy in that place, and ought not to be weakened by detachments. At Newport, in Rhode Island, the committee sought security by entering into a stipulation with the officer commanding the ships of war on that station, to furnish the requisite supplies on condition of his sparing the place. General Washington thought it necessary to remonstrate against this dangerous measure.

While the blockade of Boston was thus perseveringly maintained, other events of considerable importance occurred elsewhere.

In July, Georgia joined her sister colonies, and chose delegates to represent her in Congress; after which, the style of "the thirteen United Colonies" was assumed.

After a recess of one month, Congress reassembled at Philadelphia.

Sept. 6.   The scarcity of arms and ammunition, and the importance of a maritime force, engaged their immediate attention. It was more forcibly attracted to the latter object, by an event which, at the time, excited no ordinary degree of resentment.

Orders had been issued to the commanders of the British ships of war to proceed against those seaport towns in which any troops should be raised, or military works erected, as in the case of actual rebellion. Under color of these orders, a small naval force, commanded by Captain Mowat, was detached against Falmouth, a flourishing village on the coast of Massachusetts. After reducing the town to ashes, an attempt was made to penetrate into the country; but the militia and minute-men soon drove the party

---

What annoyance was felt by the inhabitants of the sea-coast near Boston? What state now joined the confederacy? What steps were taken for securing a naval force?

back to their ships. This measure was immediately followed by a resolution of the Convention of Massachusetts for issuing letters of marque and reprisal; and by an addition of some ships of war, on the part of Congress, to the existing naval force.

The re-enlistment of the army, next to the supply of arms and ammunition, was the subject most deeply interesting to the American government.

On the 29th of September, at the earnest solicitation of General Washington, a committee had been appointed by Congress with directions to repair to the camp at Cambridge, there to consult with the commander-in-chief and the governments of New England, "on the most effectual method of continuing, supporting, and regulating a continental army." On the return of this committee, Congress determined that the new army should consist of twenty thousand three hundred and seventy-two men, including officers. Unfortunately, an essential error was committed in constituting this first military establishment of the Union, the consequences of which ceased only with the war. The soldiers were enlisted for the term of one year, if not sooner discharged by Congress. This fatal error brought the American cause more than once into real hazard.

Other resolutions accompanied that for raising the new army, which exhibit the perilous condition of the country. The arms of those who refused to re-enlist, though private property, were detained at a valuation; two dollars were offered to every recruit who would supply himself with a blanket; cloths for the privates, (the price to be deducted from their pay,) were purchased without regard to color; and they were required to furnish their own arms, or to pay for the use of those which might be supplied by government.

That enthusiastic ardor which had brought such numbers into the field after the battle of Lexington, was already beginning to dissipate; and though the orders of the day contain the most animating exhortations to the army, and the strongest appeals to its patriotism, an ominous hesitation in forming new engagements was displayed.

At length, with much labor, the officers were arranged, and recruiting orders were issued; but the sufferings of the army had been so great, that this service advanced slowly.

General Washington had earnestly urged Congress to offer a bounty; but this expedient was not adopted till late in January; and, on the last day of December, when the old army was dis-

---

What number was fixed upon as the complement of the American army? What regulations were adopted for its continuance and efficiency? Were the troops generally willing to re-enlist?

3 *

banded, only nine thousand six hundred and fifty men had been enlisted for the army of 1776.

The General viewed with deep mortification the inactivity to which he was compelled to submit. His real difficulties were not generally known; his numbers were exaggerated; his means of acting on the offensive were magnified; the expulsion of the British army from Boston had been long since anticipated by many; and those were not wanting who insinuated that the commander-in-chief was desirous of prolonging the war, in order to continue his own importance.

Congress having manifested dispositions favorable to an attack on Boston, the general officers had been again assembled, and had again advised unanimously against the measure. Supposing that fear for the safety of the town might restrain the assault, Congress resolved, "that if General Washington and his council of war should be of opinion that a successful attack might be made on the troops in Boston, he should make it in any manner he might think expedient, notwithstanding the town and property in it might be thereby destroyed."

1776. Considering this resolution as indicating the desire of Congress, the General continued to direct his utmost efforts to that object. In January, a council of war, at which Mr. John Adams, a member of Congress, and Mr. Warren, President of the Provincial Congress of Massachusetts, assisted, resolved, " that a vigorous attempt ought to be made on the ministerial troops in Boston, before they can be reinforced in the spring, if the means can be provided and a favorable opportunity should offer;" and for this purpose that thirteen regiments of militia should be required from Massachusetts and the neighboring colonies.

The colonies complied with this requisition; but such was the mildness of the early part of the winter that the waters continued open, and of course impassable.

Early in January, the commander-in-chief received intelligence that an armament was equipping in Boston, to sail under General Clinton on a secret expedition. Believing its object to be New York, he detached General Lee with orders to raise a body of volunteers in Connecticut, and proceed with them to that city, where he was to take command of the American troops, and was instructed to put the fortifications in the best state of defence, to disarm the justly suspected, and to collect their arms and ammunition for the use of the American army.

The volunteers were raised, and Lee commenced his march to New York at the head of twelve hundred men. The inhabitants

What was determined upon, with reference to attacking the British in Boston? And what frustrated the contemplated movement? Who proceeded to New York to defend that city against the enemy?

of that place were alarmed at his approach. Captain Parker, of the Asia man-of-war, had threatened to destroy the city, should the provincials enter it. A committee of safety, exercising at the time the powers of government, addressed a letter to General Lee expressing astonishment at the report that he designed to enter their city without consulting them, and urging him not to pass the confines of Connecticut.

Lee continued his march, and represented so strongly the impolicy of leaving the military arrangements for New York under the control of the local government, that Congress appointed three of its own members to consult with him and the committee of safety concerning the defence of the place.

General Clinton arrived almost at the same instant with General Lee, but without troops. He said openly, that none were coming, that no hostilities were contemplated against New York; and that he was proceeding to North Carolina, where he expected to be joined by five regiments from Europe.

Late in February, appearances among the British troops indicated an intention to evacuate Boston. But as these appearances might be deceptive, General Washington, who had lately received a small supply of powder, determined to prosecute a plan which must force General Howe either to come to an action or to abandon the town.

Since the allowance of a bounty, recruiting had been more successful, and the regular force had been augmented to fourteen thousand men. The commander-in-chief had also called to his aid six thousand militia. Thus reinforced, he determined to take possession of the heights of Dorchester and fortify them. As the possession of this post would enable him to annoy the ships in the harbor and the soldiers in the town, he was persuaded that a general action would ensue. Should this hope be disappointed, his purpose was to make the works on the heights of Dorchester preparatory to seizing and fortifying Nook's hill, and the points opposite the south end of Boston which commanded the harbor, a great part of the town, and the beach from which an embarkation must take place in the event of a retreat.

To facilitate the execution of this plan, a heavy bombardment and cannonade were commenced on the British lines on the 2d of March, which were repeated on the succeeding nights. On the last of them a strong detachment under the command of General Thomas took possession of the heights, and labored with such

What arrangement was made, in relation to measures for the defence of New York city? What inducement facilitated the increase of the American army? What was now the effective force? What measure of annoyance to the British in Boston, was now contemplated by the commander in chief?

persevering activity through the night, that the works were suffi
ciently advanced by the morning nearly to cover them.

It was necessary to dislodge the Americans or to evacuate the
town, and General Howe determined to embrace the former part
of the alternative.   Three thousand chosen men commanded by
Lord Percy, embarked, and fell down to the Castle, in order to proceed up the river to the intended scene of action, but were scattered by a furious storm. Before they could be again in readiness
for the attack, the works were made so strong that the attempt to
storm them was thought unadvisable, and the evacuation of the
town became inevitable.

This determination was soon known to the Americans. A paper
signed by some of the select-men, and brought out by a flag, communicated the fact.   This paper was accompanied by propositions
said to be made by General Howe, relative to the security of the
town, and the peaceable embarkation of his army.

The advances of the American troops were discontinued, and
considerable detachments were moved towards New York before
the actual evacuation of Boston.   That event took place on the
17th of March; and, in a few days, the whole fleet sailed out of
Nantasket road, directing its course eastward; immediately after
which the American army proceeded by divisions to New York,
where it arrived on the 14th of April.

During the siege of Boston an altercation concerning prisoners
took place between the commanders of the respective armies,
which was viewed with great interest throughout America. The
irritations General Gage had received as governor of Massachusetts, seemed to influence his conduct as commander-in-chief. He
regarded the Americans as rebels, and viewed the great national
resistance they were making, as the act of a few turbulent individuals who would soon be quelled.   In this spirit he threw some
distinguished gentlemen of Boston, and the American officers and
soldiers who fell into his hands, into the common jail of felons,
and treated them, not as prisoners, but as state criminals.

General Washington remonstrated very seriously against this
unjustifiable measure, and declared his determination " to be regulated entirely towards the prisoners who should fall into his hands,
by the treatment which those in the power of the British General
should receive."   To this letter a haughty answer was returned,
retorting the complaints concerning the treatment of prisoners,
and affecting to consider it as an instance of clemency, that the
cord was not applied to those whose imprisonment was complained

What prevented the intended attack of the British upon Dorchester Heights?
What important movement of the British now took place?   What altercation occurred respecting prisoners of war?

of. To this answer, General Washington made a dignified reply, which was, he said, " to close their correspondence, perhaps forever;" and which concluded with saying, "if your officers, our prisoners, receive from me a treatment different from what I wished to show them, they and you will remember the occasion of it."

On the recall of General Gage, the command devolved on General Howe; and this rigorous treatment of prisoners was relaxed.

Not long after this correspondence, Colonel Ethan Allen wa captured in a rash attempt on Montreal. Under the pretext of his having acted without authority, he was put in irons and sent to England as a traitor. While he was in Canada, the commander-in-chief, at the request of Congress, addressed a letter to Sir William Howe, assuring him that General Prescot, who had been taken in Canada, and was understood to have contributed to the severities inflicted on Colonel Allen, should receive exactly the fate of that officer.

General Howe not holding any authority in Canada, declined entering into the subject, and Congress ordered General Prescot into close jail.

CHAPTER III.

Invasion of Canada.—Carlton defeated.—St. Johns taken.—Montreal capitulates.—Expedition of Arnold.—He arrives before Quebec.—Retires to Point aux Tremble.—Montgomery lays siege to Quebec.—Unsuccessful assault on that place.—Death of Montgomery.—Blockade of Quebec.—General Thomas takes command of the army.—The blockade raised.—General Sullivan takes the command.—Battle of the Three Rivers.—Canada evacuated.—General Carlton enters Lake Champlain.—Defeats the American Flotilla.—Takes possession of Crown Point.—Retires into winter quarters.

DURING these transactions, events of great interest were passing still farther north.

The discontents which prevailed in Canada, and the removal of the troops destined for its defence, to Boston, inspired Congress with the daring design of taking possession of that province.

In June 1775, General Schuyler had been directed to repair to Ticonderoga, to secure the command of the lakes, to take possession of St. Johns and Montreal, if that measure should not be disagreeable to the Canadians, and to pursue such other steps as might conduce to the peace and security of the United Colonies.

Near three thousand men from New England and New York were designed for this service, and general Schuyler hastened to Ticonderoga.

What important undertaking now engaged the attention of Congress? What instructions were given to General Schuyler, in relation to the attempt upon Canada? What was the force destined for the expedition?

Before the preparations were complete, or the soldiers assembled, the impatience expressed by the discontented in Canada, having rendered an immediate movement advisable, the troops then in readiness were ordered to the isle Aux Noix, at the junction of the Sorel with Lake Champlain, and the expected reinforcements were directed to meet at that place. General Schuyler having become dangerously sick, the command devolved on Montgomery who, late in September, at the head of near two thousand men laid siege to St. Johns.

Colonel M'Clean, with his regiment of royal Highland Emigrants and a few hundred Canadians, was posted near the junction of the Sorel with the St. Lawrence; and General Carlton had collected about a thousand men, chiefly Canadians, at Montreal. In attempting to effect a junction with M'Clean, he was encountered and entirely defeated at Longue isle, by a body of Americans under Colonel Warner. M'Clean, being immediately abandoned by his Canadians, and hearing that Arnold was approaching Point Levy, retreated to Quebec. On receiving this intelligence, St. Johns capitulated.

This first success was nearly rendered useless by the expiration of the terms for which the soldiers were engaged. Before the General could induce them to march against Montreal, he was under the necessity of stipulating that all who wished it should be discharged at that place. Having effected this compromise, he proceeded against Montreal, while his floating batteries under Colonel Easton advanced up the river. After stipulating for the rights of self-government, the town was surrendered; and Governor Carlton took refuge on board his flotilla. While preparations were making to attack the vessels, the Governor escaped in a dark night, in a boat with muffled oars, down the river to Quebec.

After garrisoning Montreal and the adjacent ports, Montgomery found the army which could follow him to Quebec, reduced to about three hundred men.

Foreseeing that the whole force of Canada would be concentrated about Montreal, General Washington had, in August, planned an expedition against Quebec, to be carried on by a detachment from his camp before Boston, which was to march by the way of Kennebec river; and passing through the then dreary wilderness lying between the settled parts of Maine and the St. Lawrence, to enter Canada about ninety miles below Montreal.

This arduous enterprise was entrusted to Colonel Arnold, and rather more than a thousand men were selected for the service.

Relate the incidents of partial success which distinguished the American invasion of Canada. What diversion did Washington contemplate, to prevent the concentration of the entire British force at Montreal?

He commenced his march about the middle of September, and after encountering almost incredible hardships, arrived with two divisions of his army, on the 3d of November, at the first settlements on the Chaudiere, which empties itself into the St. Lawrence. The rear division had been compelled by the prospect of perishing with famine, to return from the Dead River, a branch of the Kennebec.

After allowing a short respite to collect the rear and to refresh the men, Arnold resumed his line of march, and, on the 9th of November, reached Point Levi, opposite Quebec. A high wind and the want of boats rendered it impossible to cross the river, and to take advantage of the consternation excited by his first appearance. While he was thus detained on the south side of the river, Colonel M'Clean entered the city and took measures for its defence.

At length the wind moderated, and Arnold, having collected some canoes, determined to attempt passing the river. Eluding the armed vessels which guarded the passage, and conquering a rapid current, he crossed over, the night of the 14th of November, and landed a short distance above the place which is rendered memorable by the disembarkation of Wolfe. After ascending the same precipice, he, too, formed his small corps on the heights near the plains of Abraham.

Counting on surprising the place, and finding the gates open, he proposed in a council of his officers to march immediately against Quebec, but was overruled. The next day he demanded a surrender of the town, but Colonel M'Clean prevented a measure which the fears of the inhabitants would probably have induced. Being without cannon, almost destitute of ammunition, and not superior to the garrison in numbers, he determined to retire to Point aux Tremble, about twenty miles above Quebec, there to await the arrival of Montgomery.

That General, after clothing his almost naked troops, proceeded with his usual expedition at the head of about three hundred men to Point aux Tremble, whence their united forces marched against Quebec. But Governor Carlton had entered the town and was preparing for a vigorous defence. The garrison amounted to fifteen hundred men, of whom eight hundred were militia. Montgomery's effective force was stated by himself at eight hundred. Yet he determined to lay siege to the town.

His artillery was too light to make any impression on the walls, the weather was intensely cold, and a part of his army would

What were the difficulties that attended the progress of General Arnold? What was his determination, and that of General Montgomery, with reference to an assault upon Quebec?

soon be entitled to a discharge. Under these circumstances he resolved to risk an assault.

Of such materials was his little army composed, that it was necessary not only to consult the officers but the soldiers. Their approbation was obtained with some difficulty, and between four and five in the morning of the 30th of December, the several divisions moved to the assault under a violent storm of snow.

Montgomery advanced at the head of the New York troops round Cape Diamond, along the St. Lawrence to the first basin. A single piece was discharged, by which the General, with Captains M'Pherson and Cheeseman, the first of whom was his aid, together with his orderly sergeant and a private, were killed upon the spot. The whole division retreated, and left the garrison at leisure to direct its individual force against Arnold.

This officer marched at the head of his division along the St. Charles, to the first barrier on that side of the town, when he received a musket-ball in the leg which shattered the bone, and he was carried off the field. Morgan rushed forward to the battery at the head of his company, and received from one of the pieces, almost at its mouth, a discharge of grape-shot, which killed only one man. The barricade was instantly mounted, on which the battery was deserted. Morgan formed his company in the streets, but, being entirely ignorant of the town, thought it unadvisable to proceed farther until daylight should enable him to distinguish objects. He was soon joined by Colonel Greene, and Majors Bigelow and Meigs, with several fragments of companies amounting to about two hundred men. They advanced to the second barrier, where an obstinate conflict was maintained for some time. Being unable to gain it, Morgan proposed to cut their way back to the American camp. Uncertainty respecting the fate of the division led by Montgomery prevented the attempt. The number of the enemy soon increased so considerably that retreat became impossible, and the surviving Americans were made prisoners.

In this bold attack on Quebec, the loss on the part of the garrison was inconsiderable. That of the Americans was about four hundred men, three hundred and forty of whom were prisoners. It fell chiefly on Arnold's division. Captain Hendricks of Pennsylvania, Lieutenant Humphries of Virginia, and Lieutenant Cooper of Connecticut, were among the slain. Captains Lamb and Hubbard, and Lieutenants Steele and Tisdale, were among the wounded. But the loss most deplored, and most fatal to the hopes of the American army, was that of their gallant general.

Relate the circumstances of the unfortunate attack upon Quebec. What was the loss of the Americans? What distinguished commander perished in the assault?

Richard Montgomery was a native of Ireland, and had served with reputation in the late war. After its termination he settled in New York, and took a decided part with the colonies in their contest with Great Britain. His military reputation was high throughout America; and his achievements, while commanding in Canada, show the bold, skilful, and active partizan; and, so far as a judgment can be formed of the capacity for conducting a large army from the judicious management of a small one, we cannot hesitate to allow him the talents of an able general.

Congress directed a monument, expressing the circumstances of his death, and the gratitude of his country, to be erected to his memory.

The Americans retired about three miles from Quebec, where they maintained the blockade. Arnold, on whom the command devolved, though severely wounded, and though his army, which never exceeded seven hundred men, was at one time reduced by the discharge of those whose terms of service had expired, to five hundred effectives, showed no disposition to sink under adverse fortune.

While the affairs of the colonies wore this gloomy aspect in Canada, Congress was indulging sanguine hopes of annexing that province to the Union. Nine regiments were ordered to be raised for its defence, and General Thomas, an officer of reputation, was directed to take the command. The intelligence of the disaster of the 31st of December did not arrest these measures, or change these hopes. In aid of their military operations, three commissioners were deputed to Canada, with instructions to establish a free press, and to propagate the opinions which prevailed through the United Colonies.

In March, reinforcements arrived, so as to increase the army to seventeen hundred men; but this number was soon reduced by the small-pox, and was still further weakened, by being spread over a circuit of twenty-six miles, and separated by three ferries. This division was indispensable to the maintenance of the blockade.

As the season of the year approached when reinforcements from England might be expected, Arnold determined to resume the siege of Quebec. His batteries were opened on the 2d of April; but he had not weight of metal to make a breach in the wall, nor an engineer capable of directing a siege, nor artillerists who understood the management of the pieces.

On the 1st of April, General Wooster had arrived; soon after

Did Arnold persevere in his attempt against Quebec, after the repulse? What efforts were made by Congress, to give efficiency to the operations in Canada? Why was it difficult to succeed against Quebec?

4

which Arnold, believing himself to be neglected, obtained leave of absence, and took command at Montreal.

General Thomas reached the American camp on the first of May. He found an army consisting of nineteen hundred men, of whom less than one thousand were fit for duty. Among these were three hundred entitled to a discharge, who insisted on being immediately dismissed. This small force was so divided that not more than three hundred could be united at any one place. The magazines contained only one hundred and fifty barrels of powder, and provisions for six days; nor could adequate supplies be obtained from the country, as the Canadians no longer manifested a disposition to serve. The river too began to open below; and it was certain that the British would seize the first opportunity to relieve Quebec.

Amidst these unpromising appearances, General Thomas thought the hope of taking the town chimerical, and a longer continuance before it both useless and dangerous. Under this impression he called a council of war, which unanimously determined that the army was not in a condition to risk an assault, and that preparations should be made to move to a more defensible position.

May 6. The next day five ships entered the harbor and landed some troops, while the Americans were employed in the embarkation of their sick and stores.

About noon General Carlton made a sortie at the head of a thousand men, supported by six field-pieces; and General Thomas, by the advice of his field officers, ordered a retreat, which was continued to the Sorel, where he was seized with the small-pox, of which he died.

After his death reinforcements arrived which increased the army in June to four or five thousand men, commanded by General Sullivan, who entertained hopes of recovering and maintaining the post at De Chambeau.

Towards the end of May the British army was augmented to thirteen thousand men, great part of whom were on their way to the Three Rivers. A strong corps, commanded by General Frazer, had reached that place, and several armed vessels and transports full of troops lay still higher up the river.

Before the arrival of General Sullivan, General Thompson, who commanded the army after the illness of General Thomas, understanding that the party at the Three Rivers was inconsiderable, had detached Colonel St. Clair with six or seven hundred men against that place. St. Clair, being informed that the party was

What was the number of the American troops before Quebec on the 1st of May? What induced them to retreat from their position? What was the amount of the British force at the end of May?

much stronger than had been supposed, waited at Nicolet for farther orders. When his letter reached camp, General Sullivan had arrived, who immediately detached General Thompson at the head of fourteen hundred men, with orders to attack the enemy, should there be a prospect of success.

The plan was to attack the village just before day; but the troops arrived an hour later than was intended, in consequence of which they were discovered when landing, and the alarm given. To avoid the fire of some ships lying in the river, they attempted to pass what appeared to be a point of woods, but was in reality a deep morass, three miles in extent. Their detention in this morass gave General Frazer full time to prepare for their reception, while General Nesbit cut off their return to their boats. The Americans advanced to the charge, but were soon repulsed, and driven some miles through a deep swamp. General Thompson and Colonel Irwin, with about two hundred men, were made prisoners, and from twenty to thirty were killed.

Notwithstanding his very great inferiority to his enemy, General Sullivan determined to defend the post at the Sorel, and was induced only by the unanimous opinion of his officers, and a conviction that the troops would not support him, to abandon it a few hours before the British took possession of it. The same causes drew him reluctantly from Chamblée and St. Johns, where he was joined by General Arnold with the garrison of Montreal. At the Isle aux Noix he received the orders of General Schuyler to embark on the lakes for Crown Point.

The armed vessels on the St. Lawrence and the Sorel were destroyed, and the fortifications of Chamblée and St. Johns set on fire.

The British army, during this whole retreat, followed close in the rear. At Sorel, the pursuit stopped. The Americans commanded the lake, and it could not be wrested from them until vessels of war should be constructed for the purpose.

While General Carleton was preparing to enter the lakes, General Schuyler was using his utmost exertions to retain the command of them; but so great was the difficulty of obtaining workmen and materials, that he found it impossible to equip a fleet which would be equal to the exigency. It consisted of fifteen small vessels, the largest mounting twelve guns, carrying six and four pound balls. At the instance of General Washington, the command of this sqadron was given to General Arnold.

With almost incredible exertions, the British General constructed a powerful fleet; and afterwards dragged up the rapids of St.

Relate the incidents of the retreat of the Americans towards their own territory. Why did the British intermit the pursuit, upon reaching Sorel? What naval preparations were made upon the Lakes?

Therese and St. Johns a vast number of long boats and other vessels, among which was a gondola weighing thirty tons. This immense work was completed in little more than three months; and, as if by magic, General Arnold saw on Lake Champlain, early in October, a fleet consisting of near thirty vessels, the largest of which, the Inflexible, carried eighteen twelve-pounders. It proceeded immediately in quest of Arnold, who was advantageously posted between the island of Valicour and the Western main. Notwithstanding the disparity of force, a warm action ensued, which Arnold was enabled to sustain till night, by the circumstance, that a wind unfavorable to the British kept some of their largest vessels at too great a distance to render any service.

In the night Arnold attempted to escape to Ticonderoga; but was overtaken the next day about noon, and brought to action a few leagues short of Crown Point. He maintained the engagement for two hours, during which the vessels that were most ahead escaped to Ticonderoga. The galleys and five gondolas made a desperate resistance. At length one of them struck; after which Arnold ran the remaining vessels on shore and blew them up, having first saved his men.

On the approach of the British army, a small detachment which had occupied Crown Point, retired to Ticonderoga, which Schuyler determined to defend to the last extremity.

General Carlton took possession of Crown Point, and advanced a part of his fleet into Lake George, within view of Ticonderoga. His army also approached that place; but, after reconnoitring the works, he thought it too late to lay siege to the fortress. Re-embarking his army, he returned to Canada, where he placed it in winter quarters, making the Isle Aux Noix his most advanced post.

CHAPTER IV.

Transactions in Virginia.—Action at the Great Bridge.—Norfolk burnt.—Transactions in North Carolina.—Action at Moore's creek Bridge.—Invasion of South Carolina.—British fleet repulsed at fort Moultrie.—Transactions in New York.—Measures tending to Independence.—Independence declared.

WHILE the war was carried on thus vigorously in the north, the southern colonies were not entirely unemployed.

Lord Dunmore, the Governor of Virginia, who was joined by the most active of the disaffected, and by a number of slaves, had collected a small naval force with which he carried on a predatory war, and at length attempted to burn the town of Hampton.

Who conquered, in the naval action on Lake Champlain? What points were occupied by the British troops? What movement terminated the campaign? What occurrences, meanwhile, had taken place in Virginia?

Intelligence of this design having been obtained, preparations were made for his reception, and the assailants were compelled to retreat to their vessels with some loss.

In consequence of this repulse, his lordship proclaimed martial law, summoned all persons capable of bearing arms to repair to the royal standard, or be considered as traitors, and offered freedom to all indented servants and slaves who would join them.

Intelligence of these transactions being received at Williamsburg, the committee of safety ordered a regiment of regulars, an a battalion of minute-men, to march into the lower country for the defence of the inhabitants.

Hearing of their approach, Lord Dunmore selected a position on the north side of Elizabeth river, at the Great Bridge, where it was necessary for the provincials to cross in order to reach Norfolk, at which place his lordship had established himself in some force. Here he erected a small fort on a piece of firm ground surrounded by a marsh, which was accessible on either side only by a long causeway. Colonel Woodford encamped at the south end of the causeway, across which, at its termination, he erected a breast-work.

After remaining in this position for a few days, Lord Dunmore sent orders to Captain Fordyce, the commanding officer of the fort, to storm the breast-work. Between daybreak and sunrise on the morning of the 9th of December, Fordyce, at the head of about sixty grenadiers of the 15th regiment, who led the column, advanced along the causeway with fixed bayonets against the breast-work, which was immediately crowded with the bravest of the Americans, who kept up a heavy fire on the front of the British column. It was also taken in flank by a party which occupied a small eminence on its right. Captain Fordyce pressed forward under this destructive fire, until he fell dead within a few steps of the breast-work. The column immediately broke and retreated, but, being covered by the artillery of the fort, was not pursued.

In this rash attack, every grenadier was said to have been killed or wounded. The Americans did not lose a man.

The following night the fort was evacuated. The provincials proceeded to Norfolk, under the command of Colonel Howe of North Carolina, who had arrived with his regiment after the battle; and Lord Dunmore took refuge on board his vessels.

The American soldiers were in the habit of firing into the vessels from the houses near the water. To relieve himself from this practice, Lord Dunmore, on the night of the first of January,

---

What were the operations of Lord Dunmore, and where did he find the Americans in arms? What was the result of the attack of the British upon the American works at the Great Bridge?

4*

landed a body of troops under cover of a heavy cannonade, and set fire to several houses near the river. The provincials, who entertained strong prejudices against this station, made no attempt to extinguish the flames. After the fire had continued several weeks, and had consumed about four-fifths of the town, Colonel Howe, who had waited on the convention to urge the necessity of destroying the place, returned with orders to burn the remaining houses; which were carried into immediate execution.

Lord Dunmore continued for some time a predatory war on the rivers, distressing individuals, and increasing the detestation in which he was held. At length his wretched followers were sent to Florida.

In North Carolina, an extensive settlement had been made by emigrants from the highlands of Scotland, who adhered to the royal cause. By a union between them, and the numerous disaffected on the western frontier, Governor Martin, who had taken refuge on board a ship of war in Cape Fear river, hoped to make a successful struggle for the province. His confidence was increased by the assurances he had received, that a considerable amount was destined for the southern colonies.

To prepare for events, he sent commissions to the leaders of the highlanders, and granted one to a Mr. M'Donald, their chief, to act as their General. He also sent a proclamation, to be used on the proper occasion, commanding all persons, on their allegiance, to repair to the royal standard. This was raised by M'Donald at Cross creek, about the middle of February, and nearly fifteen hundred men arranged themselves under it.

Upon the first advice that the loyalists were assembling, Brigadier-General Moore, with a provincial regiment and a few militia, took a strong position within a few miles of them. M'Donald sent a letter to Moore, inclosing the Governor's proclamation, and inviting him to join the King's standard. Moore protracted the negotiation in the hope that the numerous bodies of militia who were assembling might enable him to surround his adversary. M'Donald at length perceived his danger, and endeavored by forced marches to extricate himself from it, and to join Governor Martin who had been encouraged to commence active operations by the arrival of General Clinton in the colony.

The provincial parties, however, were so alert that he found himself under the necessity of engaging Colonels Caswell and Lillington, who, with about a thousand minute-men and militia, were entrenched directly in his front, at Moore's Creek bridge. The royalists, who were compelled to cross the bridge in the face

What was the nature of the warfare carried on by Lord Dunmore against the people of Virginia? Relate the occurrences in North Carolina, which followed the attempt of Governor Martin to maintain the royal authority?

of the entrenchments occupied by the provincials, attacked with great spirit: but Colonel M'Clean, who commanded them in consequence of the indisposition of M'Donald, with several of their bravest officers, having fallen in the first onset, they fled in great disorder, leaving behind them their General and several of their leaders, who fell into the hands of the provincials.

General Clinton remained with governor Martin until the arrival of Sir Peter Parker with several ships of war. Fortunately for the province, the unsuccessful insurrection of M'Donald, had previously broken the strength and spirits of the loyalists, and deprived them of their most active chiefs. The operations which had been meditated against that colony were deferred, and Clinton determined to make an attempt on the capital of South Carolina.

Early in April, a letter from the Secretary of State to the Governor of Maryland, disclosing the designs of government against the southern colonies, had been intercepted in the Chesapeake, and communicated to Mr. Rutledge the President of South Carolina. Thus apprized of the danger, preparations were made to meet it.

In the beginning of June, the fleet came to anchor off the harbor of Charleston. The bar was crossed on the 20th, and it was determined to silence a fort on Sullivan's Island.

During the interval between passing the bar and attacking the fort, reinforcements were received from Virginia and North Carolina, which augmented the American army commanded by General Lee, to five thousand men, one half of whom were regulars.

The signal for the attack was given to the fleet by Sir Peter Parker, at half-past ten in the morning of the 28th of June, and a furious cannonade was commenced on the American works, which was continued without intermission until it was terminated by night. Its effect was not such as had been anticipated. The fort was constructed of earth and of palmetto, a soft wood, which, on being struck, does not splinter, but closes on the ball. The fire from the fort did vast execution. The Bristol and the Experiment were nearly wrecks. The first lost one hundred and eleven men, and the last seventy-nine. Several officers of distinction were killed or wounded. The Acteon frigate ran aground and was burnt. The loss of the Americans in killed and wounded was only thirty-five men.

The British did not renew the action. In a few days the troops who had been landed on Long Island previous to the attack on the fort were re-embarked, and, on the 25th of July, the fleet sailed for New York.

Great and well-merited praise was bestowed on Colonel Moul-

What circumstances of discouragement in North Carolina, induced the British commander to direct his efforts against Charleston? What was the result of the naval attack upon fort Moultrie?

trie who commanded the fort, and on the garrison. The thanks
of the United Colonies were voted by Congress to General Lee,
Colonels Moultrie and Thompson, and the officers and men under
their command.

Even before the evacuation of Boston, it had been foreseen that
New York must become the seat of war. The fortifications which
had been commenced for the defence of its capital, and those to
be erected in the passes through the highlands up the Hudson,
were, after the arrival of the commander-in-chief, objects of his
unremitting attention.

The difficulty which had been experienced in expelling the British from Boston, had determined Congress to make great exertions for the preservation of New York. The execution of this
determination was difficult and dangerous. It required an army
capable of meeting the enemy in the open field, and of acting
offensively both on York and Long Islands. Congress had not
raised such an army. The letters of the commander-in-chief,
urging measures which might bring the whole strength of the
colonies into operation, had not been disregarded, but many circumstances combined to prevent such a military establishment as
the exigency required.

Hopes had been long cherished that the differences between the
mother country and her colonies might be adjusted; and when,
at length, a conviction that the appeal must be made to arms was
forced on Congress, that body, unaccustomed to the arduous duties
of conducting a war of vast extent, could not estimate rightly the
value of the means employed, nor calculate the effect which certain causes must produce. Opinions of the most pernicious tendency prevailed, from which they receded slowly, and from which
they could be forced only by melancholy experience.

The most fatal among these was the theory that an army could
be created every campaign for the purposes of that campaign.
They relied too confidently on being able, on any emergency, to
call out a force equal to the occasion; and on the competency of
such a force to the purposes of war.

Under these impressions, the determination to form a permanent
army was too long delayed; and the measures required by the
object were deferred until their execution had become extremely
difficult.

It was not until June 1776, that the representations of the
commander-in-chief could obtain a resolution directing soldiers to
be enlisted for three years, and offering a bounty of ten dollars
for each recruit. The time when this resolution would certainly

For what reason were the Americans anxious to preserve New York?
What great error lessened the efficiency of the American arms, in the early
period of the contest?

have accomplished its purpose had passed away. The regiments voted by Congress were incomplete; and that bounty which, if offered in time, would have effected its object, came too late to fill them.

The American army was not only inferior to its adversary in numbers, but was deficient in arms, ammunition, tents, and clothes. Yet both the government and commander-in-chief were determined to defend New York. Congress passed a resolution to reinforce the army with thirteen thousand eight hundred militia; and to form a flying camp on the Jersey shore, to consist of ten thousand militia, to be furnished by Pennsylvania, Delaware, and Maryland. They were to serve till the first of December, and the commander-in-chief was also authorized to require such additional temporary aids as circumstances might make necessary.

Great and embarrassing as were the difficulties already noticed, they were augmented by the disaffection of the city of New York, and of the adjacent islands. Governor Tryon, who had taken refuge on board some ships lying in the harbor, had been permitted to continue an open intercourse with the inhabitants. This intercourse was broken off upon the arrival of the commander-in-chief: yet a plot was formed through the agency of the Mayor, to rise in favor of the British on their landing, and to seize and deliver up General Washington himself. It extended to the American army, and even to the General's guards. It was fortunately discovered in time to be defeated, and some of the persons concerned were executed. About the same time, the plan of an insurrection was discovered in the neighborhood of Albany; and there, too, executions were deemed necessary.

Although the original and single object of the war on the part of the colonies was a redress of grievances, the progress of public opinion towards independence, though slow, was certain; and measures were necessarily adopted which tended to that object. Among the first of these was the establishment of temporary governments in place of that revolutionary system which followed the suspension of the pre-existent institutions. Still, the most anxious desire to re-establish the union between the two countries on its ancient principles was openly and generally declared. However sincere these declarations might have been in the commencement, the operation of hostilities was infallible. To profess allegiance and attachment to a monarch with whom they were at open war, was an absurdity too great to be of long continuance. The prejudices in favor of a connexion with England and of the English constitution, gradually but rapidly yielded to republican principles,

What military measures were ordered by Congress? Mention the treasonable attempts against the American cause. What was the consequence of the existing hostilities, as to its bearing on national independence?

and to a desire of independence. New strength was every day added to the opinions that a cordial reconciliation had become impossible; that reciprocal jealousy, suspicion, and hate, would take the place of that affection which could alone render such a connexion beneficial; that even the commercial dependence of America on Great Britain was greatly injurious to the former; and that the government of a distant nation or sovereign, unacquainted with and unmindful of their interests, would, even if replaced in their former situation, be an evil too great to be voluntarily borne. But, victory alone could restore them to that situation; and victory would give independence. The hazard was the same; and since the risk of everything was inevitable, the most valuable object ought to be the reward of success.

It was also urged with great effect, that the probability of obtaining foreign aid would be much increased by holding out the dismemberment of the British empire to rivals of that nation, as an inducement to engage in the contest.

American independence became the common theme of conversation; and, as it became more and more the general wish, the proceedings of Congress took their complexion from the temper of the people.

At length a measure was adopted which was considered generally as deciding the question. The affairs of the several provinces had hitherto been conducted by temporary institutions; but on the 6th of May, a resolution was offered recommending the adoption of governments adequate to the exigency, to such colonies as had not already established them. This resolution was referred to Mr. John Adams, Mr. Rutledge, and Mr. Richard Henry Lee, all zealous advocates for independence, whose report in favor of the measure was adopted on the 15th of May.

The provincial conventions acted on this recommendation, and governments were generally established. Some hesitation was at first discovered in Maryland, Pennsylvania, and New York; but public opinion was in favor of it, and finally prevailed. In Connecticut and Rhode Island, the executive as well as legislature had been elected by the people, and in those colonies no change had been thought necessary.

The several colonies now exhibited the novel spectacle of matured and enlightened societies devising political systems of self-government.

The institutions received from England were admirably calculated to lay the foundation for temperate and rational republics.

Mention the reasons which influenced the public mind in deciding upon a separation from Great Britain. What resolution was adopted in Congress, indicating the great change that now seemed probable? Did the several states coincide with the views of the general Congress?

The materials in possession of the people, as well as their habits of thinking, were adapted only to governments in all respects representative; and such governments were universally adopted.

The provincial assemblies, under the influence of Congress, took up the question of independence; and many declared themselves in favor of an immediate and total separation from Great Britain.

On the 7th of June a resolution to that effect was moved by Richard Henry Lee, and seconded by John Adams. It was referred to a committee, who reported it in the following terms: " Resolved, that these United States are, and of right ought to be, free and independent states; and that all political connexion between them and the state of Great Britain is, and ought to be, totally dissolved."

This resolution was debated on Saturday the 8th and Monday the 10th of June; when, it appearing that some of the states were not yet matured for the measure, the question was adjourned to the 1st of July. In the mean time a committee* was appointed to draw the declaration of independence, which was reported on the 28th of June, and laid on the table. On the 1st of July the debate on the original resolution was resumed. The question was put on the evening of that day, and carried in the affirmative. The report of the committee was postponed till the next day, when it was agreed to. Congress then proceeded to consider the declaration of independence, which, after some amendments, was approved and signed.

This declaration was immediately communicated to the armies, who received it with enthusiasm. It was also proclaimed throughout the United States, and was generally approved by those who had opposed the claims of the British Parliament. Some few individuals who had been zealous supporters of measures having for their object a redress of grievances, relinquished with regret their connexion with Great Britain. It was also an unfortunate truth, that in the country between New England and the Potomac, which was now to become the great theatre of action, a formidable minority existed who were opposed to the revolution.

* Mr Jefferson, Mr. John Adams, Mr. Franklin, and Mr. R. R. Livingston. Mr. R. H. Lee, the mover of the resolution, had been compelled by the illness of Mrs. Lee to leave Congress, the day on which the committee was appointed.

Did the provincial assemblies respond to the action of Congress ? Mention the important resolution that was now passed by this latter body. Was this decision of Congress approved by the armies, and the people? What was that untoward fact, which had a retarding influence on the efforts of American patriots ?

CHAPTER V.

Lord and Sir William Howe arrive before New York.—Circular letter of Lord Howe.—
State of the American army.—The British land on Long Island.—Battle of Brook-
lyn.—Fruitless negotiations.—New York evacuated.—Skirmish on the heights of
Haarlem.

WHILE Congress was deliberating in Philadelphia on the great question of independence, the British fleet appeared before New York.

On evacuating Boston, General Howe had retired to Halifax, from which place he sailed for New York in June. In the latter end of that month, he arrived off Sandy Hook; and on the 3d and 4th of July his troops were landed on Staten Island. They were received with great demonstrations of joy by the inhabitants, who took the oaths of allegiance to the British crown, and embodied themselves for the defence of the island. Strong assurances were also given by the inhabitants of Long Island, and the neighboring parts of New Jersey, of the favorable disposition of a great proportion of the people to the royal cause.

The command of the fleet had been conferred on Lord Howe, the brother of the general; and they were both commissioners for restoring peace to the colonies. He arrived at Staten Island on the 12th of July.

Lord Howe was not deterred by the declaration of independence from trying the influence of his powers for pacification. He sent on shore a circular letter, dated off the coast of Massachusetts, addressed severally to the late governors under the crown, inclosing a declaration which he requested them to make public. It announced his authority to grant pardons, and to declare any colony, town, port, or place, in the peace, and under the protection of the King. Assurances were also given that the meritorious services of all persons who would aid in restoring tranquillity in the colonies would be duly considered.

These papers were immediately transmitted by the commander-in-chief, to Congress, who directed their publication, " that the good people of the United States might be informed of what nature were the Commissioners, and what the terms, with the expectation of which the insidious court of Britain had sought to amuse and disarm them."

About the same time, General Howe addressed, by a flag, a letter to "George Washington, Esquire," which the General refused to receive, " as it did not acknowledge the public character

Mention the naval and military movements near New York. What was the nature of the propositions for pacification addressed to the Americans by Lord Howe and his brother?

with which he was invested." In a resolution approving this proceeding, Congress directed "that no letter or message whatever be received by the commander-in-chief, or others, the commanders of the American army, but such as shall be directed to them in the characters they respectively sustain."

To evade the preliminary difficulty which the unwillingness of the commissioners to recognize the existing powers in America, opposed to any discussion of the terms they were authorized to propose, Colonel Patteson, Adjutant-General of the British army, was sent on shore by General Howe, with a letter directed to "George Washington," &c. &c. &c. He was introduced to the General, whom he addressed by the title of "Excellency;" and, after the usual compliments, opened the subject of his mission by saying that General Howe much regretted the difficulties which had arisen respecting the address of the letters; that the mode adopted was deemed consistent with propriety, and was founded on precedent in cases of ambassadors and plenipotentiaries, where disputes or difficulties had arisen about rank; that Lord and General Howe did not mean to derogate from his rank, or the respect due to him, and that they held his person and character in the highest esteem; but that the direction with the addition of "&c. &c. &c." implied every thing that ought to follow. Colonel Patteson then produced a letter which he said was the same that had been previously sent, and which he laid on the table.

The General declined receiving it. He said that a letter addressed to a person in a public character, should have some description or indication of that character; otherwise it would be considered as a mere private letter. It was true the et-ceteras implied every thing, and they also implied any thing; and that he should absolutely decline any letter relating to his public station, directed to him as a private person.

Colonel Patteson then said that General Howe would not urge his delicacy farther, and repeated the assertion that no failure of respect was intended.

After some conversation relative to the treatment of prisoners, Colonel Patteson said that the goodness and benevolence of the King had induced him to appoint Lord Howe and General Howe, his commissioners to accommodate the unhappy dispute at present subsisting; that they had great powers, and would derive much pleasure from effecting the accommodation; and that he wished this visit to be considered as the first advance towards so desirable an object.

General Washington replied that he was not vested with any

Name the British officer who conferred with the American commander-in-chief. State the substance of the conversation on this occasion, and mention the result of the interview.

powers on this subject; but he would observe that, so far as he could judge from what had yet transpired, Lord Howe and General Howe were only empowered to grant pardon; that those who had committed no fault wanted no pardon; and that the Americans were only defending what they deemed their indubitable rights. This, Colonel Patteson said, would open a very wide field for argument; and, after expressing his fears that an adherence to forms might obstruct business of the greatest moment and concern, took his leave.

The reinforcements expected from Europe, of whom about four hundred and fifty were captured on their passage by the American cruisers, were now chiefly arrived; and the British army was estimated at twenty-four thousand men.

To this army, aided in its operations by a numerous fleet, was opposed a force unstable in its nature, incapable from its structure of receiving discipline, and inferior to its enemy in numbers, in arms, and in every military equipment. It consisted, when General Howe landed on Staten Island, of ten thousand men, much enfeebled by sickness. At the instance of General Washington, a few regiments stationed in the different states were ordered to join him; and the neighboring militia were called into service. Yet in a letter dated the 8th of August, he stated that his army consisted of only seventeen thousand, two hundred and twenty-five men, of whom three thousand, six hundred and sixty-eight were sick. This force was rendered the more inadequate to its objects by being necessarily divided for the defence of posts, some of which were fifteen miles distant from others, with navigable waters between them.

"Under every disadvantage," continued the letter, "my utmost exertions shall be employed to bring about the great end we have in view; and, so far as I can judge from the professions and apparent dispositions of my troops, I shall have their support."

The army was soon afterwards reinforced by three regiments of regulars, and by militia, which augmented it to twenty-seven thousand men, of whom one-fourth were sick. A part of it was stationed at Brooklyn, on Long Island, under General Sullivan.

Believing that the effect of the first battle would be considerable, the commander-in-chief employed every expedient which might act upon that enthusiastic love of liberty, that indignation against the invaders of their country, and that native courage, which were believed to animate the bosoms of his soldiers, and were relied on as substitutes for discipline and experience. The orders of the day contain the most animating exhortations to both

After the British reinforcements arrived, what was the strength of the royal forces in America? Mention the numbers and condition of the American army. How did their commander endeavor to animate them?

officers and soldiers; recommending to the officers, coolness in time of action, and to the soldiers, strict attention and obedience, with becoming spirit. He directed explicitly that any soldier who should attempt to conceal himself, or retreat without orders, should instantly be shot; and solemnly promised to notice and reward those who should distinguish themselves. Thus did he, by infusing into every bosom those sentiments which would stimulate to the greatest individual exertion, endeavor to compensate for the want of arms, of discipline, and of numbers.

Early in the morning of the 22d of August, the principal part of the British army, under the command of General Clinton, landed on Long Island, under cover of the guns of the fleet, and extended from the ferry at the Narrows, through Utrecht and Gravesend, to the village at Flatbush. A large division, commanded by General Clinton, turned short to the right and approached Flatland. General Sullivan had been strongly reinforced as soon as the movements of the British fleet indicated an intention to make the first attack at this point. On the 25th, Major-General Putnam, with a reinforcement of six regiments, was directed to take command at Brooklyn, and was charged most earnestly by the commander-in-chief, to be in constant readiness for an attack, and to guard the woods between the two camps with his best troops. General Washington passed the 26th at Brooklyn, making arrangements for the expected engagement, and returned at night to New York.

The two armies were separated from each other by a range of hills covered with thick woods, which extended from east to west nearly the length of the island, and across which were three different roads leading directly to Brooklyn ferry. The British centre at Flatbush was distant scarcely four miles from the American lines, and a direct road led across the heights from one to the other. Another road, more circuitous than the first, led from Flatbush and entered the road leading from Jamaica to Bedford, a small village on the Brooklyn side of the hills; and a third, leading from the Narrows along the coast by the way of Gowan's Cove, afforded the most direct route to their left.

The direct road from Flatbush to Brooklyn was defended by a fort in the hills; and the coast and Bedford roads were guarded by detachments posted on the hills within view of the British camp. Light parties of volunteers were directed to patrol on the road leading from Jamaica to Bedford; about two miles from which, near Flatbush, Colonel Miles, of Pennsylvania, was stationed with a regiment of riflemen. The Convention of New

On what day did the royal troops debark on Long Island? Mention the preparations of the Americans, and describe the position of the two opposing armies.

York had ordered General Woodhull, with the militia of Long
Island, to take post on the high grounds, as near the enemy as
possible.

About nine at night, General Clinton drew off the right of the
British army in order to seize a pass in the heights three miles
east of Bedford, on the Jamaica road. About two in the morning
of the 27th, his patrols fell in with and captured one of the American parties directed to watch this road. Learning from his prisoners that the pass was unoccupied, he immediately seized it;
and, on the appearance of day, the whole column passed the
heights, and appeared in the level country between them and
Brooklyn.

Before Clinton had secured the passes on the road leading from
Jamaica, General Grant, in order to draw the attention of the
Americans from their left, advanced slowly along the coast, at the
head of the British left wing, supported by ten pieces of cannon,
skirmishing as he advanced with the light parties stationed on that
road. These were reinforced by Putnam; and, about three in
the morning, Brigadier-General Lord Sterling was detached to
that point, with the two nearest regiments. Major-General Sullivan, who commanded all the troops without the lines, advanced
about the same time at the head of a strong detachment, on the
road leading to Flat Bush; while another detachment occupied
the heights still farther to his left.

About break of day, Lord Sterling reached the summit of the
hills, where he was joined by the troops which had been already
engaged, soon after which the enemy appeared in sight. A warm
cannonade commenced, and some sharp but not very close skirmishing took place between parties of infantry. Lord Sterling
was content with defending the pass; and General Grant did not
wish to drive him, from it until that part of the plan which had
been entrusted to Sir Henry Clinton should be executed.

In the centre, General De Heister, soon after daybreak, began
a cannonade on the troops under Sullivan. In the mean time, in
order the more effectually to draw off the attention of the Americans from the point at which the general attack was to be made,
the fleet was put in motion, and a heavy cannonade was commenced on the battery at Red Hook.

Aug. 27.   About half-past eight, the British right having then
          reached Bedford in the rear of Sullivan's left, Gen-
eral de Heister ordered Colonel Donop's corps to attack the hills,
following himself with the centre of the army. The approach of
Clinton was now discovered by the American left, which immedi-

---

What unguarded pass was seized by the invaders? Mention the various
movements which followed, until the two armies engaged in battle, on the
morning of the 27th.

ately endeavored to regain the camp at Brooklyn. While retiring from the woods by regiments, they encountered the front of the British. About the same time the Hessians advanced from Flat Bush against that part of the army which occupied the direct road to Brooklyn, where General Sullivan commanded in person. The firing heard towards Bedford had disclosed to these troops the alarming fact that the British had turned their left flank, and were getting completely into their rear. They sought to escape the danger by regaining the camp with the utmost celerity. The sudden rout of this party enabled De Heister to detach a part of his force against those who were engaged near Bedford. In that quarter, too, the Americans were broken and driven back into the woods; and the front of the column, led by General Clinton, intercepted those who were retreating along the direct road from Flat Bush. Thus attacked both in front and rear, driven alternately by the British on the Hessians, and by the Hessians back on the British, a succession of skirmishes took place in the woods, in the course of which some parts of corps forced their way through the enemy, and regained the lines of Brooklyn; but the greater part of the detachment was killed or taken.

The fire towards Brooklyn gave the first intimation to the American right that the enemy had gained their rear. Lord Sterling immediately directed the main body of his troops to retreat across the creek; and, to secure this movement, determined to attack in person a British corps commanded by Lord Cornwallis, stationed rather above the place at which he intended to cross. The attack was made with great spirit; but the force in front increasing, and General Grant advancing in his rear, his lordship, and the survivors of this gallant corps, were made prisoners of war. This attempt, though unsuccessful, enabled a great part of the detachment to cross the creek and save themselves in Brooklyn.

The loss sustained by the American army in this battle was estimated by General Washington at one thousand men; but in this estimate he must have included only his regular troops. In the letter of General Howe, the number of prisoners is stated at one thousand and ninety-seven, among whom were Major-General Sullivan, and Brigadiers Lord Sterling and Woodhull. He computes the total loss at three thousand three hundred. He states his own loss at twenty-one officers, and three hundred and forty-six privates, killed, wounded, and taken.

As the action became warm, the commander-in-chief passed over to the camp at Brooklyn, where he saw with inexpressible anguish, the destruction in which his best troops were involved,

Describe the progress of the battle, and mention its result. What were the two differing statements of the American loss? What was the loss of the British army?

5*

without the ability to extricate them. An attempt to save them by sallying from his entrenchments, and attacking the enemy, would put the camp in imminent danger, and expose that whole division of the army to ruin. His efforts, therefore, were necessarily directed to the preservation of those that remained.

General Howe did not think it advisable to risk an immediate assault on the American lines. He encamped in front of them; and, the night of the 28th, broke ground in form, within six hundred yards of a redoubt on the left.

In this perilous state of things, General Washington determined to withdraw from Long Island. This difficult movement was effected on the night of the 28th, so silently, that all the troops and military stores were carried over in safety. Early next morning, the British out-posts perceived the rear-guard crossing the East river, out of reach of their fire. The manner in which this critical operation was executed, added greatly to the reputation of General Washington in the opinion of all military men.

The resolution to defend Long Island was so hazardous in itself, and so disastrous in its consequences, that it has been condemned by many as a great error in the commander-in-chief. But the event will not always determine the wisdom of a measure. It is necessary to consider the previous state of things; and to compare the value of the object, and the means of securing it, with the hazards attending the attempt.

It was very desirable to defend New York, or to waste the campaign in a struggle for that important place. The difficulty of effecting either of these objects would be incalculably increased by abandoning Long Island to the enemy. It was, therefore, to be maintained if possible.

The impossibility of maintaining it, was not evident until the battle had been fought. It is true that the American force on the island could not have been rendered equal to that of the British; but with the advantages of the defensible country through which the assailants were to pass, and of a fortified camp assailable only on one side, hopes might be entertained without the imputation of rashness, of maintaining the position for a considerable time, and of selling it ultimately at a high price. This opinion is supported by the fact that, even after the victory of the 27th, General Howe was unwilling to hazard an assault on the works, and chose rather to carry them by regular approaches.

With more appearance of reason the General has been censured for not having guarded the road which leads from Jamaica to Bedford.

Did General Washington maintain his position at Brooklyn? What opinion was expressed by some persons respecting the defence of Long Island? What is to be observed upon that subject?

The written instructions given to the officer commanding on Long Island, directed that the woods should be well guarded, and the approach of the enemy through them be rendered as difficult as possible. But his numbers were not sufficient to furnish detachments for all the defiles through the mountains; and if a corps sufficient for defending that pass had been posted on the Jamaica road, and a feint had been made on it, while the principal attack was by the direct road leading from Flat Bush, or that along the coast, the events of the day would probably have been equally disastrous. The column marching directly from Flat Bush would probably have been in possession of the plain in rear of the detachment posted on the road from Jamaica, so as to intercept its retreat to the camp. So great is the advantage of those who attack, in being able to select the point against which to direct their grand effort.

The most advisable plan then appears to have been to watch the motions of the enemy, to oppose with a competent force, every attempt to seize the heights, and to guard all the passes in such a manner as to receive notice of his approach through any one of them, in sufficient time to recall the troops maintaining the others.

This plan was adopted:—and the heavy disasters of the day are attributable chiefly to the failure of those charged with the execution of that very important part of it which related to the Jamaica road.

The events of this day disclosed a radical defect in the structure of the American army. It did not contain a single troop of cavalry. Had the General been furnished with a few light-horse, merely to serve as videts, it is probable that the movement so decisive of the fate of the day, would not have been made unnoticed. The troops on the lines do not appear to have observed the column which was withdrawn on the evening of the 26th, from Flat Bush, to Flatland.

Whatever causes might have led to this defeat, it gave a gloomy aspect to the affairs of America. Heretofore, her soldiers had manifested a great degree of intrepidity. A confidence in themselves, a persuasion of superiority over the enemy, arising from the goodness of their cause, and their habitual use of fire-arms, had been carefully encouraged. This sentiment had been nourished by experience. When they found themselves, by a course of evolutions in which they imagined they perceived a great superiority of military skill, encircled with unexpected dangers from which no exertions could extricate them, their confidence in themselves and in their leaders was greatly diminished, and the approach of

---

Would the result of this action have been materially different, had other plans been adopted by the American General? Mention its general influence on American affairs.

the enemy inspired the apprehension that some stratagem was concealed from which flight alone could preserve them. The impression made on the militia, was attended with consequences immediately injurious. Great numbers left the army; in some instances almost by whole regiments, in many, by companies, at a time.

The first use made by Lord Howe of this victory, was to avail himself of the impression it had probably made, by opening a negotiation with Congress. For this purpose, General Sullivan was sent on parole to Philadelphia, with a verbal message, the import of which was, that though he could not at present treat with Congress as a political body, he was very desirous of having a conference with some of its members; that, in conjunction with General Howe, he had full powers to compromise the dispute between Great Britain and America, on terms advantageous to both; and wished a compact might be settled when no decisive blow was struck, and neither party could allege being compelled to enter into an arrangement; that in case Congress were disposed to treat, many things which they had not yet asked, might, and ought to be granted them; and that, if upon the conference, they found any probable ground of accommodation, the authority of Congress must be afterwards acknowledged—otherwise the compact would not be complete.

This proposition was not without its embarrassments. Congress dreaded the effects of an opinion, that the restoration of the ancient connexion on principles formerly deemed constitutional, was practicable; and was at the same time unwilling to enter into a negotiation, which might excite a suspicion, that the determination to maintain independence was not immovable.

The answer given through General Sullivan was, "that Congress, being the representatives of the free and independent states of America, cannot with propriety send any of its members to confer with his lordship in their private characters; but that, ever desirous of establishing peace on reasonable terms, they will send a committee of their body, to know whether he has any authority to treat with persons authorized by Congress for that purpose, on behalf of America; and what that authority is; and to hear such propositions as he shall think proper to make respecting the same."

Mr. Franklin, Mr. John Adams, and Mr. Edward Rutledge, all zealous supporters of independence, were appointed to receive the communications of Lord Howe.

They waited on his lordship, and on their return reported that

---

After his victory on Long Island, what was the nature of the communication conveyed by Lord Howe to the American Congress? What were the reasons which influenced that body, in deciding upon the proper answer to this proposition? What was determined in relation to it? Who composed the committee?

he had received them, on the 11th of September on Staten Island with great politeness.

. He opened the conversation by saying, that though he could not treat with them as a committee of Congress, yet as his powers enabled him to consult with any private gentlemen of influence on the means of restoring peace, he was glad of this opportunity of conferring with them on that subject, if they thought themselves at liberty to enter into a conference with him in that character. The committee observed that, as their business was to hear, his lordship might consider them in what light he pleased, and communicate any propositions he might be authorized to make; but that they could consider themselves in no other character, than that in which they were placed by Congress. His lordship then proceeded to open his views at some length. A return to their allegiance to the British crown was the condition on which peace was offered. He gave assurances of a good disposition in the King and his ministers, to make the government easy to them; and intimated that, in case of submission, the offensive acts of Parliament would be revised, and the instructions to the Governors reconsidered.

The committee gave it as their opinion, that a return to the domination of Great Britain was not now to be expected. They mentioned the repeated humble petitions which had been treated with contempt, and answered only by additional injuries; the unexampled patience which had been shown under their tyrannical government; and that it was not until the late Act of Parliament, which denounced war against them, and put them out of the King's protection, that they declared their independence. All now considered themselves as independent states, and it was not in the power of Congress to agree for them that they should return to their former dependent state. There was no doubt of their inclination for peace, and of their willingness to enter into a treaty with Britain that might be advantageous to both countries. If the same good disposition existed on the part of Britain, his lordship might obtain powers for that purpose, much sooner than powers could be obtained from the several colonies to consent to submission.

His lordship expressed his regret that no accommodation was likely to take place, and put an end to the conference.

These fruitless negotiations produced no suspension of hostilities.

The British army, posted from Bedford to Hurlgate, fronted and threatened York island from its southern extremity to the part op-

In his conference with a committee of Congress, what views did Lord Howe express in reference to the dispute between the two countries? What was the reply of the gentlemen composing the committee?

posite to the northern boundary of Long Island, a small distance below the heights of Haarlem, comprehending a space of nine miles.

The two armies were divided only by the East river, which is generally less than a mile wide.

Immediately after the victory at Brooklyn, dispositions were made by the enemy to gain possession of New York. The movements of the fleet indicated an intention to land near Kingsbridge and take a position which would cut off the communication of the American army with the country.

Aware of his danger, General Washington began to remove such stores as were not immediately necessary, and called a council of general officers to determine whether New York should be immediately evacuated. His own opinion appears to have been in favor of immediate evacuation; but the majority of the council was opposed to it. In the hope of defending the place till the campaign should be too far wasted to admit of further operations, the advice they gave was that the army should be formed into three divisions; one to remain in New York; the second to be stationed at Kingsbridge; and the third to occupy a camp in the intermediate space, so as to support either extreme.

This opinion was soon changed. The movements of the British general indicated clearly an intention either to break their line of communication, or to inclose the whole army in York island. A second council determined, by a large majority, that it had become absolutely necessary to withdraw the army from New York.

In consequence of this determination, Brigadier-General Mercer, who commanded the flying camp on the Jersey shores, was directed to move up the North river to the post opposite fort Washington; and every effort was made to expedite the removal of the stores.

On the morning of the 15th of September, three ships of war sailed up the river as far as Bloomingdale; a movement which stopped the removal of the stores by water. About eleven o'clock on the same day, Sir Henry Clinton, with a division of four thousand men, who had embarked at the head of New Town bay, unperceived by the troops on York island, proceeded through that bay into the East river, which he crossed; and, under cover of the fire of five men-of-war, landed at Kipp's bay, about three miles above New York.

The works thrown up at this place were capable of being defended for some time; but the troops abandoned them, and fled with precipitation. On the commencement of the cannonade,

---

What appeared to be the intention of the British, after their occupation of Long Island? Mention the movements of each army, when this plan was entered upon.

General Washington ordered the brigades of Parsons and Fellows to their support, and rode in person towards the scene of action. The panic of those who had fled from the works was communicated to the troops who had been ordered to sustain them, and the commander-in-chief had the extreme mortification to meet the whole party retreating in the utmost disorder, regardless of the efforts made by their generals to stop their disgraceful flight. The only part now to be taken was to secure the posts on the heights, and to withdraw the few troops still remaining in New York. In the retreat from the town, a small skirmish took place at Bloomingdale, in which an inconsiderable loss of men was sustained; but all the heavy artillery, and a large portion of the baggage, provision, and military stores, were unavoidably abandoned.

The British army, after taking possession of New York, encamped near the American lines. Its right was at Hoven's hook, near the East river, and its left reached the North river, near Bloomingdale. Both flanks were covered by ships of war.

The strongest point of the American lines was at Kingsbridge. M'Gowan's Pass and Morris's Heights were also occupied in considerable force. A strong detachment was posted in an entrenched camp, on the heights of Haarlem, within about a mile and a half of the British lines.

The present position of the armies favored the views of the American general. He wished to habituate his soldiers, by a series of skirmishes, to meet the enemy in the field; and he persuaded himself that his detachments, knowing a strong entrenched camp to be immediately in their rear, would engage without apprehension, would display their native courage, and would soon regain the confidence they had lost.

Opportunities to make the experiments he wished were soon afforded. The day after the retreat from New York, the British appeared in considerable force in the plain between the two camps; and the general rode to his advanced posts in order to make such arrangements as this movement might require. Lieutenant-Colonel Knowlton, of Connecticut, who, at the head of a corps of rangers, had been skirmishing with this party, soon came in and stated their numbers at about three hundred.

The general ordered Colonel Knowlton with his rangers, and Major Leitch, with three companies of the third Virginia regiment, which had joined the army the preceding day, to gain their rear, while he amused them with the appearance of making dispositions to attack their front.

This plan succeeded. The British ran eagerly down a hill, in

In their abandonment of New York, what loss was sustained by the Americans? What was the relative position of the two armies, after that event? Why was this situation desirable to the American general?

order to take possession of some fences and bushes which presented
an advantageous position, and a firing commenced, but at too great
a distance to do much execution. In the mean time, Colonel
Knowlton, not being precisely acquainted with their new position,
made his attack rather on their flank than rear; and a warm action ensued.

In a short time Major Leitch, who led the detachment, was
brought off the ground mortally wounded, having received three
balls through his body; and soon afterwards the gallant Knowlton
also fell. Not discouraged by the loss of their field-officers, the
Captains continued the action with great animation. Both parties
were reinforced. The Americans drove the enemy out of a wood
into the plain, and were pressing him still farther, when the General, content with the present advantage, called back his troops into
their entrenchments.

In this sharp encounter, the British loss was double that of the
Americans; but its real importance was its operation on the spirits
of the army. To give it the more effect, the parole the next day
was Leitch; and the General, in his orders, publicly thanked the
troops under the command of that officer, who had first advanced
on the enemy, and the others who had so resolutely supported
them; contrasting, at the same time, their conduct with that which
had been exhibited the day before. He appointed a successor to
the gallant and brave Colonel Knowlton, "who would," he said,
"have been an honor to any country."

CHAPTER VI.

The British land at Frogsneck.—York Island, except fort Washington, evacuated.—
Battle of the White Plains.—General Howe returns to Kingsbridge.—General Washington crosses the North river.—Fort Washington surrenders.—Fort Lee evacuated.—
Weakness of the American army.—Ineffectual attempts to raise the militia.—Retreat
through Jersey.—Capture of General Lee.—General Washington crosses the Delaware.—The British go into winter quarters.—Battle of Trenton.—Princeton.—Firmness of Congress.

THE armies did not long retain their position on York Island.
General Howe determined to gain the rear of the American camp
by the New England road, and also to possess himself of the Hudson above Kingsbridge. Having ascertained the practicability of
passing the forts on the North river, he embarked a great part of
his army in flat-bottomed boats on the East river, and, passing
through Hurlgate into the Sound, landed on the 12th of October at
Frogsneck, about nine miles from the camp on the heights of Haar-

----

Relate the particulars of a skirmish that now took place between the royal
troops and the Americans. What project was now undertaken by General
Howe?

lem, where he remained some days waiting for his artillery, military stores, and reinforcements from Staten Island, which were detained by contrary winds.

General Washington strengthened the fort at Kingsbridge, detached some regiments to West Chester for the purpose of skirmishing with the enemy should the occasion offer, and submitted the propriety of changing his ground to a board of general officers. The necessity of moving out of the island was too apparent not to be advised; but it was also determined to hold fort Washington, and to defend it as long as possible. A resolution of Congress of the 11th of October, desiring General Washington to obstruct if possible the navigation of the river, had great influence in producing this determination.

Measures were immediately taken for moving the army up the river, so as to extend its front, or left, beyond the British right. The rear division commanded by General Lee remained a few days longer at Kingsbridge, to secure and bring up the heavy baggage and military stores.

On the 18th of October, General Howe moved through Pelham's Manor, and took post at New Rochelle, a village on the Sound. The American army occupied the heights between that place and the North river.

A corps of American loyalists, commanded by Major Rogers, lay east of the main army, and was supposed to be covered by it. A bold attempt to surprise him in the night and to bear off his whole corps, by passing between him and the British camp, was made by an American detachment commanded by Major Green of Virginia. Major Rogers was surprised, and about sixty of his regiment were killed and taken. The loss of the Americans was inconsiderable, but among the wounded was Major Green, who received a ball in his shoulder which disabled him through life.

Not long afterwards a regiment of Pennsylvania riflemen under Colonel Hand, engaged an equal number of Hessian chasseurs, with some advantage.

These evidences of enterprise on the part of his adversary served to increase the caution of the British General. He waited a few days at New Rochelle, for a division commanded by Knyphausen. After its arrival, both armies, the Brunx dividing them, moved towards the White Plains, a strong piece of ground already occupied by a detachment of militia.

General Washington took possession of the heights at White Plains, on the east side of the Brunx, seven or eight miles in

Relate the particulars of the several skirmishes that now took place. What was the consequence of this display of confidence and courage on the part of the Americans?

6

front of the British column. This stream meandered so as to cover the front as well as the flank of his right wing, which extended along the road leading towards New Rochelle, as far as the brow of the hill where his centre was posted. His left, which formed almost a right angle with his centre, and was nearly parallel to his right, extended along the hills northward, so as to keep possession of the commanding ground, and secure a retreat to a still stronger position in his rear.

General M'Dougal with about sixteen hundred men, chiefly militia, occupied a hill, on the west side of the Brunx, about a mile from the right wing, for the purpose of covering the right flank. His communication with the main body was open, the river being fordable. Entrenchments were thrown up to strengthen the lines.

Oct. 25.   General Howe having determined to attack Washington in his camp, advanced in two columns, the right commanded by Sir Henry Clinton, and the left by General Knyphausen; and, about ten, his van appeared in full view. His right formed behind a hill about a mile in front of the American centre.

After viewing Washington's situation, Howe, who accompanied Knyphausen, determined to commence the action by carrying the hill occupied by M'Dougal; and directed Colonel Rawle with a brigade of Hessians, to make a circuit so as to turn M'Dougal's right flank, while Brigadier-General Leslie with a strong corps of British and Hessian troops should attack him in front. When Rawle had gained his position, Leslie also crossed the Brunx and attacked with great animation. The militia instantly fled; but the regulars maintained their ground with great gallantry. Colonel Smallwood's regiment of Maryland, and Colonel Reitzimer's of New York, advanced boldly towards the foot of the hill to meet Leslie; but, after a sharp encounter, were compelled to retreat. The remaining troops were soon driven from the hill, but still kept up an irregular fire from the stone walls near the scene of action. General Putnam, with Beal's brigade, was ordered to support them; but, the hill being lost, the attempt to regain it was deemed unadvisable. The American loss, in this spirited action, was between three and four hundred in killed, wounded, and missing. General Smallwood was among the wounded.

A considerable part of the day having been exhausted in gaining the hill, Howe suspended further operations till the next morning; and the British army lay on their arms through the night in order of battle.

This interval was employed by General Washington in removing

How were the Americans posted at White Plains, and what did General Howe resolve to do? State the circumstances of the action which now took place.

his sick and baggage, and adapting the arrangement of his troops to existing circumstances. His right was drawn back to stronger ground. Perceiving this, Howe resolved to postpone further offensive operations until Lord Percy should come up with the rear division of the army. This reinforcement was received on the evening of the thirtieth; but a violent rain which fell that night and the succeeding day still farther postponed the meditated assault.

Having now removed his sick, provisions, and heavy baggage to stronger ground, General Washington retired, in the night or the first of November, to the heights of North Castle, about five miles from the White Plains. General Howe thought this position too strong to be attempted with prudence, and determined to change his plan of operation.

The American garrisons in forts Lee and Washington imposed a check on his movements, and rendered York Island insecure. As preliminary to an attack on these forts, he directed Knyphausen to take possession of Kingsbridge, which was defended by fort Independence. On his approach, the small garrison retired to fort Washington, and Knyphausen encamped between that place and Kingsbridge.

In the mean time General Howe retired slowly down the North river. General Washington penetrated his design, and prepared as far as was in his power to counteract it. His letter to Congress communicating his movements, states his conviction that his adversary was not about to close the campaign, but would immediately invest fort Washington, and make a descent into Jersey. A council of war determined unanimously that the troops raised on the west of the Hudson should cross that river immediately, and be soon afterwards followed by those from the eastern part of the continent, except three thousand men who were to remain for the defence of the Highlands. A letter was also addressed to the Governor of New Jersey, stating the probable invasion of that State, and urging the necessity of putting the militia in the best possible condition to reinforce his army, and to replace the new levies which were engaged only to the first of December. Immediate information of this movement was also transmitted to General Greene, who commanded in the Jerseys; and his attention was particularly pointed to fort Washington.

As the British army approached Kingsbridge, three ships of war passed up the Hudson, notwithstanding the additional obstructions placed in the channel, uninjured by the fire from the forts. This demonstration of the inefficacy of those obstructions justified, in the opinion of General Washington, the evacuation of those

When Washington retired to the heights of North Castle, what two forts did General Howe resolve to attack? What measures were taken by the Americans when they became aware of the design of the British commander?

forts. " If," said he, in his letter to General Greene, " we cannot prevent vessels from passing up, and the enemy are possessed of the
surrounding country, what valuable purpose can it answer to hold
a post from which the expected benefit cannot be derived?' I am
therefore inclined to think it will not be prudent to hazard the men
and stores at Mount Washington. But as you are on the spot, I
leave it to you to give such orders respecting the evacuation of the
place as you may think most advisable; and so far revoke the orders given to Colonel Magaw to defend it to the last."

General Washington crossed the North river on the 13th of
November, in the rear of the troops destined to act in the Jerseys,
and proceeded to the quarters of General Greene, near fort Lee.

Mount Washington is a high piece of rocky ground, very difficult of ascent, especially towards the north. The lines and out-
works, which were chiefly on the southern side, were drawn quite
across the island. The fortifications were believed to be capable
of resisting any attempt to carry them by storm; and the garrison, which consisted of about two thousand regulars and a few
militia, was commanded by Colonel Magaw, a brave and intelligent officer.

General Howe, having made the necessary preparations for an
assault, summoned the garrison to surrender on the 15th of November. Colonel M'Gaw replied, that he should defend the place
to the last extremity, and communicated the summons to General
Greene at fort Lee, who transmitted it to the commander-in-chief,
then at Hackensac. He immediately rode to fort Lee, and, though
late in the night, was proceeding to fort Washington, when, in
crossing the river, he met Generals Putnam and Greene returning
from a visit to that fort. They reported that the garrison was in
high spirits, and would make a good defence; on which he returned with them to fort Lee.

Early next morning, Colonel M'Gaw prepared for the expected
assault. Colonel Rawlings, of Maryland, commanded a party
posted on a hill towards Kingsbridge; and Colonel Cadwallader
of Pennsylvania, commanded a body of troops who were posted
in the outermost of the lines drawn across the island, and between
the lines, on the rocky and precipitous heights fronting Haarlem
river.

Nov. 16.   About ten, the assailants appeared before the works
and moved to the assault in four different quarters. The
first division consisting of about five thousand Germans, commanded by General Knyphausen advanced against the hill occu
pied by Colonel Rawlings. The second, on the east, was led by

Did Washington now cross the river to New Jersey? Describe the American works at fort Washington? What preparations were made for their
defence? What was the order of attack?

General Matthews, supported by Lord Cornwallis. These troops crossed Haarlem river in boats under cover of their artillery, and landed within the outer line which crossed the island. The third, conducted by Lieutenant-Colonel Stirling, crossed the river higher up; and the fourth, led by Lord Percy, accompanied by General Howe, assaulted the lines in front on the south side.

The attacks on the north and south were made at the same instant. While Colonel Cadwallader was engaged in the first line against Lord Percy, the second and third divisions crossed Haarlem river, made good their landing, and dispersed the troops fronting that river, as well as a detachment sent by Colonel Cadwallader to support them. As the British advanced between the fort and the lines, they were necessarily abandoned. In retreating to the fort, some of the troops were intercepted by the division under Colonel Stirling, and made prisoners.

The resistance on the north was of longer duration. After an obstinate conflict, the Germans gained the summit of the hill; and Rawlings, perceiving the danger which threatened his rear, retreated to the fort.

The summons to surrender was now repeated; and it being thought impracticable to defend the place, the garrison became prisoners of war.

The loss on this occasion was the greatest the Americans had ever sustained. That of the assailants, according to Mr. Stedman, amounted to eight hundred men. It fell chiefly on the Germans.

The determination to evacuate fort Lee was the consequence of the surrender of fort Washington, and a removal of the stores was immediately commenced. Before this operation could be completed, Lord Cornwallis with about six thousand men crossed the river, and endeavoured to enclose the garrison between the north and Hackensac rivers. A retreat from that narrow neck of land was effected, with the loss of the heavy cannon and military stores.

After crossing the Hackensac, General Washington posted his troops along its western bank, but was unable to dispute its passage. At the head of about three thousand effectives, he was in a level country, with the Passaic in his rear, which unites with the Hackensac, a small distance below the ground he occupied.

This gloomy state of things was not brightened by the prospect before him. No confidence could be placed on receiving reinforcements from any quarter. But in no situation could Washington despond. Understanding that Ticonderoga was no longer threatened, he directed General Schuyler to hasten the troops of

Describe the attack upon fort Washington. What was the result? After they lost this post, what position was held by the American troops in New Jersey? What was the prospect of American affairs at this juncture?

6.*

Pennsylvania and Jersey to his assistance, and ordered General Lee to cross the North river and be in readiness to join him. But under the same fatal cause which had acted elsewhere, their armies were melting away, and would soon be almost totally dissolved. General Mercer, who commanded part of the flying-camp stationed about Bergen, was also called in; but these troops who had engaged to serve only till the first of December, had already abandoned the army in great numbers. No hope existed of retaining them after they should be entitled to a discharge; and there was not much probability of supplying their places with other militia. To New England he looked with anxious hope; and his requisitions on those states received prompt attention. Six thousand militia from Massachusetts, and a considerable body from Connecticut, were ordered to his assistance; but some delay in assembling them was unavoidable, and their march was arrested by the appearance of danger in their immediate neighborhood. Three thousand men commanded by Sir Henry Clinton took possession, late in November, of Newport in Rhode Island.

Not intending to maintain his present position, General Washington crossed the Passaic and took post at Newark. Having now entered the open country, his purpose was to halt a few days, and endeavor to collect such a force as would keep up the semblance of an army. General Mifflin was deputed to the government of Pennsylvania, and Colonel Reid, his Adjutant-General, to that of New Jersey, with orders to represent the real situation of the army, and the certainty that, without great reinforcements the state of New Jersey would be overrun, and Philadelphia be lost. General Lee was at the same time pressed to hasten his march, and cautioned to keep high enough up the country to avoid the enemy.

This perilous state of things was rendered still more critical by indications of an insurrection in the county of Monmouth, in New Jersey. In other places, too, an indisposition to further resistance was manifested. These appearances obliged him to make detachments from the militia of his army, to overawe the disaffected of Monmouth, who were on the point of assembling in force.

As the British army crossed the Passaic, General Washington retreated to Brunswick. At this place, the levies drawn from Dec. 1. Maryland and Jersey, to compose the flying camp, became entitled to their discharge; and no remonstrances could detain them. The Pennsylvanians were engaged to serve till the first of January. So many of them deserted, that guards were placed on the roads and ferries over the Delaware, to apprehend and send them back to camp. The next day, the van of the British army appeared in sight; and General Washington retreated to Trenton. Directions had already been given to collect all the boats from Philadelphia for seventy miles up that river, in the hope that the progress of the enemy might be arrested until the arrival of reinforcements, which would enable him to dispute its passage.

The army which was thus pressed slowly through the Jerseys, at no time, during the retreat, exceeded four thousand men. On reaching the Delaware, it was reduced to less than three thousand; of whom not quite one thousand were militia of New Jersey. The regulars were badly armed, worse clad, and almost destitute of tents, blankets, or utensils for dressing their food.

In this crisis of American affairs, a proclamation was issued by Lord and General Howe, commanding all persons assembled in arms against his majesty's government, to disband, and return to their homes; and offering pardon to every person who should, within sixty days, appear before certain officers of the crown, and testify his obedience to the laws, by subscribing a declaration of his submission to the royal authority. Numbers flocked in daily to make their peace, and obtain protection.

Among the many valuable traits in the character of Washington, was that unyielding firmness which supported him under these accumulated circumstances of depression. Undismayed by the dangers which surrounded him, he did not for an instant relax his exertions, nor omit any thing which could retard the progress of the enemy. He did not appear to despair; and constantly showed himself to his harassed and enfeebled army, with a serene unembarrassed countenance, betraying no fears in himself, and inspiring others with confidence. To this unconquerable firmness —to this perfect self-possession under the most desperate circumstances, is America, in a great degree, indebted for her independence.

The exertions of General Mifflin to raise the militia of Pennsylvania, were successful in Philadelphia. A large proportion of the inhabitants of this city had associated for the general defence; and on this occasion, fifteen hundred of them marched to Trenton. A German battalion was also ordered to that place by Congress. On the arrival of these troops, General Washington moved towards Princeton; but was stopped by intelligence that Lord Cornwallis, having received large reinforcements, was advancing rapidly from Brunswick by different routes, and endeavoring to gain his rear. He immediately crossed the Delaware, and placed his army in

What was the number of the American troops, as they retreated through New Jersey? What British proclamation was issued? What was the conduct of Washington in this dispiriting condition of affairs?

such a manner as to guard its fords. As his rear passed the river, the British van appeared in sight.

From Bordentown, the course of the river turns westward, making an acute angle with its course from Philadelphia to that place; so that a British division might cross a considerable distance above Trenton, and be almost as near Philadelphia as the troops opposite to that place. Lord Cornwallis made dispositions to cross both above and below. The American army was so arranged as to counteract this design.

The commander-in-chief had ordered General Gates, with the regulars of the northern army, and General Heath, with those at Peekskill, to march to his assistance.

Although General Lee had been repeatedly urged to join him, that officer proceeded reluctantly in the execution of his orders, manifesting a strong disposition to retain his separate command, and rather to threaten the rear of the British army, than to strengthen that in its front. On the 12th of December, while passing slowly through Morris county, he was surprised in his quarters, about three miles from his army, by a detachment of cavalry, commanded by Colonel Harcourt, and was carried off in triumph.

General Sullivan, on whom the command devolved, obeyed promptly the orders which had been given to Lee, and, crossing the Delaware at Philipsburg, joined the commander-in-chief. On the same day, General Gates arrived with a few northern troops. By these and other reinforcements, the army was augmented to about seven thousand effective men.

All the attempts of the British General to get possession of boats for the transportation of his army over the Delaware having failed, he gave indications of an intention to close the campaign, and to retire into winter quarters. About four thousand men were cantoned on the Delaware, at Trenton, Bordentown, the White Horse, and Mount Holly; and the residue of the army of Jersey was distributed from that river to the Hackensac. Strong corps were posted at Princeton, Brunswick, and Elizabeth Town. General Howe hoped, by covering so large a portion of Jersey, to intimidate the people, and to impede the recruiting service. To counteract these views, three regiments from Peekskill were ordered to halt at Morristown, and to unite with the Jersey militia assembled at that place under Colonel Ford. General Maxwell was sent to take command of these troops.

The short interval between this cantonment of the British troops and the recommencement of active operations, was employed by

---

Did General Lee comply with the orders of Washington? How was Lee captured? Did his successor reinforce Washington? How were the enemy distributed in New Jersey?

General Washington in repeating the representations he had so often made to Congress respecting preparations for the ensuing campaign.

The present aspect of American affairs was gloomy in the extreme. The existing army, except about fifteen hundred men, would dissolve in a few days. New Jersey had, in a great measure, submitted; and the militia of Pennsylvania had not displayed the alacrity expected from them. General Howe would most probably avail himself of the ice, which would soon be formed, and of the dissolution of the American army, to seize Philadelphia. It was feared, and with reason, that this event would deter the American youth from engaging in a service which was becoming hopeless.

To extricate the affairs of America from this desperate situation, General Washington formed the daring plan of attacking all the British posts on the Delaware at the same instant. If successful in all or any of these attacks, he hoped to relieve Philadelphia from immediate danger—to compel his adversary to compress himself, so as no longer to cover Jersey, and above all, to restore public confidence.

The positions taken to guard the river, were equally well adapted to offensive operations. It was intended to cross, in the night of the 25th of December, at M'Konkey's ferry, about nine miles above Trenton, and to march down in two divisions, by the river and Pennington roads, the first of which enters the western part of the town, and the last towards the north. This part of the plan was to be executed by the General in person, at the head of about two thousand four hundred continental troops. It was thought practicable to pass the river by twelve, and to reach the point of destination by five in the morning. General Irvine was directed to cross at the Trenton ferry, and to secure the bridge below the town. General Cadwallader was to cross over at Dunks' ferry, and to secure the post at Mount Holly.

The cold, on the night of the 25th, was intense. Snow, mingled with hail and rain, fell in great quantities, and so much ice was made in the river, that the division commanded by the General in person could not effect its passage till three, nor commence its march till near four. As the distance to Trenton, by either road, is nearly the same, orders were given to attack at the instant of arrival, and, after driving in the outposts, to follow them rapidly into town, and prevent the main body from forming.

General Washington accompanied the upper column; and, arriving at the outpost on that road precisely at eight o'clock, drove

Mention the decisive movement by which Washington hoped to encourage his army and the people. What were the preparations made in consequence? What was the state of the weather?

it in, and followed it with such ardor that its attempts to make a
stand were unavailing. In three minutes, the fire of those who
had taken the river road was heard. Colonel Rawle, who commanded in the town, paraded his men, and met the assailants. He
fell in the commencement of the action, and his troops, in apparent
confusion, attempted to gain the road to Princeton. General
Washington threw a detachment into their front, and advanced ra
pidly on them in person. Finding themselves surrounded, an
their artillery already seized, they laid down their arms and sur
rendered themselves prisoners of war. About twenty of the enemy
were killed, and about one thousand made prisoners. The American loss was two privates killed, two frozen to death, and three
or four wounded. One officer, Lieutenant Monroe, was wounded.

The ice rendered it impracticable for General Irvine to execute
that part of the plan which devolved on him, and about five hundred men, stationed in the lower end of Trenton, crossed the bridge,
early in the action, and escaped down the river. The same cause
prevented General Cadwallader from attacking the post at Mount
Holly. With great difficulty a part of his infantry passed the
river, but returned on its being found impossible to cross with the
artillery.

General Washington, thinking it unadvisable to hazard the loss
of the very important advantage already gained, by attempting to
increase it, recrossed the river with his prisoners and military
stores.

Nothing could surpass the astonishment of the British commander at this unexpected display of vigor on the part of the American General. His condition, and that of his country, had been
thought desperate. He had been deserted by every man having a
right to leave him, and two-thirds of the continental troops still remaining with him would be entitled to a discharge on the first of
January. The spirits of the people were sunk to the lowest point
of depression. New Jersey appeared to be subdued, and the best
judges of the public sentiment thought that immense numbers in
Pennsylvania also would not permit the sixty days allowed in the
proclamation of Lord and Sir William Howe to elapse, without
availing themselves of the pardon it proffered. Instead of offensive
operations, the total dispersion of the small remnant of the American army was confidently anticipated.

Finding that he was contending with an adversary who could
never cease to be formidable, and that the conquest of America was
more distant than had been supposed, General Howe determined,
in the depth of winter, to recommence active operations; and Lord

What was the result of the attack? Were Generals Irvine and Cadwallader able to execute their part of the plan? What was the salutary effect
of Washington's victory upon the mind of the enemy?

Cornwallis, who had retired to New York, with the intention of embarking for Europe, returned to the Jerseys in great force for the purpose of recovering the ground which had been lost.

General Washington, finding himself, by a reinforcement of Pennsylvania militia, at the head of a force with which it seemed practicable to act on the offensive, determined to employ the winter in endeavoring to recover Jersey.

He directed Generals Heath and Maxwell to approach the British contonments, while he again crossed the Delaware with his continental troops, and took post at Trenton. The regulars of New England were entitled to a discharge on the last day of December. With great difficulty, and a bounty of ten dollars, many of them were induced to renew their engagements for six weeks.

The British were now collected in force at Princeton, under Lord Cornwallis. His Lordship advanced on the morning of the 2d of January; and, about four o'clock in the afternoon, his van reached Trenton. On its approach, General Washington retired across Assumpinck creek, which runs through the town. The British attempted to cross the creek at several places; but finding all the fords guarded, they desisted from the attempt, and kindled their fires. The Americans kindled their fires likewise, and a cannonade was kept up till dark. *[Jan. 1, 1777.]*

The situation of General Washington was once more extremely critical. A few days of mild foggy weather had softened the ice in the Delaware, and rendered its passage very difficult. In his present situation, he would certainly be attacked early in the morning by an overwhelming force, which must render his destruction inevitable.

In this embarrassing state of things, he formed the bold design of abandoning the Delaware, and marching by a circuitous route along the left flank of the British army, into its rear at Princeton; and, after beating the troops at that place, to move rapidly on Brunswick, where the baggage and principal magazines of the British army lay under a weak guard.

This plan being approved by a council of war, preparations were made for its immediate execution. The baggage was removed to Burlington; and about one o'clock in the morning the army decamped silently, and took a circuitous road to Princeton, where three British regiments had encamped the preceding night, two of which commenced their march early in the morning to join the rear of their army. At sunrise, after proceeding about two miles, they saw the Americans on their left; and, immediately facing about, advanced upon their van, which was conducted by General

---

Relate the progress of the winter campaign in New Jersey? By what strategy did Washington disappoint the enemy at Trenton, and strike at a distant detachment? Was he successful in this design?

Mercer. A sharp action ensued, which was not of long duration. General Mercer was mortally wounded, and the van was routed. But the fortune of the day was soon changed. The main body, led by General Washington in person, followed close in the rear and attacked with great spirit. The British in turn were compelled to give way. The two regiments were separated. Colonel Mawhood, who commanded that in front, retired to the main road, and continued his march. The fifty-fifth regiment, which was on the left, being hard pressed, fled in confusion across the fields into a back road leading towards Brunswick. General Washington pressed forward to Princeton. The regiment remaining in that place took possession of the college, and made a show of resistance, but some pieces of artillery being brought up to play upon that building, it was abandoned, and the greater part of them became prisoners.

In this engagement, the British lost rather more than one hundred killed, and near three hundred prisoners. The loss of the Americans in killed was somewhat less; but in their number was included General Mercer, Colonels Haslet and Potter, Captains Neal and Fleming, and five other valuable officers.

On perceiving that the American army had decamped in the night, Lord Cornwallis marched with the utmost expedition to the protection of Brunswick, and was close in the rear of the Americans before they could leave Princeton.

The situation of General Washington was again perilous in the extreme. His small army was exhausted with fatigue, without blankets, and many of them barefooted. He was closely pursued by a superior enemy, who must necessarily come up with him before he could accomplish his designs on Brunswick. Under these circumstances, he abandoned the remaining part of his original plan, and took the road leading up the country to Pluckamin, where his troops took some refreshment. Lord Cornwallis continued his march to Brunswick; and General Washington, finding it impracticable to continue offensive operations, retired to Morristown, in order to put his men under cover, and give them some repose.

The bold, judicious, and unexpected attacks made at Trenton and Princeton had a much more extensive influence on American affairs than would be supposed from a mere estimate of the killed and taken. They saved Philadelphia for the winter; recovered the state of Jersey; and, which was of still more importance, revived the drooping spirits of the people, and gave a perceptible impulse to the recruiting service throughout the United States.

The firmness of Congress through the gloomy period which intervened between the loss of fort Washington and the battle of

After his success at Princeton, what induced Washington to forego the attack upon Brunswick? Whither did he retire? Mention the influence of his bold achievements upon the minds of his countrymen.

Princeton, give the members of that time a just claim to the admiration of the world and to the gratitude of their fellow-citizens. Undismayed by impending dangers, they did not, for an instant, admit the idea of surrendering the independence they had declared, and purchasing peace by returning to their colonial situation.

CHAPTER VII.

American army inoculated.—State of the army.—Destruction of stores at Peekskill—at Danbury.—Expedition to Sagg Harbor.—Camp formed at Middle Brook.—British move out to Somerset Court-House.—Return to Amboy.—Attempt to cut off the retreat of the American army at Middle Brook.—Lord Cornwallis skirmishes with Lord Sterling.—General Prescot surprised and taken.—The British army embarks.

Jan. 1777. THE effect of the proclamation published by Lord and General Howe, on taking possession of Jersey, was in a great degree counteracted by the conduct of the invading army. The hope that security was attainable by submission was soon dissipated. The inhabitants were treated rather as conquered rebels than returning friends. Whatever may have been the exertions of the General to restrain his soldiers, they indulged in every species of licentiousness. The loyalists as well as those who had been active in the American cause, were the victims of this indiscriminating spirit of rapine and violence. A sense of personal wrongs produced a temper which national considerations had been too weak to excite; and, when the battles of Trenton and Princeton relieved the people from the fears inspired by the presence of their invaders, the great body of the people flew to arms. Small parties of militia scoured the country, and were collecting in such numbers as to threaten the weaker British posts with the fate which had befallen Trenton and Princeton.

To guard against this spirit, the British General found it expedient to abandon the positions taken for the purpose of recovering the country, and to confine himself to New Brunswick and Amboy.

The militia and volunteers who came in aid of the small remnant of continental troops, enabled General Washington to take different positions near the lines of the enemy, to harass him perpetually, restrain his foraging parties, and produce considerable distress in his camp.

In the midst of these operations, he came to the hazardous resolution of freeing himself and his troops from the fear of a calamity which had proved more fatal than the sword of the enemy.

The small-pox had found its way into both the northern and

Mention the circumstances which counteracted the effect of the British proclamation in New Jersey. What was the consequence, and where did the British commander now concentrate his force?

7

middle army, and had impaired the strength of both to an alarming degree. To avoid the return of this evil, the General determined to inoculate all the soldiers in the American service. This determination was carried into execution, and an army, exempt from the fear of a calamity which had, at all times, endangered the most important operations, was prepared for the next campaign. The example was followed through the country, and this alarming disease ceased to be the terror of America.

As the British army was divided between New Jersey, New York, and Rhode Island, General Washington cherished hopes of being enabled to strike a decisive blow against some one of its divisions during the winter. The state sovereignties, which possessed all the real energies of government, were incessantly urged to fill their regiments and to bring their quotas into the field; but the inherent defects of the American system rendered it impracticable to collect a force competent to those vigorous operations which had been anticipated. Some of the State Assemblies did not even complete the appointment of officers till the spring. After these arrangements were made, the difficulty of enlisting men was unexpectedly great. The immense hardships to which the naked soldiers had been exposed; the mortality resulting from those hardships, and probably from an injudicious arrangement of the hospital department which proved to be the tomb of the sick, had excited extensive disgust to the service, and a consequent unwillingness to engage in it. A letter of the 4th of March, addressed to Congress, states that the whole effective force in Jersey fit for duty, was less than three thousand, of whom not quite one thousand were regulars. Still a war of skirmishes was kept up through the winter. The British foraging parties were often attacked to advantage; and these small successes, magnified by the press into victories, served to increase the confidence of the American soldiers in themselves, and to animate the people. Hopes were even entertained that, from the scarcity of forage, neither the British cavalry nor draft horses would be fit for service when the campaign should open.

As the season for active operations approached, fresh difficulties, growing out of the organization of the American system, disclosed themselves. Every state being exposed to invasion, the attention of each was directed to itself. The spirit incident to every league was displayed in repeated attempts to give to the military force such various directions as would leave it unable to effect any great object, or to obstruct any one plan the enemy might form. The patriotism of the day, however, and the unex-

---

What was done to free the American troops from the small-pox? Mention the difficulties which impeded the effective organization of the American army. What was the sort of warfare now carried on?

ampled confidence placed in the commander-in-chief, prevented the mischiefs this spirit is well calculated to generate. His representations made their proper impression, and the intention of retaining continental troops for local defence was reluctantly abandoned. The plan of raising additional regular corps, to be exclusively under state authority, was substituted for the yeomanry of the country, as a more effectual and convenient mode of protecting the coasts from insult.

During the winter, General Howe kept his troops in their quarters. As the season for active operations approached, his first attention was directed to the destruction of the scanty supplies prepared by the Americans for the ensuing campaign. Peekskill on the Hudson, about fifty miles above New York, was generally the residence of the commander in the Highlands, and was used as a place of deposit for stores to be distributed into the neighboring posts.

Colonel Bird was detached up the river against this place, at the head of five hundred men, under convoy of a frigate and some smaller vessels. After completely destroying the magazines and barracks, he returned to New York.

An expedition was also projected against Danbury, a village on the western frontier of Connecticut, in which military stores to a considerable amount had been deposited. Governor Tryon, Major-General of the provinces in the British service, assisted by Brigadiers Agnew and Sir William Irskine, proceeded on this enterprise at the head of two thousand men.

On the 25th of April, the troops landed between Fairfield and Norwalk, and reached Danbury about two the next day. The village, with the magazines it contained, were consumed by fire, and early in the morning of the succeeding day, Tryon commenced his line of march towards his ships. The militia, however, had been alarmed, and assembled in considerable bodies to obstruct his retreat. General Wooster, who had resigned his commission in the continental army, and been appointed Major-General of the militia, fell into his rear with about three hundred men, while Arnold and Sullivan, then casually in Connecticut, gained his front at Ridgefield. Wooster attacked his rear with great gallantry, about eleven in the morning, but his troops were repulsed, and he was himself mortally wounded. Tryon proceeded on his march to Ridgefield, where he found Arnold already entrenched on a strong piece of ground. A warm skirmish ensued which continued nearly an hour, when Arnold was driven from the field. At break of day next morning, after setting fire

---

What plan was now adopted as preferable for defending the coast against British depredation? Mention the various expeditions by which the enemy endeavored to destroy the military stores and provisions of the Americans.

to Ridgefield, the British resumed their line of march. About eleven in the forenoon they were again met by Arnold whose numbers were increased to a thousand men, among whom were some continental soldiers. A continued skirmishing was kept up till five in the afternoon, when the British formed on a hill near their ships. The Americans attacked with great intrepidity, but were repulsed; and Tryon, availing himself of this respite, re-embarked his troops and returned to New York.

The loss of the British amounted to one hundred and seventy men. That of the Americans was stated at one hundred; but among these was General Wooster: lieutenant-Colonel Gould, and another field-officer, killed; and Colonel Lamb wounded.

This enterprise was not long afterwards successfully retaliated. The British had collected a considerable quantity of provisions and forage at Sagg Harbor, on the eastern end of Long Island. Believing this place to be completely secured by the vessels that were continually traversing the Sound, General Howe had confided its protection to a schooner carrying twelve guns, and a company of infantry.

General Parsons, who commanded a few recruits at New Haven, formed the design of surprising this party, which was entrusted to Lieutenant-Colonel Meigs. He crossed the Sound with one hundred and seventy men under convoy of two armed sloops, and landed near Southhold, whence the boats were conveyed across the land, about fifteen miles, into a bay where the troops re-embarked. Crossing the bay, they landed at two in the morning, four miles from Sagg Harbor, which place was completely surprised, and carried with charged bayonets. At the same time another division of the detachment secured the armed schooner, which, with the stores, were consumed by fire.

The object of his expedition being effected without the loss of a man, Colonel Meigs returned with his prisoners, "having transported his men by land and water ninety miles in twenty-five hours." Congress directed a sword to be presented to him, and passed a resolution expressing their high sense of his merit.

The exertions made during the winter by the commander-in-chief to raise a powerful army for the ensuing campaign had not been successful; but that steady and persevering courage which had supported himself and the American cause through the gloomy scenes of the preceding year, did not desert him. Supposing that Burgoyne, would either attempt to seize Ticonderoga, and join General Howe on the Hudson, or would transport his troops by water to New York, whence the combined army would proceed to

By what successful exploit did the Americans retaliate the incursions of the enemy? Were the exertions of Washington as successful as he wished in endeavoring to strengthen his army?

Philadelphia, he adopted his arrangements to meet and counteract either plan of operations. With a view to the three great points, Ticonderoga, the Highlands of New York, and Philadelphia, the troops of New England and New York were divided between Ticonderoga and Peekskill, while those from Jersey to North Carolina inclusive, were directed to assemble at a camp to be formed in Jersey. The more southern troops remained in that weak part of the Union.

As the recruits were collected, the camp at Morristown was broken up, and the army assembled, on the 28th of May, at Middlebrook, just behind a connected ridge of commanding heights, north of the road leading to Philadelphia, and about ten miles from Brunswick. These heights afforded a full view of any movements which might be made by the enemy. On the 20th of May, the total of the army in Jersey, excluding cavalry and artillery, amounted to only eight thousand three hundred and seventy-eight men, of whom upwards of two thousand were sick. More than half these were recruits, who had never looked an enemy in the face.

General Washington, anticipating a movement by land towards Philadelphia, had taken the precaution to give orders for assembling an army of militia strengthened by a few continental troops, on the western bank of the Delaware, to be commanded by General Arnold, who was then in Philadelphia employed in the settlement of his accounts.

The first object of the campaign on the part of General Howe, was Philadelphia. He intended to march through Jersey; and to cross the Delaware on a portable bridge constructed in the winter for that purpose. If the Americans could be brought to an action on equal ground, victory was inevitable. Should Washington decline an engagement, and be again pressed over the Delaware, the object would be as certainly obtained. But it would be dangerous to attack him in his lines at Middlebrook; for although his camp might be forced, victory would probably be attended with such loss as to disable the victor from reaping its fruits.

An attempt to cross the Delaware in the face of an army collected on its western bank, while that commanded by General Washington in person remained unbroken on his flank and rear, was an experiment of equal hazard. It comported with the cautious temper of Sir William Howe to devise some other plan to which he might resort, should he be unable to seduce the American General from his advantageous position.

The two great bays of Delaware and Chesapeake suggested

How was the American army divided, for the general defence of the country? Mention the number acting in New Jersey. What was now the great object of the British commander? Mention the difficulties which interfered with the immediate prosecution of his plans.

the alternative of proceeding by water, should he be unable to manœuvre General Washington out of his present encampment.

On the 12th of June, General Howe assembled the main body of his army at Brunswick, and gave strong indications of an intention to reach Philadelphia by land.

General Washington, believing this to be his design, posted a select corps of riflemen under Colonel Morgan, a partisan of distinguished merit, at Vanvichton's bridge on the Raritan, to watch the left flank of the British army, and seize every occasion to harass it.

Early in the morning of the 14th, Sir William Howe, leaving two thousand men in Brunswick, advanced in two columns towards the Delaware, which reached Somerset Court-House and Middlebrook about the same time.

On receiving intelligence that his enemy was in motion, General Washington formed his army to great advantage on the heights in front of his camp. The troops remained in order of battle during the day; and, in the night, slept on the ground to be defended. The Jersey militia took the field in great numbers, and joined General Sullivan, who had retired from Princeton behind the Lowland hills towards Flemingtown, where an army of some respectability was forming, which could co-operate with that under the immediate inspection of the commander-in-chief.

The settled purpose of General Washington was to defend his camp, but not to hazard an action on other ground. That of General Howe seems to have been, by acting on his anxiety for Philadelphia, to seduce him from his strong ground, and tempt him to approach the Delaware in the hope of defending its passage. The motives which restrained Howe from marching through Jersey, leaving the American army in full force in his rear, determined Washington to allow him to proceed to the Delaware should such be his intention. In that event, he purposed to maintain the high strong grounds north of the road to be taken by his enemy, and to watch for any opportunity which might be used to advantage.

Finding the American army could not be drawn from its strong position, General Howe determined to withdraw from Jersey, and to embark his army for the Chesapeake or the Delaware. On the night of the 19th, he returned to Brunswick, and on the 22d to Amboy, from which place, the heavy baggage and a few troops passed into Staten Island on the bridge which had been designed for the Delaware.

On the march to Amboy, some sharp skirmishing took place

Mention the various movements by which General Howe endeavored to draw the Americans from their strong position. In what way did he at length determine to reach Philadelphia?

with Morgan's corps; but the retreat was conducted with such circumspection, that no important advantage could be gained.

In order to cover and co-operate with his light parties, General Washington advanced six or seven miles to Quibbletown, on the road to Amboy; and Lord Sterling's division was pushed still further to Metucking meeting-house.

In the hope of bringing on an engagement, General Howe, on the night of the 26th, recalled his troops from Staten Island, and, early the next morning, made a rapid movement in two columns: the right, commanded by Lord Cornwallis, took the route by Woodbridge to the Scotch plains; and the left, led by Sir William Howe in person, marched by Metucking meeting-house. The left was to attack the left flank of the Americans at Quibbletown, while Lord Cornwallis should gain the heights on the left of the camp at Middlebrook.

At Woodbridge, the right column fell in with an American party of observation, which gave notice of this movement. General Washington, comprehending his danger, put the army in motion, and regained the camp at Middlebrook. Lord Cornwallis fell in with Lord Sterling, and a sharp skirmish ensued, in which the Americans lost three field-pieces and a few men; after which they retreated to the hills about the Scotch plains. Perceiving the passes in the mountains to be guarded, and the object of this skilful manœuvre to be unattainable, the British general returned to Amboy, and crossed over to Staten Island.

General Washington was again left to conjecture the plan of the campaign. Intelligence had been received of the appearance of Burgoyne on Lake Champlain, and that Ticonderoga was threatened. This strengthened the opinion, that the design of Howe must be to seize the passes in the mountains on the Hudson, secure the command of that river, and effect a junction between the two armies. Without abandoning his camp at Middlebrook, he made dispositions to repel any sudden attack on the posts in the Highlands.

While the General anxiously watched the motions of his adversary, an agreeable piece of intelligence was received from New England. The command of the British troops in Rhode Island had devolved on General Prescot. Thinking himself perfectly secure, he indulged himself in convenient quarters, rather distant from camp, and was remiss with respect to guards. Information of this negligence was communicated, and a plan was formed to surprise him. This spirited enterprize was executed with courage and address by Colonel Barton, of the Rhode Island militia.

Mention the movement made by General Howe, in the hope of forcing the Americans into a general engagement. Was this project successful? Relate the particulars of the capture of General Prescot.

On the night of the 10th of July, he embarked on board four whale-boats, at Warwick neck, with a party of about forty men, including Captains Adams and Philips. After proceeding about ten miles by water unobserved, he landed about midway between Newport and Bristol ferry, and, marching a mile to the quarters of Prescot, seized the sentinel at the door, and one of his aids. The General himself was taken out of bed, and conveyed to a place of safety.

The success of this intrepid enterprize diffused the more joy, because it was supposed to secure the liberation of General Lee.

Congress expressed a high sense of this gallant action, and presented Colonel Barton with a sword.

At last, the embarkation of the British army was completed; and the fleet put to sea.

CHAPTER VIII.

General Washington marches towards the Delaware. — Takes measures for checking Burgoyne. — British army lands at the ferry on Elk River. — General Washington advances to the Brandywine.—Retreat of Maxwell.—Defeat at Brandywine.—Skirmish on the 16th of September. — Retreat to French Creek. — General Wayne surprised—General Howe takes possession of Philadelphia.—Congress removes to Lancaster.

WHILE the British troops were embarking at New York, the utmost exertions were made by General Washington to strengthen the army of the north, which was retreating before Burgoyne. He not only pressed the Governors of the eastern states to reinforce it with all their militia, and hastened the march of those generals who were designed to act in that department, but made large detachments of choice troops from his own army, thus weakening himself in order to reinforce other generals, whose strength would be more useful.

On receiving intelligence that the British fleet had sailed, the American army, under his immediate command, commenced its march southward. On the 30th of July, the fleet appeared off the capes of Delaware, and orders were given for assembling all the several detachments in the neighborhood of Philadelphia. Scarcely were these orders given, when they were countermanded. An express brought the information that the fleet had sailed out of Delaware bay, and was steering eastward. On the 7th of August, it was again seen a few leagues south of the capes of

---

With what design was the British army withdrawn from New Jersey? Where was the fleet seen? Was the American commander uncertain as to the exact designs of the enemy?

Delaware; after which it disappeared, and was not again seen until late in that month, when it appeared in the Chesapeake.

The original design had been to proceed up the Delaware; but, on entering that bay, its obstructions were found to be so considerable, that this design was abandoned, and the resolution taken to transport the army up the Chesapeake. The fleet sailed up that bay, and proceeded up Elk river as high as it was safely navigable. On the 25th of August, the troops, estimated at eighteen thousand effectives, were landed at the ferry.

On the appearance of the fleet in the Chesapeake, the several divisions of the American army were again ordered to unite in the neighborhood of Philadelphia; and the militia of Pennsylvania, Maryland, Delaware, and the northern counties of Virginia, were directed to take the field.

The day before Sir William Howe landed, the American army marched through Philadelphia to the Brandywine. The divisions of Greene and Stephen were advanced nearer the head of Elk, and encamped behind White Clay creek. The militia of Maryland and Delaware, with Richardson's continental regiment, were assembled in the British rear, under General Smallwood; and the militia of Pennsylvania were united with the main body of the army. It was estimated by General Howe at fifteen thousand, including militia; and his estimate did not far exceed their total numbers; but the effectives, including militia, did not exceed eleven thousand.

Morgan's regiment of riflemen having been detached to the northern army, a corps of light infantry was formed for the occasion, and placed under General Maxwell. This corps was advanced to Iron Hill, about three miles in front of White Clay creek.

The British army, on landing, encamped in two divisions—the one at Elkton, the other at Cecil Court-House. On the 3d of September, they formed a junction at Pencader, or Aiken's tavern. On the march, Lord Cornwallis fell in with, and attacked Maxwell, who retreated over White Clay creek, with the loss of about forty men, killed and wounded.

The American army encamped behind Red Clay creek, on the road leading from the camp of Sir William Howe to Philadelphia.

On the 8th of September, General Howe made a show of attacking the Americans in front, while the main body attempted to turn their right flank. Perceiving his design, General Washington changed his ground early in the night, and crossing the Bran-

Why did the enemy prefer sailing up the Chesapeake? When were the British troops landed, and what was their force? What were the numbers of the Americans? What movements now took place?

dywine, took post behind that river at Chadd's ford. General Maxwell occupied the hills south of the river, on the road leading over the ford. The militia under General Armstrong guarded a ford two miles below Chadd's; and the right extended a few miles above, with a view to other fords deemed less practicable.

In the evening of the 9th, Howe moved forward in two columns, which united next morning at Kennet's Square; after which his parties were advanced on the roads leading to Lancaster, to Chadd's ford, and to Wilmington.

The armies were now within seven miles of each other, with only the Brandywine between them, which opposed no obstacle to a general engagement. This was sought by Howe, and not avoided by Washington. It was impossible to protect Philadelphia without a victory; and this object was deemed of such importance throughout America, and especially by Congress, as to require that a battle should be hazarded for its attainment.

In the morning of the 11th, soon after day, information was received that the whole British army was advancing on the direct road leading over Chadd's ford. The Americans were immediately arrayed in order of battle for the purpose of contesting the passage of the river. Skirmishing now commenced between the advanced parties; and by ten, Maxwell was driven over the Brandywine below the ford. Knyphausen, who commanded this division, paraded on the heights, and appeared to be making dispositions to force the passage of the river.

About eleven, Colonel Ross of Pennsylvania brought the information that a large column, estimated by him at five thousand men, with many field-pieces, had taken a road leading from Kennet's Square directly up the country, and had entered the Great Valley road, down which they were marching to the upper fords on the Brandywine.

On receiving this intelligence, Washington is said to have determined to detach Sullivan and Lord Sterling, to engage the left of the British army; and to cross Chadd's ford in person, and attack Knyphausen. Before this plan, if formed, could be executed, counter intelligence was received inducing the opinion that the movement on the British left was a feint, and that the column which had made it, after making demonstrations of crossing the Brandywine above its forks, had marched down the southern side of that river to reunite itself with Knyphausen.

The uncertainty produced by this contradictory intelligence was at length removed; and about two in the afternoon, it was ascertained that the left wing, commanded by Lord Cornwallis,

By what reasons was Washington influenced in determining to risk a general battle? Mention the movements of both armies, which preceded the battle of Brandywine.

after making a circuit of about seventeen miles, had crossed the river above its forks, and was advancing in great force.

A change of disposition was immediately made. The divisions of Sullivan, Sterling, and Stephen, advanced farther up the Brandywine, and fronted the British column marching down the river. That commanded by Wayne remained at Chadd's ford. Greene's division, accompanied by General Washington in person, formed a reserve between the right and left wings.

The troops detached against Lord Cornwallis, formed hastily on an advantageous piece of ground, above Birmingham meeting-house. Unfortunately Sullivan's division, in taking its ground, made too large a circuit, and was scarcely formed when the attack commenced.

About half-past four the action began, and was kept up warmly for some time. The American right first gave way. The line continued to break from the right, and in a short time was completely routed. The commander-in-chief pressed forward with Greene to the support of that wing; but before his arrival, its rout was complete, and he could only check the pursuit. For this purpose the tenth Virginia regiment commanded by Colonel Stevens, and a regiment of Pennsylvania commanded by Colonel Stewart, were posted advantageously to cover the rear of the retreating army. The impression made by their fire, and the approach of night, induced Sir William Howe, after dispersing them, to give over the pursuit.

When the action commenced on the American right, General Knyphausen crossed at Chadd's ford, and forced a small battery which defended it. The defeat of the American right being known, the left also withdrew from its ground. The whole army retreated that night to Chester, and the next day to Philadelphia.

The loss sustained by the Americans in this action has been estimated at three hundred killed and six hundred wounded. Between three and four hundred, principally the wounded, were made prisoners. Among the wounded were General Lafayette, and Brigadier-General Woodford. As must ever be the case in new-raised armies, their conduct was not uniform: some regiments, especially those who had served the preceding campaign, maintained their ground with the firmness of veterans. Others gave way as soon as they were pressed.

The official letter of Sir William Howe stated his loss at rather less than one hundred killed and four hundred wounded. As the Americans sustained very little injury in the retreat, this inequality of loss can be ascribed only to the inferiority of their arms.

Relate the progress and the result of the battle of Brandywine. What was the loss on each side? What was the general conduct of Washington's troops? Whither did the American army now retire?

The battle of Brandywine was not considered as decisive; and Congress appeared determined to risk another engagement for the metropolis of America.

Having allowed his army one day for repose and refreshment, General Washington re-crossed the Schuylkill, and proceeded on the Lancaster road, with the intention of meeting and again fighting his enemy.

Sir William Howe passed the night of the 11th on the field of battle; and on the two succeeding days advanced towards Chester, and also took possession of Wilmington, to which place his sick and wounded were conveyed.

On the 15th the American army, intending to gain the left of the British, reached the Warren tavern, on the Lancaster road, twenty-three miles from Philadelphia. Intelligence being received early next morning that Howe was approaching in two columns, Washington determined to meet and engage him in front.

Both armies prepared with alacrity for battle. The advanced parties had met, and were beginning to skirmish, when they were separated by a heavy rain, which rendered the retreat of the Americans a measure of absolute necessity. Their gun-locks not being well secured, their muskets soon became unfit for use. Their cartridge-boxes had been so inartificially constructed as not to protect their ammunition, and very many of the soldiers were without bayonets.

The design of giving battle was reluctantly abandoned, and the retreat was continued all day and great part of the night through a most distressing rain, and very deep roads. A few hours before day the troops halted at the Yellow Springs, where the alarming fact was disclosed, that scarcely one musket in a regiment could be discharged, and scarcely one cartridge in a box was fit for war. The army retired to Warwick furnace, on the south branch of the French Creek, where a small supply of muskets and ammunition might be obtained in time to dispute the passage of the Schuylkill.

The extreme severity of the weather stopped the advance of Sir William Howe for two days.

From French Creek, General Wayne was detached with his division into the rear of the British, to harass their march; while General Washington crossed the Schuylkill at Parker's Ferry, and encamped on both sides of Perkioming Creek.

General Wayne lay in the woods, about three miles in rear of the left wing of the British troops. The country was so extensively disaffected, that Sir William Howe received accurate ac-

Did Washington resolve to meet the enemy a second time, rather than relinquish the defence of Philadelphia? What circumstance prevented the battle, and rendered the American arms ineffective?

counts of his position and of his force.   Major-General Grey was detached on the night of the 20th to surprise him, and effectually accomplished his purpose.   The American piquets, driven in with charged bayonets, gave the first intimation of his approach. Wayne instantly formed his division ; and while the right sustained the shock, directed a retreat by the left.   He states his loss at one hundred and fifty killed and wounded.   It probably amounted to at least three hundred.   The British admit, on their part, a loss of only seven.

When the attack commenced, General Smallwood, who was on his march to join Wayne, was within less than a mile of him ; and, had he commanded regulars, might have given a different turn to the night ; but his militia thought only of their own safety.

Some severe animadversions on this affair having been made in the army, General Wayne demanded a court-martial, which was unanimously of opinion " that he had done every thing to be expected from an active, brave, and vigilant officer," and acquitted him with honor.

Having secured his rear by compelling Wayne to take a greater distance, Sir William Howe marched to the Schuylkill, and encamped on the bank of that river from the first land ford up to French creek, along the front of the American army.   To secure his right from being turned, General Washington moved higher up the river, and encamped with his left above the British right.

General Howe, relinquishing his purpose of bringing Washington to a battle, determined to pass the Schuylkill and take possession of Philadelphia.   The whole army crossed without much opposition on the night of the 22d, and, proceeding on its march, encamped near Swede's ford.

It was now apparent that only immediate victory could save Philadelphia.   Public opinion, which a military chief finds too much difficulty in resisting, and the opinion of Congress, required a battle ; but Washington came to the wise determination of avoiding one for the present.   His reasons for this decision were conclusive.   Wayne and Smallwood had not yet joined the army ; the continental troops ordered from Peekskill were approaching ; and a reinforcement of Jersey militia, under General Dickenson, was also expected.

A council of war concurred in his opinion not to march against the enemy, but to allow his harassed troops a few days of repose on their present ground.

The members of Congress separated on the 18th of September, in the evening, and reassembled at Lancaster on the 27th.   The British army entered Philadelphia on the 26th.

What severe loss was sustained by a detachment under General Wayne? On what day did the British army enter Philadelphia?

8

CHAPTER IX.

Measures to cut off the communication between the British army and fleet.—Battle of Germantown.—Attack on fort Mifflin.—On Red Bank.—The Augusta blown up.— General Washington takes post at White Marsh.—Fort Mifflin evacuated.- Fort Mercer evacuated.—The British open a communication with their fleet.—General Howe marches to Chesnut Hill.—Returns to Philadelphia.—General Washington goes into winter quarters.

To prevent the co-operation of the fleet with the British army in Philadelphia, works had been erected on Mud island, a low marshy piece of ground near the junction of the Schuylkill with the Delaware, and at Red Bank, on the opposite Jersey shore, which were defended with heavy artillery. In the deep channel, under cover of these batteries, several ranges of frames, resembling chevaux-de-frise, had been sunk, which were so strong and heavy as to destroy any ship that might strike against them. No attempt to open the channel could be successful until the command of the shores on both sides should be obtained.

Other ranges of machines had been sunk about three miles lower down the river; and some considerable works were in progress at Billingsport, on the Jersey side, which were in such forwardness as to be provided with artillery. These works and machines were farther supported by two floating batteries, several galleys, a number of other armed vessels, and some fire-ships.

The present relative situation of the armies gave a decisive importance to these works. Cutting off the communication of General Howe with his fleet, they intercepted his supplies by water; while the American vessels in the river above fort Mifflin, the fort on Mud island, opposed obstacles to his foraging in Jersey; and General Washington hoped to render his supplies on the part of Pennsylvania so precarious as to compel him to evacuate Philadelphia.

These advantages were considerably diminished by the capture of the Delaware frigate.

Lord Cornwallis, the day after entering Philadelphia, commenced three batteries for the purpose of acting against any American ships which might appear before the town. While incomplete, they were attacked by two American frigates, assisted by several galleys and gondolas. The largest, the Delaware, being left by the tide, grounded, and was captured. This event was the more interesting, as it not only gave the British general the command of the ferry, and free access to the Jersey shore, but also enabled him to intercept the communication between the forts below and Trenton, from which place the garrisons were to have drawn their military stores.

What precautions were adopted to prevent communication between the British fleet and army through the Delaware?

The expected reinforcements, except the state regiment and militia from Virginia, being arrived, the American army amounted to eight thousand continental troops and three thousand militia. With this force General Washington determined to approach the enemy, and seize the first opportunity of attacking him. The army took a position on the Skippack road, about sixteen miles from Germantown. The British line of encampment Sept. 30. crossed this village near its centre, and Lord Cornwallis, with four regiments of grenadiers, occupied Philadelphia. Colonel Stirling had been detached with two regiments to take possession of the fort at Billingsport and destroy the works, after which service he was directed to escort a convoy of provisions from Chester to Philadelphia. For the security of this convoy, another regiment was detached from Germantown.

General Washington determined to avail himself of this division of the British force, and to attempt to surprise the camp at Germantown. His plan was to attack both wings in front and rear at the same instant.

The divisions of Sullivan and Wayne, flanked by Conway's brigade, were to march down the main road, and attack the left wing; while General Armstrong, with the Pennsylvania militia, should turn its left flank and attack in the rear. The commander-in-chief accompanied this column.

The divisions of Greene and Stephens, flanked by M'Dougal's brigade, were to take a circuit by the Limekiln road, and attack the right wing.

The militia of Maryland and Jersey, under Generals Smallwood and Forman, were to march down the old York road, and, turning its right, to fall on its rear.

The division of Lord Sterling, and the brigades of Nash and Maxwell, formed the reserve.

Parties of cavalry were silently to scour the roads, and to keep up the communication between the heads of the several columns.

The army moved from its ground about seven in the afternoon, and before sunrise the next morning, the advance of the column led by Sullivan drove in a piquet. The main body followed close in the rear, and engaging the light infantry and the fortieth regiment, forced them to give way. Though closely pursued, Lieutenant-Colonel Musgrave, with five companies, threw himself into a large stone house belonging to Mr. Chew, which stood directly in the way of Wayne's division, and poured on the Americans an incessant and galling fire from the doors and windows.

After some unsuccessful and bloody attempts to carry the house

What were the respective positions of the two armies? Mention the circumstance which encouraged Washington to engage the enemy at Germantown. State the order of attack.

by storm, and battering it with field artillery, which was too light to make any impression on its walls, a regiment was left to observe the party within it, and Wayne moved forward, passing to the left of the house.

In rather more than half an hour after Sullivan had been engaged, the left wing came also into action, and drove the light infantry posted in front of the British right from its ground. While pursuing the flying enemy, Woodford's brigade, which was on the right of this wing, was arrested by a heavy fire from Chew's house, directed against its right flank. The brigade was drawn off to the left by its commanding officer, and the field-pieces attached to it were ordered to play on the house, but were too light to be of service. The advance of that brigade being thus retarded, this part of the line was broken, and the two brigades composing the division of Stephens were not only separated from each other, but from the other division which was led by General Greene in person. That division, consisting of the brigades of Muhlenberg and Scott, encountered and broke a part of the British right wing, entered the village, and made a considerable number of prisoners.

Thus far the prospect was flattering. Had the American troops possessed the advantages given by experience, there is yet reason to believe that the hopes inspired by this favorable commencement would not have been disappointed. But the face of the country, and the darkness of the morning produced by a fog of uncommon density, co-operating with the defective discipline of the army, and the derangements of the corps by the incidents at Chew's house, blasted these flattering appearances.

The grounds over which the British were pursued abounded in small and strong inclosures, which frequently broke the line of the pursuer's army. The two divisions composing the right wing had been separated at Chew's house, and immediately after their passing it, the right of the left wing was stopped at the same place, so as to cause a division of that wing also. The darkness of the morning rendered it difficult to distinguish objects; and it was impossible for the commander-in-chief to learn the situation of the whole, or to correct the confusion which was commencing. The same cause which obstructed the re-union of the broken parts of the American army, also prevented their discerning the real situation of the enemy, so as to improve the first impression.

The attacks on the flanks and rear which formed a part of the original plan, do not appear to have been made.

These embarrassments gave the British time to recover from the consternation into which they had been thrown. General Knyp-

---

Narrate the progress of the battle of Germantown, and mention the unfavorable occurrence which interfered with the success of the American arms.

hausen, who commanded their left, detached two brigades to meet the right of Sullivan, which had penetrated far into the village, before his left, which had been detained at Chew's house, could rejoin him; and the action became warm in that quarter. The British right also recovered from its surprise, and advanced on that part of Greene's division which had entered the town. After a sharp engagement these two brigades began to retreat, and those who were most in advance were surrounded and compelled to surrender. About the same time the right wing also began to retreat. It is understood that their ammunition was expended.

Every effort to stop this retrograde movement proved ineffectual. The division of Wayne fell back on that of Stephens, and was for some time mistaken for the enemy. General confusion prevailed, and the confidence felt in the beginning of the action was lost. With infinite chagrin General Washington found himself compelled to relinquish all hope of victory, and to turn his attention to the safety of his army. The enemy not being sufficiently recovered to endanger his rear, the retreat was made without loss under cover of the division of Stephens.

In this battle about two hundred Americans were killed, near three times that number wounded, and about four hundred made prisoners. Among the killed was General Nash, of North Carolina; and among the prisoners was Colonel Matthews of Virginia, whose regiment had penetrated into the centre of the town. The loss of the British, as stated in the official return, did not exceed five hundred, of whom less than one hundred were killed. Among the latter, were General Agnew and Colonel Bird.

The American army retreated about twenty miles to Perkiomen creek, where a small reinforcement, consisting of about fifteen hundred militia, and a state regiment, was received from Virginia; after which it again advanced towards Philadelphia, and reoccupied the ground from which it had marched to fight the battle of Germantown.

The attention of both armies was now principally directed to the forts below Philadelphia.

A garrison of continental troops was placed in the fort at Red Bank, called fort Mercer, which commanded the channel between the Jersey shore and Mud island, and afforded protection to the American flotilla. The militia of Jersey were relied upon to reinforce this garrison; and also to form a corps of observation which might harass the rear of any detachment investing the place.

General Howe was indefatigable in his preparations to attack

What was the result of the battle of Germantown? Mention the loss of each army. What position was resumed by the Americans? Whither was attention now chiefly turned?

8*

fort Mifflin from the Pennsylvania shore. He erected batteries at the mouth of the Schuylkill, which were silenced by Commodore Hazlewood; but a detachment crossed over Webb's ferry into Province Island in the following night, and constructed a slight work opposite fort Mifflin, from which they were able to throw shot and shells into the barracks. This was attacked at daylight by three galleys and a floating battery, and the garrison surrendered. While the boats were bringing off the prisoners, a large body of British troops reoccupied the fortress. The attack was renewed by the flotilla, without success; and two attempts made by Lieutenant-Colonel Smith to storm it, entirely failed. In a few nights, works were completed on the high ground of Province Island, which enfiladed the principal battery of fort Mifflin.

The aids expected from the Jersey militia not being received, Colonel Angel of Rhode Island, with his regiment, was ordered to Red Bank; and Lieutenant-Colonel John Goune of Virginia, with about two hundred men, to fort Mifflin.

Immediately after the battle of Brandywine, Admiral Howe sailed for the Delaware; but his van did not get into the river until the 4th of October. The ships of war and transports which followed, came up from the 6th to the 8th, and anchored from New Castle to Reedy Island. It was not till the middle of the month, that the frigates in advance of the fleet could make a narrow and intricate passage through the lower impediments sunk in the river. In the meantime the fire from the Pennsylvania shore had not produced all the effect expected from it; and General Howe perceived that greater exertions would be necessary for the reduction of the works than could be safely made in the present relative situation of the armies. Under this impression, he withdrew his troops from Germantown into Philadelphia, as preparatory to a combined attack by land and water on forts Mercer and Mifflin.

After effecting a passage through the works sunk in the river at Billingsport, other difficulties still remained to be encountered by the ships of war. Several rows of chevaux-de-frise had been sunk about half a mile below Mud island, which were protected by the guns of the forts, as well as by the moveable water force. To silence these works, therefore, was a necessary preliminary to the removal of the obstructions in the channel.

On the 21st of October, Colonel Count Donop, at the head of twelve hundred Hessians, crossed the Delaware at Philadelphia, with orders to storm the works at Red Bank. Late in the evening of the 22d, he appeared before the fort, and attacked it with

Narrate the events which marked the contest of the two parties for the command of the Delaware. On what expedition was Count Donop sent from Philadelphia?

great intrepidity. It was defended with equal resolution. The outer works, being too extensive to be manned by the garrison, were used only to gall the assailants while advancing. On their near approach, the Americans retired within the inner entrench-ment, whence they poured upon the Hessians a heavy and de-structive fire. Colonel Donop received a mortal wound; and Lieutenant-Colonel Mengerode, the second in command, fell about the same time. Lieutenant-Colonel Minsing, the oldest remaining officer, drew off his troops, and returned next day to Philadelphia. The loss of the assailants was estimated at four hundred men. That of the Americans amounted to only thirty-two in killed and wounded.

The ships having been ordered to co-operate with Count Donop, the Augusta and four smaller vessels passed the lower line of chevaux-de-frise opposite Billingsport, and lay above it, waiting for the assault. The flood tide setting in as the attack commenced, they moved with it up the river. The obstructions sunk in the Delaware, having in some degree changed its channel, the Au-gusta and the Merlin grounded a considerable distance below the second line of chevaux-de-frise; and a strong wind from the north so checked the rising of the tide, that they could not be floated by the flood. The next morning, their situation was dis-covered, and four fire-ships were sent to destroy them, but with-out effect. Meanwhile, a warm cannonade was kept up on both sides, in the course of which the Augusta took fire, and it was found impracticable to extinguish the flames. Most of the men were taken out, the frigates withdrawn, and the Merlin set on fire; after which the Augusta blew up, and a few of the crew were lost in her.

Congress expressed its high sense of the merits of Colonel Greene, of Rhode Island, and of Lieutenant-Colonel Smith, of Maryland, who had commanded in the forts; and of Commodore Hazlewood, who had commanded the galleys, and presented a sword to each of those officers.

This repulse inspired sanguine hopes that the posts on the Delaware might be defended so long as to induce the evacuation of Philadelphia. But their condition did not justify this confi-dence.

Having failed in every attempt to draw the militia of Jersey to the Delaware, General Washington determined to strengthen the garrisons by further drafts from his army. Three hundred Penn-sylvania militia were detached to be divided between them, and General Varnum's brigade was ordered to take a position near

What was the issue of Donop's attack upon Red Bank? Mention his loss, and that of the Americans. What marine disaster was sustained by the enemy in the river Delaware?

Red Bank, and to relieve and reinforce the garrisons of both forts. The hope was entertained, that the appearance of a respectable continental force might encourage the militia to assemble in greater numbers.

In this state of things, intelligence was received of the successful termination of the northern campaign; in consequence of which, great part of the troops who had been employed against Burgoyne might be drawn to the aid of the army in Pennsylvania. Colonel Hamilton was dispatched to General Gates, to make the proper representations to that officer, and to urge him, if he contemplated no other service of more importance, to send immediately the regiments of Massachusetts and New Hampshire to aid the army of the middle department.

On reaching General Putnam, Colonel Hamilton found that a considerable part of the northern army had joined that officer; but that Gates had detained four brigades at Albany, for an expedition intended to be carried on in the winter against Ticonderoga.

Having made arrangements with Putnam for the immediate march of a large body of continental troops, Colonel Hamilton proceeded to Albany, for the purpose of remonstrating with General Gates against retaining so large and valuable a part of the army unemployed at a time when the most imminent danger threatened the vitals of the country. Gates was by no means disposed to part with his troops. He would not be persuaded that an expedition then preparing at New York was designed to reinforce General Howe; and insisted, that by a sudden movement up the Hudson, it would be in the power of the enemy, should Albany be left defenceless, to destroy the valuable arsenal at that place, and the military stores captured with Burgoyne.

After obtaining, by repeated remonstrances, an order directing three brigades to the Delaware, Hamilton hastened back to Putnam, and found the troops which had been ordered to join General Washington, still at Peekskill. The detachment from New York had suggested to Putnam the possibility of taking that place; and he does not appear to have made any great exertions to divest himself of a force which might enable him to accomplish an object that would give so much splendor to his military character. In addition to this circumstance, an opinion had insinuated itself among the soldiers that their share of service for the campaign had been performed, and that it was time for them to go into winter quarters. Great discontent, too, prevailed concerning their pay, which the government had permitted to be more than six

After the capture of Burgoyne in the north, what endeavors were made by Washington to procure reinforcements from the unemployed American force in that quarter? Mention the obstacles that were interposed.

months in arrear; and, in Poor's brigade, a mutiny broke out, in the course of which a soldier, who was run through the body by his captain, shot the officer dead before he expired. Colonel Hamilton came in time to borrow money of the Governor of New York, to put the troops in motion; and they proceeded by brigades to the Delaware. But delays retarded their arrival until the contest for the forts on that river was terminated.

The preparations of Sir William Howe being completed, a large battery on Province Island, of twenty-four and thirty-two pounders, and two howitzers of eight inches each, opened early in the morning of the 10th of November, upon fort Mifflin, at the distance of five hundred yards, and kept up an incessant fire for several days. The block-houses were reduced to a heap of ruins; the palisades were beaten down; most of the guns disabled, and the barracks battered in every part so that the troops could not remain in them. They were under the necessity of working and watching through the night; and, if in the day a few moments were allowed for repose, it was taken on the wet earth, which incessant rains had rendered a soft mud. The garrison was relieved by General Varnum every forty-eight hours; but his brigade was so weak that half the men were constantly on duty.

In the hope that the place might be maintained till reinforcements should arrive from the northern army, General Washington ordered that it should be defended to the last extremity; and never were orders better executed.

Several of the garrison were killed, and among them Captain Treat, a gallant officer who commanded the artillery. Colonel Smith received a contusion on his hip and arm, which compelled him to give up the command, and retire to Red Bank. Major Fleury, a French officer of distinguished merit, who served as engineer, reported that the place was still defensible, but the garrison was so worn down with fatigue, and so unequal to the extent of the lines, that he dreaded the event of an attempt to carry them by storm. The command was taken first by Colonel Russell, and afterwards by Major Thayer; and the artillery, commanded by Captain Lee, continued to be well served. The besiegers were several times thrown into confusion, and a floating battery which opened on the morning of the 14th was silenced in the course of the day.

The defence being unexpectedly obstinate, the besiegers brought up their ships as far as the obstructions Nov. 15 in the river permitted, and added their fire to that of the batteries. The brave garrison, however, still maintained their ground with

Was the partial aid at length obtained from the northern army, in time to save the forts on the Delaware? Describe the obstinate attack and defence of fort Mifflin.

unshaken firmness. In the midst of this stubborn conflict, the Vigilant, and a sloop-of-war, were brought up the middle channel, between Mud and Province islands, which had, unperceived by the besieged, been deepened by the current, in consequence of the obstructions in the main channel; and taking a station within one hundred yards of the works, not only kept up a destructive cannonade, but threw hand-grenades into them; while the musketeers from the round-top of the Vigilant, killed every man that appeared on the platform.

Major Thayer applied to the Commodore to remove these vessels; and six galleys were ordered on the service; but they returned without attempting any thing. Their report was that these ships were so covered by the batteries on Province Island, as to be unassailable.

It was apparent that the fort could be no longer defended; and on the night of the 16th, the garrison was withdrawn; soon afterwards a detachment from Province Island occupied the ground that had been abandoned.

The day after receiving intelligence of the evacuation of fort Mifflin, the commander-in-chief deputed Generals De Kalb and Knox, to confer with General Varnum, and the officers at fort Mercer, on the practicability of continuing to defend the obstructions in the channel. Their report was favorable; but a council of naval officers had already been called by the commodore, in pursuance of a request made by the commander-in-chief, previous to the evacuation, who were unanimously of opinion that it would be impracticable for the fleet, after the loss of the island, to maintain its station, or to assist in preventing the chevaux-de-frise from being weighed by the ships of the enemy.

General Howe had now completed a line of defence from the Schuylkill to the Delaware, and a reinforcement from New York had arrived in the river at Chester. These two circumstances enabled him to form an army in Jersey for the reduction of fort Mercer, without weakening himself so much in Philadelphia as to put his lines in hazard. He detached Lord Cornwallis in the morning of the 17th, with a strong body of troops, who formed a junction with the reinforcement from New York, at Billingsport.

General Washington communicated the movement of Lord Cornwallis to General Varnum, with orders to defend fort Mercer to the last extremity; and, with a view to military operations in that quarter, ordered one division of the army to cross the river at Burlington, and despatched expresses to the troops who were marching from the north by brigades, directing them to move

---

What was the result of the operations against fort Mifflin? In what manner did General Howe strengthen himself in Philadelphia? What directions were given by Washington to the troops approaching from the north?

down the Delaware, on the northern side.   Major-General Greene
was selected for this service.   But before Greene could cross the
Delaware, Lord Cornwallis approached fort Mercer, and the place
was evacuted.

Washington still hoped to recover much of what had been lost.
A victory would restore the Jersey shore, and his instructions to
General Greene indicated the expectation that he would be in a
condition to fight Lord Cornwallis.

That judicious officer feared the reproach of avoiding an action less than the just censure of sacrificing the real interests of
his country by fighting on disadvantageous terms.   The numbers
of the British, unexpectedly augmented by the reinforcement from
New York, exceeded his, even counting his militia as regulars;
and he determined to wait for Glover's brigade, which was marching from the north.   Before its arrival Lord Cornwallis took post
on Gloucester Point, entirely under cover of the guns of the ships,
from which place he was embarking his baggage and the provisions he had collected, for Philadelphia.

Believing that Lord Cornwallis would immediately follow his
magazines, and that the purpose of Sir William Howe was to
attack the American army while divided, General Washington
ordered General Greene to re-cross the Delaware and to join
him.

Thus, after one continued and arduous struggle of more than
six weeks, the British army secured itself in the possession of Philadelphia, by opening a free communication with the fleet.

The opinion that Sir William Howe meditated an attack on the
American camp, was confirmed by unquestionable intelligence
from Philadelphia.   On the 4th of December, Captain M'Lane, a
vigilant officer on the lines, discovered that this design was to be
immediately carried into execution, and communicated his disco-
very to the commander-in-chief.   On the evening of the same day,
General Howe marched out of Philadelphia with his whole force;
and, about eleven at night, M'Lane, who had been detached with
one hundred chosen men, attacked his van with some success at
Three-Mile run, on the Germantown road.   He hovered on the
front and flank of the advancing army until three next morning,
when the British encamped on Chesnut Hill, in front of the American right, and distant from it about three miles.   The Pennsylvania militia, under General Irvine, had also engaged the advanced
light parties of the enemy.   The general was wounded, and the
militia dispersed.

The range of hills on which the British were encamped, ap-

The British having now opened a communication with their shipping,
what enterprise was next undertaken by their commander?   Did the Americans get information of the design?

proached nearer to those occupied by the Americans as they stretched northward.

Having passed the day in reconnoitring the right, Sir William Howe changed his ground in the course of the night, and moving along the hills to his right, took an advantageous position in front of the American left. The next day he inclined still farther to his right, and approached still nearer to the left wing of the American army. Supposing a general engagement to be approaching, Washington detached Gist, with some Maryland militia, and Morgan, with his rifle corps, to attack the flanking and advanced parties. A sharp action ensued, in which Major Morris, of Jersey, a brave officer in Morgan's regiment, was mortally wounded, and twenty-seven of his men were killed and wounded. A small loss was also sustained in the militia. The parties attacked were driven in; but the enemy reinforcing in numbers, and Washington, unwilling to move from the heights and engage on the ground which was the scene of this skirmish, declining to reinforce Gist and Morgan, they, in turn, were compelled to retreat.

Sir William Howe continued to manœuvre towards the flank and in front of the left wing of the American army. Expecting to be attacked in that quarter, Washington made such change in the disposition of his troops as the occasion required; and the day was consumed in these movements. In the course of it, the American chief rode through every brigade of his army, delivering his orders in person, exhorting his troops to rely principally on the bayonet, in the use of which weapon their higher ground would give them the advantage, and encouraging them by the steady firmness of his countenance, as well as by his words. The dispositions of the evening indicated an intention to attack him next morning; but, in the afternoon, the British suddenly filed off from their right, and retreated to Philadelphia.

The loss of the British in this expedition rather exceeded one hundred men. It was sustained chiefly in the skirmish of the 7th, in which Major Morris fell.

On no former occasion had the two armies met uncovered by works, with equal numbers. The effective force of Sir William Howe has been since stated by Mr. Stedman, who then belonged to his army, to have amounted to fourteen thousand. The American army consisted of precisely twelve thousand one hundred and sixty-one regular troops, and three thousand two hundred and forty-one militia. This equality in point of numbers rendered it a prudent precaution to maintain a superiority of position. As the two armies occupied heights fronting each other, neither could

When the enemy marched out of Philadelphia to attack the Americans, what evolutions took place? Mention the details of the severe skirmish in which Major Morris was killed. Did a general battle ensue?

attack without giving its adversary some advantage in the ground; an advantage which neither seemed willing to relinquish.

The return of Sir William Howe to Philadelphia without bringing on an action, after marching out with the avowed intention of fighting, is the best testimony of the respect he felt for his adversary.

The cold was now becoming too intense for an army, neither well clothed, nor sufficiently supplied with blankets, longer to keep the field. It had become necessary to place the troops in winter quarters; and the selection of a position had been a subject of serious reflection. They could not be placed in villages without uncovering the country, or exposing them to the hazard of being beaten in detail.

To avoid these calamities, it was determined to take a strong position in the neighborhood of Philadelphia, equally distant from the Delaware above and below that city; and there to construct huts in the form of a regular encampment. A strong piece of ground at Valley Forge, on the west side of the Schuylkill, between twenty and thirty miles from Philadelphia, was selected for that purpose; and before day, on the morning of the 11th of December, the army marched to take possession of it. Lord Cornwallis had been detached on the morning of the same day to forage on the west side of the Schuylkill. He had dispersed a brigade of Pennsylvania militia under General Potter, and, pursuing the fugitives, had gained the heights opposite Matson's ford, and had posted troops to command the defile called the Gulf, just as the van of the American army reached the bank of the river. These positions had been taken without any knowledge of the approach of the American army, for the sole purpose of covering the foraging party.

Apprehending that General Howe had taken the field with his whole army, Washington moved rather higher up the river for the purpose of discovering the real situation, force, and designs of the enemy. The next day Lord Cornwallis returned to Philadelphia; and, in the course of the night, the American army crossed the river.

Here the commander-in-chief communicated to his army the arrangements intended for the winter. He expressed in strong terms his approbation of their conduct, exhorted them to bear with continuing fortitude the hardships inseparable from their situation, and assured them that those hardships were not imposed by caprice, but were necessary for the good of their country.

The winter had set in with great severity, and the sufferings of

---

What change of weather now admonished Washington of the necessity of providing shelter for his troops? Where was the winter station fixed, and what movements were made to reach it?

the army were extreme. They were, however, soon diminished by the erection of logged huts, which formed comfortable habitations, and satisfied men long unused to the conveniences of life.

CHAPTER X.

Enquiry into the conduct of General Schuyler.—Burgoyne appears before Ticonderoga.
—Evacuation of that place.—Of Skeenborough.—Defeat of Colonel Warner.—Evacuation of Fort Anne.—Burgoyne approaches Fort Edward—Schuyler retires to Saratoga.—To Stillwater.—St. Leger invests Fort Schuyler.—Herkimer defeated.—Colonel Baum detached to Bennington.—Is defeated.—Breckman defeated.—St. Leger abandons the siege of Fort Schuyler.—Gates takes command.—Burgoyne encamps on the heights of Saratoga.—Battle of Stillwater.—Of the 7th of October.—Burgoyne retreats to Saratoga.—Capitulates.—The British take Forts Montgomery and Clinton,—Forts Independence and Constitution evacuated.—The British evacuate Ticonderoga.

WHILE, with inferior numbers, General Washington maintained a stubborn contest in the middle states, events of great variety and importance were passing in the north.

After Sir Guy Carlton had placed his army in winter quarters, General Burgoyne embarked for Europe, to assist in making arrangements for the ensuing campaign. The American army, having been formed for one year only, dissolved itself at the expiration of that time.

The defence of this frontier was assigned to the regiments to be raised in Massachusetts, New Hampshire, and the north-western parts of New York; but the recruiting service advanced so slowly, that the aid of the militia became indispensable; and the plan of the campaign, on the part of the British, was involved in so much obscurity, that General Washington thought it advisable to direct eight of the regiments of Massachusetts to rendezvous at Peekskill.

The services of General Schuyler had been more solid than brilliant. Prejudices against him had been manifested by Congress, and his head quarters had been fixed at Albany; while General Gates was ordered to take command at Ticonderoga. He had been detained in service only by the deep interest he felt in the contest. So soon as his fears for Ticonderoga were removed, he waited on Congress for the purposes of adjusting his accounts, obtaining an enquiry into his conduct, and supporting those necessary measures for defence in the north which were suggested by his knowledge of the country. The committee appointed to enquire into his conduct, were so convinced of the im-

---

Whilst Washington was contending with Howe in the middle states, was the war going on in the north? What is said respecting the conduct and services of General Schuyler?

portance of his services, that Congress deemed it essential to the public interest, to prevail on him to remain in the army. The resolution fixing his head quarters at Albany, was repealed, and he was directed to proceed forthwith to the northern department, and take the command of it.

On his arrival, he found the army not only too weak for its object, but destitute of military supplies. At the same time, a spy, who had been seized near Onion river, gave information that General Burgoyne was at Quebec, on the point of commencing his formidable plan of operations for the ensuing campaign.

After completing his arrangements for defence at Ticonderoga, he hastened to Albany for the purpose of attending to his supplies, and of expediting the march of reinforcements. While occupied with these duties, he received intelligence from General St. Clair, who commanded at Ticonderoga during his absence, that Burgoyne had appeared before that place.

In the course of the preceding winter, a plan had been digested in the cabinet of London for penetrating to the Hudson, by the way of the Lakes. Burgoyne was to lead a formidable army against Ticonderoga; while a smaller party under Colonel St. Leger, composed chiefly of provincials, aided by a powerful body of Indians, was to march from Oswego by the way of the Mohawk, and to join the grand army on the Hudson.

Burgoyne reached Quebec as soon as the river was practicable, and appeared in full force on the river Bouquet, on the western banks of Lake Champlain, earlier than the American General had supposed to be possible. At this place he met the Indians in a grand council. In his speech delivered on this occasion, he endeavored to impress on them the distinction between enemies in the field, and unarmed inhabitants, many of whom were friends. Addressing himself to their avarice, he promised rewards for prisoners, but none for scalps. It was perhaps fortunate for America, that these feeble restraints were disregarded.

The royal army now advanced on both sides of the Lake, the fleet preserving a communication between its divisions, and encamped, on the first of July, within four miles of the American works. The next day they took possession of Mount Hope, which commanded part of the lines on the northern side, and cut off the communication with Lake George. The weakness of the garrison obliged General St. Clair to give up this post without a struggle. The British lines were then extended on the western side from the mountain to the Lake so as to inclose the garrison

---

Mention the arrangements of General Schuyler for the northern campaign. What plan had been formed by the British? State the first operations of Burgoyne, in its prosecution.

on that side. Sugar Hill, which stands at the confluence of the waters that unite at Ticonderoga, and overlooks the fortress, had been thought inaccessible, was seized, and batteries constructed on it which would be ready to open the next day. The garrison was not in a condition to check their operations.

The situation of St. Clair was at its crisis. The place must be immediately evacuated, or maintained at the hazard of losing the garrison.

Between these cruel alternatives, General St. Clair did not hesitate to choose the first; and a council of general officers, convened on the 5th of July, unanimously advised the immediate evacuation of the fort.

The invalids, and such stores as could be moved in the course of the night, were put on board batteaux, which proceeded under the guard of Colonel Long, up the river to Skeensborough; and before day the main body of the army commenced its march to the same place.

The orders given by General St. Clair to observe profound silence, and to set nothing on fire, were disobeyed; and before the rear guard was in motion, the house which had been occupied by General de Fleury was in flames. This seemed as a signal to the besiegers, who immediately entered the works, and commenced a rapid pursuit.

The bridge, the beam, and those other works, the construction of which had employed ten months, were cut through by nine in the morning, so as to afford a passage for British vessels, which engaged the American galleys about three in the afternoon, near the falls of Skeensborough. It being discovered that three regiments had landed at some distance from the fort at that place, for the purpose of cutting off the retreat of its garrison, as well as that of the detachment in the boats and galleys, the works and vessels were set on fire, and the troops retired to fort Anne. The baggage and a great quantity of military stores were lost.

General St. Clair reached Castletown, thirty miles from Ticonderoga, on the night succeeding the evacuation of the fort. The rear guard under Colonel Warner, augmented to one thousand men by those who, from excessive fatigue, had fallen out of the line of march, halted six miles short of that place.

The next morning at five they were attacked by General Frazer, at the head of eight hundred and fifty men. The action was warm and well contested. Two regiments of militia, which lay within two miles of Colonel Warner, were ordered to his assistance. They consulted their own safety, and hastened to Castle-

Against what fortress did the British army direct its force? When Ticonderoga was abandoned by the Americans, in what direction and manner did they retire? Relate the incidents of the pursuit.

town. While the action was maintained with equal spirit on both sides, General Reidisel arrived with his division of Germans, and the Americans were routed.

Colonel Francis, several other officers, and upwards of two hundred men were left dead on the field. One Colonel, seven Captains, and two hundred and ten privates, were made prisoners. Near six hundred are supposed to have been wounded, many of whom must have perished in the woods.

The British state their own loss at thirty-five killed, including one field-officer, and one hundred and forty-four wounded, including two Majors. It is scarcely credible, notwithstanding the difference in arms, that the disparity in the killed could have been so considerable.

St. Clair directed his march to Rutland, where he fell in with several soldiers who had been separated from their corps; and two days afterwards, at Manchester, was joined by Warner with about ninety men. From this place he proceeded to fort Edward, where he met General Schuyler.

After taking possession of Skeensborough, Burgoyne found it necessary to suspend the pursuit, and to halt a few days in order to reassemble and arrange his army.

The ninth British regiment, under Lieutenant-Colonel Hill, had been detached against fort Anne; and, the garrison of that place being in some force, two other regiments were ordered, under Brigadier-General Powell, to support the first party. Before his arrival, Colonel Long attacked the first party, and a sharp skirmish ensued, the advantage in which was claimed by both parties. Hearing that a reinforcement was approaching, he set fire to the works at fort Anne, and retired to fort Edward.

At Stillwater, on his way to Ticonderoga, General Schuyler was informed of the events which had taken place. No officer could have exerted more diligence and skill than he displayed. Having fixed his head quarters at fort Edward, he obstructed the navigation of Wood creek, and rendered the roads impassable. He was also indefatigable in driving the live-stock out of the way, and in bringing the military stores deposited at fort George to fort Edward. Colonel Warner was posted on the left flank of the British army, with instructions to raise the militia.

The evacuation of Ticonderoga was a shock for which no part of the United States was prepared. Neither the strength of the invading army nor of the garrison had been understood. When, therefore, intelligence was received that a place believed to be of immense strength, which was considered as the key to the whole

---

What was the loss of the two parties respectively, in an attack of General Frazer upon the Americans? Relate the progress of St. Clair's retreat. What was the impression made by these disasters?

9*

north-western country, had been abandoned without a siege, that a large train of artillery had been lost, that the army, on its retreat, had been defeated and dispersed; astonishment pervaded all ranks of men; and the conduct of the officers was universally condemned. Congress recalled all the generals of the department, and directed an enquiry into their conduct. Throughout New England especially, the most bitter aspersions were cast on them, and General Schuyler was involved in the common charge of treachery.

On the representation of General Washington, the recall of the officers was suspended; and on a full inquiry afterwards made, they were acquitted of all blame.

A letter from St. Clair to the commander-in-chief, stating the motives for evacuating Ticonderoga, represented his garrison, including nine hundred militia entitled to a discharge, at three thousand effective rank and file. The lines required ten thousand to man them. He affirmed that his supply of provisions, which had been procured after General Schuyler resumed the command of the department, was sufficient for only twenty days, and that the works on the Ticonderoga side were incomplete. He justified the delay of evacuating the place by the prevalent opinion that the force in Canada was not sufficient to justify so hardy an enterprise; and by his orders, which were to defend it to the last extremity.

A court of inquiry justified his conduct, and he retained the confidence of the commander-in-chief.

General Washington made great exertions to reinforce the northern army, and to replace the military stores which had been lost. Through the dark gloom which enveloped the affairs of that department, he discerned a ray of light which cheered his hope for the future; and exhorted General Schuyler not to despair. On receiving a letter from that officer of the 11th, stating the divided situation of the British army, he seemed to anticipate the event which afterwards occurred, and to suggest the measure in which originated that torrent of misfortune with which the British general was overwhelmed.

After collecting his army, Burgoyne proceeded with ardor on the remaining objects of the campaign. Such were the delays of opening Wood creek, and repairing the roads and bridges, that he did not reach the Hudson until the 14th of July. At this place it was necessary again to halt, in order to bring artillery, provisions, batteaux, and other articles, from fort George.

Schuyler had received some reinforcements of continental troops

Mention the decision of a court of enquiry, regarding the conduct of General St. Clair. Did Washington still entertain hopes of successful operations against Burgoyne? Mention the impediments to the progress of the invaders.

from Peekskill, but was not yet in a condition to face his enemy. He therefore crossed the Hudson and retreated to Stillwater, not far from the mouth of the Mohawk. General Lincoln was ordered to join him with a corp of militia assembling at Manchester, and he fortified his camp in the hope of being able to defend it.

At this place information was obtained that Burgoyne had evacuated Castletown, and that his communication with Ticonderoga, whence his supplies were chiefly drawn, was insecure. The orders to General Lincoln were countermanded, and he was directed to place himself, with all the militia he could assemble, in the rear of the British army, and to cut off its communication with the lakes. Here, too, he was informed that Colonel St. Leger, reinforced with a large body of Indians, had penetrated to the Mohawk, had laid siege to fort Schuyler, and had totally defeated General Herkimer, who had raised the militia of Tryon county in the hope of relieving the fort. The importance of preventing the junction of St. Leger with Burgoyne, determined Schuyler to detach General Arnold with three continental regiments to raise the siege. This measure so weakened the army as to render its removal to a place of greater security indispensable; and it was withdrawn to some islands at the confluence of the Mohawk with the Hudson.

On the 3d of August, St. Leger invested fort Schuyler. The garrison consisted of six hundred continental troops, commanded by Colonel Gansevoort. The besieging army rather exceeded fifteen hundred, of whom between five and six hundred were Indians. General Herkimer assembled the militia of Tryon county, and gave notice, on the morning of the 6th, of his intention to force a passage that day through the besieging army. Gansevoort drew out two hundred men under Lieutenant-Colonel Willet, to favor the execution of this design by a sortie.

Unfortunately, St. Leger received information the preceding day of Herkimer's approach, and, early in the morning, placed a strong party in ambuscade on the road along which he was to march. Herkimer's first notice was given by a heavy discharge of small-arms, which was followed by a furious attack from the Indians with their tomahawks. He defended himself with resolution, but was defeated with the loss of four hundred men. The destruction was prevented from being still more complete by the timely sortie made by Colonel Willet. He fell on the camp of the besiegers, routed them at the first onset; and, after driving them into the woods, returned without the loss of a man. This checked the pursuit of Herkimer, and recalled those engaged in it to the defence of their own camp.

What fort was besieged by the British? Mention the American officer who attempted to relieve the fort. Did he succeed in this endeavor?

Burgoyne was aware of the advantage of effecting a junction with St. Leger, by an immediate and rapid movement down the Hudson; but the obstacles to his progress multiplied daily, and each step produced new embarrassments. The increasing difficulty of communicating with fort George furnished strong inducements to attempt some other mode of supply.

Large magazines of provisions were collected at Bennington, which place was generally guarded by militia, whose numbers varied from day to day. The possession of these magazines, and the means of transportation which might be acquired in the country, would enable him to prosecute his ulterior plans without relying on supplies from Lake George, and he determined to seize them. To try the affections of the people, to complete a corps of loyalists, and to mount Reidisel's dragoons, were subordinate objects of the expedition. Lieutenant-Colonel Baum, with five hundred Europeans, and a body of loyalists, was detached on this service.

To facilitate the enterprise, Burgoyne moved down the east side of the Hudson. His van crossed the river on a bridge of rafts, and took post at Saratoga. Lieutenant-Colonel Brechman, with his corps, was advanced to Batten Hill, in order to support Baum.

On approaching Bennington, Baum discovered that the New Hampshire militia, commanded by General Starke, had reached that place on their way to camp; and, uniting with Colonel Warner, amounted to about two thousand men. He halted four miles from Bennington, fortified his camp, and despatched an express for a reinforcement. Lieutenant-Colonel Brechman was immediately ordered to his assistance, but such was the state of the roads, that though he marched at eight in the morning of the 15th, he could not reach the ground on which Baum had encamped until four in the afternoon of the next day.

In the mean time General Starke determined to attack him in his entrenchments. The American troops were mistaken by the loyalists for armed friends coming to join them. Baum soon discovered the error, and made a gallant defence; but his works were carried by storm, and great part of his detachment killed or taken prisoners. Brechman arrived during the pursuit, and gained some advantage over the disordered militia engaged in it. Fortunately Colonel Warner came up at this critical juncture with his continental regiment, and restored and continued the action, until the militia reassembled, and came to his support. Brechman maintained the action till dark, when, abandoning his artillery and baggage, he saved his party under cover of the night.

Mention the difficulties which began to environ Burgoyne. Did he attempt to possess himself of the American magazines of provisions? What success attended the effort? Describe the encounter.

One thousand stand of arms, nine hundred swords, thirty-two officers, and five hundred and sixty-four privates, were the known fruits of this victory. The number of dead was not ascertained, because the battle with Brechman had been fought in the woods, and been continued for several miles.

This success was soon followed by another of equal influence on the fate of the campaign.

Fort Schuyler had been fortified with more skill, and was defended with more courage than St. Leger had expected. The Indians became intractable, and manifested great disgust with the service. In this temper they understood that Arnold was advancing with a large body of troops, and that Burgoyne had been defeated. Unwilling to share the misfortunes of their friends, they manifested a determination not to await the arrival of Arnold. Many of them decamped immediately, and the rest threatened to follow.

The time for deliberation was past. The camp was broken up with indications of excessive alarm.

The victory at Bennington and the flight of St. Leger, however important in themselves, were still more so in their consequences. An army which had spread terror in every direction, was considered as already beaten. The great body of the people were encouraged, the disaffected became timid, and the wavering were deterred from putting themselves and their fortunes in hazard to support an army whose fate was so uncertain.

The barbarities which had been perpetrated by the Indians excited still more resentment than terror; and their influence on the royal cause was the more sensibly felt because they had been indiscriminate. But other causes of still greater influence were in operation. The last reinforcements of continental troops arrived in camp; the harvest, which had detained the northern militia, was over; and General Schuyler, whose eminent services had not exempted him from the imputation of being a traitor, was succeeded by General Gates, who possessed a large share of the public confidence, and who had been directed by Congress to take command of the northern department.

Schuyler continued his exertions to restore the affairs of the north until the arrival of his successor, though he felt acutely the disgrace and injury of being recalled at that crisis of the campaign when the fairest prospect of victory opened to his view.

Notwithstanding the difficulties which multiplied around him, Burgoyne remained steady to his purpose. Having collected provisions for thirty days, he crossed the river on the 13th and 14th of September, and encamped on the heights and plains of Saratoga,

What salutary consequences flowed from the American victory at Bennington? Who superseded General Schuyler in the command of the northern army? Did Burgoyne still persevere in his design?

with a determination to decide the fate of the expedition by a battle.
General Gates had advanced to the neighborhood of Stillwater.

On the night of the 17th, Burgoyne encamped within four miles
of the American army; and on the morning of the 19th, advanced
in full force towards its left. Morgan was immediately detached
to harass his front and flanks. He attacked and drove in a piquet
in front of the right wing; but, pursuing with too much ardor, he
was met in considerable force, and compelled in turn to retreat in
some disorder. Two regiments being sent to his assistance, his
corps was rallied, and the action became more general. Reinforcements were continually brought up; and, and by four in the
afternoon, upwards of three thousand American troops were
already engaged with the right wing of the British army, commanded by General Burgoyne in person. The conflict was extremely severe, and only terminated with the day. At night the
Americans retired to their camp, and the British lay on their arms
near the field of battle.

The killed and wounded on the part of the Americans, were
between three and four hundred. Among the former were Colonels
Coburn and Adams, and several other valuable officers. The
British loss has been estimated at rather more than five hundred
men. The Indians, beaten in the woods by Morgan, and restrained
from scalping and plundering the unarmed by Burgoyne, seeing
before them the prospect of hard fighting without profit, grew tired
of the service, and deserted in great numbers. The Canadians
and Provincials were not much more faithful; and Burgoyne perceived that his hopes must rest on his European troops. With
reason, therefore, this action was celebrated throughout the United
States as a victory.

General Lincoln had assembled a considerable body of militia
in the rear of Burgoyne, from which he drew three parties of five
hundred men each. One, under the command of Colonel Brown,
was to proceed against a small fort at the north end of Lake
George, where some American prisoners were confined. The second, commanded by Colonel Johnson, was to march against
Mount Independence; and the third, under Colonel Woodbury,
was detached to Skeensborough to cover the retreat of both the
others. With the residue, Lincoln proceeded to the camp of Gates.

Brown surprised the post on Lake George, and also took possession of Mount Defiance and Mount Hope. He liberated one
hundred American prisoners, and captured two hundred and ninety-
three of the enemy, with the loss of three killed and five wounded.

Colonel Johnson attacked Mount Independence, but was repulsed; after which, all the parties returned to their former station.

State the particulars of the battle of Stillwater. What loss was sustained
on each side? What movements now took place in the rear of Burgoyne?

The day after the battle of Stillwater, Burgoyne took a position almost within cannon-shot of the American camp, fortified his right, and extended his left to the river. Here he received a letter from Sir Henry Clinton, stating that he should attack fort Montgomery about the 20th of September.

Both armies retained their position until the 7th of October, when Burgoyne, having heard nothing farther from Sir Henry, and being reduced to the necessity of diminishing his rations, determined to make one more trial of strength with his adversary. For this purpose, he drew out fifteen hundred choice troops on his right, whom he commanded in person, assisted by Generals Philips, Reidisel, and Frazer. They formed within three quarters of a mile of the left of the American camp ; and a corps of rangers, provincials, and Indians, was pushed forward through secret paths to show themselves in its rear.

On perceiving these movements, Gates determined to attack their left, front, and right flank at the same time. Poor's brigade, and some regiments from New Hampshire, were ordered to meet them in front, while Morgan, with his rifle corps, made a circuit unperceived, and seized a height covered with wood on their right. The attack was made in front and on the left in great force, and at the same instant Morgan poured in a deadly fire on the front and right flank.

While the British right was thus closely pressed, a distinct corps was ordered to intercept its retreat to camp. Burgoyne, perceiving its danger, formed a second line with the light infantry, under General Frazer, and part of the twenty-fourth regiment, for its security. While this movement was in progress, the left was forced from its ground, and the light infantry was ordered to its aid. In the attempt to execute this order, they were attacked by Morgan, and Frazer was mortally wounded. Overpowered by numbers, Burgoyne regained his camp with the loss of his field-pieces, and great part of his artillery corps. The Americans followed close in his rear, and assaulted his works throughout their whole extent. The entrenchments were forced on their right ; and General Arnold, with a few men, entered their works ; but his horse being killed under him, and himself wounded, the troops were forced out of them ; and the night put an end to the assault. The left of Arnold's division was still more successful. Jackson's regiment, of Massachusetts, led by Lieutenant-Colonel Brooks, turned the right of the encampment, and stormed the works occupied by the German reserve. Lieutenant-Colonel Brechman was killed, and the works carried. Darkness put an end to the action, and the

Describe the position of Burgoyne. In what manner was the battle of Saratoga brought on ? Relate the details of its progress, and mention its general result. What terminated the action ?

Americans lay all night on their arms, about half a mile from the British lines.

Burgoyne changed his position in the night, and drew his whole army into a strong camp on the river heights, extending his right up the river.

General Gates was not disposed to attack him on this strong ground. He detached a party higher up the Hudson to intercept the British army on its retreat; and posted strong corps on the other side of the river to guard its passage.

Burgoyne retired to Saratoga, from which place he detached a company of artificers, under a strong escort, to repair the roads and bridges towards fort Edward. This detachment had scarcely moved, when the Americans appeared in force, and threatened his camp. The Europeans escorting the artificers were recalled; and a provincial corps employed in the same service being attacked, ran away, and left the workmen to shift for themselves.

The British army was now almost completely environed by a superior force, and its difficulties and dangers were continually increasing. A council of general officers took the bold resolution to abandon every thing but their arms, and such provisions as the soldiers could carry, and force their way to fort George.

Gates had anticipated this movement; and had placed strong guards at the fords of the Hudson, and formed an entrenched camp on the high grounds between fort Edward and fort George. The scouts sent to examine the route returned with this information, and the plan was abandoned.

In this hopeless condition, a negotiation was opened by a proposition from General Burgoyne, which was answered by a demand that the whole army should surrender themselves prisoners of war. This demand was peremptorily rejected, but a convention was signed on the 17th of October, stipulating that the British army, after marching out of their encampment with all the honors of war, should lay down their arms, and not serve against the United States till exchanged. They were to be permitted to embark for England.

These terms were probably more advantageous than would have been granted by Gates, had he entertained no apprehensions from Sir Henry Clinton, who was, at length, making his promised diversion on the North river, up which he had penetrated as far as Æsopus and its dependencies.

The drafts made from Peekskill had left that post and its dependencies in a situation to require the aid of militia for their security. The requisitions of Putnam were complied with; but the

---

What was the situation of Burgoyne, after the battle of Saratoga? In what way was it projected to escape, and what obstacle was interposed by Gates? Mention the terms of Burgoyne's capitulation.

attack being delayed, the militia became impatient, many deserted, and General Putnam was induced to discharge the residue.

Governor Clinton ordered out half the militia of New York; but this order was executed so slowly, that the forts were carried before the militia were in the field.

Forts Montgomery and Clinton had been constructed on the west of the Hudson, on very high ground, extremely difficult of access. To prevent ships from passing the forts, chevaux-de-frise had been sunk in the river, and a boom extended from bank to bank, which was covered with immense chains stretched at some distance in its front. These works were defended by the guns of the forts, and by a frigate and galleys stationed above them.

Fort Independence was four or five miles below forts Montgomery and Clinton, on the opposite side of the river; and fort Constitution rather more than six miles above them. Peekskill, the head quarters of the commanding officer, is just below fort Independence, on the same side of the river. The garrisons had been reduced to six hundred men; and the whole force of Putnam did not much exceed two thousand. This force, if properly applied, was more than competent to the defence of the forts against any numbers which could be spared from New York. To ensure success, it was necessary to draw the attention of Putnam from the real object, and to storm the works before the garrisons could be aided by his army. This Sir Henry Clinton accomplished.

Between three and four thousand men embarked at New York, and landed, on the 5th of October, at Verplank's Point, a short distance below Peekskill, upon which General Putnam retired to the heights in his rear. On the evening of the same day, a part of these troops re-embarked, and landed the next morning, at break of day, at Stony Point, and commenced their march through the mountains into the rear of forts Clinton and Montgomery. In the mean time the manœuvres of the vessels, and the appearance of a small detachment at Verplank's, persuaded General Putnam that the meditated attack was on fort Independence. The real designs of the enemy were not suspected until a heavy firing from the other side of the river announced the assault on the forts. Five hundred men were immediately detached to reinforce the garrison; but before they could cross the river, the forts were in possession of the British.

Both posts were assaulted about five in the afternoon. The works were defended until dark, when, the lines being too extensive to be completely manned, the assailants entered them in dif-

Describe the situation of the four forts whereby the Americans defended the passage up the North river. What movements of the British were directed against these posts, and with what success?

10

ferent places. Some of the garrison were made prisoners, while their better knowledge of the country enabled others to escape. Governor Clinton passed the river in a boat; and General James Clinton, though wounded in the thigh by a bayonet, also made his escape. The loss sustained by the garrison was about two hundred and fifty men. That of the assailants was rather less than two hundred.

The continental vessels of war lying above the boom and chains were burnt; forts Independence and Constitution were evacuated; and Putnam retreated to Fishkill. General Vaughan, after burning Continental village, proceeded up the river to Draper's, which he also destroyed.

General Putnam, whose army had been augmented by militia to six thousand men, detached General Parsons with two thousand to re-possess himself of Peekskill, and of the passes in the Highlands, while he watched the progress of the enemy up the river. Gates, on the capitulation of Burgoyne, had detached five thousand men to his aid. Before their arrival General Vaughan had returned to New York, whence a reinforcement to General Howe was about to sail.

The army which surrendered at Saratoga, exceeded five thousand men. On marching from Ticonderoga it was estimated at nine thousand. In addition to this great military force, the Americans acquired a fine train of artillery, seven thousand stand of excellent arms, clothing for seven thousand recruits, with tents and other military stores to a considerable amount.

The thanks of Congress were voted to General Gates and his army; and a medal of gold, in commemoration of this great event, was ordered to be struck and presented to him by the President in the name of the United States. Colonel Wilkinson, his Adjutant-General, whom he strongly recommended, was appointed Brigadier-General by brevet.

Soon after the capitulation of Burgoyne, Ticonderoga and Mount Independence were evacuated, and the garrison retired to Isle aux Noix and St. Johns.

What acts of injury were inflicted on the villages of the North river, by the British troops from New York? What aid was sent to this quarter by Putnam and Gates? Did the enemy retire? Mention the acquisitions of the Americans from the capture of Burgoyne. In what manner did Congress testify their approbation?

CHAPTER XI.

Distresses of the army.—It is subsisted by impressment.—Combination against General Washington.—Congress send a committee to camp.—Attempt to surprise Captain Lee.—Congress determines on a second expedition to Canada.—Abandons it.—General Conway resigns.—The Baron Steuben appointed Inspector-General.—Congress forbids the embarkation of Burgoyne's army.—Plan of reconciliation agreed to in Parliament.—Rejected by Congress.—Information of treaties with France.—Great Britain declares war against France.— Treatment of prisoners.—Partia exchange.

THE army under the immediate command of General Washington, was engaged through the winter in endeavoring to stop the intercourse between Philadelphia and the country. One of the first operations meditated after crossing the Schuylkill, was the destruction of a large quantity of hay, on the islands above the mouth of Darby Creek, within the power of the British. Early in the morning, after orders for this purpose had been given, Sir William Howe marched out of Philadelphia, and encamped so as completely to cover the islands; while a foraging party removed the hay, Washington, with the intention of disturbing this operation, gave orders for putting his army in motion, when the alarming fact was disclosed that the commissary's stores were exhausted, and that the last ration had been delivered and consumed.

On receiving intelligence of the fact, General Washington ordered the country to be scoured, and provisions to be seized wherever found. In the mean time, light parties were detached to harass the enemy; but Sir William Howe, with his accustomed circumspection, kept his army so compact that an opportunity to annoy him was seldom afforded even to the vigilance of Morgan and Lee. After completing his forage, he returned with inconsiderable loss to Philadelphia.

That the American army, while the value still retained by paper bills placed ample funds in the hands of government, should be destitute of food in a country abounding with provisions, is one of those extraordinary facts which cannot fail to excite attention.

Early in the war the office of Commissary-General had been conferred on Colonel Trumbull of Connecticut, a gentleman fitted for that important station. Yet from the difficulty of arranging so complicated a department, complaints were repeatedly made of the insufficiency of supplies. The subject was taken up by Congress; but the remedy administered served only to increase the disease. The system was not completed till near midsummer;

The British possessing Philadelphia, in what way did Washington endeavor to annoy them? What circumstance prevented his efficient action? What is to be said respecting the scarcity of food in the American camp?

and then its arrangements were such that Colonel Trumbull refused the office assigned to him. The new plan contemplated a number of subordinate officers, all to be appointed by Congress, and neither accountable to, or removeable by, the head of the department.

This *imperium in imperio*, erected in direct opposition to the opinion of the commander-in-chief, drove Colonel Trumbull from the army. Congress, however, persisted in the system; and its effects were not long in unfolding themselves. In every military division of the continent, loud complaints were made of the deficiency of supplies. The armies were greatly embarrassed, and their movements suspended, by the want of provisions. The present total failure of all supply was preceded by issuing meat unfit to be eaten. Representations on this subject had been made to the commander-in-chief, and communicated to Congress. That body had authorized him to seize provisions for the use of his army within seventy miles of head-quarters, and to pay for them in money or in certificates. The odium of this measure was increased by the failure of government to provide funds to take up these certificates when presented.

At the same time, the provisions carried into Philadelphia were paid for in specie at a fair price. The temptation was too great to be resisted. Such was the dexterity employed by the inhabitants in eluding the laws, that notwithstanding the vigilance of the troops stationed on the lines, they often succeeded in concealing their provisions from those authorized to impress for the army, and in conveying them to Philadelphia.

General Washington exercised the powers confided to him only in real necessity; and Congress appeared to be as much dissatisfied with his lenity as the people were with his rigour. His forbearance was disapproved, and instructions given for the regular exertion, in future, of the power with which he was invested.

Though still retaining his opinion that such violent measures would be less offensive if executed by the civil authority, he issued a proclamation, in obedience to the will of Congress, requiring the farmers, within seventy miles of head quarters, to thresh out one half of their grain by the 1st of February, and the residue by the 1st of March, under the penalty of having the whole seized as straw.

The success of this experiment did not correspond with the wishes of Congress. It was attended with the pernicious consequences which had been foreseen and suggested by the General, to avoid which he had been desirous of reserving military impressment as a dernier resort, to be used only in extreme cases.

What vigorous measure for the procurement of provisions was authorized by the American Congress?

About this time a strong combination was forming against the commander-in-chief, in which several members of Congress, and a very few officers of the army, are believed to have entered. The splendour with which the capture of a British army had surrounded the military reputation of General Gates, acquired some advocates for the opinion that the arms of America would be more fortunate should that gentleman be elevated to the supreme command. He could not be supposed hostile himself to the prevalence of this opinion; and some parts of his conduct warrant a belief that, if it did not originate with him, he was not among the last to adopt it.

The state of Pennsylvania, too, chagrined at the loss of its capital, furnished many discontented individuals. They imputed it to General Washington as a fault that, with forces inferior to his enemy in numbers, and in every equipment, he had not effected the same result which had been produced in the north by a continental army, in itself much stronger than its adversary, and so reinforced by militia as to treble its numbers. On the report that General Washington was moving into winter quarters, the Legislature of that state addressed a remonstrance to Congress on the subject, manifesting their dissatisfaction with the commander-in-chief. About the same time a new Board of War was created, of which General Gates was appointed president; and General Mifflin, who was supposed to be of the party unfriendly to the commander-in-chief, was one of its members. General Conway, the only brigadier in the army who had joined this faction, was appointed Inspector-General, and was promoted above senior brigadiers, to the rank of Major-General.

These machinations to diminish the well-earned reputation of General Washington, could not escape his notice. They made, however, no undue impression on his steady mind. When he unbosomed himself to his private friends, the feelings and sentiments he expressed were worthy of Washington. To Mr. Laurens, the President of Congress, who, in an unofficial letter, had communicated an anonymous accusation, made to him as president, containing many heavy charges against the commander-in-chief, he said, "I was not unapprised that a malignant faction had been for some time forming to my prejudice, which, conscious as I am of having done all in my power to answer the important purposes of the trusts reposed in me, could not but give me some pain on a personal account; but my chief concern arises from an apprehension of the dangerous consequences which intestine dissensions may produce to the common cause." * * *

What machinations were formed against the commander-in-chief? By whom were they chiefly promoted? In what manner did Washington express himself on this subject?

10*

"The anonymous paper handed you exhibits many serious charges, and it is my wish that it may be submitted to Congress." * * *

" My enemies take an ungenerous advantage of me. They know the delicacy of my situation, and that motives of policy deprive me of the defence I might otherwise make against their insidious attacks. They know I cannot combat their insinuations, however injurious, without disclosing secrets it is of the utmost moment to conceal." * * *

Fortunately for America, these combinations only excited resentment against those who were believed to be engaged in them.

Soon after they were communicated, the General also discovered the failure, already mentioned, in the commissary department. On this occasion he addressed Congress in terms of energy and plainness never used before. This letter contains a faithful as well as vivid description of the condition of the army and of the country.

The distresses it describes, however, so far as respected clothing, were not attributable to the inattention of Congress. Measures for the importation of cloths had been adopted early in the war, but had not produced the effect expected from them. Vigorous but ineffectual means had also been taken to obtain supplies from the interior. The unfortunate non-importation agreements which preceded the commencement of hostilities, had reduced the quantity of goods in the country below the ordinary amount, and the war had almost annihilated foreign commerce. The progress of manufactures did not equal the consumption; and such was the real scarcity, that exactions from individuals produced great distress, without relieving the wants of the soldiers.

To recruit the army for the ensuing campaign became again an object of vital importance; and the commander-in-chief again pressed its necessity on Congress and on the states. To obtain a respectable number of men by voluntary enlistment was obviously impossible. Coercion could be employed only by the state governments; and it required all the influence of General Washington to induce the adoption of a measure so odious in itself, yet so indispensable to the successful termination of the war.

To the causes which had long threatened the destruction of the army, the depreciation of paper-money was now to be added. It had become so considerable, that the pay of an officer would not procure even those absolute necessaries which might protect his person from the extremes of heat and cold. The very few who possessed small patrimonial estates found them melting away; and others were unable to appear as gentlemen. Such circumstances

Was the scheme of supplanting the commander-in-chief attended with success? Mention the causes which led to a scarcity of manufactured articles. What is said respecting recruits, and the depreciation of paper-money?

could not fail to excite disgust with the service, and a disposition to leave it.

With extreme anxiety the commander-in-chief watched the progress of a temper which would increase, he feared, with the cause which produced it. He was therefore early and earnest in pressing the consideration of this important subject on the attention of Congress.

The weak and broken condition of the continental regiments, the strong remonstrances of the General, the numerous complaints received from every quarter, determined Congress to depute a committee to reside in camp during the winter, for the purpose of investigating the whole military establishment, and reporting such reforms as the public good might require.

This committee repaired to head quarters in the month of January. The commander-in-chief laid before them a general statement, taking a comprehensive view of the condition of the army, and detailing the remedies necessary for the correction of existing abuses, as well as those regulations which he deemed essential to its future prosperity. This paper discloses defects of real magnitude in the existing arrangements. In perusing it, the reader is struck with the numerous difficulties in addition to those resulting from inferiority of numbers, with which the commander-in-chief was under the necessity of contending. The neglect of the very serious representation it contained respecting a future permanent provision for the officers, threatened, at an after period, the most pernicious effects.

The wants and distresses of the army actually seen by the committee, made a much deeper impression than could have been received from a statement of them. They endeavored to communicate their impressions to Congress, and urged a correction of the errors they perceived.

Much of the sufferings of the army was attributed to mismanagement in the quarter-master's department. This subject was taken up early by the committee, and proper representations made respecting it. But Congress still remained under the influence of those opinions which had produced such mischievous effects, and were still disposed to retain the subordinate officers of the department in a state of immediate dependence on their own body.

While the reforms proposed were under consideration, the distresses of the army approached their acme. Early in February the commissaries gave notice that the country, to a great distance, was actually exhausted; and that it would be impossible to obtain supplies longer than to the end of that month. General Wash-

Mention the method adopted by Congress to obtain exact information respecting the distresses of the army. What was communicated by this committee? State the extent of the destitution.

ington found it necessary again to interpose his personal exertions
to procure provisions from a distance.

In the apprehension that the resources of the commissary department might fail before these distant supplies could reach him,
and that the enemy designed to make another foraging incursion
into the country around Philadelphia, he detached General Wayne
with orders to seize every article required by his troops within
fifteen miles of the Delaware, and to destroy the forage on the
islands between Philadelphia and Chester. The inhabitants concealed their provisions and teams; and before sufficient aid could
be procured by these means, the bread as well as the meat was
exhausted, and famine prevailed in camp.

In an emergency so pressing, the commander-in-chief used
every effort to feed his hungry army. Parties were sent out to
glean the country; officers of influence were deputed to Jersey,
Delaware, and Maryland; and circular letters were addressed to
the Governors of States, describing the wants of the troops, and
urging the greatest exertions for their immediate relief.

Fortunately for America, there were features in the character
of Washington which, notwithstanding the discordant materials
of which his army was composed, attached his officers and soldiers so strongly to his person, that no distress could weaken their
affection nor impair the respect and veneration in which they held
him. To this sentiment is to be attributed, in a great measure,
the preservation of a respectable military force, under circumstances but too well calculated for its dissolution.

In a few days the army was rescued from the famine with
which it had been threatened. It was perceived that the difficulties which had produced such melancholy effects, were occasioned
more by the want of due exertion in the commissary department,
and by the efforts of the people to save their stock for a better
market, than by a real deficiency of food in the country.

This same demonstration seems to have convinced Congress
that their favorite system was radically vicious; and the subject
was taken up with the serious intention of remodelling the commissary department on principles recommended by experience.
But such were the delays inherent in the organization of that
body, that the new system was not adopted until late in April.

The vigilance of the parties on the lines throughout the winter
intercepted a large portion of the supplies intended for Philadelphia; and corporal punishment was often inflicted on those who
were detected in attempting this infraction of the laws. As Captain Lee was particularly active, a plan was formed late in January

Mention the circumstance that had so great an influence in reconciling
the American troops to their numerous privations. Were they able to intercept supplies intended for the British?

to surprise him in his quarters. A large body of cavalry, having made an extensive circuit and seized four of his patroles without communicating an alarm, appeared at his quarters about break of day. The troopers in the houses were immediately placed at the doors and windows, and, without the loss of a man, repulsed the assailants. Lieutenant Lindsay and one private were wounded. The whole number in the house did not exceed ten. That of the British was supposed to be two hundred. They lost a serjeant and three men, with several horses killed; and an officer and three men wounded.

The result of this affair gave great pleasure to the commander-in-chief, who had formed a high opinion of Lee's talents as a partisan. He mentioned it with approbation in his orders, and in a private letter to the Captain. For his merit through the preceding campaign, Congress promoted him to the rank of Major, and gave him an independent partisan corps, to consist of three troops of horse.

While the deficiency of the public resources was felt in all the military departments, a plan was matured in Congress and in the board of war, for a second irruption into Canada. It was proposed to place the Marquis de Lafayette at the head of this expedition, and to employ Generals Conway and Starke as second and third in command.

The first intimation to General Washington that the expedition was contemplated, was given in a letter of the 24th of January, from the President of the board of war, inclosing one of the same date for the Marquis, requiring the attendance of that nobleman on Congress to receive his orders. The commander-in-chief was requested to furnish Colonel Hazen's regiment for the expedition; his advice and opinion respecting which were asked. The northern States were to furnish the necessary troops.

General Washington, without noticing the marked want of con fidence betrayed in this whole transaction, ordered Hazen's regiment to Albany; and the Marquis proceeded immediately to the seat of Congress. At his request, he was to remain under the orders of Washington. He then repaired to Albany, where the troops for the expedition were to assemble. On finding that no preparations had been made, that nothing which had been promised was in readiness, he abandoned the enterprise as impracticable. It was soon afterwards relinquished by Congress also

While his army lay at Valley Forge, the Baron Steuben arrived in camp. This gentleman was a Prussian officer, who came to the United States with ample recommendations, and was well

---

What expedition, without the knowledge of Washington, was now projected? Was it persisted in, or abandoned? Who was the foreign officer of distinction, that now offered his services to Congress?

qualified to instruct raw troops in that system of field exercise which the great Frederick had introduced. He offered to render his services as a volunteer; and, after a conference with Congress, proceeded to Valley Forge.

Although the office of Inspector-General had been bestowed on Conway, he had never entered on its duties. His promotion over senior officers had given much umbrage, and, added to the know ledge of his being in a faction hostile to the commander-in-chief had made his situation in the army so uncomfortable, that h withdrew to York, in Pennsylvania, then the seat of Congress. Not being directed to rejoin the army when the expedition to Canada was abandoned, and entertaining no hope of being permitted to exercise the functions of his new office, he resigned his commission and returned to France. On his resignation, the Baron Steuben, who had performed the duties of Inspector-General, as a volunteer, was, on the recommendation of General Washington, appointed to that office with the rank of Major-General. This gentleman was of real service to the American troops.

During the winter, Congress was occupied with several matters of great interest. Among them was the stipulation in the convention at Saratoga, for the return of the British army to England.

The facility with which the convention might be violated on the part of the British, and the captured army be employed in the United States, seems to have suggested itself to the American government as soon as the first rejoicings were over; and a resolution was passed early in November, directing General Heath to transmit to the board of war, a descriptive list of all persons comprehended in the convention. The hope was entertained, that as the port of Boston, the place of embarkation, was often rendered extremely difficult of access early in the winter, it might be closed before a sufficient number of vessels for the transportation of the troops to Europe could be collected.

Contrary to expectation, a fleet of transports reached Rhode Island early in December. Several circumstances had combined to ripen the previous suspicions of Congress into conviction. General Burgoyne had addressed a letter to General Gates, in which he complained of the inconvenient quarters assigned his officers, as a breach of the convention—a complaint supposed to be made for the purpose of letting in the principle, that the breach of one article of the treaty discharges the injured party from its obligations. This suspicion derived strength from the indiscreet hesitation of General Burgoyne to permit the resolution requiring a descriptive list of his troops to be executed.

Mention the circumstances which induced a suspicion on the part of Congress, that General Burgoyne might ultimately violate that part of the convention which prohibited the British prisoners from serving in America?

It was also alleged that the number of transports was not sufficient to convey the troops to Europe; and that General Howe
could not possibly have laid in a sufficient stock of provisions for
the voyage. The objections were strengthened by some trivial
inadvertent infractions of the convention, which, it was contended,
gave Congress a strict right to detain the troops.

The whole subject was referred to a committee, on receiving
whose report, Congress resolved "that the embarkation of Lieu-
tenant-General Burgoyne and the troops under his command be
suspended until a distinct and explicit ratification of the convention of Saratoga shall be properly notified by the court of Great
Britain to Congress." A request subsequently made by General
Burgoyne, to be permitted to embark for England in consideration
of the state of his health, was readily granted.

The impression made on the British nation by the capitulation
of Burgoyne, at length made its way into the cabinet, notwithstanding the persevering temper of the king; and Lord North
moved for leave to bring in two bills having conciliation for their
object. The first surrendered the principle of taxation, and the
second empowered the crown to appoint commissioners to treat
of peace.

General Washington received early intimation of their arrival,
and immediately forwarded copies of them to Congress, in a letter
suggesting the policy of preventing their pernicious influence on
the public mind by all possible means.

This letter was referred to a committee consisting of Messrs.
Morris, Drayton, and Dana, by whom a report was made, investigating the bills with much acuteness and asperity. The report
and resolutions founded on it were ordered to be published.

During these transactions, a frigate arrived with the important
intelligence that treaties of alliance and of commerce had been
formed between the United States of America and France. This
event had been long anxiously expected; and had been so long
delayed as to excite serious apprehensions that it might not take
place.

France, still sore under the wounds which had been inflicted
during the war of 1756, had viewed the growing discontents between Great Britain and her colonies with secret satisfaction; but
rather as a circumstance to be encouraged from motives of general policy, than as one from which any definite advantage was
to be derived. The system on which the cabinet of Versailles
appears to have acted, for a time, was to aid and encourage the
colonies secretly, in order to prevent a reconciliation with the

What two bills on American affairs were enacted by Parliament? What
report respecting them was made by a committee of Congress? Mention
the important alliance that was at length effected.

mother country, and to prepare privately for hostilities, but to avoid every thing which might give occasion for open war.

During the public demonstration of dispositions favorable to England, means were taken to furnish aids of ammunition and arms, and to facilitate the negotiation of loans to the United States; and the owners of American privateers, though forbidden to sell their prizes, or to procure their condemnation, found means to dispose of them privately.

Matters remained in a fluctuating state until December 1777, when intelligence of the convention of Saratoga reached France. The American deputies took that opportunity to press the treaty which had been under consideration for twelve months; and to urge the importance at this juncture, when Britain would most probably make proposals for an accommodation, of communicating to Congress precisely what was to be expected from France and Spain.

They were informed by M. Girard, one of the secretaries of the king's Council of State, that it was determined to acknowledge the independence of the United States, and to make a treaty with them.

A courier was despatched to his Catholic Majesty with information of the line of conduct about to be pursued by France; on whose return, a treaty of friendship and commerce was concluded. This was accompanied by a treaty of alliance, eventual and defensive, stipulating that if war should break out between France and England during the existence of that with the United States, it should be made a common cause; and that neither party should conclude either truce or peace with Great Britain, without the formal consent of the other.

In a few weeks the Marquis de Noailles announced officially to the court of London, the treaty of friendship and commerce France had formed with the United States. The British government, considering this notification as a declaration of open war, published a memorial for the purpose of justifying to all Europe the hostilities it had determined to commence.

The despatches containing these treaties were received by the President on Saturday the 2d of May, after Congress had adjourned. That body was immediately convened, the despatches were opened, and their joyful contents communicated.

From this event, the attention must be directed to the proceedings respecting the exchange of prisoners.

General Gage, in the harshness of spirit which had been excited while governor of Massachusetts, not only threw all his prisoners into a common jail, but rejected every proposition for an

---

What mutual obligations were imposed by the treaty between the United States and France? What was the determination of Britain, on learning the existence of this treaty?

exchange of them. General Howe abandoned this absurd system; but the Americans did not possess a sufficient number of prisoners to relieve all their citizens, and many of them still remained in confinement. Representations were continually received from these unfortunate men, describing in strong terms the severity of their treatment. When charged with conduct so unworthy of his character, Sir William Howe positively denied its truth.

The capture of General Lee furnished an additional ground of controversy. The resignation of his commission in the British service not having been received when he entered into that of America, a disposition was at first manifested to consider him as a deserter, and he was closely confined. Congress directed General Howe to be assured that Lieutenant-Colonel Campbell and five Hessian field-officers should experience precisely the fate of General Lee. These officers were taken into close custody, and informed that the resolution announced by General Howe would be strictly enforced.

The resolutions of Congress not to observe a convention respecting the prisoners taken at the Cedars, was also the source of much embarrassment to the commander-in-chief. Alleging that the capitulation had been violated on the part of the enemy, they withheld their sanction from the agreement entered into by General Arnold, and refused to allow other prisoners to be returned in exchange for those liberated under that agreement, until the Indians alleged to have murdered some of the prisoners should be given up, and compensation made for the baggage said to have been plundered. As the fact alleged was not clearly proved, Sir William Howe continued to press General Washington on the subject, and to urge the importance of a punctilious observance of faith plighted in such engagements.

The remonstrances of General Washington to Congress could not, for a long time, procure a change of their resolution.

After the sufferings of the prisoners in New York had been extreme, and great numbers had perished in confinement, the survivors were liberated for the purpose of being exchanged; but so miserable was their condition, that many of them died on their way home. For the dead as well as the living, General Howe claimed a return of prisoners; while General Washington contended that reasonable deductions should be made for those who were actually dead of diseases under which they labored when permitted to leave the British prisons. Until this claim should be admitted, General Howe rejected any partial exchange.

Information was continually received that the American prison-

Mention the differences which arose between the commanders of the two armies, respecting the exchange of prisoners. What is said respecting the American prisoners at New York?

ers suffered almost the extremity of famine. The British General answered the repeated remonstrances on this subject by a denial of the fact. He continued to aver that the same food was issued to the prisoners as to British troops while in transports, or elsewhere, not on actual duty; and yielded to a request to permit a commissary to visit the jails. Mr. Boudinot, the American commissary of prisoners, was met by Mr. Ferguson, the British commissary, and informed that General Howe thought it unnecessary for him to come into the city, and would himself inspect the situation and treatment of prisoners. There is reason to believe that their causes of complaint of complaint were considerably diminished, at least so far as respected provisions. But clothes and blankets were also necessary. General Howe would not permit the purchase of those articles in Philadelphia, and they could not be procured elsewhere.

To compel him to abandon this distressing restriction, and to permit the use of paper-money within the British lines, Congress resolved that no prisoner should be exchanged until all the expenditures made in paper, for the supplies they received from the United States, should be paid in specie, at the rate of four-and-six-pence for each dollar. They afterwards determined that, from the 1st day of February, no British commissary should be permitted to purchase any provisions for the use of prisoners west of New Jersey; but that all supplies should be furnished from British stores.

Sir William Howe remonstrated against the last resolution, as a decree which doomed a considerable number of prisoners to a slow and painful death by famine. Its severity was, in some degree, mitigated by a resolution that each British commissary of prisoners might receive provisions from the American commissary of purchases, to be paid for in specie, according to the resolution of the 19th of December, 1777.

About the same time, an order was hastily given by the Board of War, which produced no inconsiderable embarrassment.

General Washington had consented that a quartermaster, with a small escort, should come out of Philadelphia with clothes and other comforts for prisoners. He had expressly stipulated for their security, and had given them a passport.

While they were travelling through the country, information was given to the Board of War that Sir William Howe had refused to permit provisions to be sent to the American prisoners by water. This information was not correct. The board, however, ordered Lieutenant-Colonel Smith to seize the party, their carriages and provisions, and detain them.

By what methods did Congress endeavor to secure good treatment to American prisoners in the hands of the British?

General Washington despatched one of his aids, with directions for the immediate release of the persons and property seized; but the officers refused to proceed on their journey, and returned to Philadelphia.

After all hope of inducing General Howe to recede from the high ground he had taken respecting the compensation for prisoners released in Philadelphia had been abandoned, he suddenly relinquished it himself, and acceded completely to the proposition made by General Washington. Commissaries were mutually appointed, who were to meet on the 10th of March in Germantown, to arrange the details of a general cartel. On the 4th of that month, a resolution of Congress appeared in a newspaper, calling on the several states for the amount of supplies furnished the prisoners, that they might be adjusted according to the rule of the 10th of December, before the exchange should take place.

This embarrassing resolution obliged General Washington to request a postponement of the meeting of the commissaries till the 21st of the month. The interval was successfully employed in procuring a repeal of the resolution.

The commissioners met according to the second appointment; but, on examining their powers, it appeared that those given by General Washington were expressed to be in virtue of authority vested in him; while those given by Sir William Howe contained no such declaration.

This omission produced an objection on the part of the United States; and General Howe refusing to change the language, the negotiation was broken off. Some time afterwards Sir William Howe proposed that all prisoners, actually exchanged, should be sent into the nearest posts, and returns made of officer for officer, and soldier for soldier; and that if a surplus of officers should remain, they should be exchanged for an equivalent in privates.

On the application of General Washington, Congress acceded to this proposal, so far as related to the exchange of officer for officer, and soldier for soldier; but rejected the part which admitted an equivalent in privates for a surplus of officers, because the officers captured with Burgoyne were exchangeable. Under this agreement an exchange took place to a considerable extent.

Did the British General at length accede to the wishes of Washington, respecting the prisoners? Mention the resolution of Congress which impeded the negotiation, and the point of formality which caused it to be broken off. What arrangement was at length effected upon this embarrassing subject?

CHAPTER XII.

Incursion into Jersey.—General Lacy surprised.—Attempt on Lafayette at Barren Hill.—General Howe resigns.—Is succeeded by Sir Henry Clinton.—He evacuates Philadelphia.—Marches through Jersey.—Battle of Monmouth.—General Lee arrested.—Sentenced to be suspended.—Thanks of Congress to General Washington and the army.

As the spring opened, several expedients were undertaken by the British. Colonel Mawhood made an incursion into Jersey, at the head of twelve hundred men. Governor Livingston was immediately requested to call out the militia in order to join Colonel Shreeve, whose regiment was detached for the protection of that state. The legislature had omitted to make provision for paying them, and the governor could not bring them into the field. Mawhood of course was unrestrained; and the devastation committed by his party was wantonly distressing. After completing his forage, unmolested, he returned to Philadelphia. During the continuance of this incursion, which lasted six or seven days, not more than two hundred militia could be collected.

Not long afterwards, an expedition was undertaken against General Lacy, who, with a small body of Pennsylvania militia, varying in its numbers, watched the roads on the north side of the Schuylkill.

Colonel Abercrombie, who commanded this expedition, avoided all Lacy's posts of security, and threw a detachment into his rear before he discovered the approach of an enemy. After a short resistance, he escaped with a loss of a few men, and all his baggage. His corps was entirely dispersed, and he was soon afterwards replaced by General Potter.

To cover the country more effectually on the north side of the Schuylkill, to form an advance guard for the security of the main army, and to be in readiness to annoy the rear of the enemy should he evacuate Philadelphia, the Marquis de Lafayette was detached on the 18th of May, with more than two thousand choice troops, to take post near the lines.

He crossed the Schuylkill, and encamped near Barren Hill church eight or ten miles in front of the army. Immediate notice of his arrival was given to Sir William Howe, who reconnoitred his position, and formed a plan to surprise him. On the night of the 19th, General Grant with five thousand select troops, marched on the road leading up the Delaware, and after making a considerable circuit, reached Plymouth meeting-house, rather more than a mile in rear of the Marquis, between him and Valley Forge,

Mention the incursions of the British into New Jersey, and their surprise of General Lacy. What attempt was made on Lafayette at Barren Hill?

before sunrise next morning. In the course of the night, General Grey with a strong detachment, had advanced up the Schuylkill, on its south side, and taken post at a ford, two or three miles in front of the right flank of Lafayette, while the residue of the army encamped at Chesnut hill.

Captain M'Clane, a vigilant partisan, was posted some distance in front of Barren hill. In the course of the night, he fell in with two British grenadiers at Three-Mile run, who communicated to him the movement made by Grant, and also the preparations for that made by Grey. Conjecturing the object, M'Clane detached Captain Parr with a company of riflemen to harass and retard the column advancing up the Schuylkill, and hastened in person to the camp of Lafayette. That officer instantly put his troops in motion, and passed the Schuylkill at Watson's ford, which was rather nearer to Grant than himself, with the loss of only nine men.

General Grant followed his rear, and appeared at the ford just after the Americans had crossed it. Finding them advantageously posted, he did not choose to attack them; and the whole army returned to Philadelphia.

This was the last enterprise attempted by Sir William Howe. He resigned the command of the army to Sir Henry Clinton, and embarked for Great Britain. About the same time, orders were received for the evacuation of Philadelphia. The great naval force of France rendered that city a dangerous position, and determined the administration to withdraw the army from the Delaware.

The preparations for this movement indicated equally an embarkation of the whole army, or its march through Jersey. The last was believed to be most probable, and every exertion was made to take advantage of it.

General Maxwell with the Jersey brigade was ordered over the Delaware, to Mount Holly, to join Major-General Dickenson, who was assembling the militia for the purpose of co-operating with the continental troops.

On the 17th of June, intelligence was received that great part of the British army had crossed the Delaware, and that the residue would soon follow. The opinion of the general officers was required on the course to be pursued. General Lee, who had been lately exchanged, and whose experience gave great weight to his opinions, was vehement against risking either a general or partial engagement. General Du Portail, a French officer of considerable reputation, maintained the same opinions; and the Baron de Steuben concurred in them. The American officers seem to

---

When Sir William Howe left the army and sailed for Europe, what important measure was determined on, regarding Philadelphia? In leaving this city, what was the line of march of the enemy?

11*

have been influenced by the counsels of the Europeans; and, of seventeen Generals, only Wayne and Cadwallader were decidedly in favor of attacking the enemy. Lafayette appeared inclined to that opinion without openly embracing it; and General Greene was inclined to hazard more than the counsels of the majority would sanction.

On the morning of the 28th, Philadelphia was evacuated; and by two in the afternoon, all the British troops were encamped on the Jersey shore. As their line of march, until they passed Crosswick's, led directly up the Delaware, General Washington found it necessary to make an extensive circuit, and to cross the river at Coryell's ferry, after which he kept possession of the high grounds; thereby retaining the choice of bringing on or avoiding an action.

As Sir Henry Clinton encamped at Allentown, the main body of the American army lay in Hopewell township. Major-General Dickenson, with one thousand militia and Maxwell's brigade, hung on his left flank; General Cadwallader with Jackson's regiment and a few militia was in his rear; and Colonel Morgan with a regiment of six hundred men watched his right.

Notwithstanding the almost concurrent opinion of his general officers against risking an action, Washington appears to have been strongly inclined to that measure. A council was therefore once more assembled, who were asked whether it would be advisable to hazard a general action? If it would, ought it to be brought on by a general or partial attack, or by taking a position which must compel the enemy to become the assailants?

Should a general action be unadvisable, he asked what measures could be taken to annoy the enemy on his march?

The proposition respecting a general action was decidedly negatived. But it was advised to reinforce the corps on the left flank of the enemy with fifteen hundred men; and to preserve with the main body of the army a relative position, which would enable it to act as circumstances might require.

In pursuance of this opinion, the troops on the lines were strengthened with fifteen hundred select men commanded by General Scott; and the army moved forward to Kingston.

Knowing that several officers whose opinions were highly valued wished secretly for something more than skirmishing, General Washington, who was still in favor of an engagement, determined to take his measures on his own responsibility; and ordered General Wayne with one thousand men to join the advanced corps. The continental troops of the front division now amounting to at least four thousand men, it was proper that they should be com-

Did the American army follow the British, in their march through Jersey towards New York? Was Washington desirous of attacking them, and what steps were favored by him, with the intention of bringing on an action?

manded by a Major-General. Lee had a right to claim this tour of duty; but, supposing that nothing important was to be attempted, he showed no inclination to assert his claim, and yielded it to Lafayette. The orders given to this General, were to gain the enemy's left flank and rear; give him every practicable annoyance; and attack by detachment, or with his whole force, as the occasion might require. General Washington moved forward to Cranberry for the purpose of supporting his front division, which had pressed forward and taken a position about five miles in rear of the British army, with the intention of attacking it next morning on its march.

Lafayette had scarcely taken command of the front division, when Lee, perceiving that great importance was attached to it by the general officers, began to regret having yielded it. To relieve his feelings without wounding those of Lafayette, General Washington detached him with two additional brigades to Englishtown, to which place the Marquis had been directed to march. It was expressly stipulated that any enterprise already formed by Lafayette should be carried into execution as if the commanding officer had not been changed. Lee acceded to this condition; and, with two additional brigades, joined the front division, now amounting to five thousand continental troops. The rear division moved forward, and encamped about three miles in his rear. Morgan still hovered on the right flank of the British, and General Dickenson on the left.

The position of Sir Henry Clinton on the heights about Monmouth Court-House was unassailable, and he was within twelve miles of the high grounds about Middletown, after reaching which he would be perfectly secure. Lee was therefore ordered to attack the British rear as soon as it should move from its ground.

About five in the morning, intelligence was received that the front of the enemy was in motion. Lee was ordered to attack the rear "unless there should be powerful reasons to the contrary," and was at the same time informed that the rear division would be on its march to support him.

Sir Henry Clinton had observed the appearances on his flanks and rear, and had changed the order of his march. The baggage was placed in front under the care of Knyphausen, while the flower of his army formed the rear division under the particular command of Lord Cornwallis, who was accompanied by the commander-in-chief.

Soon after the rear had moved from its ground on the 28th, Lee prepared to execute the orders he had received, and directed Ge-

What preparations were made by Washington, to attack the British? What was the position of Sir Henry Clinton? Mention the American officer who was ordered to attack the rear of the enemy?

neral Wayne to attack the rear of their covering party with sufficient vigor to check its march, but not to press it so closely as either to force it up to the main body, or draw reinforcements to its aid. In the meantime he continued to gain the front of this party by a shorter road, and, intercepting its communication with the line, to bear it off before it could be assisted.

While in the execution of this design, a gentleman in the *suite* of General Washington came up to gain intelligence; and Lee communicated his object.

Before he reached his destination, there was reason to believe that the British rear was much stronger than had been conjectured.

Sir Henry Clinton, perceiving that his rear was followed by a strong corps, that a cannonade was commenced upon it, and that a respectable force showed itself at the same time on both his flanks, suspected a design on his baggage, and determined to attack the troops in his rear so vigorously as to compel the recall of those on his flanks.

Lee now discovered the strength of the British rear division; but was still determined to engage on the ground his troops occupied, though his judgment disapproved the measure, there being a morass immediately in his rear.

This was about ten. While both armies were preparing for action, General Scott (as stated by General Lee) mistook an oblique march of an American column for a retreat, and repassed the ravine in his rear.

Being himself of opinion that the ground was unfavorable, Lee did not correct the error he alleges Scott to have committed, but ordered the whole detachment to regain the heights. He was closely pressed, and some slight skirmishing ensued, without much loss on either side.

As soon as the firing announced the commencement of the action, the rear division advanced rapidly to support the front. General Washington, to his astonishment and mortification, met the troops retiring before the enemy, without having made an effort to maintain their ground. The only answer they could make to his enquiries was, that, in obedience to the orders of their General, they had fled without fighting. In the rear of the division he met Lee, to whom he spoke in terms implying disapprobation of his conduct.

Colonel Stewart and Lieutenant-Colonel Ramsay were ordered to check the pursuit with their regiments; and General Lee was directed to stop the British column on the ground then occupied. These orders were executed with firmness and effect; and the

Describe the military movements which brought on the battle of Monmouth. What was Lee's conduct on that occasion, and what directions were issued by Washington to retrieve the battle?

troops, when forced from the field, were formed in the rear of Englishtown.

This check afforded time to draw up the second line on an eminence covered by a morass in front. The artillery, under Lieutenant-Colonel Carrington, played with considerable effect on a division of the British which had passed the morass and was pressing forward. They stopped the advance of the enemy.

Finding themselves warmly opposed in front, the British attempted to turn first the left, and afterwards the right, flank of the American army, but were repulsed. At this moment General Wayne was advanced with a body of infantry to engage them in front, who soon drove them behind the ravine.

The position now taken by the British army was very strong. Both flanks were secured by thick woods and morasses; and their front was accessible only through a narrow pass. Yet General Washington was determined to renew the engagement. Poor, with his own and the North Carolina brigade, was ordered to gain their right flank, while Woodford should turn their left. The artillery was ordered to advance and play on their front.

The impediments on the flanks were so considerable that, before they could be overcome, it was nearly dark. Farther operations were, therefore, deferred till the morning, and the troops lay on their arms. General Washington passed the night in his cloak, in the midst of his soldiers. About midnight the British withdrew in such silence that their retreat was not discovered until day.

It was certain that they would gain the high grounds about Middletown before they could be overtaken; and the face of the country did not justify an attempt to oppose their embarkation. Leaving a detachment to hover on their rear, the army moved towards the Hudson.

The loss of the Americans in the battle of Monmouth was eight officers and sixty-four privates killed, and one hundred and sixty wounded. Among the slain were Lieutenant-Colonel Bonner of Pennsylvania, and Major Dickenson of Virginia, both much regretted. One hundred and thirty were missing; but many of them rejoined their regiments. Of the British, four officers and two hundred and forty-five privates were buried on the field. Some were afterwards found, increasing their dead to nearly three hundred. Sir Henry Clinton, in his official letter, states his wounded at sixteen officers and one hundred and fifty-four privates. The uncommon heat of the day proved fatal to several on both sides.

In addition to the loss sustained in the action, the British army was considerably weakened in its march from Philadelphia to

What were the impediments that prevented a general attack upon the British? What was the loss of the two armies respectively, in the battle of Monmouth? Did the weather increase the loss?

New York. About one hundred prisoners were made, and near one thousand soldiers, chiefly foreigners, deserted.

The conduct of Lee was generally disapproved. It is, however, probable that explanations would have rescued him from the imputations cast on him, could his haughty temper have brooked the indignity he believed to have been offered to him on the field of battle. General Washington had taken no measures in consequence of the events of that day, when he received from Lee a letter expressed in very unbecoming terms, requiring reparation for the injury sustained "from the very singular expressions" used on the day of the action.

This letter was answered by an assurance, that as soon as circumstances would admit of an enquiry, he should have an opportunity of justifying himself to the army, to America, and to the world in general; or of convincing them that he had been guilty of disobedience of orders, and of misbehavior before the enemy. On his expressing a wish for a court-martial, he was arrested—

First, for disobedience of orders, in not attacking the enemy on the 28th of June, agreeably to repeated instructions.

Secondly, for misbehavior before the enemy on the same day, in making an unnecessary, disorderly, and shameful retreat.

Thirdly, for disrespect to the commander-in-chief in two letters.

Before this correspondence had taken place, strong and specific charges of misconduct had been made against General Lee by several officers, particularly by Generals Wayne and Scott.

A court-martial, of which Lord Sterling was president, found him guilty of all the charges exhibited against him, and sentenced him to be suspended for one year. This sentence was afterwards, though with some hesitation, approved almost unanimously by Congress. The court softened in some degree the severity of the second charge, by finding him guilty, not in its very words, but "of misbehavior before the enemy, by making an unnecessary, and in some few instances, a disorderly retreat."

Lee defended himself with his accustomed ability; and suggested a variety of reasons in justification of his retreat, which, if they do not absolutely establish its propriety, give it so questionable a form as to render it probable that a public examination would not have taken place, could his proud spirit have stooped to offer explanation instead of outrage to the commander-in-chief.

His suspension gave general satisfaction to the army. Without being master of his conduct as a military man, they perfectly understood the insult offered to their General by his letters, and believed his object to have been to disgrace Washington, and elevate himself to the supreme command.

What were the charges brought against General Lee? What sentence was passed upon him by a court-martial?

The battle of Monmouth gave great satisfaction to Congress. A resolution was passed unanimously, thanking General Washington for the activity with which he marched from Valley Forge in pursuit of the enemy; for his distinguished exertions in forming the line of battle, and for his great good conduct in the action. He was also requested to signify the thanks of Congress to the officers and men under his command.

After remaining a few days on the high grounds of Middletown, Sir Henry Clinton proceeded to Sandy Hook, whence his army passed over to New York.

CHAPTER XIII.

Count D'Estaing arrives with a French fleet.—Meditates an attack on the British fleet in the harbor of New York.—Relinquishes it.—Sails to Rhode Island.—Is followed by Lord Howe.—Both fleets dispersed by a storm.—General Sullivan lays siege to Newport.—D'Estaing returns.—Sails for Boston.—Dissatisfaction of Sullivan.—He raises the siege of Newport.—Action on Rhode Island.—Sullivan retreats to the continent.—Exertions of Washington to assuage the irritations of Sullivan and D'Estaing.—Lord Howe resigns.—Colonel Baylor surprised.—Skirmish between Colonel Butler and Captain Donop.—Pulaski surprised.

EARLY in July, intelligence was received that a powerful French fleet, commanded by the Count D'Estaing, had appeared off Chingoteague inlet, the northern extremity of the coast of Virginia. The Count had sailed from Toulon on the 13th of April, with twelve ships of the line and six frigates, having on board a respectable body of land forces. His destination was the Delaware; and the extraordinary length of his voyage, occasioned by adverse winds, saved the British fleet and army.

Having failed in accomplishing his first object, he proceeded along the coast of New York, in the hope of being able to attack the British fleet in the harbor of that place.

At Paramus, in Jersey, on the 13th of July, General Washington received a letter from the President of Congress, advising him of this important event, requesting him to concert measures with the Count for conjoint and offensive operations, and empowering him to call out the militia from New Hampshire to Jersey inclusive. He determined to proceed immediately to the White Plains, whence his army might more readily co-operate with the fleet; and despatched Lieutenant-Colonel Laurens, one of his aids, to the French Admiral, with all the information that could be useful to him.

The Count, on arriving off the Hook, communicated his strength

---

How did Congress testify its approbation of Washington's conduct in the affair of Monmouth? When did a powerful French fleet arrive on the American coast? What movements followed?

and his views to General Washington. His first object was to attack New York. Should this be found impracticable, his second was Rhode Island.

Fearing that the water on the bar might not be of sufficient depth to admit the passage of the largest French ships, General Washington had turned his attention to other eventual objects; and, on the 21st of July, had directed General Sullivan, who commanded the troops in Rhode Island, to prepare for an enterprise against Newport; and had reinforced him with two brigades commanded by the Marquis de Lafayette. The next day he received the final determination of the Admiral to relinquish the meditated attack on the fleet in the harbor of New York.

On the 25th of July, the fleet appeared off Newport, and cast anchor just without Brenton's Ledge; soon after which General Sullivan went on board the Admiral, and concerted with him a conjoint plan of operations. The French and American troops were to land at the same time on opposite sides of the island.

Aug. 8. As the militia of New Hampshire and Massachusetts approached, the continental troops were united at Tiverton; and it was agreed with the Admiral that the fleet should enter the main channel immediately, and that the descent should be made the succeeding day. The militia not arriving precisely at the time they were expected, General Sullivan could not hazard the movement which had been concerted, and stated to the Count the necessity of postponing it till the next day. Meanwhile, General Pigot, having observed preparations for a descent, drew his troops in the night from the north end of the island into Newport. In the morning Sullivan determined to avail himself of this circumstance; and, crossing the east passage, took possession of the works which had been abandoned. This movement gave great offence to the Admiral, who resented the indelicacy committed by Sullivan in landing before the French, and without consulting him. Unfortunately, some differences on subjects of mere punctilio had previously arisen.

At this time a British fleet appeared, which came to anchor off Point Judith, just without the narrow inlet leading into the harbor.

So soon as the destination of Count D'Estaing was ascertained, he was followed by a squadron of twelve ships of the line, under Admiral Byron. The vessels composing the squadron, were dispersed in various storms; and arrived, after lingering through a tedious passage, on different and remote parts of the American coast. Four ships of sixty-four and fifty guns arrived separately at Sandy Hook, within a few days after the departure of D'Estaing from that place.

Mention the naval and military operations near Newport. What British naval force now appeared on the coast?

This reinforcement, though it left the British considerably inferior to the French fleet, determined Lord Howe to attempt the relief of Newport. He sailed from New York on the 6th of August; and appeared on the 9th in sight of the French fleet. D'Estaing determined to stand out to sea and give battle. Lord Howe also stood out to sea, and both fleets were soon out of sight.

The militia who had now arrived augmented Sullivan's army to ten thousand men; and he determined to commence the siege immediately. Before this determination could be executed, a furious storm blew down all the tents, rendered the arms unfit for immediate use, and greatly damaged the ammunition. The soldiers suffered extremely; and several perished in the storm, which continued three days. On the return of fair weather, the siege was commenced, and was carried on without any material occurrence for several days. On the 19th the French fleet reappeared.

The admirals had consumed two days in manœuvring. When on the point of engaging, they were separated by the storm which had been felt so severely on shore. Both fleets were dispersed, and retired in a shattered condition, the one into the harbor of New York, and the other into that of Newport. A letter from D'Estaing informed Sullivan that, in pursuance of orders from the King, and of the advice of all his officers, he had determined to carry the fleet to Boston.

This communication threw Sullivan and his army into despair. Generals Greene and Lafayette were directed to wait on the Admiral with a letter, remonstrating against this resolution. The remonstrances of Sullivan, and the representations made by these officers, were ineffectual.

Sullivan made another effort to retain the fleet. In his second letter he pressed the Admiral, in any event, to leave his land forces. The bearer of this letter was also charged with a protest signed by all the general officers, except Lafayette, the only effect of which was to irritate D'Estaing, who sailed immediately for Boston. Sullivan was so indiscreet as to express his dissatisfaction in general orders, insinuating a suspicion that the French nation and their Admiral were indisposed to promote the interests of the United States.

A council of general officers were in favor of attempting an assault, if five thousand volunteers, who had seen nine months' service, could be obtained. But this number could not be procured; and in a few days the army was reduced by desertion to little more than five thousand men. The British being estimated at six thousand, it was determined to retire to the north end of the island,

What circumstance frustrated the contemplated action between the English and French fleets? Mention the difference which arose between General Sullivan and Admiral D'Estaing.

12

there to wait the result of another effort to induce D'Estaing to return.

On the night of the 28th the army retired by two roads, having its rear covered by Colonels Livingston and Laurens, who commanded light parties on each.

Early next morning the British followed in two columns, and were engaged on each road by Livingston and Laurens, who retreated slowly, until the British were brought within view of the American army, drawn up in order of battle on the ground of their encampment. The British formed on Quaker hill, rather more than a mile in front of the American line.

The two armies cannonaded each other for some time, and a succession of skirmishes was kept up till two in the afternoon, when the British advanced in force against a redoubt in front of the right wing. It was supported by General Greene, and a short engagement ensued, which was continued about half an hour, when the British retreated to Quaker hill.

The loss of Sullivan in killed, wounded, and missing, was two hundred and eleven. That of the British was stated by General Pigot at two hundred and sixty.

The next day the cannonade was renewed; but neither army was inclined to attack the other. The British waited for reinforcements, and Sullivan had determined to retire from the island.

The commander-in-chief had been induced, by some movements among the British transports, to suggest to Sullivan the necessity of securing his retreat. A fleet of transports soon put to sea, of which notice was given to the commanding officer in Rhode Island, in a letter recommending his immediate return to the continent. The whole army passed over unobserved by the enemy, and disembarked by two in the morning of the 31st, about Tiverton.

Never was retreat more fortunate. Sir Henry Clinton, who had been detained by adverse winds, arrived the next day with a reinforcement of four thousand men.

The complete success of this expedition had been confidently anticipated throughout America; and the chagrin produced by disappointment was proportioned to the exaltation of their hopes. In the first moments of vexation, several evidences of ill-humor were exhibited both by the civil departments and the army, from which the most disastrous consequences were apprehended. The discontent in New England generally, and in Boston particularly, was so great as to inspire fears that the means of repairing the French ships would not be supplied. In its commencement, General Washington foresaw the evils with which it was fraught, and la-

Describe the military operations on Rhode Island, after the departure of the French fleet. Was it necessary for Sullivan to retreat to the main land? Why was this a fortunate movement?

bored to prevent them. He addressed letters not only to General Sullivan, but also to General Heath, who commanded at Boston, and to several individuals of influence in New England, urging the necessity of restraining the intemperance of the moment. For the same objects, General Hancock repaired from camp to Boston; and Lafayette followed him on a visit to D'Estaing.

The General also seized the first opportunity to recommence his correspondence with the count, and his letters were calculated to soothe every angry sensation which might have been excited. A letter from the Admiral, stating the whole transaction, was answered in terms so perfectly satisfactory, that the irritation which threatened such serious mischief appears to have entirely subsided.

Congress, too, in a resolution which was made public, expressed their full approbation of the conduct of the count; and directed their President to assure him that they entertained the highest sense of his zeal and attachment.

These prudent and temperate measures restored harmony to the allied armies.

On receiving information that the Count D'Estaing was proceeding towards Boston, Lord Howe sailed for the same port, in the hope of reaching it before him. Being disappointed in this expectation, he returned to New York, and resigned the command to Admiral Gambier.

General Clinton, finding that Sullivan had retreated to the continent, returned to New York, leaving the troops on board the transports, under the command of General Grey, with orders to conduct an expedition eastward, as far as Buzzard's bay.

Grey destroyed a number of vessels in Acushnet river; and having reduced part of the towns of Bedford and Fairhaven, together with some stores, to ashes, he re-embarked his troops, before the militia could be assembled, and sailed to Martha's Vineyard, where he destroyed several vessels, and some salt-works, and levied a heavy contribution on the inhabitants.

Soon after the return of General Grey from New England, the British army moved up the Hudson in Sept. 22. great force, and encamped on both sides of the river. Their ships of war maintained the communication between their columns.

Colonel Baylor, with his regiment of cavalry, crossed the Hackensack early in the morning of the 27th, and took quarters at Herringtown, a small village near New Taupaun, where some militia were posted. Immediate notice of his position was given to Lord Cornwallis, the commanding officer on the south side of the Hudson, who formed a plan to cut off both the cavalry and

---

Mention the conciliatory measures adopted by Washington with respect to D'Estaing. What British expeditions were sent along the New England coast and up the North river?

militia. The party designed to act against Baylor was conducted
by General Grey, and the other by Lieutenant-Colonel Campbell.
Notice of the approach of Campbell was given by a deserter,
and the militia saved themselves by flight. But the corps commanded by General Grey, guided by some of the country people,
eluded the patroles, cut off a guard posted at a bridge over the
Hackensack, and completely surprised the regiment. Of one
hundred and four privates, sixty-seven were killed, wounded, and
made prisoners. The number of prisoners was ascribed to the
humanity of one of Grey's captains, who gave quarter to the
whole of the fourth troop. Colonel Baylor and Major Clough,
who were both wounded, the first dangerously, the last mortally,
were among the prisoners.

Three days afterwards, Colonel Richard Butler, with a detachment of infantry, assisted by Major Lee with a part of his cavalry,
fell in with a party of chasseurs and yagers, commanded by Captain Donop, whom he instantly charged, and, without the loss of
a man, killed ten on the spot, and took one officer and eighteen
privates prisoners. Some interest was taken at the time in this
small affair, because it served to revenge, in some measure, the
loss of Colonel Baylor.

After completing their forage, the British army returned to New
York. This movement had been designed in part to cover an expedition against Little Eggharbor, which was completely successful. The works and store-houses, as well as several vessels, and
a large quantity of merchandize, were destroyed.

The Count Pulaski, a Polish nobleman, had obtained permission
to raise a legionary corps, which he officered chiefly with foreigners. In this corps, one Juliet, a deserter, had obtained a commission. The Count had been ordered towards Little Eggharbor,
and was lying a few miles from the coast, when Juliet again deserted, and gave intelligence of Pulaski's situation. A plan to
surprise him succeeded so far as respected his infantry, who were
put to the bayonet.

Admiral Byron reached New York, and took command of the
fleet about the middle of September. After repairing his shattered
vessels, he sailed for Boston; but, soon after entering the bay, a
furious storm drove him out to sea, and damaged his ships so
much, that he found it necessary to put into the port of Rhode
Island to refit. The Count D'Estaing seized this favorable moment, and sailed, on the 3d of November, for the West Indies.

The Marquis de Lafayette, expecting a war on the continent of

Mention the particulars of the skirmish wherein Colonel Baylor was defeated by the British, and of that one wherein the Americans were successful. What was done at Little Eggharbor? What is said of Count Pulaski?

Europe, was anxious to return to France, and to tender his services to his king and native country.

From motives of friendship as well as of policy, General Washington was desirous of preserving the connexion of this nobleman
with the American army. He therefore expressed to Congress
his wish that Lafayette might have unlimited leave of absence,
and might carry with him every mark of the confidence of the
government. This policy was adopted by Congress.

A detachment from the British army, of five thousand men,
commanded by Major-General Grant, sailed, early in November,
for the West Indies; and, towards the end of the same month, a
second detachment, commanded by Lieutenant-Colonel Campbell,
escorted by Commodore Hyde Parker, was destined for the southern states.

In December, the American army retired into winter quarters.
The main body was cantoned in Connecticut, about West Point
and at Middlebrook. The troops again wintered in huts.

CHAPTER XIV.

Terms of reconciliation proposed by the British Commissioners.—Answer of Congress
—Attempts of Mr. Johnson to bribe some members of Congress.—Manifesto of Commissioners.—Arrival of Monsieur Girard, Minister of France.—Irruption of the Indians into Wyoming. — Battle of Wyoming. — Colonel Dennison capitulates for the
inhabitants.—Colonel Clarke surprises Vincennes. — Plan for the invasion of Canada.—General Washington induces Congress to abandon it.

ABOUT the last of November, the commissioners ap- 1778.
pointed to give effect to the late conciliatory acts of Parliament, embarked for Europe. Their utmost exertions to accomplish the object of their mission, had been unsuccessful. Great
Britain required that the force of the two nations should be united
under one common sovereign; and America was no longer disposed, or even at liberty, to accede to this proposition.

On their arrival in Philadelphia, they addressed a letter "To
the President and other members of Congress," inclosing copies
of their commission and of the acts of Parliament, together with
propositions founded on those acts, drawn in the most conciliatory
language.

Some expressions having been introduced into it, reflecting on
the conduct of France, the reading was interrupted, and a motion
made to proceed no further. A debate took place, and Congress
adjourned. The following day, the letter was read, and commit-

---

Upon the closing of the campaign, whither did the British send a part of
their force? What was the nature of the chief proposition of the British
commissioners to the American Congress?

12 *

ted after some opposition. The report of the committee, which was transmitted to the commissioners, declared that "nothing but an earnest desire to prevent the further effusion of blood, could have induced them to read a paper containing expressions so disrespectful to his Most Christian Majesty, the good and great ally of these states, or to consider propositions so derogatory to the honor of an independent nation."

The resolutions proceeded to declare, that the propositions were totally inadmissible; but that Congress would be ready to enter upon the consideration of a treaty of peace and commerce not inconsistent with treaties already subsisting.

On the 13th of July, after arriving at New York, the commissioners addressed a second letter to Congress, in terms well calculated to make an impression on those who had become weary of the contest. On receiving it, that body resolved that, as neither the independence of the United States was explicitly acknowledged, nor the fleets and armies withdrawn, no answer should be given to it.

The first packet contained several private letters written by Governor Johnson, one of the commissioners, in which he blended, with flattering expressions of respect, assurances of the honors and emoluments to which those would be entitled who should contribute to restore peace and harmony to the two nations.

In compliance with a resolution requiring that all letters of a public nature, received by any member, from any subject of the British crown, should be laid before Congress, these letters were produced; and Mr. Read stated a direct offer which had been made to him by a third person, of a considerable sum of money, and of any office in the gift of the crown, to use his influence for the restoration of peace. Congress published a solemn declaration, in which, after reciting the offensive paragraphs of the private letters, and the conversation stated by Mr. Read, they expressed their opinion, "that these were direct attempts to bribe the Congress of the United States, and that it was incompatible with their honor to hold any manner of correspondence or intercourse with the said George Johnson, esquire." After an unsuccessful attempt to involve the other commissioners in the same exclusion, this declaration was transmitted to them. On receiving it, Mr. Johnson withdrew from the commission. The other commissioners, without admitting the construction put by Congress on his letter, or the authority of the person who held the conversation with Mr. Read, denied all knowledge of those letters or of that conversation. They at the same time repeated their detail of

What was the reply of Congress to these propositions? What overtures from one of the British commissioners, gave offence to Congress? Mention the action of that body, in reference to this subject.

the advantages to be derived by America from acceding to the propositions they had made.

In the hope that a knowledge of the terms they had offered, would make an impression on the people, they published a manifesto before their departure, addressed to Congress, the Provincial Assemblies, and all the inhabitants of the colonies, recapitulating the several steps they had taken, and the refusal of Congress even to open a conference with them. They declared their readiness still to proceed in the execution of their powers, and proclaimed a general pardon to all who should, within fifty days, withdraw from their opposition to the British government, and conduct themselves as faithful subjects. Thirteen copies of the manifesto were executed, one of which was transmitted by a flag of truce to each state. A vast number of copies were printed, and great exertions were made to disperse them among the people.

Congress declared this measure to be contrary to the law of nations, and recommended it to the executive departments of the several states, to secure in close custody every person who, under the sanction of a flag or otherwise, was found employed in circulating those manifestoes. They at the same time directed a publication of the manifesto in the American papers; taking care however that it should be accompanied with comments made by individuals calculated to counteract its effect.

Thus ended this fruitless attempt to restore a connexion which had been wantonly broken, the reinstatement of which had become impracticable.

In the midst of these transactions with the commissioners of Great Britain, the Sieur Girard arrived in the character of minister plenipotentiary of his Most Christian Majesty. The joy produced by this event was unbounded; and he was received by Congress with great pomp. July 14.

While these diplomatic concerns employed the American cabinet, and the war seemed to languish on the Atlantic, it raged to the west in its most savage form.

About three hundred white men commanded by Colonel John Butler, and about five hundred Indians led by the Indian Chief Brandt, entered the valley of Wyoming near its northern boundary, late in June. The inhabitants capable of bearing arms assembled, on the first alarm, at Forty fort, on the west side of the Susquehanna, four miles below the camp of the invading army. The regular troops, amounting to about sixty, were commanded by Colonel Zebulon Butler; the militia by Colonel Dennison. The combined forces, amounting to about four hundred men, marched

Mention the ineffectual endeavor of the British commissioners to appeal more directly to the American people. What foreign minister now arrived? Relate the incidents that marked the massacre of Wyoming.

on the third of July from Forty fort to attack the enemy. The British and Indians were prepared to receive them. Their line extended from the river about a mile to a marsh at the foot of the mountain. The Americans advanced in a single column, without much interruption, until they approached the enemy, when they received a fire which did not much mischief. The line of battle was instantly formed, and the action commenced with spirit. The Americans rather gained ground on their right where Colonel Butler commanded, until a large body of Indians, passing through the skirt of the marsh, turned their left flank, which was composed of militia, and poured a most destructive fire on their rear. The fate of the day was decided, and a flight commenced on the left which was soon followed by the right. The Indians, rushing on them with the tomahawk, completed the confusion. Rather less than sixty men escaped, some to Forty fort, some by swimming the river, and some to the mountain. Very few prisoners were made, only three of whom were carried alive to Niagara.

Terms of capitulation were granted to the inhabitants. Colonel Butler, with his few surviving soldiers, fled from the valley. The inhabitants generally abandoned the country, and wandered into the settlements on the Lehigh and the Delaware. The Indians, after laying waste the whole settlement, withdrew from it before the arrival of the continental troops who were detached to meet them.

On the first intelligence of the destruction of Wyoming, the regiments of Hartley and Butler, with the remnant of Morgan's corps commanded by Major Posey, were detached to the protection of that distressed country. They were engaged in several sharp skirmishes, made separate incursions into the Indian country, broke up their nearest villages, destroyed their corn, and, by compelling them to remove to a greater distance, gave some relief to the inhabitants.

While the frontiers of New York and Pennsylvania were suffering the calamities incident to savage warfare, a fate equally severe was preparing for Virginia. The western militia of that state had taken some British posts on the Mississippi, which were erected into the county of Illinois; for the protection of which a regiment of infantry and a troop of cavalry had been raised, to be commanded by Colonel George Rogers Clarke, a gentleman whose capacity for Indian warfare had crowned his enterprises against the savages with repeated success. A part of this corps remained with Colonel Clarke at Kaskaskia.

Colonel Hamilton, the Governor of Detroit, was at Vincennes

To what extent were the Americans able to retaliate the devastation at Wyoming? What danger now menaced the frontier of Virginia? What American officer planned the defence?

with six hundred men, chiefly Indians, preparing an expedition first against Kaskaskia, and then up the Ohio to Pittsburg; after which he purposed to devastate the frontiers of Virginia. Clarke anticipated and defeated his designs by one of those bold and decisive measures, which mark the military genius of the man who plans and executes them.

While preparing for his defence, he received information that Hamilton had detached his Indians on an expedition, reserving at the post he occupied only eighty regulars. Clarke instantly resolved to seize this favorable moment. After detaching a small galley up the Wabash, with orders to place herself a few miles below Vincennes, and to permit nothing to pass her, he marched in the depth of winter, at the head of one hundred and thirty men through a wilderness, from Kaskaskia to Vincennes. This march required sixteen days, five of which were employed in crossing the drowned lands of the Wabash. The troops were under the necessity of wading five miles in the water, frequently up to their breasts. The town was completely surprised, and readily agreed to change its master. Hamilton, after defending the fort a short time, surrendered himself and his garrison prisoners of war.

The plan which Congress had formed in the preceding winter for the conquest of Canada, seems to have been suspended, not abandoned. The alliance with France revived the latent wish to annex that territory to the United States; and, towards autumn, a plan was completely digested for a combined attack on all the British dominions on the continent, and on the adjacent islands of Cape Breton and Newfoundland. This plan was matured about the time the Marquis de Lafayette obtained leave to return to his own country, and was to be transmitted by him to Doctor Franklin with instructions to induce the French cabinet to accede to it. In October 1778, it was sent to General Washington with a request that he would enclose it by the Marquis to Doctor Franklin, with his observations on it.

This very extensive plan of operations, prepared in the cabinet without consulting a single military man, consisted of various parts.

Two detachments, consisting of sixteen hundred men each, were to march from Pittsburg, and Wyoming, against Detroit, and Niagara.

A third was to seize Oswego, and to secure the navigation of Lake Ontario.

A fourth was to penetrate into Canada by the St. Francis, and to reduce Montreal and the posts on Lake Champlain; while a fifth should guard against troops from Quebec.

What western post was captured by Clarke? Give the details of a plan formed by Congress for an attack upon all the British possessions in North America.

But Upper Canada being subdued, another campaign would be necessary for the reduction of Quebec, whose garrison might in the meantime be largely reinforced. It was therefore essential to the success of the enterprise that France should be induced to embark in it.

It was proposed to request his Most Christian Majesty to furnish four or five thousand troops, to sail from Brest, the beginning of May, under convoy; the troops to be clad as if for service in the West Indies, and thick clothes to be sent after them in August. A large American detachment was to act with this French army. It was supposed that Quebec and Halifax might be reduced by the middle of October, after which the conquest of Newfoundland might be accomplished.

General Washington was forcibly struck with the impracticability of executing that part of this magnificent plan, which was to be undertaken by the United States, should the British armies continue in their country; and with the serious mischief which would result, as well from diverting so large a part of the French force to an object he thought so unpromising, as from the ill impression that would be made on the court and nation by the total failure of the American Government to execute its part of a plan originating with itself.

A plan, too, consisting of so many parts, to be executed both in Europe and America, by land and by water, which required such a harmonious co-operation of the whole, such a perfect coincidence of events, appeared to him to be exposed to too many accidents, to risk upon it interests of such high value.

In a long and serious letter to Congress, he apologized for not obeying their orders; and, entering into a full investigation of the plan, demonstrated the dangers with which it was replete. This letter was referred to a committee, whose report admits the force of the reasons urged by the commander-in-chief against the expedition, and their own conviction that it ought not to be attempted, unless the British armies should be withdrawn from the United States.

Men, however, recede slowly and reluctantly from favorite projects on which they have long meditated; and the committee proceeded to state the opinion that the posts held by the British in the United States would probably be evacuated before the active part of the ensuing campaign; and that eventual measures for the expedition ought to be taken. For this purpose, the commander-in-chief was still required to write to the Marquis de Lafayette and

Mention the reasons which induced the American commander-in-chief to disapprove this extensive project. Did he urge upon Congress its impracticability? Was that body ready to relinquish the scheme decidedly, or did they consent only to postpone it?

to Dr. Franklin, that the subject might be laid before the cabinet of Versailles.

This report, which was approved by Congress and transmitted to the commander-in-chief, embarrassed him greatly. In his answer, he repeated his objections to the plan, stated the difficulties he felt in performing the duties assigned to him, and requested, if they still persisted in their purpose, that they would give him more definite and explicit instructions.

In the same letter he expressed his desire to make a full exposition of the condition of the army, and of the requisites necessary for carrying into execution an undertaking that might involve the most serious consequences. "If," he added, "Congress think this can be more satisfactorily done in a personal conference, I hope to have the army in such a situation before I can receive their answer, as to afford me an opportunity of giving my attendance."

This request was acceded to; and, on his arrival at Philadelphia, a committee was appointed to confer with him. The result was that the expedition against Canada was entirely, though reluctantly, given up.

CHAPTER XV.

Invasion of Georgia.—General Howe defeated by Colonel Campbell.—Savannah taken.
—Sunbury surrenders.—Georgia reduced.—General Lincoln takes command of the
Southern army.—Major Gardener defeated.—Tories in South Carolina defeated.—
Ash surprised and defeated.—Prevost marches to Charleston.—Battle at Stono ferry.
—Invasion of Virginia.

IT being no longer practicable to engage soldiers by vo- 1779. luntary enlistment, and government not daring to force men into the service for three years, or during the war, the vacant ranks were scantily supplied by drafts for nine, twelve, and eighteen months. A great proportion of the troops were discharged in the course of each year; and, except that the veteran officers remained, almost a new army was to be formed for every campaign.

Although the commander-in-chief pressed Congress and the state governments continually and urgently to take timely measures for supplying the places of those who were leaving the service, the means adopted were so slow and ineffectual in their operation, that the season for action always arrived before the preparations for it were completed. It was not until the 23d of January that Congress passed the resolution authorizing the commander-in-chief to re-enlist the army, nor until the 9th of March that the requisition was made on the several states for their quotas.

Was the plan at last entirely abandoned? What difficulties occurred with respect to filling up the ranks of the army?

The British arms had heretofore been chiefly directed against the Northern and Middle states—the strongest and most populous parts of the Union. Anticipating confidently the recovery of all the colonies, the government had formed no plan of partial conquest. The loss of the army commanded by Burgoyne, the alliance of America with France, and the unexpected obstinacy with which the contest was maintained, had diminished this confidence; and, when the pacific overtures made in 1778 were rejected, the resolution seems to have been taken to change the object of their military operations, and to direct their arms against the Southern states, on which, it was believed, a considerable impression might be made.

With this view, Lieutenant-Colonel Campbell sailed from the Hook about the last of November, 1778. He reached the isle of Tyber on the 23d of December, and, in a few days, the fleet passed the bar, and anchored in the Savannah.

The troops of South Carolina and Georgia were commanded by General Robert Howe, who, in the preceding summer, had invaded East Florida. The diseases incident to the climate having forced him to hasten out of the country, his army, consisting of six or seven hundred continental troops, and a few hundred militia, encamped in the neighborhood of the town of Savannah, situated on the southern bank of the river bearing that name.

Lieutenant-Colonel Campbell effected a landing on the 29th, about three miles below the town; upon which Howe formed his line of battle. His left was secured by the river; and a morass, believed to be impassable, stretched along the whole extent of his front, so far to the right as, in the opinion of the General, to cover that wing.

Campbell advanced on the great road leading to Savannah; and, about three in the afternoon, appeared in sight of the American army. While making dispositions to dislodge it, he was informed by a negro of a private path leading through the swamp round the right of the American line to its rear. A party was detached under Sir James Baird, which entered the morass by this path, unperceived by Howe.

Sir James, on emerging from the swamp, attacked and dispersed a body of militia, which gave the first notice to the American General of the danger which threatened his rear. At the same instant, the British in his front were put in motion, and their artillery began to play upon him. A retreat was immediately ordered, and the flying troops were exposed to a most destructive fire from the detachment which had gained their rear. The few who escaped crossed the Savannah at Zubly's ferry, and took refuge in South Carolina.

The war being turned on the Southern states, what defeat was sustained by the Americans near Savannah?

The victory was complete. About one hundred Americans were killed, and thirty-eight officers and four hundred and fifteen privates, were taken. Forty-eight pieces of cannon, twenty-three mortars, and all the military stores, were the fruits of this victory, which was obtained at the expense of seven killed and nineteen wounded.

No military force remained in Georgia, except the garrison of Sunbury, whose retreat to South Carolina was cut off. All the lower part of the state was in possession of the British, who, to secure the conquest they had made, treated the people with a lenity as wise as it was humane. In pursuance of a proclamation inviting the inhabitants to repair to the British standard, and promising protection, military corps were formed, and posts of loyalists established for a considerable distance up the river.

The northern frontier being supposed to be settled into a state of quiet, Colonel Campbell was about to proceed against Sunbury, when he received intelligence that the place had surrendered to General Prevost.

Sir Henry Clinton had ordered that officer to co-operate from East Florida with Colonel Campbell. He entered the southern frontier of Georgia, and invested Sunbury, which surrendered at discretion. He then took command of the army, and detached Colonel Campbell to Augusta, which fell without resistance, and the whole state of Georgia was reduced.

While the expedition commanded by Lieutenant-Colonel Campbell was preparing at New York, Congress was meditating the conquest of East Florida.

In compliance with the solicitations of the delegates from South Carolina and Georgia, Howe had been ordered, in September 1778, to repair to the head quarters of General Washington; and Lincoln, whose military reputation was high, had been directed to take command in the southern department. In pursuance of this resolution, Lincoln repaired to Charleston, where he found the military affairs of the country in utter derangement. Congress had established no continental military-chest, and the army was dependent for supplies entirely on the state. The militia, too, though in continental service, were governed by the military cod of the state.

When Lincoln received intelligence that the British fleet ha appeared off the coast, the militia of North Carolina had reached Charleston; but were unarmed, and Congress had been unable to provide magazines. Arms were not delivered to them by the states, until it was too late to save the capital of Georgia. On re-

Did the British subdue the State of Georgia? What American General was invested with the command of the southern department, and what was the condition of affairs when he reached Charleston?

ceiving them, he proceeded towards the scene of action. On his march, he was informed of the victory gained over Howe; and was soon afterwards joined by the remnant of the defeated army, at Purysburg, a small town on the north side of the Savannah, where he established his head quarters on the 30th of January.

The effective force of Prevost must have amounted to at least three thousand British, and this number was augmented by loyalists who joined him in Georgia. The American army rather exceeded three thousand six hundred men, of whom about one thousand were continental troops, part of them new levies; and the rest militia.

Major Gardner, who had been detached with two hundred men to take possession of the island of Port Royal, was attacked by General Moultrie, and compelled to retreat with considerable loss. This repulse checked the designs of Prevost on South Carolina.

The loyalists of the west had been invited to assemble and join the king's standard at Augusta. About seven hundred embodied themselves on the frontiers of South Carolina, and were marching for that place when they were attacked at Kittle Creek, by Colonel Pickens, and defeated with considerable loss. Colonel Boyd, their leader, was killed, and five of those who escaped were executed as traitors. About three hundred reached Augusta. This defeat broke the spirits of the tories for a time.

As the American army gained strength by reinforcements of militia, General Lincoln began to contemplate offensive operations. He had meditated an attempt on Augusta; but before he was in readiness to make it, Prevost withdrew his troops from that place to Hudson's ferry. Lincoln then ordered General Ash to cross the Savannah, and take post near the confluence of Briar Creek with that river. This camp was believed to be unassailable.

Prevost, having determined to dislodge the Americans from this position, drew the attention of General Lincoln to his preparations for crossing the Savannah, and amused General Ash with a feint on his front, while Lieutenant-Colonel Prevost made a circuit of about fifty miles, and, crossing Briar Creek fifteen miles above the ground occupied by Ash, came down unsuspected on his rear, and was almost in his camp before his approach was perceived. The continental troops under General Elbert were drawn out to oppose him, and aided by one regiment of North Carolina militia, commenced the action with great gallantry, but were soon overpowered by numbers, and the survivors became prisoners of war. The main body of the militia threw away their arms and fled in confusion. The killed and taken amounted to between three and

---

What defeat was sustained by the loyalists in Georgia? In what manner was General Lincoln deceived by Prevost at Briar Creek, and what was the result of the action?

four hundred men. General Elbert and Colonel M'Intosh were among the prisoners.

This victory was supposed to give the British such complete possession of Georgia, that a proclamation was issued the succeeding day, for the establishment of civil government.

These disasters animated the state of South Carolina to still greater exertions. The legislature passed an act authorizing the executive to do whatever should be thought necessary for the public good; and the militia were called out in great numbers.

General Lincoln resumed his plan for the recovery of the upper posts of Georgia; and, on the 23d of April, marched up the Savannah. The high waters seemed to present an impassable barrier to an invading army; and a small military force was thought insufficient for the defence of the country. Eight hundred militia and two hundred continental troops were left with General Moultrie for this purpose.

In the hope of recalling Lincoln by alarming him for Charleston, Prevost crossed the Savannah with three thousand men, and obliged Moultrie to retreat. The militia would not defend the passes, and deserted in numbers. An express was despatched to Lincoln, but he, not believing that Prevost had any real designs on Charleston, detached three hundred light troops to the aid of Moultrie, and crossing the Savannah, continued his march down the south side of that river towards the capital of Georgia.

Though the original purpose of Prevost had been limited to the defence of Georgia, the opposition he encountered was so inconsiderable, and the assurances of the favorable dispositions of the people were so confidently given by those who flocked to his standard, that he was emboldened to hazard the continuation of his march to Charleston.

On receiving intelligence of this threatening aspect of affairs, Lincoln recrossed the Savannah, and hastened to the relief of South Carolina.

Had Prevost continued his march with the rapidity with which it was commenced, Charleston must have fallen; but he consumed two or three days in deliberating on his future measures; and while he deliberated, that state of things which determined him to proceed was rapidly changing. Fortifications on the land-side were vigorously prosecuted, the neighboring militia were called into town, the reinforcements detached by Lincoln, with the remnant of the legion of Pulaski, arrived, and the Governor, on the 19th of May, entered the town at the head of some troops who had been stationed at Orangeburg. The next day Prevost crossed

Mention the various movements connected with the advance of the British army upon Charleston, and the means of defending the city possessed by the Americans.

Aug. 19. Ashly river, and encamped just without cannon-shot of the works. The town was summoned to surrender, and the day was spent in sending and receiving flags. The terms of capitulation not being agreed on, the garrison prepared to sustain an assault. But Prevost came to the prudent resolution of decamping that night and recrossing Ashly river.

The British army retired slowly through the islands south of Charleston. Soon after the commencement of their retreat, General Lincoln arrived; and, on the 28th of June, attacked a fortified camp on the main, at Stono ferry, which was defended by eight hundred men, commanded by Colonel Maitland. Strong reinforcements arriving from the island, the assailants retired with the loss of twenty-four officers and one hundred and twenty-five privates killed and wounded. That of the British was stated to be rather less.

The heat now became too excessive for active service; and Prevost, after establishing a post on the island contiguous to Port Royal and St. Helena, retired into Georgia and East Florida.

The American militia dispersed, leaving General Lincoln at the head of about eight hundred men, with whom he retired to Sheldon, where his primary object was to prepare for the next campaign.

Orders had been given to reinforce the southern army with Bland's and Baylor's regiments of cavalry, and the new levies of Virginia. The execution of these orders was suspended by the invasion of that state.

On the 9th of May, a fleet, commanded by Sir George Collier, convoying a body of troops commanded by General Matthews, entered the Chesapeake, and anchored the next day in Hampton Roads.

Virginia had raised a regiment of artillery for the performance of garrison duty; which had been distributed along the eastern frontier in slight fortifications, defensible only on the side of the water. Fort Nelson, garrisoned by about one hundred and fifty soldiers, commanded by Major Matthews, was designed for the protection of Norfolk and Portsmouth, and a marine yard at Gosport, a little above them.

On the 10th the fleet entered Elizabeth river, and landed a body of troops three miles below the fort, which was evacuated in the night. From his head quarters at Portsmouth, General Matthews detached small parties to the neighboring towns, who took possession of military and naval stores to a great amount, and of several vessels richly laden. After destroying what could not be removed, he returned to New York.

When the British force was in retreat from Charleston, what action took place? Relate the particulars of the invasion of Virginia by an expedition under Sir George Collier.

CHAPTER XVI.

Discontents in a part of the American army.—Colonel Van Schaick destroys an Indian settlement.—Fort Fayette surrenders to the British.—Invasion of Connecticut.—General Wayne storms Stony Point.—Expedition against Penobscot.—Powles' Hook surprised by Major Dean.—Arrival of Admiral Arbuthnot.—Of the Count D'Estaing.—Siege of Savannah.—Unsuccessful attempt to storm the place.—Siege raised.—Victory of General Sullivan over the Indians.—Spain declares war against England.—The army goes into winter quarters.

THE barbarities committed by the Indians during the preceding year had added motives of resentment and humanity to those of national interest for employing a large force in the protection of the western frontier. The state governments also took a strong interest in the subject; and Connecticut, New York, and Pennsylvania, had severally applied to Congress, urging the adoption of vigorous measures in that quarter. These papers were referred to the committee appointed to confer with General Washington, in conformity with whose report, it was resolved, "that the commander-in-chief be directed to take efficient measures for the protection of the inhabitants, and the chastisement of the savages." 1779.

General Washington had always believed that it was impossible to defend the immense western frontier by any chain of posts; and that the country could be protected only by offensive war. His ideas had been communicated to, and approved by, Congress.

The Six Nations had made some advances towards acquiring the comforts of civilized life. Some few of their towns were attached to the United States, but most of them were under the influence of the British. It was determined to lead a sufficient force into these villages, and to destroy their settlements.

As the army destined for this expedition was about to move, alarming symptoms of discontent appeared in a part of it. The Jersey brigade, which had been stationed during the winter at Elizabethtown, was ordered, early in May, to march by regiments. This order was answered by a letter from General Maxwell, stating that the officers of the first regiment had delivered a remonstrance to their Colonel, addressed to the legislature of the state, declaring, that unless their complaints on the subjects of pay and support should obtain the immediate attention of that body, they were, at the expiration of three days, to be considered as having resigned. General Maxwell expressed his conviction that this step would be taken by all.

This intelligence made a serious impression on the commander-

What were the views of Washington with respect to the best method of proceeding against the Indians? What was determined on, and what cause delayed the expedition?

13*

in-chief. He was strongly attached to the army and to its interests—had witnessed its virtue and its sufferings; and could no more deny the justice of the complaints made by the officers, than he could approve the measure they had adopted. In his letter to General Maxwell, designed to be laid before them, he made the strongest appeals to their patriotism, their honor, their military pride, and their real interest; and urged them, by these powerfu motives, to abandon the resolution they had taken, and continue in the performance of their duty. He suggested, too, the rea difficulties with which government was surrounded—difficulties which ought to excuse, to a considerable extent, its apparent inattention to their wants. It required all his influence to prevent the mischief threatened by this rash measure. While the officers still remained with their regiment, but no definitive step was taken, the legislature of Jersey, alarmed at this state of things, was at length induced to make some provision for them, they consenting to withdraw their remonstrance; and the troops marched according to their orders.

In communicating this transaction to Congress, General Washington took occasion to repeat his remonstrances on the necessity of some general and adequate provision for the officers of the army.

Before the troops destined for the grand expedition could be put in motion, an enterprise was undertaken against the towns of the Onondagas, the nearest of the hostile tribes of Indians. Colonel Van Schaick marched from fort Schuyler in the morning of the 19th of April, at the head of between five and six hundred men, and on the third day, reached the point of destination. The whole settlement was destroyed; and the detachment returned without the loss of a single man. The thanks of Congress were voted to Colonel Van Schaick and the officers and soldiers under his command.

The relative strength and situation of the parties rendered it improbable that any other offensive operation than that against the Indians could be carried on by the Americans, in the course of the present campaign. The British troops in New York and Rhode Island were computed at between sixteen and seventeen thousand men. The grand total of the American army, exclusive of those in the south and west, including officers of every description, amounted to about sixteen thousand; of whom three thousand were in New England, under the command of General Gates. On their part, therefore, the plan of the campaign was necessarily defensive.

<hr>

What successful expedition was carried on against the Onondaga Indians? What was the respective force of the British and American armies, at this time?

After the destruction of forts Clinton and Montgomery, in 1777 it had been determined to construct the fortifications intended for the future defence of the North river, at West Point; a position which, being more completely embosoned in the hills, was deemed more defensible. The works had been prosecuted with industry, but were far from being completed.

Some miles below West Point, about the termination of the highlands, is King's ferry, where the great road affording the most convenient communication between the middle and eastern states crosses the river. The ferry is commanded by the two opposite points of land. That on the west side, a rough and elevated piece of ground, is denominated Stony Point. The other, a flat neck, projecting far into the water, is called Verplank's Point. Washington had comprehended these points in his plan of defence for the highlands. A small but strong work termed fort Fayette, was completed at Verplank's, and was garrisoned by a company commanded by Captain Armstrong. The works on Stony Point were unfinished. Sir Henry Clinton determined to open the campaign by a brilliant *coup de main* up the North river.

His preparations were communicated to General Washington, who penetrated his designs, and took measures to counteract them. Putnam and M'Dougal, who commanded on the north side of the Hudson, were ordered to hold themselves in readiness to march; and, on the 29th of May, the troops at Middlebrook moved by divisions towards the highlands. On the 30th, the British army, convoyed by Sir George Collier, proceeded up the river. The largest division, led by General Vaughan, landed next morning about eight miles below Verplank's; and another division under the particular command of General Patterson, but accompanied by Sir Henry Clinton, landed on the west side within three miles of Stony Point. That place was abandoned, and General Patterson took immediate possession of it. The next morning he opened a battery on fort Fayette within one thousand yards. Two galleys passed the fort in the night, and prevented the escape of the garrison, which surrendered to the enemy. Immediate directions were given for completing the works at both posts. After their completion, Sir Henry Clinton placed a strong garrison in each, and finding the position of the Americans at West Point too strong to be forced, returned down the river to Philipsburg.

The relative situation of the hostile armies presenting insuperable obstacles to any great operation, they could act offensively only in detached expeditions. Connecticut was particularly exposed to invasion; and the activity of his cruisers in the Sound,

Mention the posts held by the Americans on the North river. Did the British general form a plan for attacking these forts? To what extent was he successful?

as well as the large quantity of provisions with which she supplied the army, furnished great inducements to Sir Henry Clinton
to direct his enterprises against that state. An expedition was
therefore fitted out against Connecticut, the command of which
was given to Governor Tryon. He reached New Haven bay on
the 5th of July, with about two thousand six hundred men; and
his appearance gave the first intimation of his approach.

The militia assembled in considerable numbers with alacrity;
but the military and naval stores found at New Haven were destroyed; after which Tryon proceeded to Fairfield, which was
reduced to ashes. The good countenance showed by the militia
is attested by the apology made by Tryon for this destruction of
private property. "The village was burnt," he says, "to resent
the fire of the rebels from their houses, and to mask our retreat."

About the same time a still larger detachment from the British
army directed its course towards Horse Neck, and made demonstrations of a design to penetrate into the country in that direction.

On the night of the 11th, Tryon sailed from Huntington bay
and landed at the Cow Pasture, a peninsula on the east side of the
bay of Norwalk. On the morning of the 12th, as soon as his
troops were in motion, he was attacked by General Parsons, at the
head of about one hundred and fifty continental troops supported
by considerable numbers of militia. Parsons kept up an irregular
distant fire throughout the day; but being too weak to protect any
particular town on the coast, Norwalk was reduced to ashes; after
which the British re-embarked and returned to Huntingdon bay,
there to wait for reinforcements. Before their arrival, Tryon was
directed to meet Sir Henry Clinton at the White Stone, where it
was determined to proceed against New London with an increased
force. But before this determination could be carried into execution, Sir Henry Clinton found it necessary to recall Tryon to the
Hudson.

General Washington had planned an enterprise against the posts
at King's ferry; but the difficulty of a perfect co-operation of detachments incapable of communicating with each other, determined him to postpone the attack on Verplank's, and to make that
part of the plan dependent on the success of the other.

The execution of this enterprise was entrusted to General
Wayne, who commanded the light infantry of the army. The
night of the 15th, and the hour of twelve, were chosen for the
assault.

Stony Point is a commanding hill, projecting far into the Hudson, which washes three-fourths of its base. The remaining fourth

Mention the several predatory expeditions which were sent along the coast
by the British in New York. What enterprise was now undertaken by
General Washington?

is, in a great measure, covered by a deep marsh, over which there is but one crossing-place; but at its junction with the river, is a sandy beach, passable at low tide. The place was skilfully fortified, and garrisoned by six hundred men commanded by Colonel Johnson.

General Wayne arrived about eight in the afternoon at Spring Steel's, one and a half miles from the fort; and made his dispositions to attack the works on the right and left flanks at the same instant. The regiments of Febiger and of Meigs, with Major Hull's detachment, formed the right column; and Butler's regiment with two companies under Major Murfree, formed the left. One hundred and fifty volunteers, led by Lieutenant-Colonel Fleury and Major Posey, constituted the van of the right; and one hundred volunteers under Major Stewart composed the van of the left. At half-past eleven the two columns moved to the assault, the van of each with unloaded muskets and fixed bayonets, preceded by a forlorn hope of twenty men, the one commanded by Lieutenant Gibbon, and the other by Lieutenant Knox. They reached the marsh undiscovered, and at twenty minutes after twelve commenced the assault.

Both columns rushed forward under a tremendous fire. They entered the works at the point of the bayonet; and, without discharging a single musket, obtained possession of the fort.

The humanity displayed by the conquerors was not less conspicuous, nor less honorable, than their courage. Not an individual suffered after resistance had ceased.

All the troops engaged in this perilous service manifested a high degree of ardour and impetuosity; and all distinguished themselves, whose situation enabled them to do so. Colonel Fleury was the first to enter the fort, and strike the British standard. Major Posey mounted the works almost at the same instant, and was the first to give the watch-word—"The fort's our own." Lieutenants Gibbon and Knox performed the service allotted to them with a degree of intrepidity which could not be surpassed. Of the twenty men who constituted the party of the former, seventeen were killed or wounded.

Sixty-three of the garrison were killed, including two officers. The prisoners amounted to five hundred and forty-three, among whom were one Lieutenant-Colonel, four captains, and twenty subalterns. The military stores taken in the fort were considerable.

The loss sustained by the assailants did not exceed one hundred men. General Wayne, who marched with Febiger's regiment, received a slight wound in the head which stunned him for a short

What fort was stormed by the Americans under General Wayne? Was the attack successful? Mention the number of killed and wounded on each side?

time, but did not compel him to leave the column. Supported by his aids, he entered the fort with the regiment. Lieutenant-Colonel Hay was also among the wounded.

According to the original plan, the attack on Verplank's was immediately to have followed the surrender of Stony Point. In consequence of some inadvertencies which cannot be accounted for, it was not made. Notice of the success at Stony Point was not given to the detachment ordered on this service, in consequence of which the favorable moment was not seized; and before preparations were made for regular operations, Sir Henry Clinton relinquished his designs on Connecticut, and by a rapid movement relieved fort Fayette.

The possession of Verplank's Point by the enemy, closing the road leading over King's ferry, General Washington determined to evacuate Stony Point, and retire to the highlands. Sir Henry repossessed himself of that post; and, after placing a stronger garrison in it, retired first to Philipsburg, and afterwards to York Island.

Colonel M'Clean with between six and seven hundred men had penetrated, early in June, from Nova Scotia into the eastern part of Maine, where he had taken possession of a peninsula on the eastern side of the Penobscot, and had thrown up entrenchments on the isthmus connecting it with the continent. The state of Massachusetts determined to dislodge him. A respectable fleet commanded by Commodore Saltonstal, and an army of near four thousand men under General Lovell, were prepared with so much celerity, that the whole armament appeared in the Penobscot as early as the 25th of July.

General Lovell effected a landing on the western part of the peninsula, where he ascended a precipice of two hundred feet; and, with the loss of fifty men, drove the party which defended it from the ground. A battery was erected within seven hundred and fifty yards of the main work of the besieged, and a warm cannonade was kept up for several days on both sides.

On the application of the government of Massachusetts, General Gates ordered Jackson's regiment to Penobscot, and preparations were made to storm the works on his arrival.

Such was the posture of affairs on the 13th of August, when Lovell received information that Sir George Collier had entered the river with a superior naval force. He re-embarked his whole army; and, in the hope of gaining time until the transports might convey his land forces up the river, drew up his flotilla, as if determined to maintain his position. The British Admiral was too confident in his strength to permit this stratagem to succeed; and, as he approached, the Americans sought for safety in flight. A general chase, and unresisted destruction, ensued. The troops landed in a wild uncultivated country, and were obliged to explore their way through a pathless wilderness, for more than a hundred miles. Exhausted with famine and fatigue, they at length gained the settled parts of the state.

While Sir Henry Clinton was encamped just above Haarlem, and the American army continued in the highlands, Major Lee, who was employed to watch the enemy on the west side of the Hudson, obtained intelligence which suggested the idea of surprising and carrying off the garrison at Powles' Hook, a neck of land immediately opposite the town of New York, penetrating deep into the river. Some works had been constructed on the point nearest New York, which were garrisoned by five or six hundred men.

A deep ditch which could be passed only at low water, had been cut across the isthmus. Thirty paces within it was a row of abatis running into the river, and some distance in front of it a creek fordable only in two places. This difficulty of access, added to the remoteness of the nearest corps of the American army, impressed the garrison with the opinion that they were perfectly secure, and this opinion produced an unmilitary remissness in the commanding officer, which did not escape the vigilance of Lee.

General Washington withheld his assent from this enterprise until satisfied that the assailants could make good their retreat. The long and narrow necks of land formed by the water courses which run almost parallel with the North river, along which the British troops were encamped above Powles' Hook, afforded points of interception of which the enemy would certainly avail himself should the American party be discovered. To diminish this danger, it was intended to occupy the roads leading through the mountains of the Hudson to the Hackensack.

Early preparatory arrangements being made, a detachment from the division of Lord Sterling was ordered down as a foraging party. His lordship followed with the residue of his division, and encamped at the New Bridge, on the Hackensack.

Major Lee, at the head of three hundred men, part of the foraging detachment, took the road through the mountains which run parallel to the North river; and, having guarded the passes into York Island, reached the creek which surrounds the Hook, between two and three in the morning. About three he entered the main work, and with the loss of only two

Aug. 18.

What post, opposite the city of New York, was carelessly garrisoned by the British? Mention the American officer who led his corps against it. Was the attempt attended with success?

killed and three wounded, made one hundred and fifty-nine prisoners, including three officers. Very few of the British were killed. Major Sutherland who commanded the garrison, saved himself with forty or fifty Hessians in a strong redoubt. Major Lee hastened to bring off his prisoners and his detachment. The retreat was effected with immense toil and great address.

This critical enterprise reflected much honor on the partisan with whom it originated, and by whom it was conducted. General Washington announced it to the army in his orders with much approbation; and Congress bestowed upon it a degree of applause more apportioned to the talent displayed in performing the service, than to its magnitude.

A few days after the surprise of Powles' Hook, Admiral Arbuthnot arrived at New York with a strong reinforcement to the British army. He was soon followed by the Count D'Estaing, who arrived on the southern coast of America with twenty-two ships of the line, having on board six thousand soldiers; after which Sir Henry Clinton deemed it necessary to turn his attention to his own security. Rhode Island was evacuated, and the whole army was collected in New York.

It was immediately determined to lay siege to Savannah, the head quarters of General Prevost. D'Estaing was to land three thousand men at Beaulieu on the 11th of September, and Lincoln was to cross the Savannah on the same day with one thousand Americans and to effect a junction with him.

On the 11th, General Lincoln reached Zubly's ferry, and on the 15th was assured that the French had disembarked in force. A junction of the two armies was formed the next day.

After bringing up the heavy ordnance and stores from the fleet, the besieging army broke ground; and, by the first of October, had pushed their sap within three hundred yards of the abatis on the left of the British lines.

The situation of D'Estaing was becoming critical. More time had already been consumed on the coast of Georgia than he had supposed would be required for the destruction of the British force in that state. He became uneasy for the possessions of France in the West Indies, and apprehensive for the safety of his ships. The naval officers remonstrated strenuously against longer exposing his fleet on an insecure coast, at a tempestuous season.

In a few days the lines of the besiegers might have been carried into the works of the besieged, which would have rendered the capture of the town and garrison inevitable. But D'Estaing declared that he could devote no more time to this object; and it

Where did the British concentrate their troops? What accessions of strength to each of the belligerents arrived from Europe? What place was besieged by the French and Americans?

only remained to raise the siege, or to attempt the works by storm. The latter part of the alternative was adopted.

On the left of the allied army was a swampy hollow way, which afforded a cover for troops advancing on the right flank of the besieged, to a point within fifty yards of their principal work. It was determined to march to the main attack along this hollow; and, at the same time, to direct feints against other parts of the lines.

Before day on the 9th of October, a heavy cannonade was commenced as preliminary to the assault. Three thousand five hundred French, and one thousand Americans, of whom between six and seven hundred were regulars and the residue militia of Charleston, advanced in columns led by D'Estaing and Lincoln, aided by the principal officers of both nations, and made a furious assault on the British lines. Their reception was warmer than had been expected. The fire from the batteries of the besieged did great execution. Yet the assailants advanced with unabated ardor, passed through the abatis, crossed the ditch, and mounted the parapet. Both the French and Americans planted their standards on the walls, and were killed in great numbers, while endeavouring to force their way into the works. For near an hour the contest was extremely obstinate: at length, the columns of the assailants began to pause, and the vigor of the assault to relax.

At this critical moment Major Glaziers, at the head of a body of grenadiers and marines, rushing from the lines, on those who had made their way into the redoubts, drove them over the ditch and abatis into the hollow through which they had marched to the attack. It became apparent that farther perseverance could produce no advantage, and a retreat was ordered.

In this unsuccessful attempt, the French lost in killed and wounded about seven hundred men. Among the latter were the Count D'Estaing, Major-General de Fontanges, and several other officers of distinction. The continental troops lost two hundred and thirty-four men, and the Charleston militia had one captain killed and six privates wounded. The loss of the garrison, in killed and wounded, amounted only to fifty-five. So great was the advantage of the cover afforded by their works.

After this repulse, the Count D'Estaing announced to General Lincoln his determination to raise the seige. The remonstrances of that officer were unavailing; and both armies moved from their ground on the 18th of October. The Americans recrossing the Savannah, again encamped in South Carolina, and the French re-embarked. The militia dispersed; and the affairs of the

State the order of attack, when the French and Americans assaulted Savannah. What was the result of the attempt? Mention the loss of the parties respectively. Was the siege persisted in, or abandoned?

southern states wore a more gloomy aspect than at any former period.

Congress passed resolutions requesting General Washington to order the troops of North Carolina, and such others as could be spared from the northern army, to the aid of that in the south; and assuring the states of South Carolina and Georgia, of the attention of government to their security.

During these transactions in the South, the long-meditated expedition against the Indians was prosecuted with success.

The largest division of the western army was to assemble at Wyoming. Another passed the winter on the Mohawk. On the 22d of August, these two divisions, amounting to five thousand men, united, and marched up the Tioga, which led into the heart of the Indian country. They resolved to risk a battle in defence of their settlements, and selected their ground with judgment.

About a mile in front of Newtown, the Indians collected their whole force, estimated by General Sullivan at fifteen hundred men, by themselves at eight hundred. Five companies of whites, amounting to two hundred men, were united with them. They had constructed a breastwork half a mile in length, on a piece of rising ground. The right flank of this work was covered by the river, which, bending to the right, and winding round their rear, exposed only their front and left to an attack. On the left was a high ridge nearly parallel to the general course of the river, terminating somewhat below the breastwork; and, still farther to the left, was another ridge running in the same direction, and leading to the rear of the American army. The ground was covered with pine, interspersed with low shrub oaks, many of which, for the purpose of concealing their works, had been cut up and stuck in front of them, so as to exhibit the appearance of being still growing. The road, after crossing a deep brook at the foot of the hill, turned to the right, and ran nearly parallel to the breastwork, so as to expose the whole flank of the army to their fire, if it should advance without discovering their position. Parties were stationed on both hills, so as to fall on the right flank and rear of Sullivan, so soon as the action should commence.

About eleven in the morning of the 29th of August, this work was discovered by Major Par, who commanded the advance guard of the army; upon which General Hand formed the light infantry in a wood, about four hundred yards distant from the enemy, and waited the arrival of the main body. A continual skirmishing was kept up between Par's rifle corps and small parties of Indians

What expedition was now arranged, for the chastisement of the savages? State their numbers, and defensive works. What officer first came in contact with the Indians, and how was the battle brought on?

who sallied from their works, and suddenly retreated, apparently with the hope of being incautiously pursued.

Sullivan ordered General Poor to take possession of the hill which led into his rear, and, thence, to turn the left, and gain the rear of the breastwork, while Hand, aided by the artillery, should attack in front. These orders were promptly executed. While the artillery played on the front, Poor pushed up the mountain and commenced a sharp conflict with the Indians occupying it, which was sustained for some time with considerable spirit. Poor continued to advance rapidly, pressing the enemy with the bayonet, until he gained the summit of the hill. The savages perceiving that their flank was uncovered, and that they were in danger of being surrounded, abandoned their breastwork, and fled with the utmost precipitation.

This victory cost the Americans thirty men. The loss of the Indians was also inconsiderable; but they were so intimidated that every idea of farther resistance was abandoned; and, as Sullivan advanced, they continued to retreat before him.

He penetrated into the heart of the country, which his parties laid waste in every direction. Houses, corn-fields, gardens, and fruit-trees, shared one common fate; and Sullivan executed strictly the severe but necessary orders he had received, to render the country uninhabitable.

The object of the expedition being accomplished, the army returned to Easton in Pennsylvania, having lost only forty men. Congress passed a resolution approving his conduct and that of his army.

While Sullivan laid waste the country on the Susquehanna, another expedition under Colonel Brodhead was carried on from Pittsburg up the Alleghany. He advanced two hundred miles up the river, and destroyed the villages and corn-fields on its head branches. Here, too, the Indians were unable to resist the invading army; and after one unsuccessful skirmish, abandoned their villages to a destruction which was inevitable, and sought for personal safety in their woods.

Although these great exertions did not afford complete security to the western frontier, they were attended with considerable advantages. The savages were intimidated; and their incursions became less formidable, as well as less frequent.

The summer of 1777 passed away without producing any circumstance in America having a material influence on the issue of the war. In Europe, however, an event took place which had been long anxiously expected, and was believed to be of decisive im-

Mention the result of the action, and the loss of each party. What expedition, of a similar nature, was despatched from Pittsburg? State the result. Did these punishments check the savages?

portance. Spain at length determined to make one common cause with France against Great Britain. Despatches giving notice of this determination were forwarded to Don Galvez, the governor of Louisiana, who collected a considerable military force at New Orleans, and reduced the settlements held by the British crown on the Mississippi, which had not been apprized of the war.

On receiving information that D'Estaing had sailed for the West Indies, Sir Henry Clinton resumed his plan of active operations against the southern states. A large body of troops commanded by himself sailed from the Hook, towards the end of December, convoyed by a fleet commanded by Admiral Arbuthnot. The defence of New York and its dependencies was entrusted to General Knyphausen.

The preparations made in New York for some distant enterprise were communicated to General Washington, who conjectured the object, and hastened the march of the troops designed to reinforce General Lincoln.

The season for action in a northern climate being over, the commander-in-chief turned his attention to the distribution of his troops in winter quarters. One division of the army, commanded by General Heath, was to be encamped in huts in the highlands of the North river. Its chief object was the security of West Point, and of the posts on the river as low as King's ferry. Subordinate to this was the protection of the country on the Sound, and down the Hudson to the neighborhood of Kingsbridge. The other and principal division, under the immediate command of General Washington, was put under cover, late in December, in the neighborhood of Morristown.

CHAPTER XVII.

South Carolina invaded.—The British fleet passes the bar and enters the harbor of Charleston.—Opinion of General Washington that the place should be evacuated.—Sir Henry Clinton invests the town.—Tarlton surprises an American corps at Monk's Corner.—Fort Moultrie surrendered.—Tarlton defeats Colonel White.—Charleston capitulates.—Buford defeated.—Arrangements for the government of South Carolina and Georgia.—Sir Henry Clinton embarks for New York.—General Gates takes command of the southern army.—Is defeated near Camden.—Death of De Kalb.—Success of Sumpter.—He is defeated.

1780. ADMIRAL ARBUTHNOT arrived off Savannah on the 31st of January. One of his transports had been brought into Charleston harbor, on the 23d of that month; and the prisoners gave the first certain intelligence that the expedition from New York was destined against the capital of South Carolina.

What European power now joined France and America in hostilities against Britain? What was now the design of General Clinton?

Before the middle of February, the fleet entered the inlet of North Edisto; and the troops were landed on St. John's Island. A part of the fleet was sent round to blockade the harbor of Charleston, while the army proceeded slowly and cautiously from Stono creek to Wappoo cut, and through the islands of St. John and St. James.

This delay was employed to the utmost advantage in improving the defences of Charleston. Six hundred slaves were employed on the works; and vigorous though not very successful measures were taken by the executive to assemble the militia.

The American army being too weak to make any serious opposition to the progress of the enemy through the country, the cavalry, with a small corps of infantry, were directed to hover on their left flank, and the other troops, consisting of about fourteen hundred regulars and a few militia, were drawn into the town, and employed on the works.

Lieutenant-Colonel Tarlton had been ordered to cover the march of a reinforcement from Georgia, under the command of General Patterson. In one of the excursions of this active officer to disperse the militia, his cavalry encountered Lieutenant-Colonel Washington, who commanded the remnant of Baylor's regiment, and was driven back with loss; but the want of infantry prevented Washington from pressing his advantage.

The command of the harbor is of great importance to the defence of Charleston. To procure this advantage, Congress had ordered four frigates to South Carolina, which, with the marine force of the state, and two French vessels, were placed under the command of Commodore Whipple. It had been understood that the bar was impassable by a ship of the line, and that even a large frigate could not be brought over it without first taking out her guns, or careening her so much that the crew would be unable to work her.

This naval force, it was hoped, might defend the entrance into the harbor; but, on sounding within the bar, it was discovered that the water was too shallow for the frigates to act with effect, and that they would be exposed to the batteries which the assailants had erected.

The intention of disputing the passage over the bar was abandoned, and Commodore Whipple moved his squadron in a line with fort Moultrie, in a narrow passage between Sullivan's Island and the middle ground. The British ships, without their guns, passed the bar, and anchored in five-fathom hole.

It being now thought impossible to prevent the fleet from passing

---

What military and naval preparations were made by the Americans for the defence of Charleston? What difficulty as to depth of water lessened the capacity to act efficiently?

14*

fort Moultrie and entering Cooper river, the plan of defence was once more changed, and the armed vessels were sunk in that river, in a line from the town to Shute's folly.

This was the critical moment for evacuating the town. The loss of the harbor rendered the defence of the place, if not desperate, too improbable to have been persisted in by a person who was not deceived by the expectation of much more considerable aids than were received.

In reply to a letter from Lieutenant-Colonel Laurens, communicating the actual state of things, General Washington said, "The impracticability of defending the bar, I fear, amounts to the loss of the town and garrison. At this distance it is impossible to judge for you. I have the greatest confidence in General Lincoln's prudence; but it really appears to me, that the propriety of attempting to defend the town depended on the probability of defending the bar; and that when this ceased, the attempt ought to have been relinquished. In this, however, I suspend a definitive judgment, and wish you to consider what I say as confidential." Unfortunately, this letter did not arrive in time to influence the conduct of the besieged.

On the night of the 1st of April, Sir Henry Clinton broke ground within eight hundred yards of the American lines.

While the besiegers were employed on their first parallel, General Woodford, who had marched from Morristown, in December, entered the town with the old continental troops of the Virginia line, now reduced to seven hundred effectives. General Hogan, with the line of North Carolina, had arrived before him. The garrison consisted of rather more than two thousand regular troops, of one thousand North Carolina militia, and of the citizens of Charleston. The exertions of the Governor to bring in the militia of South Carolina had not succeeded.

By the 9th of April, Sir Henry Clinton completed his first parallel; and about the same time, Admiral Arbuthnot passed Sullivan's Island, under a heavy fire from fort Moultrie, then commanded by Colonel Pinckney, and anchored under James's Island, just out of gun-shot of the American batteries.

Being now in complete possession of the harbor, the British General and Admiral sent a joint summons to General Lincoln, demanding a surrender; to which he returned this firm and modest answer: "Sixty days have elapsed since it has been known that your intentions against this town were hostile, in which time has been afforded to abandon it; but duty and inclination point to the propriety of defending it to the last extremity."

What is to be said respecting the propriety of standing a siege in Charleston? Mention the first operations of the British against the city, and state the reply of General Lincoln when summoned to surrender.

On receiving this answer, the besiegers opened their batteries; but seemed to rely principally on proceeding by sap quite into the American lines.

The communication with the country north-east of Cooper river had hitherto remained open, and was protected by the cavalry commanded by General Huger, stationed at Monk's Corner, and by some corps of militia posted at different places on the Cooper and Santee. After Woodford had entered Charleston, Lincoln, as an additional security, detached a body of regulars to throw up some works about nine miles above the town, on Wando, the eastern branch of Cooper, and on Lamprere's Point. The hope was entertained that the militia might be drawn to these posts.

After the completion of his first parallel, Sir Henry Clinton turned his attention to the country on the east **April 14.** of Cooper, to acquire the possession of which it was necessary to disable the American cavalry. This service was committed to Lieutenant-Colonel Webster, who detached Tarlton with the horse and a corps of infantry to execute it. He succeeded completely. Conducted in the night through unfrequented paths to the American videttes, he entered the camp with them, killed and took about one hundred men and dispersed the residue, who saved themselves on foot in a swamp. This decisive blow gave Lieutenant-Colonel Webster possession of the whole country between Cooper and Wando.

The besiegers had now commenced their second parallel, and it was apparent that the town must ultimately yield to their regular approaches. An evacuation was proposed, and Lincoln is understood to have favored the measure, but the opposition of the civil government and of the inhabitants deterred him from pursuing the only course which afforded even a probability, by saving his army, of saving the southern states.

Soon after the affair at Monk's Corner, Sir Henry Clinton received a reinforcement of three thousand men from New York. This addition enabled him to send large detachments to the east side of Cooper river, under the command of Lord Cornwallis.

Lincoln, who appears to have been still inclined to an evacuation of the town, called another council of war. A number of fortunate circumstances must have concurred to render a retreat possible; and the attempt was prevented by the opposition of the civil government. The opinion seems to have prevailed that the escape of the garrison would have been followed by the destruction of the town, and the ruin of the inhabitants. Terms of ca-

Narrate the progress of the siege, and mention the manner in which the American cavalry was routed at Monk's Corner. What reinforcement now increased the strength of the besiegers? Mention the chief reason that prevented General Lincoln from evacuating Charleston.

pitulation were proposed which were rejected by the besiegers, and hostilities recommenced.

The besiegers had begun their third parallel, when Colonel Henderson made a vigorous sally on their right, which was attended with some success.

In this state of things, General Du Portail, chief of the engineers, was conducted through secret ways into the town. Confident that the place could not be defended, he repeated the proposition for attempting a retreat, which was again rejected. Every day added to the difficulties of the besieged. The Admiral took possession of Mount Pleasant, which induced the evacuation of Lamprere's Point; soon after which, the cavalry who had escaped the disaster at Monk's Corner, and had been reassembled under Colonel White of New Jersey, was again surprised and defeated by Lieutenant Tarlton at Lanneau's ferry.

The investment of the town was now complete, and its condition desperate. The garrison was summoned a second time to surrender, but the terms proposed by Lincoln were refused, and hostilities recommenced.

The besiegers now advanced their works in front of their third parallel, crossed the canal, pushed a double sap to the inside of the abatis, and approached within twenty yards of the American works. Preparations were making for an assault by sea and land. The inhabitants prepared a petition to General Lincoln, entreating him to surrender the town on the terms which had been offered by the beseigers.

Convinced that successful resistance was impossible, he made the proposition, and it was accepted. The capitulation was signed on the 12th of May.

The town and all public stores were surrendered. The garrison, including the citizens who had borne arms, were to be prisoners of war. The militia were to retire to their homes on parole, and their persons and property, as well as the persons and property of the inhabitants of the town, to be secure while they adhered to their parole.

The defence of Charleston, though obstinate, was not bloody. The loss of the British was seventy-six killed, and one hundred and eighty-nine wounded. That of the Americans was ninety-two killed, and one hundred and forty-two wounded.

From the official returns made to Sir Henry Clinton, the number of prisoners, exclusive of sailors, amounted to five thousand six hundred and eighteen men. This report, however, presents a very incorrect view of the real strength of the garrison. It

---

Was it at length thought advisable to surrender the city? Mention the terms of capitulation. What was the loss of the Americans? State also that of the besiegers.

includes every male adult inhabitant of the town. The precise number of privates in the continental regiments, according to the report made to Congress by General Lincoln, was one thousand nine hundred and seventy-seven; of whom five hundred were in the hospital.

Aware of the impression his conquest had made, and of the value of the first moments succeeding it, Sir Henry Clinton made three large detachments from his army;—the first, towards the frontiers of North Carolina; the second to Ninety-Six; and the third up the Savannah.

Lord Cornwallis, who commanded the northern detachment, received intelligence that Colonel Buford, with about four hundred men, was retreating in perfect security towards North Carolina. He directed Lieutenant-Colonel Tarlton with his legion, the infantry being mounted, to pursue this party. That officer, by moving near one hundred miles in two days, overtook Buford, in a line of march, at the Waxhaws, and demanded a surrender. This was refused. While the flags were passing, Tarlton continued to make his dispositions for the assault; and the instant the truce terminated, his cavalry made a furious charge on the Americans, who, having received no orders, seem to have been uncertain whether to defend themselves or not. Some fired on the assailants, while others threw down their arms and begged for quarters. None was given. Colonel Buford escaped with a few cavalry; and about one hundred infantry who were in advance saved themselves by flight; but the regiment was almost demolished. The loss of the British was five killed and fourteen wounded.

Tarlton gives a different account of the circumstances which preceded this massacre. He says that the demand for a surrender was made long before Buford was overtaken; that it was answered by a defiance; and that both parties prepared for action.

Scarcely the semblance of opposition remained in South Carolina and Georgia. The spirit of resistance seemed entirely broken; and a general disposition to submit was manifested. The two other detachments, seeing no appearance of an enemy, received the submission of the inhabitants, who either became neutral by giving their paroles not to bear arms against his Britannic Majesty, or took the oaths of allegiance.

To give stability to the conquest which had been made, small garrisons were posted at different stations, and a series of measures adopted for the purpose of settling the civil affairs of the province.

So entirely was Sir Henry Clinton convinced of the favorable

After General Clinton occupied Charleston, whither did he send three detachments? Mention the particulars of the action wherein Colonel Buford was defeated. Were Georgia and South Carolina entirely subdued?

disposition of the inhabitants, that he ventured to issue a proclama
tion on the third of June, in which he discharged the militia from
their paroles, with the exception of those taken in Charleston and
fort Moultrie, and restored them to all the rights and duties of
British subjects; declaring, at the same time, that those who should
neglect to return to their allegiance should be considered and
treated as rebels.

This proclamation disclosed to the inhabitants their real situa
tion; that a state of neutrality was not within their reach; an
that the only alternative presented to them was, to drive the enemy
out of their country, or to take up arms against their countrymen.

With sanguine hopes that the southern states would be reunited
to the British empire, Sir Henry Clinton embarked for New York
on the 5th of June, leaving four thousand British troops in South
Carolina, under the command of Lord Cornwallis.

The intense heat, and the impossibility of supporting an army
in North Carolina before harvest, induced his lordship to suspend
an expedition which he meditated against that state. In the meantime he despatched emissaries to his friends, requesting them to remain quiet until late in August or early in September, when the
King's troops would be ready to enter the province.

The impatience of the royalists could not be restrained by this
salutary counsel. Anticipating the immediate superiority of their
party, they could not brook the necessary severities of the government, and broke out into ill-concerted insurrections, which were
vigorously encountered, and generally suppressed. One body of
them, however, amounting to near eight hundred men, led by
Colonel Bryan, marched down the east side of the Yadkin, to a
British post at the Cheraws, whence they proceeded to Camden.

Lord Cornwallis, impatient to derive active aids from the conquest of the state, pursued the system adopted by Sir Henry
Clinton, admitting of no neutrality. For some time his measures
seemed to succeed, and professions of loyalty were made in every
quarter. But under this imposing exterior lurked a mass of concealed discontent to which every day furnished new aliment, and
which waited only for a proper occasion to show itself.

Late in March, General Washington had obtained the permission
of Congress to reinforce the Southern army with the troops of
Maryland and Delaware, and with the first regiment of artillery.
This detachment was commanded by the Baron de Kalb. Such
was the deranged state of American finances, that some time
elapsed before it could move, and its progress was afterwards delayed by the difficulty of obtaining subsistence. The troops were

What proclamation was issued by Sir Henry Clinton? Why did the British defer operations in North Carolina? What force was ordered by Washington to proceed southward?

under the necessity, while passing through the upper parts of North Carolina, of spreading themselves over the country to collect corn for their daily food. In this manner they reached Deep river, and encamped near Buffalo ford in July.

The Baron halted at this place, and was meditating on leaving the direct road, which led through a country exhausted by a body of militia under General Caswell, when the approach of Major General Gates was announced.

Alarmed at the danger which threatened the Southern states, Congress sought for a general in whom military talents should be combined with that weight of character which would enable him to draw out the resources of the country. They turned their eye on Gates; and, on the 13th of June, he was called to the command in the Southern department. He entered with alacrity on its duties; and, on the 25th of July, reached the American camp.

The approach of this army revived the hopes of South Carolina. As the prospect of being supported by regular troops brightened, a small body of exiles, amounting to less than two hundred, who had sought an asylum in North Carolina and Virginia, assembled together, and choosing Colonel Sumpter, a continental officer, for their chief, entered South Carolina. They skirmished with the royal militia, and with small corps of regulars on the frontiers, and were soon augmented to six hundred men. Such a disposition to resume their arms showed itself in various parts of the state, that the British General deemed it prudent to draw in his outposts, and to collect his troops in larger bodies.

On the 27th of July the American army moved from its ground, and took the nearest route to the advanced post of the enemy on Lynch's creek, a few miles from Camden. The assurances Gates had received that supplies would overtake him, and would be prepared for him on the road, were not fulfilled; and his distress was extreme. The soldiers subsisted on a few lean cattle found in the woods, and a very scanty supply of green corn and peaches. On the 13th of August, after being joined by General Caswell and Lieutenant-Colonel Porterfield, Gates reached Clermont, sometimes called Rugely's mills. Lord Rawdon had drawn in his outposts, and assembled his forces at Camden.

The American army was reinforced the day after its arrival at Clermont, by seven hundred militia from Virginia, commanded by Brigadier-General Stevens, an officer of experience and merit. On the same day, an express from Colonel Sumpter brought the information that an escort of military stores for the garrison of Camden was on its way from Ninety-Six, and must pass the

---

What officer of reputation was appointed by Congress to command the southern army? Mention the various movements by which the American force approached the British in South Carolina.

Wateree at a ferry which was covered by a small redoubt on the opposite side of the river. One hundred regular infantry, with two brass field-pieces, were immediately detached to join Sumpter, who was ordered to reduce the redoubt, and intercept the convoy. To co-operate with Sumpter, it was determined, in a council of general officers, to put the army in motion that evening, and to take post about seven miles from Camden, with a deep creek in front.

About ten at night the line of march was taken up, and the army had advanced about half-way to Camden, when a firing commenced in front.

On receiving intelligence of the approach of the Americans, and of the defection of the country between Pedee and the Black river, Lord Cornwallis had determined to hasten to Camden; which place he reached the day Gates arrived at Clermont.

The British army did not much exceed two thousand men, of whom about nineteen hundred were regulars; but, as the whole country was rising, his Lordship apprehended that every day would strengthen his adversary; and, therefore, determined to attack him in his camp. By one of those caprices of fortune on which great events often depend, he marched from Camden to attack Gates in Clermont, at the very hour that Gates moved from that place towards Camden.

Aug. 16. At about half-past two in the morning, the advanced parties of the hostile armies, to their mutual surprise, met in the woods, and began to skirmish with each other. Some of Armand's cavalry being wounded at the first fire, threw the others into disorder, and the whole recoiled so suddenly, that the front of the column was broken, and the whole line thrown into consternation. From this first impression the raw troops never recovered. The light infantry, however, particularly Porterfield's corps, behaved so well as to check the advance of the British. Unfortunately, their gallant commander received a mortal wound, and could no longer lead his troops.

As soon as order could be restored, the line of battle was formed. The Maryland division, including the troops of Delaware, were on the right; the North Carolina militia in the centre, and the Virginia militia on the left.

The ground on which the army was drawn up was so narrowed by a marsh on each flank, as to admit of removing one of the Maryland brigades so as to form a second line about two hundred yards in rear of the first. The artillery was placed in the centre of the first line, and Armstrong's light infantry covered the flank of the left wing.

By what coincidence of movement did the armies of Gates and Cornwallis come in contact? State the order of battle.

At dawn of day the British appeared, advancing in column. Captain Singleton opened some field-pieces on its front, at the distance of about two hundred yards, and the American left was ordered to commence the action. As Stevens led on his brigade, Colonel Williams advanced in front with a few volunteers, hoping by a partial fire to extort that of the enemy at some distance, and to diminish its effect on the militia. The experiment did not succeed. The British rushed forward with great impetuosity, and the terrified militia, disregarding the exertions of their General, threw down their loaded muskets, fled from the field, and were followed by the light infantry of Armstrong. The whole North Carolina division, except one regiment, commanded by Colonel Dixon, followed the shameful example. Their General, while endeavoring to rally them, was dangerously wounded.

Tarlton's legion charged them as they broke, and pursued them in their flight. Gates, assisted by their generals, made several efforts to rally them; but the alarm in their rear continuing, they poured on in a torrent, and bore him with them.

After a vain endeavor to stop a sufficient number at Clermont to cover the retreat of the continental troops, he gave up all as lost, and retreated with a few friends to Charlotte, about eighty miles from the field of battle, where he left General Caswell to assemble the neighbouring militia, and proceeded himself to Hillsborough, in order to concert some plan of future defence with the government.

Deserted by the centre and left wing, the continental troops, with the Baron de Kalb at their head, were left without orders, under circumstances which might have justified a retreat. But, taking counsel from their courage, and seeing only their duty, they preferred the honorable and dangerous part of maintaining their position. They were charged about the time the left was broken, but the charge was received with firmness. The bayonet was occasionally resorted to by both parties; and the conflict was maintained for near three quarters of an hour with equal obstinacy.

The reserve was flanked by the British right wing, which wheeled on that brigade, and, attacking it in front and round the left flank, threw it into some disorder. The soldiers were, however, quickly rallied, and renewed the action with unimpaired spirit.

The fire of the whole British army was now directed against these two devoted brigades. They had not lost an inch of ground, when Lord Cornwallis, perceiving that they were without cavalry,

Narrate the details of the battle of Camden. What part of the American army first gave way? What portion maintained the fight with devoted gallantry? Who were the victors?

15

pushed his dragoons upon them, and at the same instant charged them with the bayonet. These gallant troops were broken; and, as they did not give way until intermingled with the enemy, were totally dispersed. Before they were reduced to this last extremity the Baron de Kalb, who fought on foot with the Maryland brigade, in the front line, fell under eleven wounds. His aid-de-camp, Lieutenant-Colonel Dubuysson, received him in his arms, announced his rank and nation, and begged that his life might be spared. He received several wounds, and was taken prisoner with his General.

Never was victory more complete. Every corps was broken and dispersed. The general officers were divided from their men, and reached Charlotte at different times. The loss of men could never be accurately ascertained. Between three and four hundred of the North Carolina division were made prisoners, and between sixty and one hundred were wounded. Three of the Virginia militia were wounded on the field. Not many were taken.

The loss sustained by the regulars was considerable for the numbers engaged. It amounted to between three and four hundred men, of whom a large portion were officers. The British accounts state their own loss at three hundred and twenty-five, of whom two hundred and forty-five were wounded.

On his retreat, General Gates received information of the success of Sumpter. That officer had reduced the redoubt on the Wateree, captured the guard, and intercepted the escort with the stores. This gleam of light cheered the dark gloom which enveloped his affairs but for a moment. He was soon informed that this corps also was defeated and totally dispersed.

On hearing the disaster which had befallen Gates, Sumpter retreated up the south side of the Wateree. While giving his troops some refreshments, he was overtaken near the Catawba ford by Tarlton, who entered the camp so suddenly as in a great measure to cut off the men from their arms. Some slight resistance made from behind the wagons, was soon overcome, and the Americans fled precipitately to the river and woods. Between three and four hundred of them were killed and wounded; and the prisoners and stores they had taken were recovered.

Intelligence of the defeat of the American army reached Charlotte the next day. Generals Smallwood and Gist were then arrived at that place; and about one hundred and fifty stragglers, half-famished officers, and soldiers, had also dropped in. It was thought advisable to retreat immediately to Salisbury. From that place General Gates directed the remnant of the troops to march

---

What was the respective loss in the battle of Camden? Mention the momentary success of Sumpter, and the disastrous action which destroyed his corps. To what place did the discomfited Americans retreat?

to Hillsborough, where he was endeavoring to assemble another army, which might enable him to continue the contest for the southern states.

CHAPTER XVIII.

Distress in camp.—Requisitions on the States.—New scheme of finance.—Resolution to make up depreciation of pay.—Mutiny in the line of Connecticut.—General Knyphausen enters Jersey.—Sir Henry Clinton returns to New York.—Skirmish at Springfield.—Bank established at Philadelphia.—Contributions of the ladies.—Arrival of a French armament in Rhode Island.—Changes in the Quarter-Master's department.—Naval superiority of the British.

WHILE disasters thus crowded on each other in the South, the commander-in-chief was surrounded with difficulties which threatened calamities equally distressing. His earnest requisitions for men to supply the places of those whose terms of service had expired, were not complied with; and the soldiers who remained could scarcely be preserved from perishing with cold and hunger, or dispersing and living on plunder. 1780.

General Greene and Colonel Wadsworth, who had been placed at the head of the Quarter-Master and Commissary department, possessed distinguished merit. Yet, during the campaign, the rations were frequently reduced; and, on coming into winter quarters, the exhausted magazines furnished neither meat nor flour.

The rapid depreciation of the currency, ascribed truly to the quantity in circulation, induced Congress, among other expedients, to withhold from the public agents the money necessary for public purposes, and thus oblige them to purchase on credit. The difference between the value of money at the time of contract and of payment, being soon perceived, had its influence on contracts; and the failure of the government to provide funds to meet the demands, destroyed the credit of public agents. Towards the close of the year 1779, they found it impracticable to obtain supplies for the subsistence of the army. Early in January, notice was given by the Commissary that it was absolutely impossible longer to supply the army, as he was without money and had totally exhausted his credit.

To relieve the immediate and pressing wants of his soldiers the commander-in-chief was under the necessity of requiring from each county in Jersey, a supply of provisions proportioned to its resources, to be forwarded to the camp in six days. Though the country had been much exhausted, the supplies required were instantly furnished.

Mention the difficulty of subsisting the army of Washington, and the measure which at length he was compelled to adopt.

Congress had solemnly resolved to limit the emission of bills on credit of the continent, to two hundred millions of dollars. This emission was completed, and the money expended in November 1779.

The requisitions on the states for money not being fully complied with, it became necessary to devise other means for the prosecution of the war. So early as December 1779, Congress had determined to change the mode of supplying the army from purchases to requisitions of specific articles on the several states. This subject was under deliberation till the 25th of February, when sundry resolutions were passed apportioning on the states their respective quotas. To induce a compliance with these requisitions, a resolution was also passed, declaring " that any state which shall have taken the necessary measures for furnishing its quota, and have given notice thereof to Congress, shall be authorized to prohibit any continental Quarter-Master or Commissary from purchasing within its limits."

These resolutions received the anxious attention of the commander-in-chief, who communicated to Congress, with sincere regret, the serious defects he perceived in their arrangements.

In addition to the radical objection felt by all men of experience to the abandonment of the national and the adoption of the state system for the conduct of the war, and of that to the obvious inadequacy of all the estimates to the demand, the total omission to provide means for supplying occasional deficiencies from the resources of any particular state, and the principle which enabled any state complying with the requisition to prohibit continental agents from purchasing within its territory, appeared to him to present insurmountable obstacles to the new scheme, which must inevitably produce its failure.

The legislature of New Jersey, in which the largest division of the army was stationed, adopted means for complying with the requisition, and not only passed an act prohibiting the purchase of provisions within its jurisdiction by the continental staff, but refused to authorize its own agents to provide for any emergency however pressing.

These suggestions, however, with others less material, did not change the plan of Congress. A disposition in its members, growing inevitably out of the organization of the government, to yield implicitly to the supposed will of their respective states, had discovered itself at an early period, and had strengthened with time.

Whatever might be the future operation of this system, it was unavoidably suspended. The legislatures of the respective states

What was the limit of the issue of continental paper-money? When this sum was exhausted, what expedients were resorted to by Congress for the support of the troops? Mention the objections to these plans.

to whom it was to be submitted, were not, all of them, in session; and were to meet at different times through the ensuing spring. Meanwhile, bills to the amount of £200,000 sterling, payable six months after sight, were drawn on ministers, who were empowered to negotiate loans in Europe.

Accompanying these requisitions was a new scheme of finance, which was a second essay to substitute credit for money.

The several states were required to continue to bring into th continental treasury, monthly, from February to April inclusive their quotas of fifteen millions of dollars. The bills were to be destroyed, and others, not to exceed one dollar for every twenty paid into the treasury, were to be emitted.

These bills were to be redeemable in six years, and were to bear an interest of five *per centum per annum*, to be paid at the time of their redemption, in specie, or, at the election of the holder, annually, in bills of exchange drawn by the United States on their commissioner in Europe, at four shillings and six-pence sterling for each dollar.

The operation of this scheme, too, depended on the sanction of the several states, and was necessarily suspended.

The value of the proposed currency would depend, it was believed, on arresting all future emissions of paper by the states, and on inducing them to call in that which was already in circulation. The exertions of Congress to produce these results did not succeed.

The distresses of the army for food soon returned. The supplies of forage, too, had failed, and a great proportion of the horses had perished. The Quartermaster-General, possessing neither funds nor credit to purchase others, was unable to transport provisions from the distant magazines into camp. The commander-in-chief was again reduced to the painful necessity of calling on the patriotism of private citizens, under the penalty of military impressment.

To the want of food, other distressing privations were added, which increased the irksomeness of the service. From the depreciation of the money, the pay of an officer had become merely nominal, and would no longer supply the smallest of his wants.

Under these complicated embarrassments, it required all that enthusiastic patriotism which originally brought them into the field, and all the influence of the commander-in-chief, whom they almost adored, to retain in the service men who felt themselves neglected, and who believed themselves to be objects of the jealousy of their country, rather than of its gratitude.

Mention the several financial schemes by which Congress hoped to replenish the treasury, and particularize the inconvenience and suffering which were consequent upon its exhausted condition.

15*

Among the privates, causes of disgust grew out of the very composition of the army, which increased the dissatisfaction produced by their multiplied wants.

The first efforts made to enlist troops for the war had, in some degree, succeeded. While these were obliged to continue in service without compensation, the vacant ranks were filled by men who were to serve for a few months, and who received for that short time bounties which appeared to soldiers not well acquainted with the real state of depreciation to be immense. They could no fail to repine at engagements which deprived them of advantages they saw in possession of others. Many were induced to contest those engagements, many to desert, and all felt with the more poignant indignation, those distressing failures in the commissary department which so frequently recurred.

To relieve this gloomy state of things by infusing into it a ray of hope for the future, a resolution was passed declaring that Congress would make good the deficiency of their original pay, which had been occasioned by depreciation; and that the money, or other articles heretofore received, should be considered as advanced on account.

This resolution was published in general orders, and had considerable influence, but not sufficient to remove the various causes of dissatisfaction which were continually multiplying.

This long course of suffering had unavoidably produced some relaxation of discipline, and had gradually soured the minds of the soldiers to such a degree that their discontents broke out into mutiny.

On the 25th of May, two regiments belonging to Connecticut, paraded under arms, with a declared resolution to return home, or to obtain subsistence at the point of the bayonet. By great exertions on the part of the officers, aided by the appearance of a neighboring brigade of Pennsylvania, the leaders were secured, and the mutineers brought back to their duty.

The discontents of the army, and the complaints excited in the country by frequent requisitions on the people, had induced an opinion in New York that the American soldiers were ready to desert their standards, and the people of New Jersey to change their government. To countenance these dispositions, General Knyphausen landed in the night of the 6th of June at Elizabethtown Point, at the head of five thousand men, and marched towards Springfield. The militia assembled with alacrity, and aided the small patrolling parties of continental troops in harassing him on his march to the Connecticut Farms, a distance of five or

Did Congress adopt a resolution with a view of reconciling the soldiery to their present privations? Mention the mutiny and discontents that occurred and the British movement into New Jersey.

six miles, where a halt was made. In a spirit of revenge, more in the character of Tryon who was with him, than of the general who commanded, this settlement was reduced to ashes.

From the Farms, Knyphausen proceeded to Springfield. The Jersey brigade, and the militia of the adjacent country, showing a determination to defend that place, he halted in its neighborhood, and remained on his ground till night.

General Washington put his army in motion early in the same morning that Knyphausen marched from Elizabethtown Point, and advanced to the Short Hills, in the rear of Springfield, as the British encamped near that place. Dispositions were made for an engagement next day; but Knyphausen retired in the night to the place of disembarkment. General Washington continued on the hills near Springfield, too weak to hazard an engagement but on ground chosen by himself. His continental troops did not exceed three thousand men. June 8.

While Knyphausen remained at Elizabethtown, Sir Henry Clinton returned from the conquest of South Carolina; and the design of acting offensively in the Jerseys was resumed. To divide the American force, demonstrations were made of an intention to seize West Point. Greene was left at Springfield, with two brigades, and the Jersey militia; while General Washington proceeded slowly towards Pompton, watching the movements of his enemy. He had not marched farther than Rockaway, eleven miles beyond Morristown, when the British army advanced towards Springfield in great force. He immediately detached a brigade to hang on their right flank, and returned with the residue of his army five or six miles, in order to be in a situation to support Greene. June 18.

Early in the morning of the 23d, the British army moved rapidly in two columns towards Springfield. Every possible exertion to check their march was made by Major Lee and Colonel Dayton, who severally commanded a party detached on each road for the purpose, while General Greene concentrated his little army at Springfield. Scarcely had he made his dispositions when the British front appeared, and a cannonade commenced between their van and the American artillery, which defended a bridge over Rahway, guarded by Colonel Angel with two hundred men. Major Lee, supported by Colonel Ogden, was directed to defend a bridge on the Vauxhall road, along which the right column of the enemy advanced. The residue of the American troops were drawn up on high ground in the rear of the town.

Both bridges were attacked nearly at the same time, and de-

Describe the movements of the two armies consequent upon the advance of the British into New Jersey, and relate the details of a partial engagement near Springfield.

fended with persevering gallantry for about half an hour. When overpowered by numbers, these advanced parties retired in good order, and brought off their wounded. The English then took possession of the town and reduced it to ashes.

The obstinate resistance which had been encountered, the strength of Greene's position, and the firm countenance maintained by his troops, all contributed to deter Sir Henry Clinton from a farther prosecution of his original plan. He retired that afternoon to Elizabethtown; and in the following night passed over to Staten Island. It is probable that the caution manifested during this expedition is to be ascribed, too, in some degree, to the intelligence that a French fleet and army were daily expected on the coast.

The Marquis de Lafayette had been well received at the court of Versailles, and had employed all his influence in impressing on the cabinet, the importance and policy of granting succours to the United States. Having succeeded in this favorite object, and finding no probability of active employment in Europe, he obtained permission to return to America, and arrived late in April at Boston, whence he proceeded to head quarters, and thence to the seat of government, with the information that his Most Christian Majesty had consented to employ a considerable land and naval armament in the United States for the ensuing campaign. On receiving this intelligence, Congress required the states, from New Hampshire to Virginia inclusive, to pay into the continental treasury within thirty days, ten millions of dollars, part of their quotas which became due on the first of March; and drew specie bills on Messrs. Franklin and Jay to the amount of fifty thousand dollars.

The defects which had been suggested in the requisition system were corrected, and the several state legislatures, from New Hampshire to Virginia inclusive, were requested to invest the executives with powers sufficiently ample to comply with such applications as might be made to them by the committee in camp. Letters equally stimulating were written by that committee, and by the commander-in-chief.

The state legislatures, generally, passed the laws which were required, but the energy displayed in their passage was not maintained in their execution. The Assemblies, following the example of Congress, apportioned on the several counties or towns within the state, the quota to be furnished by each, and these were again subdivided into classes, each of which was to furnish a man by contributions or taxes imposed on itself.

Why were the British disinclined to force an engagement? What measures were adopted by Congress, with a view to efficient co-operation with the armament expected from France?

These operations were slow and unproductive.

The merchants, and other citizens of Philadelphia, with a zeal guided by that sound discretion which turns expenditure to the best account, established a bank with a capital of £315,000 in specie, the principal of which was to supply the army with provisions and rum. The members of this bank were to receive no emolument. They required only that Congress should pledge the faith of the Union to reimburse the costs and charges of the transaction, and should aid its execution so far as might be in their power.

The ladies of Philadelphia, too, gave a splendid instance of patriotism by large donations for the immediate relief of the suffering army, and this example was extensively followed. But it is not by the contributions of the generous that a war can or ought to be maintained. The purse of the nation alone can supply the expenditures of a nation. The sufferings of the army continued to be extreme, and attest its patriotism. One heroic effort, however it may dazzle the mind, is an exertion most men are capable of making; but continued patient suffering, and unremitting perseverance in a service promising no personal emolument, and exposing the officer unceasingly, not only to wants of every kind, but to those circumstances of humiliation which seem to degrade him in the eyes of others, demonstrate a fortitude of mind, a strength of virtue, and a firmness of principle, which ought never to be forgotten.

As the several legislative acts for bringing the army into the field, did not pass till June and July, General Washington remained uninformed of the force on which he might rely, and was consequently unable to prepare any certain plan of operations.

This suspense was the more embarrassing, as, in the event of an attempt on New York, it was of the utmost importance that the French fleet should, on its arrival, take possession of the harbor, which was then weakly defended. But this measure, if followed by a failure to furnish the requisite support, would not only be ineffectual, but might sacrifice the fleet itself.

Should the attempt on New York be unadvisable, other objects presented themselves against which the allied arms might be directed with advantage. To avoid the disgrace and danger of attempting what could not be effected, and the reproach as well as injury of neglecting any attainable object, equally required a correct knowledge of the measures which would be taken by the states. The commander-in-chief stated his embarrassments on this interesting subject with great strength to Congress.

The tardy proceedings of the states were not less perplexing to

Did the merchants of Philadelphia devise means of relief to the suffering army? How did the ladies of the same city testify their patriotic sympathy? What uncertainty embarrassed Washington?

that body than to their General. They had assured the minister
of his Most Christian Majesty, in the preceding January, that the
United States could rely confidently on bringing into the field for
the next campaign, an army of twenty-five thousand men, with
such aids of militia as would render it competent to any enterprise
against the posts occupied by the British in the United States; and
that ample supplies of provisions for the combined armies should
be laid up in magazines.

The French Minister addressed Congress on this subject, and
Congress renewed their urgent requisitions on the states.

On the 13th of July, while the result of the measures adopted
by the several states remained uncertain, the French fleet entered
the harbor of Newport, soon after which letters were received
from the Count de Rochambeau, and the Chevalier de Ternay, the
General and Admiral, transmitting to General Washington an
account of their arrival, of their strength, their expectations, and
their orders.

The troops designed to serve in the United States had assembled
at Brest; but the transports of that place having been chiefly employed for an armament destined for the West Indies, and the ports
from which it was intended to draw others being blockaded, only the
first division consisting of five thousand men had sailed; but letters from France contained assurances that the second might soon
be expected.

Late as was the arrival of the French troops, they found the
Americans unprepared for active operations. Not even at that time
were the numbers ascertained which would be furnished by the
states. Yet it was necessary to communicate a plan of the campaign to the Count de Rochambeau.

The season was already so far advanced that preparations for the
operations contemplated eventually on the arrival of the second division of the French fleet, must be immediately made, or there would
not be time to execute the design against New York. Such a state of
things so ill comported with the engagements of Congress and the
interests of the nation, that, trusting to the measures already taken,
General Washington determined to hazard much rather than forego
the advantages to be derived from the aids afforded by France.

A decisive naval superiority was, however, considered as the
basis of any enterprise to be undertaken by the allied armies.
This naval superiority being assumed, the outlines of the plan for
an attempt on New York were drawn, and committed to the Marquis de Lafayette, who was authorized to explain the situation of
the American army, and the views of the General, to the Count

With what number of troops did Congress undertake to aid the French
army, when it should reach the United States? Mention the causes of delay
which occurred in assembling the promised force?

de Rochambeau. It was to be considered as an indispensable preliminary that the fleet and army of France should continue their aid until the enterprise should succeed or be abandoned by mutual consent.

The Chevalier de Ternay did not long maintain his superiority at sea. Three days after he reached Newport, Admiral Greaves arrived with six ships of the line, and transferred it to the British. The hostile fleet proceeded to Rhode Island and cruised off the harbor.

As the commanders of the allied forces still cherished the hope of acquiring a superiority at sea, the design on New York was only suspended. In this crisis of affairs, a derangement took place in a most important department, which threatened to disconcert the whole plan of operations, though every other circumstance should prove favorable.

The reciprocal disgusts and complaints produced by the immense expenditures of the Quartermaster's Department, and the inadequacy of the funds with which it was supplied, had determined Congress to make still another radical change in the system. This subject had been taken up early in the winter; but the report of the committee was not made until March, nor finally decided on, until the middle of July.

This interesting subject engaged the anxious attention of the commander-in-chief. While the army lay in winter quarters, the Quartermaster-General, at his request, repaired to Philadelphia, for the purpose of giving Congress all the information that he possessed. His proposition was, to withdraw the direct management of the department from the civil government, and to place it under the control of the person who should be at its head, subject to the direction of the commander-in-chief.

The views of Congress were entirely opposed to this proposition. While the subject was suspended, it was taken up by the committee of co-operation, at head quarters, and a system digested by the combined talents and experience of Generals Washington, Schuyler, and Greene, which was recommended to the government. To give the more weight to his opinion, General Greene offered to discharge the duties assigned to him, without other extra emolument than his family expenses. This plan was unacceptable to Congress. A system was at length completed by that body, which General Greene believed to be incapable of execution; and, therefore, determined to withdraw from a station in which he despaired of being useful.

Apprehending the worst consequences from his resignation, at

What arrival from England gave to the British the naval superiority near New York? What matter now threatened serious consequences to the efficiency of the alliance?

so critical a moment, General Washington pressed him to suspend this decisive step, until the effect of an application from himself and from the committee of co-operation should be known. Their representations were of no avail. The resolution to make this bold experiment was unalterable. General Greene's resignation was received, and Colonel Pickering was appointed to succeed him. A more judicious selection could not have been made but there was a defect of means, for which neither talents nor ex ertions could compensate.

In the commissary department, the same distress was experienced. General Washington was reduced to the necessity of emptying the magazines at West Point, and of foraging on a people, whose means of subsisting themselves were already nearly exhausted by the armies on both sides. So great were the embarrassments produced by the difficulty of procuring subsistence, that although the second division of the French fleet was daily expected, he found it necessary to countermand the orders under which the militia were marching to camp.

Such was the state of preparation for the campaign, when intelligence was brought, by the Alliance frigate, that the port of Brest was blockaded. In the hope, however, that the combined fleets of France and Spain would be able to raise the blockade, General Washington adhered to his purpose respecting New York. The details of a plan of co-operation continued to be the subject of a correspondence with the Count de Rochambeau and the Chevalier de Ternay; and at length, a personal interview was agreed upon, to take place on the 21st of September, at Hartford, in Connecticut.

In this interview, ulterior eventual measures, as well as a detailed arrangement for acting against New York, were the subjects of consideration. No one of the plans, however, then concocted, was carried into execution. They depended on a superiority at sea, which was rendered hopeless by the arrival of Admiral Rodney, at New York, with eleven ships of the line and four frigates.

Who succeeded General Greene in the Quartermaster's Department? To what straits was the American commander-in-chief reduced, in order to subsist his troops? To what circumstance is to be attributed the non-arrival of the second division of the French fleet? What was done in reference to a combined attack upon the British at New York? What further reinforcements confirmed the naval preponderance of the enemy?

CHAPTER XIX.

Treason and escape of Arnold.—Execution of Major André.—Proceedings of Congress respecting the army.—Major Talmadge destroys the British stores at Coram.—The army retires into winter quarters.—Irruption of Major Carlton into New York.—European transactions.

WHILE the public was anticipating great events from the combined arms of France and the United States, treason lay concealed in the American camp.

The great military services of General Arnold had secured to him a high place in the opinion of the army, and of his country. Not having recovered from his wounds, and having large accounts to settle, which required leisure, he was, on the evacuation of Philadelphia, appointed to the command in that place. Unfortunately, he did not possess that strength of principle, and correctness of judgment, which would have enabled him to resist the seductions to which his rank and reputation exposed him, in the metropolis of the Union. His expenses having swelled his debts to an amount which it was impossible to discharge, he entered into speculations which were unfortunate, and took shares in privateers which were unsuccessful. He relied on his claims against the United States, for the means of extricating himself from embarrassments in which his indiscretion had involved him; but they were greatly reduced by the commissioners, to whom they were referred; and, on his appeal to Congress, a committee reported that the commissioners had allowed more than he was entitled to receive.

He was charged with various acts of extortion on the citizens of Philadelphia, and with peculating on the funds of the continent. Soured by these various causes of resentment, he indulged himself in angry reproaches against what he termed the ingratitude of his country; which provoked those around him, and gave great offence to the government. The executive of Pennsylvania exhibited formal charges against him to Congress, who directed that he should be brought before a court-martial.

In January, 1779, he was sentenced to be reprimanded by the commander-in-chief; which sentence, being approved by Congress, was carried into execution. His proud, unprincipled spirit revolted from the cause of his country, and determined him to seek an occasion to make the objects of his hatred the victims of his vengeance. Turning his eyes to West Point, as an acquisition which would give value to treason, he sought the command of that fortress, and addressed himself to the delegation of New

To what must be attributed the disposition of Arnold to treason against his country? With the purpose of betrayal, what important command did he seek?

16

York. One of the members recommended him to General Washington for that station; and soon afterwards, General Schuyler mentioned a letter from Arnold, intimating his wish to rejoin the army, but stating his inability to perform the active duties of the field. General Washington said that if, with a knowledge that West Point would be garrisoned by invalids and a few militia, he still preferred that situation to a command in the field, his wishes should certainly be indulged. Arnold caught at the proposition; and, in the beginning of August, repaired to camp, where he renewed the solicitations which had before been made indirectly; and was invested with the command he solicited.

He had previously, in a letter to Colonel Robinson, signified his change of principles, and his wish to restore himself to the favor of his prince by some signal proof of his repentance. This letter opened the way to a correspondence with Sir Henry Clinton, the immediate object of which, after obtaining the command of West Point, was to concert the means of betraying that important post to the British General. This business was entrusted to Major John André, an aid-de-camp of Sir Henry Clinton, and Adjutant-General of the British army. A correspondence was carried on between that officer and Arnold, under a mercantile disguise, in the feigned names of Gustavus and Anderson; and at length, to facilitate their communications, the Vulture sloop of war moved up the North river, and took a station convenient for the purpose.

The time when General Washington met the Count de Rochambeau at Hartford, was selected for the final adjustment of the plan and Major André came up the river and went on board the Vulture. Both parties repaired in the night to a house, without the American lines, which had been selected for the interview—André being brought under a passport for John Anderson, in a boat despatched from the shore. While the conference was yet unfinished, daylight appeared, and Arnold proposed that André should remain concealed till the succeeding night. When, in the following night his return to the Vulture was proposed, the boatmen refused to carry him, because she had shifted her station in consequence of a gun which had been moved to the shore without the knowledge of Arnold, and brought to bear upon her. Being thus reduced to the necessity of endeavoring to reach New York by land, he put on a plain suit of clothes, and received a pass from General Arnold, authorizing him, under the name of John Anderson, to proceed on the public service to the White Plains, or lower if he thought proper.

What arrangements were made by the enemy for the convenience of plotting with Arnold, and who was the British officer sent to confer with him? What incident interfered with André's return?

With this permit he had passed all the guards and posts on the road, and was proceeding to New York, when one of their militia men employed between the lines of the two armies, springing from his covert, seized the reins of his bridle and stopped his horse. André, instead of producing his pass, asked the man where he belonged? He replied, "to below;" a term implying that he was from New York. "And so," said André, "am I." He then declared himself to be a British officer, on urgent business, and begged that he might not be detained. The appearance of the other militia men disclosed his mistake too late to correct it. He offered a purse of gold and a valuable watch, with promises of ample reward from his government if they would permit his escape; but his offers were rejected, and his captors proceeded to search him. Papers in Arnold's hand-writing, containing valuable information concerning West Point, were found concealed in his boots. To Lieutenant-Colonel Jameson, who commanded the scouting parties on the lines, he still maintained his assumed character; and requested Jameson to inform his commanding officer that Anderson was taken. On receiving the express conveying this communication, Arnold took refuge on board the Vulture. When sufficient time for his escape was supposed to have elapsed, André acknowledged himself to be the Adjutant-General of the British army. Jameson, seeking to correct the mischief of his indiscreet communication to Arnold, immediately despatched a packet to the commander-in-chief, containing the papers which had been discovered, with a letter from André.

Every precaution was immediately taken for the security of West Point; after which a board of general officers was called to report a state of André's case, and to determine on his character and punishment. The board reported the essential facts which had appeared, with their opinion, that he was a spy, and ought to suffer death. The execution of this sentence was ordered to take place on the succeeding day. André wished to die like a soldier, not as a criminal, and requested this mitigation of his sentence, in a letter replete with the feelings of a man of sentiment and honor; but the occasion required that the example should make its full impression, and this request could not be granted. He met his fate with composure and dignity.

Great exertions were made by Sir Henry Clinton to have André considered, first as protected by a flag of truce, and afterwards as a prisoner of war. Even Arnold had the hardihood to interpose. He stated, among other arguments, that many of the most distinguished citizens of South Carolina who had forfeited their lives,

Mention the manner of André's capture. How did Arnold make his escape? What was determined as to the fate of André? Mention the unavailing interposition to save his life.

and had hitherto been spared, could no longer be the subjects of clemency, should André suffer.

It may well be supposed that the interposition of Arnold could have no influence on Washington. He conveyed Mrs. Arnold to her husband in New York, and transmitted his clothes and baggage for which he had written. In no other respect were his letters noticed.

From motives of policy or of respect for his engagements, Sir Henry Clinton conferred on Arnold the commission of a brigadier-general, which he preserved throughout the war.*

When the probable consequences of this plot, had it been successful, were considered; and the combination of apparent accidents by which it was defeated, was recollected, all were filled with awful astonishment; and the devout perceived in the transaction, the hand of Providence guiding America to independence.

The thanks of Congress were voted to John Paulding, David Williams, and John Vanwert, the three militia men who had rendered this invaluable service; and a silver medal, with an inscription expressive of their fidelity and patriotism, was presented to each of them. As a farther evidence of national gratitude, a resolution was passed granting to each two hundred dollars per annum during life, to be paid in specie, or an equivalent in current money.

The efforts of General Washington to obtain a permanent military force, or its best substitute, a regular system for filling the vacant ranks with drafts who should join the army on the first day of January in each year, were still continued. Great as were the embarrassments with which the governments of the states as well as that of the Union were surrounded, it is not easy to find adequate reasons for the neglect of representations so vitally interesting.

Private letters disclose the fact, that two parties still agitated Congress. One entered fully into the views of the commander-in-chief. The other, jealous of the army, and apprehensive of its hostility to liberty, were unwilling to give stability to its constitution. They seemed to dread the danger from the enemy to which its fluctuations must expose them, less than that which might be apprehended from its permanent character. They caught with avidity at every intelligence which encouraged the hope of a speedy peace, but entered reluctantly into measures founded on the supposition that the war might be of long duration. Perfectly acquainted with the extent of the jealousies entertained on this subject, although, to use his own expressions, in a private letter, " Heaven

* General Washington used great exertions to cause Arnold to be seized in New York and conveyed to the American camp. John Champ, sergeant-major in Lee's legion, was employed in this important and critical service, and was near effecting it.

How did Congress reward the captors of André? Did Washington still persevere in his endeavors to put the army in a condition of greater efficiency?

knows how unjustly," General Washington had forborne to press his opinions on it so constantly as his own judgment directed. But the uncertainty of collecting a force to co-operate with the auxiliaries from France, was so peculiarly embarrassing that he at length resolved to conquer the delicacy by which he had been in some degree restrained, and to open himself fully on a subject which he deemed all-important to the success of the war.

In August, while looking anxiously for a reinforcement to th Chevalier de Ternay, which would give him the command of the American seas, and apprehensive that a failure on the part of the United States might disappoint the hopes founded on that superiority, he transmitted a letter to Congress, freely and fully imparting his sentiments on the state of things.

This very interesting letter contains an exact statement of American affairs, and a faithful picture of the consequences of the ruinous policy which had been pursued, drawn by the man best acquainted with them.

After long delays, a committee, which had been appointed for the purpose, presented their report for the reorganization of the army. This report being approved, was transmitted to the com mander-in-chief for his consideration. His objections to it were stated at length and with great respect. Among them was its omission to make an adequate provision for the officers. " This," he said, " should be the basis of the plan. He was aware of the difficulty of making a present provision sufficiently ample to give satisfaction; but this only proved the expediency of making one for the future, and brought him to that which he had so frequently recommended as the most economical, the most politic, and the most effectual that could be devised; this was half-pay for life." He then enters into a full defence of this measure, and an examination of the objections to it.

This letter was taken into serious consideration; and the measures it recommended were pursued in almost every particular. Even the two great principles which were viewed with most jealousy—an army for the war, and half-pay for life—were adopted. It would have greatly abridged the calamities of America, could these resolutions have been carried into execution.

To place the officers of the army in a situation which would hold out to them the prospect of a comfortable old age in a country saved by their blood, their sufferings, and the labors of their best years, was an object which had been always dear to the heart of General Washington, and he had seized every opportunity to press it on Congress. That body had approached it slowly, taking step after step with apparent reluctance.

Upon what important subject did General Washington address a letter to Congress? Mention the two chief features of his plan.

16,*

The first resolution on the subject, passed in May, 1778, allowed to all military officers who should continue in service during the war, and not hold any office of profit under the United States, or any of them, half-pay for seven years, if they lived so long. At the same time, the sum of eighty dollars was granted to every non-commissioned officer and soldier who should serve to the end of the war. In 1779, this subject was resumed. After much debate, its farther consideration was postponed, and the officers and soldiers were recommended to the attention of their several states, with a declaration that their patriotism, valor, and perseverance, in defence of the rights and liberties of their country, had entitled them to the gratitude, as well as the approbation of their fellow-citizens.

In 1780, a memorial from the general officers, depicting in strong terms the situation of the army, and requiring present support, and future provision, was answered by a reference to what had been already done, and by a declaration " that patience, self-denial, fortitude, and perseverance, and the cheerful sacrifice of time and health, are necessary virtues, which both the citizen and soldier are called to exercise, while struggling for the liberties of their country; and that moderation, frugality, and temperance, must be among the chief supports, as well as the brightest ornaments of that kind of civil government which is wisely instituted by the several states in this Union."

This unfeeling, cold, philosophic lecture on the virtues of temperance to men who were often without food, and always scantily supplied, was ill calculated to assuage irritations fomented by past neglect. In a few days afterwards a more conciliating temper was manifested. The odious restriction, limiting the half-pay for seven years to those who should hold no post of profit under the United States, or any of them, was removed; and the bounty allowed the non-commissioned officers and privates was extended to the widows and orphans of those who had died, or should die in the service. At length the vote passed which has been stated, allowing half-pay for life to all officers who should serve in the armies of the United States to the end of the war.

Resolutions were also passed recommending it to the several states to make up the depreciation on the pay that had been received by the army; and declaring that their future services should be compensated in the money of the new emission, the value of which, it was supposed, might be kept up by taxes and by loans.

While the government was employed in maturing measures for the preservation of its military establishment, the season for ac-

Did there appear a favorable disposition in Congress, to relieve the distresses of the army? What enactments by that body at length promised relief and permanence to the military force?

tion passed away. Towards the close of the campaign, a handsome enterprise was executed by Major Talmadge, of Sheldon's regiment of light dragoons, who had been generally stationed on the east side of the North river. He obtained information that a large magazine of forage had been collected at Coram, on Long Island, which was protected by the militia of the country, a small garrison in its neighborhood, and the cruisers in the Sound.

At the head of a detachment of eighty dismounted and ten mounted dragoons, he passed the Sound, where it was twenty miles wide, marched across the island in the night, surprised the fort, and entered the works without resistance. The garrison took refuge in two houses, and commenced a fire from the doors and windows. These were instantly forced open, and the whole party, amounting to fifty-four, among whom were a lieutenant-colonel, captain, and a subaltern, were killed or taken. The fort was demolished, and the magazines consumed by fire. The object of the expedition being accomplished, Major Talmadge returned without the loss of a man. On the recommendation of General Washington, Congress passed a resolution expressing a high sense of the merits of those engaged in the enterprise.

Nearly at the same time, Major Carlton, at the head of one thousand men, composed of Europeans, tories, and Indians, made a sudden irruption into the northern parts of New York, and took possession of forts Ann and George, with their garrisons. At the same time, Sir John Johnson, at the head of a corps composed of the same materials, appeared on the Mohawk. Several sharp skirmishes were fought; and General Clinton's brigade was ordered to that quarter, but before his arrival the invading armies had retired, after laying waste the country through which they passed.

In December the troops were distributed in winter quarters, near Morristown, at Pompton, at West Point and its vicinity, and at Albany.

While the disorder of the American finances, and the debility of the government, determined Great Britain to persevere in offensive war against the United States, Europe assumed an aspect not less formidable to the permanent grandeur of that nation than hostile to its present views. In the summer of 1780, Russia, Sweden, and Denmark, entered into the celebrated compact which has been generally denominated "THE ARMED NEUTRALITY." Holland had also declared a determination to accede to the same confederacy; and it is not improbable that this measure hastened the declaration of war which was made by Great Britain against that power towards the close of the present year. Had it been

What gallant exploit on Long Island was performed by Major Talmadge? What partial operations took place in northern New York? Mention the European powers that composed the Armed Neutrality.

delayed till the actual accession of Holland to the league, Great Britain must have allowed her immense navigation to be employed in the transportation of belligerent property, or have engaged in war with the whole confederacy.

CHAPTER XX.

Transactions in South Carolina and Georgia.—Defeat of Ferguson.—Lord Cornwallis enters North Carolina.—Retreats out of that state.—Major Wemys defeated.—Tarleton repulsed.—Greene appointed to command the Southern army.—Arrives in camp. —Detaches Morgan over the Catawba,—Battle of the Cowpens.—Greene retreats into Virginia.—Lord Cornwallis retires to Hillsborough.—Greene recrosses the Dan. —Loyalists under Colonel Pyle cut to pieces.—Battle of Guilford.—Lord Cornwallis retires to Ramsay's mills.—To Wilmington.—Greene advances to Ramsay's mills.— Determines to enter South Carolina.—Lord Cornwallis resolves to enter Virginia.

1780.   In the South, Lord Cornwallis found it necessary to suspend the new career of conquest on which he had intended to enter. In addition to the difficulty of obtaining food, a temper so hostile to British interests had appeared in South Carolina as to require great part of his force to subdue the spirit of insurrection against his authority. General Marion had entered the north-eastern parts of that state with only sixteen men, and was rousing the well-affected inhabitants to arms, when the defeat of the 16th of August chilled the growing spirit of resistance. With the force he had collected, he rescued about one hundred and fifty continental troops who had been captured at Camden, and were on their way to Charleston. He made repeated excursions from the swamps in which he concealed himself, and skirmished successfully with the militia who had joined the royal standard, and the small parties of regulars who supported them.

The interval between the victory of the 16th of August and the invasion of North Carolina, was employed in quelling what was termed the spirit of revolt in South Carolina. The efforts of the people to recover their independence were considered as new acts of rebellion. Several of the most active militiamen who had taken protections as British subjects, and entered into the British militia, having been made prisoners in the battle of Camden, were executed as traitors; and orders were given to officers commanding at different posts to proceed in the same manner against persons of a similar description.

While pursuing these measures to break the spirit of insurrection, Lord Cornwallis was indefatigable in urging his preparations for the expedition into North Carolina. Major Ferguson, who had

What disposition, impeding the full triumph of the British arms in South Carolina, was now made manifest? Mention the celebrated partisan who harassed the enemy. What occurred in North Carolina?

been employed in the district of Ninety-Six, to train the most loyal inhabitants, and to attach them to his own corps, was directed to enter the western parts of North Carolina for the purpose of em bodying the royalists in that quarter.

On the 8th of September, Lord Cornwallis moved from Cam den and reached Charlotte in North Carolina late in that month. At this place he expected to be joined by Ferguson; but that officer was arrested by an event as important as it was unexpected.

Colonel Clarke, a refugee from Georgia, had invested Augusta, but was compelled by the approach of Colonel Cruger from Ninety-Six to abandon the enterprise, and save himself by a rapid retreat. To favor the design of intercepting Clarke, Ferguson remained longer in the country than had been intended; and this delay gave an opportunity to several volunteer corps to unite. The hardy mountaineers inhabiting the extreme western parts of Virginia and North Carolina, assembled on horseback with their rifles under Colonels Campbell, M'Dowell, Cleveland, Shelby, and Sevier, and moved with their accustomed velocity towards Ferguson, who pressed his march for Charlotte. His messengers announcing his danger to Lord Cornwallis were intercepted, and no movement was made to favor his retreat.

Colonel Campbell of Virginia was chosen to command the American parties. At the Cowpens, they were joined by Colonels Williams, Tracy, and Branan, of South Carolina. About nine hundred men were selected, by whom the pursuit was continued through the night, and through a heavy rain. The next day about three in the afternoon, they came within view of Ferguson, encamped on the summit of King's Mountain—a ridge five or six hundred yards long and sixty or seventy wide.

The Americans, who had arranged themselves into three columns, the right commanded by Colonel Sevier Oct. 7. and Major Winston, the centre by Colonels Campbell and Shelby, and the left by Colonels Cleveland and Williams, attacked the front and flanks of the British line. Ferguson made several impetuous charges with the bayonet; but before any one of them could completely disperse the corps against which it was directed, the destructive fire of the others called off his attention, and the broken corps was rallied, and brought again to the attack. Before the fate of the day was absolutely decided, Ferguson received a mortal wound, and instantly expired. The courage of his party fell with him, and quarter was immediately demanded.

In this sharp action, one hundred and fifty of Ferguson's party were killed on the spot, and about the same number were wounded.

Mention the circumstance which favored the assembling of the Americans who pursued and attacked Ferguson at King's Mountain. What were the result of the action, and the loss of the enemy?

Eight hundred and ten, of whom one hundred were British, were made prisoners; and fifteen hundred stand of excellent arms were taken.

The Americans, as is usual with riflemen, fought under the cover of trees, and their loss was inconsiderable. As cruelty begets cruelty, the example set by the British was followed, and ten of the most active of the royalists were hung on the spot. The victorious mountaineers returned to their homes.

Lord Cornwallis, fearing for the posts in his rear, retreated to Wynnsborough, where he waited for reinforcements from New York.

Sir Henry Clinton had determined to send a large detachment to the South, and had ordered the officer commanding it to enter the Chesapeake, and to take possession of the lower parts of Virginia, after which he was to obey the orders he should receive from Lord Cornwallis. This detachment, amounting to near three thousand men, commanded by General Leslie, sailed on the 6th of October, and, entering James river, took possession of the country on its south side as high as Suffolk, and began to fortify Portsmouth. At this place he received orders from Lord Cornwallis to repair to Charleston by water.

While his lordship waited at Wynnsborough for this reinforcement, the light corps of his army were employed in suppressing the parties that were rising throughout the country. Marion having become so formidable as to endanger the communication between Camden and Charleston, Tarlton was detached against him, and Marion took refuge in the swamps. From the unavailing pursuit of him, Tarlton was called to a different quarter, where an enemy, supposed to be entirely vanquished, had reappeared in considerable force.

Sumpter had again assembled a respectable body of mounted militia, and was advancing on the British posts. Major Wemyss who marched against him with a regiment of infantry, and about forty dragoons, reached his camp several hours before day, and instantly attacked it. At the first fire Wemyss was disabled by two dangerous wounds. The assailants fell into confusion, and were repulsed with the loss of their commanding officer and twenty men. Sumpter was joined by Clarke and Branan, and threatened Ninety-Six. Tarlton was recalled and ordered to proceed against him.

Nov. So rapid was the movement of that officer, that he had nearly gained the rear of his enemy before notice of his return was received. In the night, Sumpter was apprised of the approaching danger by a deserter, and began his retreat. Tarlton overtook his rear guard at the ford of the Ennoree, and cut it to pieces. Fearing that Sumpter might save himself by crossing the Tyger, he pressed forward with about two hundred and eighty cavalry and mounted infantry, and, in the afternoon, Nov. 20. came within view of the Americans, who were arranged in order of battle on the banks of the Tyger. Their right flank was secured by the river, and their left by a barn of logs, in which a considerable number of men were placed.

Tarlton rushed to the charge with his usual impetuosity. After several ineffectual attempts to dislodge the Americans, he retired with great precipitation, leaving ninety-two dead and one hundred wounded. Sumpter crossed the Tyger; and, having been severely wounded, his troops dispersed. His loss was only three killed and four wounded.

The shattered remains of the army defeated near Camden, had been slowly collected at Hillsborough. It amounted, with its reinforcements, to about fourteen hundred continental troops. To these were added the militia of the country.

While Lord Cornwallis remained at Charlotte, Gates detached Smallwood to the ford of the Yadkin, with orders to take command of all the troops in that quarter. As Lord Cornwallis retreated, Gates advanced to Charlotte, Smallwood moved down the Catawba, and Morgan, now a brigadier, was pushed forward some distance in his front. This was the arrangement of the troops when their General was removed.

On the 5th of November, Congress passed a resolution requiring the commander-in-chief to order a court of enquiry on the conduct of General Gates, and to appoint some other officer to command the southern army, until the enquiry should be made.

Washington selected Greene for that important service. In a letter to Congress recommending him to their support, he said General Greene was "an officer in whose abilities, fortitude, and integrity, from a long and intimate experience of them, he had the most entire confidence." About the same time the legion of Lee was ordered into South Carolina.

Greene reached Charlotte on the 2d of December; and was soon afterwards gratified with the intelligence of a small success obtained by the address of Colonel Washington.

Smallwood, having received information that a body of royal militia had entered the country in which he foraged, ordered Morgan and Washington against them. The militia retreated; but Washington, being able to move with more celerity than the in-

---

Mention the repulse of Tarleton. Where were the remains of the American force collected, after the battle of Camden? What General superseded Gates in command of the Southern army?

fantry, resolved to make an attempt on another party, which was stationed at Rugely's farm within thirteen miles of Camden. He found them posted in a logged barn, unassailable by cavalry, on which he resorted to the following stratagem. Having painted the trunk of a pine, and mounted it on a carriage so as to resemble a field-piece, he paraded it in front, and demanded a surrender. The whole party, consisting of one hundred and twelve men, with Colonel Rugely at their head, became prisoners of war.

To narrow the limits of the British army, and to encourage the inhabitants, Greene directed Morgan to take a position near the confluence of the Pacolet with the Broad river. His party consisted of rather more than three hundred chosen continental infantry, commanded by Lieutenant-Colonel Howard, of Maryland, of Washington's light dragoons amounting to eighty men, and of two companies of Virginia militia, commanded by Captains Triplet and Taite, which were composed almost entirely of old continental soldiers. He was also to be joined on Broad river by seven or eight hundred volunteers, and by militia commanded by General Davidson and by Colonels Clarke and Few. The activity of his troops, and the enterprising temper of their commander rendered him extremely formidable to the parties of the royal militia who were embodying in that part of the country.

Lord Cornwallis detached Tarlton with some infantry and artillery added to his legion, so as to amount in the whole to a thousand men, for the purpose of affording protection to Ninety-Six. His lordship, having completed his preparations to enter North Carolina by the upper route, advanced northward between the Catawba and Broad rivers. Leslie, who had halted at Camden, was ordered to move up the banks of the former; and Tarlton was ordered to strike at Morgan. Should that officer escape Tarlton, the hope was entertained that he might be intercepted by the main army which would be between him and Greene.

Jan. 1781.

These combined movements were communicated to Morgan on the 14th of January. He retired across the Pacolet, the fords of which he was desirous of defending. Tarlton having effected a passage of that river about six miles below him, he made a precipitate retreat; and his pursuers occupied the camp he had abandoned. Believing that he should be overtaken on his retreat, while his men were fatigued and discouraged, and thinking it more advisable to exhibit the appearance of fighting from choice, he determined to risk a battle at the Cowpens.

At three in the morning of the 17th, Tarlton recommenced the pursuit. He found his enemy prepared to receive him.

Mention the position and force of General Morgan. State also the preparations to attack him. Where did the encounter take place?

On an eminence in an open wood, Morgan drew up his continental troops, and Triplet's corps, deemed equal to continentals, amounting to between four and five hundred men, commanded by Lieutenant-Colonel Howard. In their rear, on the descent of the hill, Lieutenant-Colonel Washington was posted with his cavalry, and a small body of mounted Georgia militia, commanded by Major Call. On these two corps rested his hopes of victory, and with them he remained in person. The front line was composed of militia under the command of Colonel Pickens. Major M'Dowell with a battalion of North Carolina volunteers, and Major Cunningham, with a battalion of Georgia volunteers, were advanced about one hundred and fifty yards in front of this line, with orders to give a single fire, and then to fall back into the interval left for them in the centre of the first line. The militia were ordered to keep up a retreating fire by regiments until they should pass the continental troops, on whose right they were to form. His whole force amounted to eight hundred men.

Soon after this disposition was made, the British van appeared in sight. Their line of battle was instantly formed, and they rushed forward, shouting as they advanced.

After a well-directed fire, M'Dowell and Cunningham fell back on Pickens, who, after a short but warm conflict, retreated into the rear of the second line. The British pressed forward with great eagerness; and, though received by the continental troops with firmness, continued to advance. Tarlton ordered up his reserve. Perceiving that his enemy extended beyond him both on the right and left, and that his right flank especially was on the point of being turned, Howard ordered the company on his right to change its front, so as to face the British on that flank. This order being misunderstood, the company fell back; and the rest of the line, supposing a change of ground to have been directed, began to retire in perfect order. At this moment, General Morgan rode up, and directed the infantry to retreat over the summit of the hill and join the cavalry. This judicious but hazardous movement was made in good order, and extricated the flanks from immediate danger. Believing the fate of the day to be decided, the British pressed forward with increased ardor, and in some disorder; and when the Americans halted, were within thirty yards of them. The orders given by Howard to face the enemy were executed as soon as they were received; and the whole line poured in a fire as deadly as it was unexpected. Some confusion appearing in the ranks of the enemy, Howard seized the critical moment, and ordered a charge with the bayonet. These orders were instantly obeyed, and the British line was broken.

Mention the order of battle at the Cowpens, and the several movements which terminated in breaking the British line.

17

At the same moment, the corps of cavalry on the British right was routed by Washington. The militia of Pickens were closely pursued by the cavalry, who had passed the flank of the continental infantry, and were cutting down the scattered militia in its rear. Washington directed his dragoons to charge them with drawn swords. A sharp conflict ensued, but it was not of long duration. The British were driven from the ground with slaughter, and were closely pursued. Both Howard and Washington pressed their advantage until the artillery and great part of the infantry had surrendered.

In this engagement, upwards of one hundred British, including ten commissioned officers, were killed. Twenty-nine commissioned officers and five hundred privates were taken. Eight hundred muskets, with a number of baggage-wagons and dragoon horses, fell into the hands of the conquerors. The victory cost the Americans less than eighty men in killed and wounded.

Tarlton retreated to the head quarters of Lord Cornwallis, then about twenty-five miles distant, at Turkey creek, on the east side of Broad river. This camp was as near as the Cowpens to the ford at which Morgan was to cross the Catawba. Comprehending the full danger of being intercepted, he abandoned the baggage, left his wounded under the protection of a flag, detached the militia as an escort to his prisoners, and brought up the rear in person with his regulars. Passing Broad river in the evening, he hastened to the Catawba, which he passed at Sherwood's ford on the 23d, and encamped on its eastern bank.

Lord Cornwallis, having formed a junction with Leslie, reached Ramsay's mills on the 25th, where, to accelerate his future movements, he destroyed his baggage; and, after collecting a small supply of provisions, resumed his line of march. He reached Sherald's ford on the evening of the 29th; and, in the night, an immense flood of rain rendered the river impassable. While Morgan remained on the Catawba, General Greene arrived and took command of the detachment. He had left the other division to be commanded by General Huger.

In his camp on the Pedee, he had been joined by Lee's legion, which he detached the next day to join Marion for the purpose of attempting to carry a British fort at Georgetown. The fort was surprised, but the success was only partial.

Greene directed the Virginia militia under Stevens, whose terms of service were about to expire, to escort the prisoners taken at the Cowpens to Charlottesville in Virginia, while he directed his whole attention to the effecting of a junction with Huger.

Did Morgan find it necessary to retreat, after his victory at the Cowpens? What movements were made by Lord Cornwallis, with the view of intercepting the retiring Americans?

On the 1st of February, Lord Cornwallis forced a passage over the Catawba, at a ford which was defended by General Davidson, with three hundred North Carolina militia. Davidson was killed, and his troops dispersed. They were followed by Tarlton, who, hearing that the militia were assembling at a town about ten miles from the ford, hastened to the place of rendezvous, and, killing some, dispersed the residue.

Greene retreated along the Salisbury road, and, on the evening of the 3d, crossed the Yadkin at the trading ford. His rear which was impeded by the baggage of the whigs, was overtaken by the van of the British army about midnight, and a skirmish ensued in which some loss was sustained.

The boats being now collected on the northern side of the Yadkin, and the river unfordable, the pursuit was suspended; and General Greene continued his march to Guilford Court-house, where he joined General Huger on the 9th. The infantry of the American army, including six hundred militia, amounted to about two thousand effectives, and the cavalry to between two and three hundred.

Lord Cornwallis marched up the Yadkin, which he crossed on the morning of the 8th, and encamped the next day twenty-five miles above Greene, at Salem, with an army estimated at from twenty-five hundred to three thousand men, including three hundred cavalry. His object was to place himself between Greene and Virginia, so as to force that officer to a general action before he should be joined by the reinforcements preparing for him in that state.

Greene was indefatigable in his exertions to cross the Dan, without exposing himself to the hazard of a battle. To effect this object, his cavalry, with the flower of his infantry, amounting together to rather more than seven hundred men, were formed into a light corps for the purpose of impeding the advance of the enemy until the baggage, with the military stores, should be secured. Morgan being rendered incapable of duty by illness, the command of this corps was given to Colonel Otho H. Williams.

Lord Cornwallis had been informed that it would be impossible to obtain boats for the transportation of the American troops across the Dan before he could overtake them. He had, therefore, supposed that, by retaining his position above them, so as to prevent their gaining the shallow fords, he would secure his object. Dix's ferry, on the direct road, was equidistant from the two armies. Considerably below were two other ferries, Boyd's and Irwin's, contiguous to each other; and by taking the road leading to them, the distance between the two armies was so much ground gained. At the suggestion of Lieutenant-Colonel Carrington, quartermaster-general for the southern department, Greene resolved to direct his march to these lower ferries, and to dispatch a light party to Dix's, in order to bring the boats at that and the intermediate ferries down the river to meet him.

Feb. 10. The next morning both armies resumed their march. Williams took a road between them; and such were the boldness and activity of his corps, that Lord Cornwallis found it necessary to move with caution; yet he marched near thirty miles each day. On the third day he attempted to surprise the Americans, by detaching from his rear while his front moved slowly; but Lieutenant-Colonel Lee charged his advanced cavalry with such impetuosity as to cut a troop nearly to pieces. A captain and several privates were made prisoners. So rapid were the movements of both armies that, in the last twenty-four hours, the Americans marched forty miles; and the rear had scarcely touched the northern bank when the British van appeared on the opposite shore.

Having driven Greene out of North Carolina, Lord Cornwallis turned his attention to the re-establishment of regal authority in that state. At Hillsborough, then its capital, he erected the royal standard, and issued a proclamation inviting the inhabitants to repair to it, and to assist him in restoring the ancient government. It was understood that seven independent companies were formed in a single day.

Soon after entering Virginia, Greene was joined by six hundred militia drawn from the neighboring counties, who were commanded by General Stevens. Alarmed at the progress made by the British general in embodying those who were attached to the royal cause, he determined, on receiving this small reinforcement, to re-enter North Carolina, and, avoiding a general action, to discourage this spirit of disaffection by showing himself in the field. The legion of Lee had repassed the Dan on the 18th, the light infantry on the 21st, and they were followed by the residue of the army on the 23d.

A large body of royalists had begun to embody themselves on the branches of the Haw river; and Colonel Tarlton was detached from Hillsborough to conduct them to the British army. Greene ordered Lieutenant-Colonel Lee, with his legion cavalry, and General Pickens, with between three and four hundred militia, to move against both parties.

Lee, whose cavalry was in front, came up with the loyalists in

Did the Americans succeed in crossing the river Dan with safety? After thus leaving North Carolina, what considerations urged General Greene to a speedy return? Upon what service did he send Lee and Pickens?

a long lane, and was supposed to be a British officer. Perceiving their mistake, he purposed to avail himself of it by making propositions to their colonel which might enable him to proceed in his design of surprising Tarlton. As he was about to make his communications, some of the militia who followed close in his rear were recognised by some of the insurgents, and a firing began. The alarm being thus given, Lee changed his plan, and turning on the loyalists, cut them to pieces while they were making protestations of loyalty. More than one hundred, among whom was Colonel Pyle, their leader, fell under the swords of his cavalry. This terrible but unavoidable carnage broke the spirits of the tories in that quarter of the country.

The hope of surprising Tarlton being thus disappointed, the attack on him was postponed, and Pickens and Lee took a position between him and a body of militia which was advancing under Colonel Preston from the western parts of Virginia. Tarlton had meditated an attempt on this corps; but at midnight, when his troops were paraded for the purpose, he received an express, directing his immediate return to the army.

On the 27th, Lord Cornwallis, to approach more nearly the great body of the loyalists, crossed the Haw and encamped on Allimance-creek. As the British army retired, General Greene advanced, still carefully avoiding a general action; but, by the activity of his light troops, intimidating the disaffected.

On the 6th of March, Lord Cornwallis moved out in full force in the hope of surprising the light infantry under cover of a thick fog. A sharp skirmish ensued, but the advance of the British army obliged Williams to retire. The further designs of his lordship were disappointed by the junction of General Greene with his light infantry on the north-eastern bank of the Haw.

At length his reinforcements were received, and Greene, in his turn, sought a battle. He dissolved the corps of light infantry, and encamped within eight miles of his enemy, March 14. at Guilford Court-house. His army, including officers, amounted to four thousand five hundred men, of whom not quite two thousand were continental troops. Of the four regiments composing the continental infantry, only one, the first Maryland, was veteran. The other three consisted of new levies, among whom a few old continental soldiers were interspersed. The officers were veteran.

Early in the morning of the 15th, the fire of his reconnoitring parties announced the approach of the enemy on the great Salisbury-road, and his army was immediately arranged in order of battle. It was drawn up in three lines on a large hill, chiefly covered with trees and underwood.

The first line was composed of the North Carolina militia, who were posted on the edge of the wood, behind a strong rail fence, with an open field in front.

The Virginia militia formed the second line. They were drawn up in the wood, on either side of the great road, about three hundred yards in rear of the first.

The third line was placed about three hundred yards in rear of the second, and was composed of continental troops.

Washington's dragoons, Kirkwood's company of light infantry, and Lynch's militia riflemen, formed a corps of observation for the security of the right flank, which was commanded by Lieutenant-Colonel Washington. The legion, and a body of militia riflemen, commanded by Colonels Campbell and Preston, formed a corps of observation for the security of the left flank, which was placed under Lieutenant-Colonel Lee. The artillery was in the front line, in the great road leading through the centre.

Lord Cornwallis, though sensible that the numbers of his adversary were augmented by troops who could not be kept long in the field, deemed it so important to maintain the appearance of superiority, that he resolved to hazard a general engagement. Early on the morning of the 15th, he moved from his ground, determined to attack the adverse army wherever it should be found. About four miles from Guilford Court-house, his advance, under Tarlton, fell in with Lee, and a sharp skirmish ensued, which terminated on his appearance in force. On coming within view of the American army, his disposition for the attack was made, and the British troops advanced to the charge with the cool intrepidity which discipline inspires.

The North Carolina militia broke instantly; and, throwing away their arms, fled through the woods, seeking their respective homes.

The second line received the charge with more firmness; and maintained their ground for some time. Lord Cornwallis, observing the corps on his flanks, brought up the whole of his reserved infantry into the line.

The British continuing to advance, and it being well understood that the militia could not stand the bayonet, the brigade of Stevens, who had maintained their ground, were ordered to retreat, and the enemy advanced boldly on the third line.

The several divisions of the British army had been separated from each other by extending themselves in order to engage the

State the dispositions on each side for the battle at Guilford Court-house. What part of the American force immediately fled? What then took place, as respects the second line?

distinct corps which threatened their flanks; and by advancing in regiments at different times, as the different parts of the second line had given way. The thickness of the wood increased the difficulty of restoring order. They pressed forward with great eagerness, but with considerable irregularity.

Greene entertained the most sanguine hopes of victory. His continental troops were fresh, in perfect order, and about to engage an enemy broken into distinct parts. This fair prospect was blasted by the misconduct of a single corps. The second regiment of Maryland was posted at some distance from the first, its left forming almost a right angle with the line, so as to present a front to any corps which might attack on that flank. The second battalion of guards, following close on the brigade of Stevens, rushed on the second regiment of Maryland which broke in the utmost confusion. By pursuing them the guards were thrown into the rear of the first regiment of Maryland, then engaged with Webster, but concealed from their view by the unevenness of the ground, and by a skirt of wood.

About this time Webster had retired across a ravine into an adjoining wood. This critical respite enabled the corps that had been engaged with him to face the guards, who were called off from the pursuit of the second Maryland regiment, and brought against them by Lieutenant-Colonel Stuart. A very animated fire took place, during which the Americans gained ground.

In this critical moment, Lieutenant-Colonel Washington made a furious charge on the guards and broke their ranks. Almost at the same instant, the infantry rushed upon them with the bayonet, and following the horse through them were masters of the whole battalion. After passing through the guards, Howard, who then commanded the regiment, Colonel Gunby having been separated from it by his horse being killed under him and by the rapidity of its advance, perceived several British columns with some pieces of artillery. Believing his regiment to be the sole infantry remaining in the field, he retreated in good order, bringing off some prisoners, and was followed by the cavalry.

Greene observing the flight of the second Maryland regiment, and being unwilling to risk his remaining three regiments, only one of which could be relied on, had ordered Colonel Greene of Virginia to take a position in the rear, for the purpose of covering the retreat of the two regiments which still remained in the field. About the time that Howard withdrew from the action, the remaining Virginia regiment commanded by Colonel Hawes, and Kirkwood's company, were also ordered to retire. The retreat was con-

Did Greene, at this juncture, hope to gain the battle? Relate the misconduct of two Maryland regiments, and the incidents of the contest on the right and centre of the Americans.

ducted in good order, and General Greene brought up the rear in person.

Though the action was over on the right and centre, Campbell's riflemen still continued it on the extreme left.

After the first battalion of guards and the regiment of Bose had routed Lawson's brigade, they were attacked by Campbell's riflemen and the legion infantry, and the action was maintained with great obstinacy until the battle was decided on the right. Lieutenant-Colonel Tarlton was ordered to charge the Americans, and they retired from the field.

Two regiments of infantry and a corps of cavalry pursued the right and centre of the Americans for a short distance, but were ordered to return. Lord Cornwallis found himself too much weakened in the action to hazard its renewal, or to continue the pursuit. General Greene halted about three miles from the field of battle for the purpose of collecting stragglers, and then retired twelve miles to the iron works on Troublesome creek.

The loss of the continental troops in killed, wounded, and missing, was fourteen officers, and three hundred and twelve non-commissioned officers and privates. Major Anderson of Maryland was killed; and General Huger was wounded. The loss of the militia was stated at four Captains and seventeen privates killed. One Brigadier-General, one Major, three Captains, eight subalterns, and sixty privates, were wounded. Official accounts state the loss of the British army at five hundred and thirty-two men, among whom were several officers of distinguished merit. Lieutenant-Colonel Stuart was killed; and Lieutenant-Colonel Webster mortally wounded. The loss, compared with the numbers brought into the field, was very considerable. Lord Cornwallis stated his rank and file at fourteen hundred and forty-five.

No battle in the course of the war reflects more honor on the courage of the British troops than that of Guilford. On no other occasion have they fought with such inferiority of numbers or disadvantage of ground. General Greene's army, estimating his first line at nothing, consisted of three thousand two hundred men, posted on ground chosen by himself; and his disposition was skilfully made.

The American General prepared for another engagement, but Lord Cornwallis found it necessary to retreat to a place of greater security, where provisions might be obtained.

When the expedition into North Carolina was meditated, Major Craig took possession of Wilmington on Cape Fear river, Lord

What was the termination of the engagement, and why did Cornwallis hesitate to renew the fight or engage in pursuit? What was the respective loss? Whither did each army now retire?

Cornwallis now looked to a communication with this post, for aids which had become indispensable to his farther operations. On the 18th of March, he broke up his encampment and proceeded by slow and easy march, to Wilmington, where he arrived on the 7th of April.

General Greene resolved to follow him, but was so delayed by the necessity of waiting for a supply of ammunition, and by the difficulty of subsisting his troops, that he did not reach Ramsay's mills till the 28th of March.

At this place he gave over the pursuit; and formed the bold and happy resolution to carry the war into South Carolina.

This unexpected movement gave a new aspect to affairs, and produced some irresolution in the British General respecting his future operations. He finally determined to advance into Virginia.

CHAPTER XXI.

Virginia invaded by Arnold.—He destroys the stores at Westham and at Richmond.—Retires to Portsmouth.—Mutiny of the Pennsylvania line.—Sir H. Clinton attempts to negotiate with the mutineers.—They compromise with the Government.—Mutiny in the Jersey line.—Mission of Colonel Laurens to France.—Congress recommends a system of revenue.—Reform in the Executive departments.—Confederation adopted.—Military transactions.—Lafayette detached to Virginia.—Cornwallis arrives.—Presses Lafayette.—Expedition to Charlottesville, to Point of Fork.—Lafayette forms a junction with Wayne.—Cornwallis retires to the lower country.—General Washington's letters intercepted.—Action near Jamestown.

THE evacuation of Portsmouth by Leslie afforded Virginia but a short interval of repose. On the 30th of December 1780, a fleet of transports, having on board between one and two thousand men, commanded by General Arnold, anchored in Hampton roads, and proceeded next day up James' river, under convoy of two small ships of war. On the 4th of January, they landed at Westover, about twenty-five miles from Richmond, the metropolis of the state, and Arnold commenced his march the next day for that place at the head of about nine hundred men.

A few continental troops who were at Petersburg, were ordered to the capital; and between one and two hundred militia, collected from the town and its immediate vicinity, were directed to harass the advancing enemy. This party being too feeble for its object, Arnold entered Richmond on the 5th, where he halted with about five hundred men. The residue proceeded under Lieutenant-Colonel Simcoe to Westham, where they burnt several public buildings with military stores to a considerable amount, and many valuable

---

What resolution was formed by General Greene, and whither did Cornwallis determine to proceed? Relate the particulars of an inroad into Virginia, by a British force commanded by the traitor Arnold?

papers which had been carried thither as to a place of safety. This service being effected, Simcoe rejoined Arnold at Richmond; where the public stores, and a large quantity of rum and salt belonging to private individuals, were destroyed.

The army returned to Westover on the 7th, and re-embarking on the 10th, proceeded down the river. It was followed by the Baron Steuben with a few new levies and militia. Near Hood's, Colonel Clarke drew a party of them into an ambuscade, and gave them one fire with some effect, but, on its being partially returned, the Americans fled in the utmost confusion.

Arnold reached Portsmouth on the 20th, where he manifested an intention to establish a permanent post.

The loss of the British in this expedition was stated in the New York Gazette at seven killed, including one subaltern; and twenty-three wounded, among whom was one captain. This small loss was sustained almost entirely in the ambuscade near Hood's.

In the North, the year commenced with an event which, for a time, threatened the American cause with total ruin.

The accumulated sufferings and privations of the army constitute a large and interesting part of the history of that war which gave independence to the United States. In addition to these, the Pennsylvania line complained of grievances almost peculiar to itself.

When Congress directed enlistments to be made for three years or during the war, the recruiting officers of Pennsylvania, in some instances, instead of engaging their men definitively for the one period or the other, engaged them generally for three years or the war. This ambiguity produced its natural effect. The soldier claimed his discharge at the expiration of three years, and the officer insisted on retaining him during the war.

The discontents, which had been long fomenting, broke out on the 1st of January in an open and almost universal revolt of the line. On a signal given, the non-commissioned officers and privates paraded under arms, avowing their determination to march to the seat of government and obtain redress, or serve no longer. In attempting to suppress the mutiny, six or seven mutineers were wounded on the one side; and, on the other, Captain Billings was killed, and several other officers were dangerously wounded. The authority of General Wayne availed nothing; and the whole line, consisting of thirteen hundred men, marched under the command of their serjeants, with six field-pieces, towards Princeton.

The next day they were followed by General Wayne, accompanied by Colonels Butler and Stewart; and overtaken near Mid-

What was the loss of the enemy, in this predatory expedition? Mention the cause which produced so much dissatisfaction in the American army, and at length ended in the revolt of the Pennsylvania line.

diebrook. A sergeant was deputed from each regiment, on a written invitation from Wayne, with whom a conference was held; and, on the succeeding day, the soldiers proceeded to Princeton. At that place the propositions of the general and field-officers were communicated to them, and referred to a committee of sergeants, who stated their claims. But these could not be acceded to.

A committee of Congress, united with the Governor and some members of the Executive Council of Pennsylvania, proceeded to Princeton for the purpose of endeavoring to accommodate this dangerous commotion.

At his head quarters at New Windsor, on the North river, General Washington received intelligence of this alarming mutiny. Accustomed as he had been to contemplate hazardous and difficult situations, it was not easy, under existing circumstances, to resolve instantly on the course it was most prudent to pursue. His first impression—to repair to the camp of the mutineers—soon gave place to opinions which were formed on more mature reflection; and he thought it advisable to leave the negotiation with the civil power, and to prepare for those measures which ought to be adopted in the event of its failure. After sounding the disposition of the troops on the North river, and finding them to be favorable, a detachment of eleven hundred men was ordered to be in readiness to move at a moment's warning. The militia of New Jersey were assembled under General Dickenson, and measures were taken to call out those of New York.

To avail himself of an event so auspicious to the royal cause, Sir Henry Clinton despatched three emissaries with tempting offers to the revolters, and instructions to invite them, while the negotiation was depending, to take a position behind the South river, where they could be covered by detachments from New York. Meanwhile, he kept his eye on West Point.

His emissaries were seized, and their proposals communicated to General Wayne, but they were not surrendered; nor could the revolters be induced to cross the Delaware, or to march from Princeton. Their former officers, except those already mentioned, were not permitted to enter their camp; and Generals St. Clair and Lafayette, and Lieutenant-Colonel Laurens, were ordered to leave Princeton.

Such was the state of things when the committee of Congress, and President Read, with a part of his executive council, arrived in the neighborhood of the revolters. The former having delegated their power to the latter, a conference was held with the serjeants, after which proposals were made and distributed among the troops for consideration. The government offered—

What committee proceeded to confer with the mutineers? Mention the arrangements of Washington to quell them. Were the emissaries from Sir Henry Clinton listened to with favor?

MARSHALL'S

1st. To discharge all those who had enlisted indefinitely for three years, or during the war, the fact to be examined into by three commissioners to be appointed by the executive; and to be ascertained, when the original enlistment could not be produced, by the oath of the soldier.

2d. To give immediate certificates for the depreciation on their pay, and to settle the arrearages as soon as circumstances would admit.

3d. To furnish them immediately with certain specified articles of clothing.

On receiving these propositions, the troops agreed to march to Trenton, where they were accepted, with the addition that three commissioners, to be deputed by the line, should be added to the board authorized to determine on the claims of soldiers to a discharge. The British emissaries were then surrendered, and were executed as spies.

While the investigation was depending, the serjeants retained their command. Under this irksome state of things, the business was pressed with so much precipitation, that almost the whole of the artillery, and of the five first regiments of infantry, were discharged on the oaths of the soldiers, before the enlistments could be brought from their huts. When they were produced, it was found that not many of those whose claims remained to be examined were entitled to a discharge; and that, of those actually dismissed, the greater number had been enlisted for the war. The discharges given, however, were not cancelled, and the few who were to remain in service received furloughs for forty days.

Thus ended a mutiny, of which a voluntary performance of much less than was extorted, would have prevented.

The dangerous policy of yielding even to the just demands of soldiers with arms in their hands, was soon illustrated. On the night of the 20th, a part of the Jersey brigade, which had been stationed at Pompton, many of whom were also foreigners, rose in arms; and, making the same claims which had been yielded to the Pennsylvanians, marched to Chatham, where a part of the same brigade was cantoned, in the hope of exciting them also to join in the revolt.

General Washington, who had been extremely chagrined at the issue of the revolt in the Pennsylvania line, ordered a detachment of the eastern troops, who were natives, to march against the mutineers, and to bring them to unconditional submission. General Howe, who commanded, was ordered to make no terms with them while in a state of resistance; and, as soon as they should sur-

What terms were at last made with the revolters? Mention the fraud practised by many of them. What second mutiny followed this evil example? What was Washington's determination?

render, to seize a few of the most active and execute them on the spot. These orders were obeyed, and the Jersey mutineers returned to their duty. This mutiny was crushed too suddenly to allow time for the operation of the measures taken by Sir Henry Clinton to avail himself of it.

The vigorous measures taken in this instance, were happily followed by such attention on the part of the states to their respective quotas, as, in some measure, to check the progress of discontent.

Although the resources of the government were inadequate to its exigencies, the discontents of the people were daily multiplied by the contributions which they were required to make, and by the irritating manner in which those contributions were drawn from them. Every article for public use was obtained by impressment, and the taxes were either unpaid, or collected by coercive means. Strong remonstrances were made against this system; and the dissatisfaction which pervaded the mass of the community was scarcely less dangerous than that which had been manifested by the army.

To relieve the United States from their complicated embarrassments, a foreign loan seemed an expedient of indispensable necessity; and from France they hoped to obtain it. Congress selected Lieutenant-Colonel Laurens for this interesting service, and instructed him also to urge the advantage of maintaining a naval superiority in the American seas. Before his departure, he received from General Washington, in the form of a letter, the result of his reflections on the existing state of things.

With much reason the commander-in-chief urged on the cabinet of Versailles the vital policy of affording powerful aids to the United States through the next campaign. Deep was the gloom with which their political horizon was overcast. The British, in possession of South Carolina and Georgia, had overrun great part of North Carolina also; and a second detachment from New York was making a deep impression on Virginia.

The restoration of credit was indispensable to their affairs, and the establishment of a revenue, subject to the exclusive control of the continental government, was connected inseparably with the restoration of credit. The efforts therefore to negotiate a foreign loan were accompanied by resolutions recommending to the several states to vest a power in Congress to levy for the use of the United States, a duty of five *per centum ad valorem* on all goods imported into any of them; and also on all prizes condemned in the courts of admiralty. This plan, though unequal to the public exigencies, was never adopted.

How was the Jersey mutiny suppressed? Upon what mission was Laurens sent? In addition to these efforts to procure a foreign loan, what measures were adopted by Congress?

18

About the same time a reform was introduced into the administration, the necessity of which had been long perceived. All the great executive duties had been devolved either on committees of Congress, or on boards consisting of several members. This unwieldy and expensive system had maintained itself against all the efforts of reason and utility. But the scantiness of the public means at length prevailed over prejudice, and the several committees and boards yielded to a secretary for foreign affairs, a superintendant of finance, a secretary of war, and a secretary of marine. But so miserably defective was the organization of Congress, that the year was far advanced before this measure could be carried into complete execution.

About this time the articles of confederation were ratified. Much difficulty had been encountered in obtaining the adoption of this instrument. At length, in February 1781, to the great joy of America, this interesting compact was rendered complete. Like many other human institutions, it was productive, neither in war nor in peace, of all the benefits which its sanguine advocates had anticipated.

Such was the defensive strength of the positions taken by the adverse armies on the Hudson, that no decisive blow could be given by either. The anxious attentions of General Washington, therefore, were directed to the South. One of those incidents which fortune occasionally produces, presented an opportunity which he deemed capable of being improved to the destruction of the British army in Virginia.

Late in January, a part of the British fleet sustained so much damage by a storm, as to destroy for a time the superiority which Arbuthnot had uniformly pursued. To turn this temporary advantage to account, Monsieur Destouches detached a ship of the line with two frigates to the Chesapeake; a force which the delegation of Virginia had assured him was sufficient for the object.

Confident that the critical moment must be seized, and that the co-operation of a land and naval force was indispensable to success, General Washington had ordered a detachment of twelve hundred men under the command of the Marquis de Lafayette, to the head of the Chesapeake, there to embark for that part of Virginia which was to become the theatre of action, under convoy of a French frigate for which he applied to the Admiral. He immediately communicated this measure to the Count de Rochambeau and to Monsieur Destouches, with his conviction that no serious advantage could be expected from a few ships unaided by land

What change was made in the administration of American affairs? When were the articles of confederation ratified? What reason prevented active measures in the north? What naval operations took place in the Chesapeake?

troops. He recommended that the whole fleet, with a detachment of one thousand men, should be employed on the expedition.

His representations did not prevail. Monsieur de Tilley had sailed for the Chesapeake with a sixty-four gun ship and two frigates; and, as some of the British ships had been repaired, the Admiral did not think it prudent to put to sea with the residue of his fleet.

As had been foreseen by General Washington, De Tilley found Arnold in a situation not to be assailed with any prospect of success, and returned to Newport.

After the return of De Tilley, the French General and Admiral proposed in a letter to General Washington, to make a second expedition to the Chesapeake with the whole fleet, and with eleven hundred men. He hastened to Newport; and on the 6th of March met the Count de Rochambeau on board the Admiral, and it was determined that the armament should put to sea as soon as possible. The fleet did not sail till the evening of the 8th.

Two days after Destouches had sailed, he was followed by Arbuthnot, who overtook him off the capes of Virginia. A partial engagement ensued which continued about an hour, when the fleets were separated. The French Admiral called a council of war in which it was declared unadvisable to renew the action, and he returned to Newport.

Late in March, General Philips arrived in Virginia with two thousand men, and took command of the British forces in that state. After completing the fortifications at Portsmouth, he commenced offensive operations. Two thousand five hundred men spread themselves over the lower end of that narrow neck of land which is made by York and James' river, and after destroying some public property in the neck, and the vessels in the rivers, re-embarked and proceeded to City Point, where they landed in the afternoon of the 24th of April. The next day they marched against Petersburg, where immense quantities of tobacco, and some other stores, were deposited.

The Baron Steuben was not in a condition to check their progress. The levies of Virginia had marched to the aid of General Greene; and the whole number of militia in the field did not much exceed two-thousand men. One thousand of them were placed a mile below the town, for the purpose of skirmishing with the advancing enemy. They were employed two or three hours in driving this party over the Appamattox; on passing which the bridge was taken up, and farther pursuit became impracticable. The Baron retreated towards Richmond, and Philips took posses-

Mention the ineffectual movements of the French naval force. When did a British force invade Virginia? What town was taken by the enemy, and what mischief done?

sion of Petersburg, where he destroyed a considerable quantity of tobacco and all the vessels lying in the river.

Arnold was then detached to Warwick against a small naval force which had been collected between that place and Richmond, for the purpose of co-operating with the French fleet; and Philips took the road by Chesterfield Court-house, the place of rendezvous for the new levies of Virginia, in order to destroy the barracks and public stores. Each party having effected its object, they re-united on the 30th, and marched to Manchester on the southern bank of James' river, opposite to Richmond, where the warehouses were set on fire and all the tobacco destroyed.

On the preceding evening, the Marquis de Lafayette, who had made a forced march from Baltimore, arrived in Richmond, and saved that place, in which a great proportion of the military stores of the state were then collected. His detachment was joined by about two thousand militia and sixty dragoons.

General Philips retired to Bermuda Hundred, where his troops re-embarked and fell down the river to Hog island. At this place he received a letter from Lord Cornwallis, directing him to take his station at Petersburg.

General Lafayette, on being informed that Lord Cornwallis was marching northward, and that General Philips had landed at Brandon on the south side of James' river, was persuaded that a junction of the two armies was intended, and hastened to take possession of Petersburg. Being anticipated in this design by the British General, he recrossed James' river, and used his utmost exertions to remove the military stores from Richmond.

Lord Cornwallis, after effecting a junction with Arnold, who had succeeded by the death of Philips to the command of the British forces in Virginia, determined on a vigorous plan of offensive operations. He crossed James' river at Westover, where he was joined by a reinforcement from New York, and attempted, by turning the left flank of the Marquis, to get into his rear.

Lafayette was not in a condition to risk an engagement. His objects were to save the public stores, and to effect a junction with the Pennsylvania line, which was marching southward under the command of General Wayne.

The fine horses found in the stables of private gentlemen enabled the British General to mount so many infantry, as to move large detachments with unusual rapidity. He was so confident of overtaking and destroying his enemy as to say exultingly, " the boy cannot escape me." His hopes, however, were disappointed, and, after marching some distance up the northern side of North-

---

What further destruction was effected by the British? Who approached them from the north? What induced Lafayette to avoid a battle? Was he pursued, and did he escape?

anna, he relinquished the pursuit, and turned his attention to other objects.

Military stores had been collected, among other places, at the Point of Fork, the confluence of the Rivanna and Fluvanna, the two branches of James' river, which were protected by between five and six hundred new levies, and a few militia, commanded by the Baron Steuben. Colonel Simcoe was detached against this post at the head of five hundred men; and Tarlton, with about two hundred and fifty cavalry and mounted infantry, was ordered against Charlottesville, where the General Assembly was in session. Notice of his approach was given by a private gentleman, Mr. Jouiette, on a fleet horse, and nearly all the members of the legislature escaped, and re-assembled at Staunton. Tarlton, after destroying the stores, proceeded down the river to the Point of Fork.

The Baron Steuben, hearing of the expedition to Charlottesville, had employed himself in removing the military stores from the Point of Fork to the south side of the Fluvanna. On the approach of Tarlton and Simcoe, he withdrew precipitately in the night, and the stores which had not been removed, were destroyed by a few men who crossed the Rivanna in canoes.

To secure his junction with Wayne, Lafayette had crossed the Rapidan. The movements of the two armies had placed Lord Cornwallis between him and a large quantity of military stores, which had been transported up the river from Richmond, and deposited at Albemarle old court-house. To this place, Lord Cornwallis directed his march.

The Marquis, after effecting a junction with the Pennsylvania line, amounting to eight hundred men, advanced with celerity towards the British army, and encamped within a few miles of it. While upwards of a day's march from its point of destination, Lord Cornwallis encamped at Elk Island, and advanced his light parties to a position commanding the road by which it was supposed the Americans must pass. Lafayette, however, in the night, discovered a nearer road, which had been long disused; and next morning, the British general had the mortification to perceive that the American army had crossed the Rivanna, and taken a strong position behind Mechunk creek, which commanded the route leading to Albemarle old court-house. At this place, a considerable reinforcement of mountain militia was received.

Lord Cornwallis, desirous of transferring the war to the lower country, retired first to Richmond, and afterwards to Williamsburg.

Whither, and for what purpose, were the British officers Simcoe and Tarlton sent? To what extent was each successful? Mention the several movements of Cornwallis and Lafayette.

The Marquis followed, with cautious circumspection. On the 18th of June, he was reinforced by four or five hundred new levies, under the Baron Steuben, which augmented his army to four thousand men, of whom two thousand were regulars.

As the British army retreated, Lafayette pressed its rear with light parties. Colonel Simcoe, who covered the retreat, was overtaken by Colonel Butler, about six miles from Williamsburg, and a sharp action ensued. The approach of large reinforcements to the British, compelled the Americans to retire.

Although, from various causes, Lord Cornwallis had encountered less resistance in his bold and rapid march through Virginia than was to be expected, no disposition was manifested to join the royal standard, or to withdraw from the contest. The Marquis complained "of much slowness and much carelessness in the country; but the dispositions of the people," he said, "were good, and they required only to be awakened." This, he thought, would be best effected by the presence of General Washington. But Washington deemed it of more importance to remain on the Hudson, for the purpose of digesting and conducting a grand plan of combined operations then meditated against New York.

An express, carrying letters communicating to Congress the result of his consultations, on this subject, with the commanders of the land and naval forces of France, was intercepted in Jersey. The disclosure made by these letters alarmed Sir Henry Clinton for New York, and determined him to require the return of part of the troops in Virginia. Supposing himself too weak, after complying with this requisition, to remain in Williamsburg, Lord Cornwallis took the resolution of retiring to Portsmouth.

He marched from Williamsburg on the 4th of July, and a part of his troops crossed over into the island of Jamestown on the same evening. The two succeeding days were employed in passing over the baggage. Lafayette pushed his best troops within nine miles of the British camp, with the intention of attacking their rear, when the main body should have passed into Jamestown.

Suspecting his design, Lord Cornwallis encamped the greater part of his army compactly on the main, and displayed a few troops on the island, so as in appearance to magnify their numbers. Believing that the greater part of the British had passed over in the night, Lafayette detached some riflemen to harass their outposts, while he advanced on their rear with his continental troops.

The piquets were forced by the riflemen, without much resistance; but an advanced post, which covered the camp from the

---

What were the dispositions of the people in Virginia? Mention the project of Washington against New York, and its consequences as to the British army in the south. Where did Cornwallis now repair?

view of the Americans, was perseveringly maintained, though three of the officers commanding it were successively picked off by the riflemen. Lafayette, who arrived a little before sunset, suspecting that this post covered more than a rear-guard, determined to reconnoitre the camp. From a tongue of land, stretching into the river, he perceived that the enemy was in much greater force than had been supposed, and hastened to call off his men.

He found Wayne closely engaged. In the attempt to seize a piece of artillery, purposely exposed, that officer discovered the whole British army moving out against him, in order of battle. To retreat was impossible; and Wayne, with his detachment, not exceeding eight hundred men, made a gallant charge on the whole line of the enemy. A warm action ensued, which was kept up till the arrival of Lafayette, who ordered Wayne to retreat, and form in a line with the light infantry, which was drawn up half a mile in his rear. The whole party then saved itself behind a morass.

Lord Cornwallis, suspecting an ambuscade, would allow no pursuit; and in the night crossed over into the island, whence he proceeded to Portsmouth.

In this action, the Americans lost one hundred and eighteen men, among whom were ten officers. The British loss was less considerable.

The campaign in Virginia enhanced the military reputation of Lafayette, and raised him in the general esteem. That with a decided inferiority of effective force, and especially of cavalry, he had been able to keep the field in an open country, and to preserve a considerable proportion of his military stores, as well as his army, was believed to furnish unequivocal evidence of his prudence and vigor.

CHAPTER XXII.

State of affairs in the beginning of 1781.—Measures of Mr. Morris.—Designs of General Washington against New York.—Rochambeau marches to the North River.—Intelligence from the Count de Grasse. — Plan of operations against Lord Cornwallis. — Naval engagement. — The combined armies march for the Chesapeake. — Yorktown invested.—Surrender of Lord Cornwallis.

THE total incompetency of the political system which had been adopted by the United States, to their own preservation, became every day more apparent. Each state seemed 1781.

By what means did Lord Cornwallis draw into action a part of Lafayette's force? Mention the prudent conduct of the latter commander, in retrieving the error; and state the estimation in which he was held.

fearful of doing too much, and of taking upon itself a larger portion of the common burden than was borne by its neighbor.

The requisitions of Congress for men were made too late, and were never completely executed by the states. The regular force drawn, from Pennsylvania to Georgia inclusive, at no time, during this active and interesting campaign, amounted to three thousand effective men. That drawn from New Hampshire to New Jersey inclusive, exhibited, in the month of May, a total of not quite seven thousand, of whom rather more than four thousand might be relied on for action.

The prospects for the campaign were rendered still more unpromising by the failure of supplies. The requisitions made on the states had been neglected to such a degree, as to excite fears that the soldiers must be disbanded from the want of food.

The Quartermaster Department was destitute of funds, and unable to transport provisions or other stores from place to place, but by means of impressment, supported by a military force. This measure had been repeated, especially in New York, until it excited so much irritation, that the commander-in-chief was seriously apprehensive of resistance to his authority.

While in this state of deplorable imbecility, intelligence from every quarter announced increasing dangers.

Information was received, that an expedition was preparing in Canada against Fort Pitt; and it was understood that many, in the country threatened with invasion, were ready to join the British standard. The Indians, too, had entered into formidable combinations, endangering the western frontier in its whole extent.

A correspondence of a criminal nature was discovered between some persons in Albany and in Canada. A letter intercepted by Generals Schuyler and Clinton, stated the disaffection of particular settlements, the provision made in them for an invading army, and their readiness to join it.

This intelligence derived increased interest from the ambiguous conduct of that country which now constitutes Vermont. Early in the war, its inhabitants had declared themselves independent, and had exercised the powers of self-government. The state of New York, however, still continued to assert her claim of sovereignty, and the controversy had become so violent as to justify the most serious apprehensions. The declaration was openly made that, if not admitted into the Union as an independent state, they held themselves at liberty to make a separate peace; and some negotiations for carrying this threat into execution, had been commenced.

Mention the difficulty of procuring men and supplies, under the confederation which bound together the American states. Point out the danger which threatened the west, the treasonable correspondence in the north, and the difficulty in Vermont.

Early in May, the Count de Barras, who had been appointed to the command of the French fleet on the American coast, arrived in Boston, and brought the long-expected information respecting the naval armament designed to act in the American seas. Twenty ships of the line, to be commanded by the Count de Grasse, were destined for the West Indies, twelve of which were to proceed to the continent of America in the month of July.

An interview between General Washington and the Count de Rochambeau immediately took place, in which it was determined to unite the troops of France to those of America on the Hudson, and to proceed against New York.

Though the prospect now opening roused the northern states from that apathy into which they appeared to be sinking, yet, in the month of June when the army took the field at Peekskill, its effective numbers did not exceed five thousand men.

To supply even this army with provisions required greater exertions than had been made. The hope of terminating the war produced these exertions. The legislatures of the New England states took up the subject in earnest, and passed resolutions for raising the necessary supplies. But, till these resolutions could be executed, the embarrassments of the army continued; and there was reason to apprehend, either that the great objects of the campaign must be relinquished for want of provisions, or that coercion must still be used.

New England not furnishing flour, this important article was to be drawn from New York, New Jersey, and Pennsylvania. The two first states were much exhausted; and the application to Pennsylvania did not promise to be very successful. Respecting this article, therefore, serious fears existed.

These were removed by the activity and exertions of an individual. The management of the finances had been committed to Mr. Robert Morris. This gentleman united considerable political talents to a degree of mercantile enterprise, information, and credit, seldom equalled in any country. He had accepted this arduous appointment on the condition of being allowed time to make his arrangements. But the critical state of public affairs furnished irresistible motives for changing his original determination, and entering immediately on the duties of his office. The occasion required that he should bring his private credit in aid of the public resources, and pledge himself extensively, for articles of absolute necessity which could not be otherwise obtained. Condemning the system of violence and of legal fraud which had been too long practised, he sought the gradual restoration of confidence by a

What information was now received respecting aid from France? Mention the chief difficulty in the way of conjoint operations, and the name of the individual who now undertook to manage the American finances.

punctual and faithful compliance with his engagements. It is in no inconsiderable degree to be attributed to him, that the very active and decisive operations of the campaign were not impeded, perhaps defeated, by a failure of the means for transporting military stores, and feeding the army.

On determining to assume the duties of his office, Mr. Morris laid before Congress the plan of a national bank, whose notes were to be receivable from the respective states as specie. Congress passed an ordinance for the incorporation of this valuable institution.

Important as was this measure to future military operations, a contract with the state of Pennsylvania was of still more immediate utility.

After furnishing flour to relieve the wants of the moment on his private credit, Mr. Morris proposed to assume a compliance with all the specific requisitions made on Pennsylvania, and to rely for reimbursement on the tax imposed by law, to be collected under his authority. This proposition being accepted, supplies which the government was unable to furnish, were raised by an individual.

The American army was joined by the Count de Rochambeau at Dobbs' ferry, on the 6th of July ; and the utmost exertions were made for the grand enterprise against New York. But the execution of this plan depended so much on events, that the attention of General Washington was also directed to other objects.

Early in August, letters from the Marquis de Lafayette announced that a large portion of the troops in Virginia were embarked, and that their destination was believed to be New York. This intelligence induced him to think seriously of southern operations. To conceal from Sir Henry Clinton this eventual change of plan, his arrangements were made secretly, and the preparations for acting against New York were continued. A reinforcement from Europe of near three thousand men had induced Sir Henry Clinton to countermand the orders he had given to Lord Cornwallis to detach a part of the army in Virginia to his aid ; and also to direct that nobleman to take a strong position on the Chesapeake, from which he might he enabled to execute the designs meditated against the states lying on that bay, so soon as the storm which threatened for the moment should blow over. In a few days after the arrival of this reinforcement, the Count de Barras gave the interesting information that De Grasse was to have sailed for the Chesapeake on the 3d of August, with from twenty-five to twenty-nine ships of the line, having on board three thousand two hundred soldiers ; and that he had made engagements to return to the West Indies by the middle of October.

What judicious and efficient steps were taken by Mr. Morris? Did Washington resolve on southern operations ? What news came from France ?

This intelligence decided General Washington in favor of operations to the South; and Lafayette was directed to make such a disposition of his army as should prevent Lord Cornwallis from saving himself by a sudden march to Charleston.

The Count de Grasse arrived in the Chesapeake late in August, with twenty-eight ships of the line and several frigates. At Cape Henry, he found an officer despatched to meet him with the information that Lord Cornwallis was fortifying Yorktown and Gloster Point; and that the Marquis had taken a position on James' river.

In consequence of this information, detachments from the fleet, which lay at anchor within the capes, blocked up the mouth of York river, and conveyed the land forces brought from the West Indies under the Marquis de St. Simon, up the James' to join Lafayette, who, on receiving this reinforcement, took post at Williamsburg. On the 25th of August, the Count de Barras sailed from Newport for the Chesapeake.

Admiral Rodney, not suspecting that the whole fleet of De Grasse would come to the United States, supposed that a part of his squadron would be sufficient to maintain an equality in the American seas, and detached Sir Samuel Hood to the continent with only fourteen sail of the line. That officer arrived at Sandy Hook on the 28th of August.

Admiral Greaves, who had succeeded Arbuthnot, lay in the harbor of New York with seven ships of the line, only five of which were fit for service. On the day that Hood appeared and gave information that De Grasse was probably on the coast, intelligence was also received that De Barras had sailed from Newport. The ships fit for sea were ordered out of the harbor; and Greaves proceeded in quest of the French with nineteen sail of the line, hoping to fight their squadrons separately.

Early in the morning of the 5th of September, the French admiral descried the British squadron, and immediately ordered his fleet, then at anchor just within the Chesapeake, to form the line and put to sea. About four in the afternoon the action commenced between the foremost ships, and continued until sunset. The hostile fleets continued within view of each other until the 10th, when De Grasse returned to his former station, where he found De Barras with the squadron from Newport, and fourteen transports laden with heavy artillery and military stores proper for carrying on a siege. The British admiral, on approaching the capes, perceived a force with which he was unable to contend, and bore away for New York.

General Washington had determined to command the southern

When it was determined to act against Cornwallis, what naval operations took from the British the command of the Chesapeake, and allowed the allies to transport thither their force?

expedition in person. All the French, and rather more than two thousand continental troops, were destined for this service.

On the 16th of August, the Jersey line and Hazen's regiment were ordered to pass the Hudson, and take a position between Springfield and Chatham, in order to excite fears for Staten Island. The whole army was put in motion on the same day, and on the 25th the passage of the river was completed. The march of the army was continued until the 31st, in such a direction as to keep up fears for New York. The letters which had been intercepted by Sir Henry Clinton favored this deception; and so strong was the impression they had made, that he did not suspect the real object of his adversary until it had become too late to obstruct the progress of the allied army towards Virginia. He then determined to make every exertion in his power to relieve Lord Cornwallis; and, in the mean time, to act offensively in the North. An expedition was planned against New London, in Connecticut, and a strong detachment, under the command of General Arnold, was landed on the 6th of September on both sides of the harbor, about three miles from the town.

New London, a seaport town on the west side of the Thames, was defended by fort Trumbull and a redoubt, a small distance below it, and by fort Griswold, opposite to it, on Croton hill. General Arnold advanced with the troops that landed on the west side of the harbor, against the posts on that side, which, being untenable, were evacuated on his approach. Lieutenant-Colonel Eyre, with the troops that landed on the Croton side of the harbor, was ordered to storm fort Griswold, which was defended by a garrison of one hundred and sixty men. On the refusal of Colonel Ledyard to surrender, the British assaulted it on three sides, made a lodgement on the ditch and fraized work, and entered the embrasures with charged bayonets. Further resistance being hopeless, the action ceased on the part of the Americans, and Colonel Ledyard delivered his sword to the commanding officer of the assailants. Irritated by the loss sustained in the assault, the British officer on whom the command had devolved, tarnished the glory of victory by the inhuman use he made of it. Instead of respecting, with the generous spirit of a soldier, the gallantry he had subdued, he indulged the vindictive feelings which had been roused by the slaughter of his troops. The sword presented by Colonel Ledyard was plunged into his bosom; and the carnage was continued until the greater part of the garrison was killed or wounded.

In this fierce assault, Colonel Eyre was killed; and Major Montgomery, the second in command, also fell. The total loss of the

How was Sir Henry Clinton deceived as to the real design of Washington? Mention the British attack on New London, and the disgraceful cruelty which characterized the assailants.

assailants was not much less than two hundred men. The town, and the stores contained in it, were consumed by fire.

General Washington, having made arrangements for the transportation of his army down the Chesapeake, proceeded in person to Virginia. He reached Williamsburg on the 14th of September; and, accompanied by Rochambeau, Chatelleux, Knox, and Duportail, repaired immediately on board the admiral's ship, where a plan of co-operation was adjusted, conforming to his wish in every respect, except that the Count de Grasse declined complying with a proposition to station some ships above Yorktown, thinking it too hazardous.

On the 25th of September, the last division of the allied troops arrived; soon after which the preparations for the siege were completed.

York is a small village on the south side of the river which bears that name, where the long peninsula between the York and the James is only eight miles wide. On the opposite shore is Gloucester Point, a piece of land projecting deep into the river. Both these posts were occupied by Lord Cornwallis. The communication between them was commanded by his batteries, and by some ships of war which lay under his guns. The main body of his army was encamped on the open grounds about Yorktown, within a range of outer redoubts and field-works.

On the 28th, the combined army moved by different roads towards Yorktown. About noon the different columns reached their ground, and, after driving in the piquets and some cavalry, encamped for the evening. The next day the right wing, consisting of Americans, occupied the ground east of Beaver Dam creek, while the left wing, consisting of French, was stationed on the west side of that stream. In the course of the night Lord Cornwallis withdrew from his outer lines, which were occupied by the besieging army; and the town on that side was completely invested.

Two thousand men were stationed on the Gloucester side for the purpose of keeping up a rigorous blockade. On their approaching the lines, a sharp skirmish took place, which terminated unfavorably for the British; after which they remained under cover of their works.

On the night of the 6th of October, the first parallel was commenced within six hundred yards of the British lines. Before th return of daylight disclosed the operation to the garrison, the trenches were in such forwardness as to cover the men. Several batteries were opened; and by the 10th, the fire became so heavy that the besieged withdrew their cannon from the embrasures, and

State the dispositions of the French and Americans for the siege of Yorktown, and describe the position of Cornwallis. How were operations begun, and with what success?

19.

scarcely returned a shot.   The shells and red-hot balls reached the ships in the harbor, and set fire to the Charon of forty-four guns, and to three large transports, which were entirely consumed. The second parallel was opened on the night of the 11th, within three hundred yards of the British lines.   The three succeeding days were devoted to its completion, during which the fire of the garrison, from several new embrasures, became more destructive than at any previous time.   The men in the trenches were particularly annoyed by two redoubts, advanced three hundred yards in front of the British works, which flanked the second parallel of the besiegers.   Preparations were made on the 14th to carry them by storm.   The attack of the one was committed to a detachment of Americans, led by the Marquis de Lafayette, and that of the other to a detachment of French, commanded by the Baron de Viominel.   Towards the close of the day, both detachments marched to the assault.   Colonel Hamilton led the advanced corps of the Americans, and Colonel Laurens turned the redoubt at the head of eighty men.   The troops rushed to the charge without firing a gun; and, passing over the abatis and palisades, assaulted the works on all sides, and entered them with such rapidity that their loss was inconsiderable.   Major Campbell, a captain, and seventeen privates were made prisoners.   Eight privates were killed while the assailants were entering the works.   They were defended by forty-five privates, besides officers.

The redoubt attacked by the French was defended by a greater number of men; and the resistance, being greater, was not overcome with so little loss.   One hundred and twenty men, commanded by a lieutenant-colonel, were in this work, eighteen of whom were killed, and forty-two, including a captain and two subaltern officers, were made prisoners.   The assailants lost, in killed and wounded, near one hundred men.

The commander-in-chief was highly gratified with the intrepidity displayed in these assaults; and, in the orders of the succeeding day, expressed in strong terms, his approbation of the judicious dispositions and gallant conduct of both the Baron de Viominel and the Marquis de Lafayette, and the officers and soldiers under their respective command.

During the same night, these redoubts were included in the second parallel.

The situation of Lord Cornwallis was becoming desperate.   To suspend a catastrophe which appeared almost inevitable, he resolved on attempting to retard the completion of the second parallel by a vigorous sortie against two batteries which were in the greatest

Describe the attack of the allies upon the two British redoubts, and mention the loss of the parties.   What were the prospects of the besieged, and upon what did Cornwallis resolve?

forwardness. A party led by Lieutenant-Colonel Abercrombie attacked them with great impetuosity about four in the morning of the 16th, and carried both with inconsiderable loss; but the guards from the trenches immediately advancing on the assailants, they retreated without effecting any thing of importance.

About four in the afternoon, the besiegers opened several batteries in their second parallel; and it was apparent that the works of the besieged were not in a condition to sustain so tremendous a fire as was to be expected on the succeeding day. In this extremity Lord Cornwallis formed the bold design of forcing his way to New York.

His plan was to leave his sick and baggage behind, and, crossing over in the night to Gloucester shore, to attack De Chóisé. After cutting to pieces or dispersing the troops under that officer, he intended to mount his infantry on horses, and by forced marches to gain the fords of the great rivers, and forcing his way through the states of Maryland, and Pennsylvania, and New Jersey, to form a junction with the army in New York.

Boats were held in readiness to receive the troops at ten in the morning; and the first embarkation was landed at the point, unperceived, when a violent storm drove the boats down the river. It continued till near daylight, when the boats returned. But the enterprize was necessarily abandoned, and the troops brought back.

In the morning of the 17th, several new batteries were opened in the second parallel which poured in a weight of fire not to be resisted. The place being no longer tenable, Lord Cornwallis beat a parley, and proposed a cessation of hostilities for twenty-four hours, that commissioners might meet to settle terms for the surrender of the posts of York and Gloucester. To this letter General Washington returned an immediate answer, declaring his "ardent desire to spare the further effusion of blood, and his readiness to listen to such terms as were admissible;" but as in the present crisis, he could not consent to lose a moment in fruitless negotiations, he desired that, "the proposals of his lordship might be transmitted in writing, for which purpose a suspension of hostilities for two hours should be granted." The proposals being such as led to the opinion that no difficulty would occur in adjusting the terms, the suspension of hostilities was prolonged for the night. In the mean time, the commander-in-chief drew up such articles as he would be willing to grant, which were transmitted to Lord Cornwallis, accompanied by a declaration that, if he approved them, commissioners might be immediately appointed to digest them into form.

In his exigency at Yorktown, what bold plan of extrication was formed by Cornwallis? Mention the circumstance which frustrated the design.

The Viscount de Noailles, and Lieutenant-Colonel Laurens, were met next day by Colonel Dundass and Major Ross; but being unable to adjust the terms of capitulation definitively, only a rough draft of them was prepared, to be submitted to the consideration of the British General. General Washington, determined not to permit any suspense on the part of Lord Cornwallis, immediately directed the rough articles to be fairly transcribed, and sent them to his lordship early the next morning with a letter, expressing his expectation that they would be signed by eleven, and that the garrison would march out by two in the afternoon. Finding all attempts to obtain better terms unavailing, Lord Cornwallis submitted to a necessity no longer to be avoided, and, on the 19th of October, surrendered the posts of Yorktown and Gloucester Point with their garrisons, and the ships in the harbor with their seamen, to the land and naval forces of America and France.

The army, artillery, arms, military-chest, and stores of every description, were surrendered to General Washington; the ships and seamen to the Count de Grasse. The total number of prisoners, excluding seamen, rather exceeded seven thousand. The loss sustained by the garrison during the siege, amounted to five hundred and fifty-two, including six officers.

The allied army, including militia, may be estimated at sixteen thousand men. In the course of the siege, they lost in killed and wounded about three hundred.

The whole army merited great approbation; but, from the nature of the service, the artillerists and engineers were enabled to distinguish themselves particularly. Generals Du Portail and Knox were each promoted to the rank of Major-General; and Colonel Govion and Captain Rochfontaine, of the corps of engineers, were each advanced a grade by brevet. In addition to the officers belonging to those departments, Generals Lincoln, De Lafayette, and Steuben, were particularly mentioned by the commander-in-chief in his orders issued the day after the capitulation; and terms of peculiar warmth were applied to Governor Nelson, who continued in the field during the whole siege, at the head of the militia of Virginia; and also exerted himself greatly to furnish the army with those supplies that the country afforded. The highest acknowledgments were made to the Count de Rochambeau; and several other French officers were named with distinction.

The day on which the capitulation of the British army was signed at Yorktown, Sir Henry Clinton sailed from the Hook at the head of seven thousand of his best troops, convoyed by a fleet of twenty-five ships of the line, and appeared off the capes of Vir-

Did Cornwallis at length surrender? Mention the terms of capitulation. State the numbers of each army, and their loss during the siege. What officers distinguished themselves? What reinforcement arrived too late?

ginia on the 24th of October. On receiving unquestionable intelligence that Lord Cornwallis had surrendered, he returned to New York.

The exultation manifested throughout the United States at the capture of this formidable army was equal to the terror it had inspired. Congress expressed their sense of the great event in various resolutions, returning thanks to the commander-in-chief, to the Count de Rochambeau, to the Count de Grasse, to the officers of the allied army generally, and to the corps of artillery and engineers particularly. In addition to these testimonials of gratitude, they resolved that a marble column should be erected at Yorktown, with emblems of the alliance between the United States and his Most Christian Majesty, and inscribed with a succinct narrative of the surrender of Earl Cornwallis to his Excellency General Washington, the commander-in-chief of the combined forces of America and France; to his Excellency the Count de Rochambeau, commanding the auxiliary troops of his Most Christian Majesty in America; and to his Excellency Count de Grasse, commanding-in-chief the naval armament of France in the Chesapeake. Two stand of colors taken in Yorktown were presented to General Washington; two pieces of field ordnance, to the Count de Rochambeau; and application was made to his Most Christian Majesty to permit the Admiral to accept a testimonial of their approbation similar to that presented to the Count de Rochambeau. A proclamation was issued appointing the 13th day of December for general thanksgiving and prayer, on account of this signal interposition of divine providence.

The superiority of the allied force opened a prospect of still further advantages. The remaining posts of the British in the southern states were too weak to be defended against the army which had triumphed over Lord Cornwallis, and must inevitably be surrendered should the fleet co-operate against them. Although the Admiral had explicitly declared his inability to engage in any enterprise subsequent to that against Yorktown, the siege of that place had employed so much less time than he had consented to appropriate to it, that the General cherished the hope of prevailing on him to join in an expedition which must terminate the war. Every argument which might operate on his love of fame, or his desire to promote the interests of the allies, was urged in support of the application, but urged in vain. The Count acknowledged his conviction of the advantages to be expected from the enterprise, but said that "the orders of his court, ulterior projects, and his engagements with the Spaniards, rendered it impossible for him to

In what way did Congress testify their approbation of the result at Yorktown? What favorable prospect was now opened to the allied arms, and what officer withheld his co-operation?
19*

remain on the coast during the time which would be required for the operation." As he also declined taking on board the troops designed to reinforce General Greene, preparations were made for their march by land; and Major-General St. Clair, who commanded the detachment, was ordered to take Wilmington in his route, and to gain possession of that post.

The Count de Grasse, having consented to remain in the bay a few days, for the purpose of covering the transportation of the eastern troops to the head of Elk, they were embarked early in November, under the command of General Lincoln, who was directed to canton them for the winter in New Jersey and New York. The French troops remained in Virginia; the Count de Grasse sailed for the West Indies; and the commander-in-chief proceeded to Philadelphia.

CHAPTER XXIII.

Greene invests Camden.—Battle of Hobkirk's hill.—Progress of Marion and Lee.—Lord Rawdon retires into the lower country.—Greene invests Ninety-Six.—Is repulsed.—Retires from that place.—Activity of the armies.—Movements suspended by the heat.—They resume active operations.—Battle of Eutaw.—The British army retires towards Charleston.

1781. In South Carolina and Georgia, the campaign of 1781 was uncommonly active.

When Lord Cornwallis entered North Carolina, the command of the more southern states was committed to Lord Rawdon. For the preservation of his power, a line of posts, slightly fortified, had been continued from Charleston, by the way of Camden and Ninety-Six, to Augusta, in Georgia. The spirit of resistance was still kept alive in the north-western and north-eastern parts of the state, by Generals Sumpter and Marion; but neither of them was formidable.

Such was the situation of the country, when General Greene formed the bold resolution of endeavoring to reannex it to the American Union. His army consisted of about eighteen hundred men. The prospect of procuring subsistence was unpromising, and the chance of reinforcements precarious.

The day preceding his march southward, he detached Lee to join General Marion, and communicated his intention of entering South Carolina to General Pickens, with a request that he would assemble the western militia, and lay siege to Ninety-Six and Augusta.

Where were the French and American forces stationed, after the surrender at Yorktown? What was the state of affairs in the South? Mention the bold determination of General Greene.

Having made these arrangements, he moved from Deep river on the 7th of April, and encamped before Camden on the 19th of the same month, within half a mile of the British works. Lord Rawdon had received early notice of his approach, and was prepared to receive him. Being unable to storm the works, or to invest them on all sides, he contented himself with lying before the places, in the hope of being reinforced by militia, or of some event which might bring on an action in the open field. With this view, he retired about a mile and a half from the town, and encamped on Hobkirk's hill.

While in this situation, he received information that Colonel Watson was marching up the Santee, with four hundred men. To intercept him while at a distance from Camden, Greene crossed Sandhill creek, and encamped on the road leading to Charleston. It being impossible to transport artillery and baggage over the deep marshes adjoining the creek, Colonel Carrington, with the North Carolina militia, was directed to convey them to a place of safety, and to guard them till further orders.

In a few days, Greene found himself compelled, by the want of provisions, to relinquish his position; and on the 24th, returned to the north side of the town, and again encamped on Hobkirk's hill. Colonel Carrington was ordered to rejoin him. Before the arrival of that officer, a deserter informed Lord Rawdon that the artillery and militia had been detached. His Lordship determined to seize this favorable occasion; and marched out of town, on the morning of the 25th, at the head of nine hundred men, to attack the American army.

By keeping close to the swamp, and making a circuit of some distance, Lord Rawdon gained the American left, without being perceived. About eleven, his approach was announced by the fire of the advanced piquets, half a mile in front of Greene's encampment; and the American line of battle was immediately formed.

The parties advanced in front were driven in, after a gallant resistance; and Rawdon continued his march through the wood, until he reached the road, when he displayed his columns.

Perceiving that the British advanced with a narrow front, Greene ordered Colonel Ford, from his extreme left, and Lieutenant-Colonel Campbell, from his extreme right, severally to attack their flanks, while the regiments of Granby and Hawes should charge them in front with the bayonet. To complete their destruction, Lieutenant-Colonel Washington was directed to pass their left flank, and charge their rear.

Before what town did General Greene encamp? What British officer defended it? What circumstance induced Lord Rawdon to sally forth and attack the Americans? Relate the movements which ensued.

The regiments commanded by Ford and Campbell, being composed chiefly of new levies, did not perform the duties assigned to them with the requisite rapidity and precision; in consequence of which, Rawdon had time to extend his front, by bringing the volunteers of Ireland into his line.

This judicious movement disconcerted the design on his flanks; and the regiments of Ford and Campbell were thrown into some confusion by the abortive attempt.

Colonel Washington, too, was compelled, by the obstructions in his direct course, to make so extensive a circuit, that he came into the rear of the British at a greater distance from the scene of action than was intended; in consequence of which, he fell in with their staff, and with the followers of the army who took no part in the engagement. Too humane to cut his way through this crowd, he employed so much time in taking their paroles, that he did not reach the rear of the British line, until the battle was ended.

The artillery, however, which had arrived in the morning, with Colonel Carrington, played on the enemy with considerable effect, and the regiments of Gunby and Hawes advanced on the British front with resolution. This fair prospect of victory was blasted by one of those incidents against which military prudence can make no provision.

Captain Beaty, who commanded on the right of Gunby's regiment, was killed; upon which, his company, with that adjoining it, got into confusion, and dropped out of the lines. Gunby ordered the other companies to fall back, and form with the two companies behind the hill the British were ascending. The retrograde movement was mistaken for a retreat, and the regiment gave way. The British pressed forward with increased ardor, and all the efforts of the officers to rally the Americans, were ineffectual. This veteran regiment, equally distinguished for its discipline and courage, was seized with an unaccountable panic, which, for a time, resisted all the efforts of their officers.

The flight of the first Maryland regiment increased the confusion which the change of ground had produced in the second; and, in attempting to restore order, Colonel Ford was mortally wounded. Lord Rawdon improved these advantages to the utmost. His right gained the summit of the hill, forced the artillery to retire, and turned the flank of the second Virginia regiment, commanded by Lieutenant-Colonel Haines, which had advanced some distance down the hill. By this time, the first Virginia regiment, which Greene had endeavored to lead on in person

Mention the unsuccessful attempt against the British flank, and the cause which detained Colonel Washington from the field of battle. What circumstance of panic and mistake frustrated the hopes of General Greene?

against the left flank of the British, being also in some disorder, began to give ground. Greene, knowing that he could not depend on his second line, which was composed of militia, thought it most advisable to withdraw the second Virginia regiment.

The Maryland brigade was in part rallied; but Lord Rawdon had gained the hill; and it was thought too late to retrieve the fortune of the day. Greene determined to reserve his troops for a more auspicious moment, and directed a retreat.

Finding that the action was over, Colonel Washington also retreated, with the loss of only three men, bringing with him about fifty prisoners, among whom were all the surgeons of the army.

The Americans retired in good order, about four miles from the field of battle, and proceeded next day to Rugely's mills. The pursuit was continued about three miles. In the course of it, some sharp skirmishing took place; which was terminated by a vigorous charge made by Washington, which broke a corps of horse that led their van; on which, the infantry in its rear retreated into Camden.

The loss of the Americans, in killed, wounded, and missing, was two hundred and sixty-eight; that of the British was stated at two hundred and fifty-eight, of whom thirty-eight were killed in the field.

General Greene remained in the vicinity of Camden; and, by the activity of his cavalry, straitened its communications with the country. The distress of the garrison for provisions had been considerably increased by the progress of Marion and Lee.

As soon as Lee could join Marion, they commenced their operations against the line of communication from Camden to Charleston, by capturing fort Watson. This acquisition enabled them to interrupt the intercourse between those places, and to obstruct the retreat of Lord Rawdon, should that measure become necessary. But his lordship was relieved from the difficulties of his situation on the 7th of May, by the arrival of Colonel Watson. That officer had eluded the vigilance of Marion and Lee, who, for the purpose of intercepting him, had taken possession of the fording places on the creeks it was necessary to pass, by returning down the Santee, crossing it near its mouth, and marching up its southern side until he had passed his watchful enemy. This reinforcement having given the British general a decided superiority, Greene, on the day of its arrival, withdrew from the neighborhood of Camden, and took a strong position behind Sawney's creek. On the following night Lord Rawdon marched out of Camden for the purpose of attacking the Americans in their camp; but he found them so ju-

Did General Greene retire from the field of battle? What was the loss on each side? Mention the two partisan officers who harassed the British. What reinforcement was received by Lord Rawdon?

diciously posted, that he despaired of being able to force it, and returned to Camden.

His lordship had been induced to relinquish his designs upon Greene by a conviction that a temporary surrender of the upper country had become necessary. Marion and Lee had crossed the Santee, and permitted no convoy from Charleston to escape them. On the 8th they laid siege to Mott's house, which had been made the depot of all the supplies designed for Camden. The safety of the lower posts required that he should take a position which would enable him to support them. He had, therefore, determined to evacuate Camden, unless a battle with Greene should remove all fears of future danger. After failing in his hope of bringing on an engagement, he carried this determination into execution, and marched down the river to Neilson's ferry, where he received the unwelcome intelligence that Mott's house had surrendered on the 12th, and that its garrison, consisting of one hundred and sixty-five men, had become prisoners. The post at Orangeburg had surrendered to Sumpter on the preceding day.

On the evening of the 14th, Lord Rawdon marched to Monk's Corner, a position which enabled him to cover those districts from which Charleston drew its supplies.

Meanwhile the American force was exerted with increased activity. Marion reduced Georgetown on the Black river; and Lee laid siege on the 14th to fort Granby, a post garrisoned by three hundred and fifty-two men, chiefly militia, who surrendered the next morning. He was then ordered to march against Augusta, while Greene invested Ninety-Six.

This post was fortified. The principal work, called the Star, was on the right of the village, and was surrounded by a dry ditch, fraize, and abatis. On the left was a block-house and a stockade fort. The garrison, commanded by Lieutenant-Colonel Cruger, was ample for the extent of the place.

On the 22d of May, the American army, consisting of about one thousand continental troops, encamped within cannon-shot of the place, and, on the following night, broke ground within seventy yards of the British works; but the besieged made a vigorous sally under the protection of their guns; drove the advanced party from their trenches, put several of them to the bayonet, and retired into the fort before Greene could support them. After this check, the siege was conducted with more caution, but with indefatigable industry.

On the 8th of June, Lee rejoined the army. The day after the fall of fort Granby, that active officer proceeded to join General

Mention the three British posts which successively surrendered to the Americans. What were the defences of Ninety-Six? Who invested it, and what repulse was received by the besiegers?

Pickens, and lay siege to Augusta. On the 21st of May, he took possession of fort Golphin, immediately after which the operations against Augusta were commenced. The place was surrendered on the 5th of June; and the prisoners, amounting to three hundred, were conducted by Lee to the main army.

While the siege of Ninety-Six was pressed in the confidence that the place must soon surrender, Lord Rawdon received a reinforcement of three regiments from Ireland, which enabled him once more to overrun South Carolina. On the 11th, Greene received intelligence that his lordship was approaching at the head of two thousand men. Sumpter, to whose aid the cavalry was immediately detached, was ordered to continue in his front, and to impede his march to the utmost. But his lordship passed Sumpter below the junction of the Saluda and Broad rivers.

Greene, finding it impossible to draw together such aids of militia as might enable him to meet Lord Rawdon and fight him at a distance from Ninety-Six, hoped to press the siege so vigorously as to compel a surrender before his lordship could arrive. The garrison was reduced to extremities, when the approach of the British army was communicated to Cruger by a loyalist who passed through the American lines. The hope of obtaining a surrender by capitulation being thus extinguished, Greene determined to attempt carrying the place by storm. As preparatory to an assault on the Star, it was deemed indispensable to make a lodgement on one of the curtains of the redoubt, and at the same time to carry the fort on the left.

Lieutenant-Colonel Lee, at the head of the legion infantry and Kirkwood's company, was ordered to assault the works on the left of the town; while Lieutenant-Colonel Campbell was to lead the first regiment of Maryland and the first of Virginia against the Star redoubt. The lines were manned, and the artillery opened on the besieged.

About noon on the 18th, the detachments marched to the assault. Lee took possession of the works on the left; but the resistance on the right was greater, and Campbell was less fortunate. Lieutenants Duval of Maryland, and Selden of Virginia, led the forlorn hope with great intrepidity. They entered the ditch; but the height of the parapet opposed obstructions not to be surmounted. After a severe conflict of more than half an hour, during which Lieutenants Duval and Selden were both badly wounded, and nearly all the forlorn hope were killed or wounded, the assault was relinquished, and the few who remained were recalled from the ditch. The next day Greene raised the siege, and, crossing the

When was Augusta reduced? What reinforcement enabled Lord Rawdon to advance to the relief of Ninety-Six? Did this induce General Greene to assault the place by storm? What was the result?

Saluda, encamped on Little river. The loss of the besieging army, in killed and wounded, amounted to one hundred and fifty-five men. That of the garrison has been stated at eighty-five.

On the morning of the 21st, Lord Rawdon arrived at Ninety-Six; and, on the evening of the same day, marched in quest of the American army. He pursued Greene, who retreated towards Virginia, as far as the Ennoree; whence he returned to Ninety-Six.

Still retaining the opinion that circumstances required him to contract his posts, he left the principal part of his army under the command of Lieutenant-Colonel Cruger, to protect the loyalists while removing within those limits which were to be maintained, and with less than one thousand men, marched in person, on the 29th of June, towards the Congaree.

Early in July, Greene marched with the utmost expedition for Friday's ferry, at which place Lord Rawdon had arrived two days before him. As Greene drew near his enemy, a detachment of the legion under Captain Eggleston, announced his approach by attacking a foraging party within a mile of the British camp, and bringing off a troop consisting of forty-five men. Rawdon retreated the next day to Orangeburg, where he formed a junction with a detachment from Charleston, commanded by Lieutenant-Colonel Stuart.

On the Congaree, Greene was reinforced by Sumpter and Marion, with a thousand men; and, on the 11th of July, marched to Orangeburg with the intention of attacking the British army; but found it so strongly posted as to be unassailable.

At this place, intelligence was received of the evacuation of Ninety-Six, and that Cruger was marching down to Orangeburg. The north branch of the Edisto, which was passable only at the place occupied by Rawdon, interposed an insuperable obstacle to any attempt on this party; and Greene thought it most advisable to force the British out of the upper country by threatening their lower posts. On the 13th, Sumpter, Marion, and Lee were detached on this service, and, on the same day, the residue of the army moved towards the high hills of Santee.

The detachments ordered against the north-eastern posts held by the British, were not so completely successful as their numbers, courage, and enterprise deserved. Some sharp skirmishes were fought; several prisoners were made; a considerable quantity of ammunition was taken; and baggage and military stores, to a large amount, were destroyed. But Sumpter, though brave to excess, did not display the combining talents of Greene. After

Was the British commander compelled, notwithstanding his late accession of force, to reduce his posts? Mention the various movements of General Greene, and those of Sumpter, Marion, and Lee.

being disappointed in the hope of getting possession of Monk's Corner, some discontents prevailed among the several corps. Marion returned to his swamps, Sumpter recrossed the Santee, and Lee rejoined the army, July 18th.

The intense heat demanded some relaxation from unremitting toil. From the month of January, the southern army had been engaged in one course of incessant fatigue and hardy enterprise. All were entitled to great praise; but the successful activity of one corps will attract particular attention. The legion, from its structure, was peculiarly adapted to the partisan war of the southern states; and, being detached against the weaker posts of the enemy, had opportunities for displaying all the energies it possessed. In that extensive sweep which it made from the Santee to Augusta, which employed from the 15th of April to the 5th of June, this corps, acting in conjunction, first with Marion, afterwards with Pickens, and sometimes alone, had constituted an essential part of the force which carried five British posts, and made upwards of eleven hundred prisoners.

The whole army had exhibited a degree of activity, courage, and patient suffering, surpassing any expectation which could have been formed of troops composed chiefly of new levies; and its general had manifested great firmness, enterprise, prudence, and skill.

The suffering sustained in this ardent struggle for the southern states, was not confined to the armies. The inhabitants of the country felt all the miseries which are inflicted by war in its most savage form. Being almost equally divided between the contending parties, reciprocal injuries had sharpened their mutual resentments, and had armed neighbor against neighbor, until it became a war of extermination. As the parties alternately triumphed, opportunities were alternately given for the exercise of their vindictive passions.

Greene was too humane, as well as too judicious, not to discourage this exterminating spirit. Perceiving, in its progress, the total destruction of the country, he sought to appease it, by restraining the excesses of those who were attached to the American cause.

At the high hills of Santee, the reinforcements expected from North Carolina were received; which augmented the army to two thousand six hundred men: but its effective force did not exceed sixteen hundred.

Lord Rawdon, having been induced by ill health, to avail himself of a permit to return to Europe, the command of the British

Why did the American forces require relaxation? Mention their military merits and capacities. What was the nature of the warfare which afflicted the Southern states? What reinforcements joined the American army?

forces in South Carolina devolved on Lieutenant-Colonel Stuart. He again advanced to the Congaree, and manifested a disposition to establish himself, at the junction of that river, with the Wateree.

Early in September, Greene broke up his camp at the high hills of Santee, and, crossing the Wateree near Camden, marched towards his enemy. On being informed of his approach, the British army retired to Eutaw, where it received a reinforcement from Charleston. Greene followed by easy marches. In the afternoon of the 7th, he was joined by Marion; and determined to attack the British camp next day.

At four, in the morning of the 8th, the army moved from its ground, which was seven miles from Eutaw, having the legion of Lee and the troops of South Carolina in advance. About four miles from the British camp, the van fell in with and attacked a body of horse and foot, who were escorting a foraging party. The British were instantly routed. Several were killed, and about forty, including their captain, were made prisoners. Supposing this party to be the van of the English, Greene formed his order of battle.

The militia, commanded by Marion and Pickens, composed his first line. The second consisted of the continental infantry. The North Carolina brigade, commanded by General Sumner, was placed on the right; the Virginians, commanded by Lieutenant-Colonel Campbell, formed the centre; and the Marylanders, commanded by Colonel Williams, the left. The legion of Lee was to cover the right flank; the state troops of South Carolina, commanded by Colonel Henderson, the left; and the cavalry of Washington, with the infantry of Kirkwood, formed the reserve. Captain-Lieutenant Gaines, with two three-pounders, was attached to the first line, and Captain Brown, with two sixes, to the centre.

The British line, which was also immediately formed, was drawn up across the road, in a wood on the heights, having its right flank on Eutaw creek. It was also covered by a battalion commanded by Major Majoribanks, which was posted in a thicket. The left was protected by the cavalry, commanded by Major Coffin, and by a body of infantry, held in reserve. A corps of infantry was pushed forward about a mile.

As the American van encountered this advanced party, the first line was ordered up, and the legion, and the state troops of South Carolina, formed on its flanks. The advanced party was soon driven in; and the Americans, still pressing forward, were engaged with the main body. The militia, having many of them

<hr />

Did Greene advance towards his enemy? Was the latter reinforced? Where did the two armies come into contact? Mention General Greene's disposition of his force for the battle.

frequently faced an enemy, and being commanded by generals of experience and courage, exhibited a degree of firmness not common to that species of force, and maintained their ground with obstinacy. When they gave way, Lee and Henderson still maintained the engagement on the flanks. General Sumner was ordered up to fill the place from which Marion and Pickens were receding; and his brigade came into action with great intrepidity. Stuart ordered the corps of infantry posted in the rear of his left wing into the line, and directed Major Coffin, with his cavalry, to guard that flank. About this time, Colonel Henderson received a dangerous wound, and the command of his regiment devolved on Colonel Hampton.

After sustaining the fire of the enemy for some time, Sumner's brigade began to give way, and the British rushed forward in some disorder. Greene then directed Williams and Campbell to charge with the bayonet, and ordered Washington to act on his left. Williams charged without firing a musket. The soldiers of Campbell's regiment, being chiefly new levies, returned the fire of the enemy, as they advanced. In this critical moment, Lee, perceiving that the American right extended beyond the British left, ordered Captain Rudolph, of the legion infantry, to turn their flank, and give them a raking fire. This order being executed with precision and effect, the British broke successively on their left, till the example was followed by all that part of their line. The Marylanders had already used the bayonet; and many had fallen on both sides, transfixed by that weapon.

The British left retreated towards Eutaw creek, near which stood a brick house, surrounded with offices, into which Major Sheridan threw himself with the New York volunteers. The Americans pursued them closely, and took three hundred prisoners and two field-pieces. The legion infantry pressed their rear so eagerly, as to make a serious struggle to enter the house with them. The door was shut in their faces, and several British were excluded, who were made prisoners; and, being mixed with the Americans, saved them from the fire of the house, while retiring from it.

As the British left gave way, Washington was directed to charge their right. He advanced with his accustomed impetuosity; but found it impossible, with cavalry, to penetrate the thicket occupied by Majoribanks. In attempting to force it, Lieutenant Stewart, who commanded the leading section, was wounded, his horse killed under him, and every man in his section killed or wounded. Captain Watts fell, pierced with two balls. Colonel Washington was wounded, and his horse was killed. They fell together; and before he could extricate himself, he was made a prisoner.

Relate the circumstances of the battle of Eutaw, and state particularly the manner in which the British left was broken.

After a large portion of the regiment was killed or wounded, the residue was drawn off by Captain Parsons, assisted by Lieutenant Gordon. Lieutenant-Colonel Hampton and Captain Kirkwood soon afterwards came up and renewed the attack on Majoribanks; but finding it impossible to dislodge him, they relinquished the attempt.

Greene ordered up the artillery to batter the house in which Sheridan had taken refuge. The guns were too light to make a breach in the walls; and, having been brought within the range of the fire from the house, almost every artillerist was killed, and the pieces were abandoned.

The firm stand made by Majoribanks, and the disorder among a part of the American right, gave Stuart an opportunity to rally his broken regiments, and bring them again into action. Perceiving that the contest was maintained under circumstances extremely disadvantageous to the Americans, Greene withdrew them a small distance, and formed them again in the wood in which the battle had been fought. After collecting his wounded, he retired with his prisoners to the ground from which he had marched in the morning, determined again to attack the British army when it should retreat from Eutaw.

Every corps engaged in this hard-fought battle received the applause of the General. Almost every officer whose situation enabled him to attract notice was named with distinction.

The loss on both sides bore a great proportion to their respective numbers. That of the Americans was five hundred and fifty-five, including sixty officers. One hundred and thirty were killed on the spot. Seventeen commissioned officers, including Lieutenant-Colonel Campbell, were killed, and four mortally wounded.

The loss of the British was stated by themselves at six hundred and ninety-three men, of whom only eighty-five were killed in the field. This disparity in the killed is to be ascribed to the carnage of the Americans during their unavailing efforts to dislodge the enemy from the house, and strong adjoining grounds.

Each party had pretensions to the victory. If the consequences be taken into the account, it belonged to Greene. The result was, the expulsion of the hostile army from the territory which was the immediate object of contest.

The thanks of Congress were voted to every corps in the army; and a resolution was passed for "presenting to Major-General Greene, as an honorable testimony of his merit, a British standard and golden medal emblematic of the battle and of his victory."

Mention the attack upon the British right, and its result. What enabled the enemy to rally his broken troops? Mention the loss on each side. Was the battle of Eutaw decisive, or might either party claim the victory? What was its consequence?

On the succeeding day, Colonel Stuart marched from Eutaw to meet Major M'Arthur, who was conducting a body of troops from Charleston. This movement saved M'Arthur from Marion and Lee, who had been detached in the morning to intercept any reinforcement from below. Stuart was followed to Monk's Corner by Greene, who, on reconnoitring the numbers and position of his enemy, returned to the high hills of Santee.

The ravages of disease were added to the loss sustained in battle, and the army remained for some time in too feeble a condition for active enterprise.

As the cool season approached, disease abated in the American camp, and Greene marched towards the Four Holes, a branch of the Edisto. Leaving the army to be conducted by Colonel Williams, he proceeded in person with a detachment of cavalry and infantry against the British post at Dorchester. Though his march was conducted with the utmost secrecy, intelligence of his approach was given, and the garrison, after burning the stores, retired with inconsiderable loss to the Quarter House, where their main body was encamped. Greene returned to the army at the Round O, where he purposed to wait the arrival of the reinforcement marching from the North under General St. Clair.

On the 4th of January, that officer arrived; and, five days afterwards, General Wayne with his brigade, and the remnant of the third regiment of dragoons commanded by Colonel White, was detached over the Savannah for the recovery of Georgia.

General Greene crossed the Edisto, and encamped on the Charleston road six miles from Jacksonborough, for the purpose of covering the legislature who were convened at that place. Thus was civil government re-established in South Carolina, and that state restored to the Union.

It is impossible to review this active and interesting campaign without feeling that much is due to General Greene. He found the country completely conquered, and defended by a regular army estimated at four thousand men. The inhabitants were so divided as to leave it doubtful to which side the majority was attached. At no time did his effective continental force amount to two thousand men; and of these a considerable part were raw troops. Yet he could keep the field without being forced into action, and, by a course of judicious movement and hardy enterprise, he recovered the Southern states. It is a singular fact, well worthy of notice, that, although well-merited victory was uniformly snatched by fortune from his grasp, he obtained to a considerable extent, even when defeated, the object for which he fought.

<hr>

What movements succeeded the battle of Eutaw? To what must be attributed the inactivity for some time after? What reinforcements arrived, and what position was taken? What is to be said respecting Greene's army?

20 *

A large portion of this praise is unquestionably due to the troops he commanded. These real patriots bore every hardship and privation, with a degree of patience and constancy which cannot be sufficiently admired, and never was a General better supported by his inferior officers.

CHAPTER XXIV.

Preparations for another campaign.—Proceedings in the Parliament of Great Britain.—Conciliatory conduct of General Carlton.—Transactions in the South.—Negotiations for peace.—Preliminary and eventual articles of peace between the United States and Great Britain.—Discontents of the American army.—Peace.—Mutiny of a part of the Pennsylvania line.—Evacuation of New York.—General Washington resigns his commission and retires to Mount Vernon.

1782. THE splendid success of the allied arms in Virginia, and the great advantages obtained still further south, produced no disposition in General Washington to relax those exertions which might yet be necessary to secure the great object of the contest. He was detained in Philadelphia by the request of Congress, in order to aid the consultations of a committee appointed to report the requisitions to be made on the states for the establishment of the army. The secretaries of war, of finance, and of foreign affairs, also assisted at these deliberations; and the business was concluded with unusual celerity.

As a superiority at sea was indispensable to the success of offensive operations, the commander-in-chief pressed its importance on the minister of France, and commanding officers of the French troops, as well as on the Marquis de Lafayette who was about to return to his native country.

The first intelligence from Europe was not calculated to diminish the anxieties still felt in America by the enlightened friends of the revolution. The Parliament of Great Britain had reassembled .n November. The speech from the throne breathed a settled purpose to continue the war; and the addresses of both houses, which were carried by large majorities, echoed the sentiment. The debates indicated a determination to maintain the posts then held in the United States, and to press the war vigorously against France and Spain. This development of the views of administration furnished additional motives to the American government for exerting all the faculties of the nation to expel the British garrisons from those posts; and the efforts of the commander-in-chief to produce those exertions were unremitting, but not successful. The state legislatures declared the inability of their constituents to pay taxes.

Was Washington anxious to make efficient preparations for the next campaign? What seemed the determination of the British Parliament with respect to the continuance of hostilities?

Instead of filling the continental treasury, some were devising means to draw money from it; and some of those who passed bills imposing heavy taxes, directed that the demands of the state should be first satisfied, and that the residue only should be paid to the continental receiver. At the commencement of the year, not a dollar remained in the treasury; and, although Congress had required the payment of two millions on the first of April, not more than twenty thousand dollars had reached the treasury. In July, when the second quarter annual payment of taxes ought to have been received, the minister of finance was informed by some of his agents that the collection of the revenue had been postponed by some of the states, so that the month of December would arrive before any money could come into their hands.

Fortunately for the United States, the temper of the British nation on the continuance of the war, did not accord with that of its sovereign. It had now become almost universally unpopular. Motions against the measures of administration respecting America were repeated by the opposition; and on every experiment the strength of the minority increased. At length, on the 27th of February, a resolution disapproving the further prosecution of offensive war against America was carried, and an address to the crown in conformity with it, was presented by the whole house. The answer of the King being deemed inexplicit, it was, on the 4th of March, resolved " that the house will consider as enemies to his Majesty and the country, all those who should advise or attempt a further prosecution of offensive war on the continent of North America."

These votes were soon followed by a change of ministers, and by instructions to the officers commanding the forces in America, which conformed to them.

Early in May, Sir Guy Carlton, who had succeeded Sir Henry Clinton, arrived at New York. Having been also appointed, in conjunction with Admiral Digby, a commissioner to negotiate a peace, he lost no time in forwarding copies of the votes of the House of Commons, and of a bill founded on them, which had been introduced on the part of administration. But the bill had not yet become a law; nor was any assurance given that the present commissioners were authorized to offer other terms than those which were formerly rejected. General Carlton could not expect that negotiations would open on such a basis.

But the public votes which have been stated, and probably his private instructions, restrained General Carlton from offensive war; and General Washington was too weak to make any attempt

What was the condition of the continental treasury? Mention the votes in the British Parliament which restrained the further prosecution of hostilities. What communication was now made by Sir Guy Carlton?

on the posts in his possession. The summer of 1782 consequently passed away without furnishing any military operations of moment between the armies under the immediate direction of the respective commanders-in-chief.

Early in August, a letter was received by General Washington from Sir Guy Carlton and Admiral Digby, containing the information that Mr. Grenville was at Paris, invested with full powers to treat with all the parties at war; and that his Majesty had commanded his minister to direct Mr. Grenville, that the independence of the thirteen provinces should be proposed by him, in the first instance, instead of being made a condition of a general treaty. This letter was followed by one from Sir Guy Carlton, declaring that he could discern no farther object of contest, and that he disapproved of all further hostilities by sea or land, which could only multiply the miseries of individuals, without a possible advantage to either nation.

These communications appear to have alarmed the jealousy of the minister of France. To quiet his fears, Congress renewed the resolution " to enter into no discussion of any overtures for pacification, but in confidence and in concert with his Most Christian Majesty;" and again recommended to the several states to adopt such measures as would most effectually guard against all intercourse with any subjects of the British crown during the continuance of the war.

The same causes which produced this inactivity in the North, operated to a considerable extent in the South.

When General Wayne entered Georgia, the British troops retired to Savannah, and the Americans advanced to Ebenezer.

Propositions for the suspension of hostilities were made in the Southern department about the time that they were rejected in the North. The same motives continuing to influence Congress, they were rejected in the South also, and the armies still continued to watch each other. While the whole attention of Wayne was directed towards Savannah, an unlooked-for enemy came upon his rear, entered his camp in the night, and had not his army been composed of the best materials, must have dispersed it.

A strong party of Creeks, marching entirely in the night, guided by white men through unfrequented ways, subsisting on meal made of parched corn, reached the neighborhood of the American army undiscovered; and, emerging in the night from a deep swamp which had concealed them, entered the rear of the camp about three in the morning of the 23d of June. The sentinel was killed before he could sound the alarm, and the first notice of danger was

Did this change in the views of the British government, cause the summer of 1782 to pass away in comparative inactivity? What movements were made in the South? Describe the night-attack on General Wayne.

given by the fire and yell of the enemy. They rushed into the camp, and, killing the few men they met with, seized the artillery. Fortunately, some time was wasted in attempting to turn the pieces. Captain Parker, with his company, had returned that evening from a fatiguing tour of duty, and they were asleep in the rear, near the artillery, when the Indians entered the camp. Roused by the fire, and perceiving the enemy, he drew off his men in silence, and formed them, with the quarter-guard, behind the general's house. Wayne was instantly on horseback, believing the whole garrison of Savannah to be upon him. Parker was directed to charge immediately with the bayonet, and orders were despatched to Posey to bring up the troops in camp without delay. The orders to Parker were executed so promptly, that Posey could not reach the scene of action in time to join in it. The Indians, unable to resist the bayonet, soon fled; leaving their chief, his white guides, and seventeen of his warriors, dead on the spot. Only twelve prisoners were made. The general's horse was shot under him, and twelve privates were killed and wounded.

This sharp conflict terminated the war in Georgia. Savannah was evacuated on the 11th of July, and Wayne rejoined General Greene.

While the two armies continued to watch each other in South Carolina, occasional enterprises were undertaken by detachments, in some of which a considerable degree of merit was displayed. In one of them, the corps of Marion, their general being absent in the legislature, was surprised and dispersed by the British Colonel Thompson; and in another, an English guard-galley, mounting twelve guns, and manned with forty-three seamen, was captured by Captain Rudolph of the legion.

From the possession of the lower country, the army had anticipated more regular supplies of food than it had been accustomed to receive. This hope was disappointed by the measures of the government.

The war having been transferred to the South at a time when the depreciation of paper-money had deprived Congress of its only fund, subsistence for the troops could often be obtained only by coercive means. Popular discontent was the necessary consequence of this odious measure, and the feelings of the people were communicated to their representatives. The Assembly of South Carolina, during its session at Jacksonborough, passed a law forbidding impressment, and enacting "that no other persons than those who shall be appointed by the Governor for that purpose, shall be allowed or permitted to procure supplies for the army."

What other partial conflicts took place in the South? Mention the difficulty which occurred in procuring provisions for the Southern army, and the resolution of the South Carolina Assembly.

The effect of this measure was soon felt. Subsistence was not procured; and General Greene, after a long course of suffering, was compelled to relieve his urgent wants by an occasional recurrence to means forbidden by law.

Privations which had been borne without a murmur under the excitement of active military operations, produced great irritation when that excitement had ceased; and the discontents in the Pennsylvania line, composed chiefly of foreigners, were aggravated to such a point as to produce a treasonable intercourse with the enemy, the object of which was to seize General Greene, and deliver him to a detachment of British troops which would march out of Charleston to favor the design. It was discovered when supposed to be on the point of execution, and a serjeant was condemned and executed on the 22d of April. Twelve others deserted that night.

Charleston was held until the 14th of December. The proposal of General Leslie for a cessation of hostilities, and the supply of his troops with fresh provisions, in exchange for articles of the last necessity in the American camp, being rejected, the British general continued to supply his wants by force. This produced several skirmishes, to one of which, importance was given by the death of Lieutenant-Colonel Laurens, whose loss was universally lamented.

Such were the prospects of peace in 1782, that a reduction of the army was contemplated, by which many of the officers would be discharged. In a confidential letter to the Secretary of War, after expressing his conviction of the alacrity with which they would return to private life, could they be placed in situations as eligible as they had left at entering the service, the General added, " Yet, I cannot help fearing the result of the measure, when I see such a number of men, goaded by a thousand stings of reflection on the past, and of anticipation on the future, about to be turned on the world, soured by penury, and what they call the ingratitude of the public; involved in debt, without one farthing to carry them home, after having spent the flower of their days, and many of them, their patrimonies, in establishing the freedom and independence of their country, and having suffered every thing which human nature is capable of enduring on this side death. But you may rely on it, the patience and long-sufferance of this army are almost exhausted; and there never was so great a spirit of discontent as at this instant."

To judge rightly of the motives which produced this uneasy temper, it must be recollected, that the resolution of October, 1780,

---

What conspiracy was formed against General Greene? When was Charleston evacuated? State the substance of a letter from General Washington touching the disbandment of a part of the army.

granting half-pay for life to the officers, stood on the mere faith of a government, possessing no funds enabling it to perform its engagements. From requisitions alone, to be made on sovereign states, supplies were to be drawn; and the ill success of these, while the dangers of war were impending, furnished melancholy presages of their unproductiveness in time of peace. Other considerations, of decisive influence, were added to this reflection. The dispositions manifested by Congress itself, were so unfriendly to the half-pay establishment, as to extinguish the hope, that any funds the government might acquire would be applied to that object. Since the passage of the resolution, the articles of confederation, which required the assent of nine states to any act appropriating money, had been adopted; and nine states had never been in favor of the measure.

In October, the French troops marched to Boston, in order to embark for the West Indies; and the Americans retired into winter quarters. General Washington felt the utmost confidence that no military operations would be undertaken during the winter, which would require his presence in camp; but the irritable temper of the army furnished cause for serious apprehension : and he determined to forego every gratification to be derived from a suspension of his toils, in order to watch its discontents.

Eventual and preliminary articles of peace, between the United States and Great Britain, were signed on the 30th of November, 1782; but their effect was suspended until peace should also be concluded between that power and France. This was delayed by the persevering endeavors of Spain to recover Gibraltar. At length, the formidable armament which had invested that fortress was defeated, with immense slaughter; after which, negotiations were commenced in earnest; and preliminary articles for a peace between Great Britain, France, and Spain, were signed on the 20th of January, 1783.

In America, the officers could not look with indifference at the prospect which was opening to them. In December, they presented a petition to Congress, proposing a commutation of the half-pay for a sum in gross, which they flattered themselves would encounter fewer prejudices.

In consequence of the divisions in Congress, the question on this petition remained undecided in March, 1783; when intelligence was received of the signature of the preliminary and eventual articles of peace between the United States and Great Britain.

The officers, soured by their past sufferings, their present wants, and their gloomy prospects—exasperated by the neglect

When were articles of peace signed between the United States and Great Britain? What delayed for a while the full consummation of peace? Mention the cause of dissatisfaction among the officers of the American army.

they experienced, and the injustice they apprehended, manifested
an irritable and uneasy temper, which required only a slight impulse to give it activity. Early in March, a letter was received
from a committee, attending on their behalf in Philadelphia, showing that the objects they solicited had not been obtained. On the
10th of that month, an anonymous paper was circulated, requiring
a meeting of the general and field-officers at the public building,
at eleven in the morning of the succeeding day; and announcing
that an officer from each company, and a delegate from the medical staff would attend, " to consider the late letter from their representatives in Philadelphia, and what measures (if any) should be
adopted, to obtain that redress of grievances which they seemed
to have solicited in vain."

On the same day, an address to the army was privately circulated, which was admirably well caculated to work on the passions
of the moment, and to lead to the most desperate resolutions.

Persuaded, as the officers generally were, of the indisposition
of Congress to remunerate their services, this eloquent and im-
passioned address, dictated by genius and by feeling, found in
almost every bosom a kindred, though latent sentiment, prepared
to receive its impression.

Fortunately, the commander-in-chief was in camp. His cha-
racteristic firmness and decision did not forsake him in this crisis.
The occasion required that his measures should be firm, but prudent and conciliatory—evincive of his fixed determination to oppose any rash proceedings, but calculated to assuage the irritation
which had been excited, and to restore confidence in government.

Knowing well that it was much easier to avoid intemperate
measures, than to correct them, he thought it essential to prevent
the immediate meeting of the officers; but, knowing also that a
sense of injury, and a fear of injustice, had made a deep impression
on them, and that their sensibilities were all alive to the proceedings of Congress on their memorial, he thought it more advisable
to guide their deliberations on that interesting subject, than to dis-
countenance them.

With these views, he noticed the anonymous paper in his orders; and expressed his conviction, that their good sense would
secure them from paying any " attention to such an irregular invitation; but his own duty, he conceived, as well as the reputation and true interest of the army, required his disapprobation of
such disorderly proceedings." At the same time, he requested a
similarly constituted meeting to convene on the 15th, to hear the
report of the committee deputed by the army to Congress. " After

---

What anonymous address was circulated, calculated to inflame the officers?
State the sentiments of General Washington upon this subject, and the course
he adopted to prevent mischief.

mature deliberation, they will devise what further measures ought to be adopted, as most rational, and best calculated to obtain the just and important object in view." The senior officer present was directed to preside, and to report the result of their deliberations to the commander-in-chief. The interval between his orders and the general meeting, was employed in impressing on those who possessed the largest share of general confidence, a just sense of the true interest of the army; and the whole weight of his influence was exerted to calm the agitations of the moment. It was all required by the occasion.

On the 15th, the convention of officers assembled, and General Gates took the chair.

The commander-in-chief then addressed them, in terms well calculated to assuage the irritation which had been excited, and to give to their deliberations the direction which he wished. After animadverting with just severity on the irregular and unmilitary mutiny which had been invited, and on the dangerous and criminal anonymous paper which had been circulated through camp, he entered with affectionate warmth on their meritorious services and long sufferings, which had been witnessed with much approbation by himself, and which entitled them to the gratitude of their country, and the admiration of the world. He stated his own earnest endeavors to promote their just claims on the public, and his firm belief that Congress would make every exertion honorably to perform the engagements which had been made, and to pay the debt of gratitude and justice which had been contracted. He exhorted them to avoid the criminal measures which had been suggested; and concluded with saying, "Let me conjure you, in the name of our common country, as you value your own honor, as you respect the rights of humanity, and as you regard the military and national character of America, to express your utmost horror and detestation of the man who wishes, under any specious pretences, to overturn the liberties of our country, and who wickedly attempts to open the flood-gates of civil discord, and deluge our rising empire in blood.

"By thus determining, and thus acting, you will pursue the plain and direct road to the attainment of your wishes. You will defeat the insidious designs of our enemies, who are compelled to resort from open force to secret artifice. You will give one more distinguished proof of unexampled patriotism and patient virtue rising superior to the pressure of the most complicated sufferings; and you will, by the dignity of your conduct, afford occasion for posterity to say, when speaking of the glorious

When did the meeting of officers take place, and by whom were they addressed? State the substance of the address which General Washington delivered on this critical occasion.

example you have exhibited to mankind, had this day been want ing, the world had never seen the last stage of perfection to which human nature is capable of attaining."

These sentiments from the man whom the army had been accustomed to love, to revere, and to obey, could not fail to be irresistible. The general impression was apparent. A resolution moved by General Knox, and seconded by Brigadier-General Putnam, " assuring him that the officers reciprocated his affectionate expressions with the greatest sincerity of which the human heart is capable," was unanimously voted. A committee was then appointed to prepare resolutions on the business before them, and to report in half an hour.

The report embodied the sentiments which had been expressed by the commander-in-chief, mingling the most fervent assurances of their patriotism and devotion to their country, with their hope and expectation that Congress would speedily decide on the subject of their late application to that body.

The storm, which had been raised so suddenly, being thus happily dissipated, the commander-in-chief exerted all his influence in support of the application the officers had made to Congress.

These proceedings produced a concurrence of nine states in favor of the resolution commuting the half-pay into a sum in gross, equal to five years' full pay; immediately after the passage of which, the fears that the war might continue were dissipated by a letter from the Marquis de Lafayette, announcing a general peace; and orders were immediately issued recalling all armed vessels cruising under the authority of the United States. Early in April, an authenticated copy of the declaration announcing the exchange of ratifications of the preliminary articles between France and Great Britain was received; and, on the 19th of that month, the cessation of hostilities was proclaimed.

The reduction of the army, in the empty state of the treasury, was a critical operation. Large arrears were due to them, the immediate receipt of part of which was required by the most urgent wants; and Congress was unable to advance the pay of a single month. At the close of the year 1782, the expenditures of the Superintendent of the Finances had exceeded his receipts, including foreign loans, four hundred and four thousand seven hundred and thirteen dollars and nine-ninetieths; and the excess continued to increase rapidly.

Congress urged the states to enable him to advance a part of the arrears due to the soldiers; but, as the foreign danger diminished, they became still less attentive to there requisitions; and the

What effect was produced by Washington's speech, and what resolution and report were adopted? What arrangement was made respecting the officers' pay? Mention the condition of the national treasury.

financier was under the necessity of making farther anticipations of the revenue. Measures were taken to advance three months' pay in his notes; but, before they could be prepared, orders were issued for complying with a resolution of Congress, granting unlimited furloughs to the non-commissioned officers and privates who were engaged for the war.

The superior officers presented an address to the commander-in-chief, in which the most ardent affection to his person, and confidence in his attachment to the interests of the army, were mingled with expressions of profound duty and respect for the government. But they declared that they had confidently expected that their accounts would be liquidated, and adequate funds for the payment of the balances provided, before they should be dispersed or disbanded.

The general was equally induced by sentiment and by prudence to regard this application. Declaring "that as no man could possibly be better acquainted than himself with the past merits and services of the army, so no one could possibly be more strongly impressed with their present ineligible situation; feel a keener sensibility at their distresses; or more ardently desire to alleviate or remove them." He added, that although it was not for him, a servant of the public, to dispense with orders; yet, as furloughs are a matter of indulgence, not of compulsion, he would not hesitate, "until the farther pleasure of Congress shall be known, to comply with the wishes of the army, under this reservation only, that officers sufficient to conduct the men who choose to receive furloughs will attend them, either on furlough or on detachment."

This answer satisfied the officers; and the arrangements were made without a murmur. In October, a proclamation was issued by Congress, declaring all soldiers who had engaged for the war, to be discharged on the 3d of December.

While these excellent dispositions were manifested by the veterans serving under the eye of their patriot chief, the government was exposed to insult and outrage from the mutinous spirit of a small party of new levies.

About eighty men of this description, belonging to Pennsylvania, who were stationed at Lancaster, marched in a body to Philadelphia, with the avowed purpose of obtaining a redress of their grievances from the executive of the state. After augmenting their numbers by the junction of a few troops stationed in the barracks, they marched with fixed bayonets to the State House; and, after placing sentinels at the doors, sent in a written message, threatening the executive of the state with the vengeance of enraged sol-

On what day were the soldiers of the American army discharged by Congress? Mention the outrage offered to that body, by a small party of the Pennsylvania line.

diers if their demands were not gratified in twenty minutes. Although these threats were not directed against Congress, that body was grossly insulted, and its members were blockaded for three hours, after which they separated, to reassemble at Princeton.

On receiving information of this outrage, the commander-in-chief detached fifteen hundred men, under the command of General Howe, to suppress the mutiny. His indignation and his mortification were strongly expressed in his letter to Congress.

Before this detachment could reach Philadelphia, the disturbances were, in a great degree, quieted without bloodshed.

At length the British troops evacuated New York; and, on the 25th of November, a detachment from the American army took possession of that town. General Washington, accompanied by Governor Clinton, and attended by many civil and military officers, and a large number of respectable inhabitants, made his public entry on horseback into the city, where he was received with every mark of attention.

His military course was now on the point of terminating, and he was about to bid adieu to his comrades in arms. This affecting interview took place on the 4th of December. The principal officers assembled at Frances's tavern at noon; soon after which their beloved commander entered. His emotions were too strong to be concealed. After an affectionate embrace, and a strong manifestation of deep feeling, he left the room, and, passing through a corps of light infantry, walked to White Hall, where a barge waited to convey him to Powles Hook. The whole company followed in mute and solemn procession. Having entered the barge, he turned to the company, and, waving his hand, bid them a silent adieu. They paid him the same affectionate compliment, and returned in the same solemn manner to the place where they had assembled.

On the 19th of December, the General arrived at Annapolis, then the seat of Congress, and the next day informed that body that he attended for the purpose of resigning the commission he had the honor of holding in their service. They determined that his resignation should be received on Tuesday the 23d, at twelve, at a public audience.

When the hour arrived for performing a ceremony which recalled to the memory so many interesting scenes, the gallery was crowded with spectators, and several persons of distinction were admitted on the floor of Congress. The General was introduced by the Secretary, and conducted to a chair. After a short pause, the President informed him that "the United States in Congress

When did Washington enter New York city, after its evacuation by the enemy? Relate the particulars of his interview with his officers, and his departure towards the South. What took place when he arrived at Annapolis?

assembled were prepared to receive his communications." The General rose, and, in a short and impressive speech, tendered his commission. After retiring to his chair, he received, standing, the flattering answer of Congress, which was delivered by the President.

This interesting scene being closed, the American chief withdrew from the hall of Congress, leaving the silent and admiring spectators deeply impressed with those sentiments which its solemnity and dignity were calculated to inspire.

Divested of his military character, General Washington retired to Mount Vernon, followed by the enthusiastic love, esteem, and admiration of his countrymen. Relieved from the agitations of a doubtful contest, and from the toils of an exalted station, he returned with increased delight to the duties and the enjoyments of a private citizen. He indulged the hope that, in the shade of retirement, under the protection of a free government, and the benignant influence of mild and equal laws, he might taste that felicity which is the reward of a mind at peace with itself, and conscious of its own purity.

CHAPTER XXV.

General Washington devotes his time to agriculture, to the duties of friendship, and to institutions of public utility.—Resolves of Congress and of the Legislature of Virginia for erecting statues to his honor.—He recommends the improvement of internal navigation.—Declines accepting a donation offered by his native state.—The Society of the Cincinnati.—The causes which led to a change of the government of the United States.—Circular letter to the Governors of the several states.

WHEN an individual, long in possession of great power, and almost unlimited influence, retires from office with alacrity, and resumes the character of a private citizen with pleasure, the mind is gratified in contemplating the example of virtuous moderation, and dwells upon it with approving satisfaction. Such was the example exhibited by General Washington. His feelings were thus described in his letter to his friend Lafayette:—"I have not only retired from all public employments, but am retiring within myself, and shall be able to view the solitary walk, and tread the paths of private life, with heartfelt satisfaction. Envious of none, I am determined to be pleased with all; and this, my dear friend, being the order of my march, I will move gently down the stream of life, until I sleep with my fathers."

Every day brought to Mount Vernon testimonials of the grateful and ardent affection universally felt by his fellow-citizens. Con-

---

Mention the course of life adopted by Washington, after his resignation. What sentiments did he express in a letter to Lafayette? How did his countrymen testify their gratitude?

21*

gress, soon after peace was proclaimed, unanimously passed a resolution for the erection of an equestrian statue of their General, at the place which should be established as the seat of government. The legislature of Virginia, too, at its first session after his resignation, passed the following resolution.

"Resolved that the executive be requested to take measures for procuring a statue of General Washington, to be of the finest marble and best workmanship, with the following inscription on its pedestal :

"The general assembly of the commonwealth of Virginia have caused this statue to be erected as a monument of affection and gratitute to George Washington, who, uniting to the endowments of the hero, the virtues of the patriot, and exerting both in establishing the liberties of his country, has rendered his name dear to his fellow-citizens, and given the world an immortal example of true glory."

This statue stands in the capitol of his native state.

The time of Washington was now chiefly devoted to agriculture, that great source of national prosperity. The energies of his active mind were directed to its improvement. His energies were extended beyond his own country ; and he entered into a correspondence on this interesting subject with those foreigners who had been most distinguished for their additions to the stock of agricultural science.

Mingled with this favorite pursuit, were the multiplied avocations resulting from the high office he had lately filled. But their numerous occupations could not withdraw his mind entirely from objects tending to promote and secure the prosperity of his country.

A person looking beyond the present moment, could not inspect the map of the United States, without perceiving the importance of connecting the west with the east, by facilitating the intercourse between them.

The attention of General Washington had been directed to this subject in early life ; and he had obtained the passage of a bill for opening the Potomac and the James. This business was in a train which promised success when the war of the revolution diverted the attention of its patrons from internal improvements to the still greater objects of liberty and independence. As that war approached its termination, internal navigation reclaimed its just place with the wise and thinking part of society.

Accustomed to contemplate America as his country, Washington now took a more enlarged view of the advantages to be derived from opening both the eastern and western waters. After peace had been proclaimed, he traversed the western parts of New

To what was the time of Washington chiefly devoted ? What other pursuit claimed a share of his attention ? Did he, at an early period, perceive the advantages of easy internal communication ?

England and New York; and saw with prophetic eye the immense advantages which have since been derived from executing the plans he meditated.

Scarcely had he answered those spontaneous offerings of the heart which flowed in upon him from every part of a grateful nation, when his views were seriously turned to this interesting subject. In the autumn of 1784, he made a tour as far west as Pittsburg; after returning from which, his first moments of leisure were devoted to the task of engaging his countrymen in a work which appeared to him to merit still more attention from its political, than from its commercial influence on the Union. In a long and interesting letter to the Governor of Virginia, he detailed the advantages which might be derived from opening the great rivers, the Potomac and the James, as far as should be practicable. His plan also extended to the navigable waters of the west, and to a communication with the great lakes of that region. By these means alone, he thought, could the connexion of the western with the Atlantic country be preserved. This idea was pressed with much earnestness in his letters to several members of Congress.

His letter to the Governor of Virginia was communicated to the legislature, and the internal improvements it recommended were zealously supported by the wisest members of that body. While the subject remained undecided, General Washington, accompanied by the Marquis de Lafayette, who had crossed the Atlantic for the purpose of devoting a part of his time to the delights of an enthusiastic friendship, paid a visit to the capital of the state. Amidst the festivities which were produced by the occasion, the great business of internal improvement was assiduously pressed; and the ardour of the moment was seized to conquer those objections to the plan which still lingered in the bosoms of members who thought that no future advantages could compensate for the present expense.

An exact conformity between the acts of Virginia and Maryland being indispensable to the improvement of the Potomac, a resolution was passed soon after the return of General Washington to Mount Vernon, requesting him to attend the legislature of Maryland, in order to agree on a bill which might receive the sanction of both states. This agreement being happily completed, those bills were enacted which form the first essay towards connecting the navigation of the eastern with the western waters of the United States.

These acts were succeeded by one which conveys the liberal wishes of the legislature with a delicacy not less honorable to its

What views of internal navigation were expressed in Washington's letter to the Governor of Virginia? Who came from Europe, to visit Washington? What acts were passed by Virginia and Maryland?

framers than to him who was its object. The treasurer had been
instructed to subscribe, in behalf of the state, for a specified number of shares in each company. At the close of the session, a
bill was suddenly brought in, and passed unanimously by both
houses, authorizing the treasurer to subscribe for the benefit of
General Washington, the same number of shares in each company
as were to be taken for the state. A preamble was prefixed to the
enacting clause of this bill, which enhanced its value. With sim-
ple elegance it conveyed the sentiment that, in seizing this occasion
to make a donation which would in some degree testify their sense
of the merits of their most favored and most illustrious citizen,
the donors would themselves be the obliged.

This delicate and flattering testimony of the affection of his
fellow-citizens was not without its embarrassments. From his
early resolution to receive no pecuniary compensation for his services, he could not permit himself to depart; and yet this mark
of the gratitude and attachment of his country could not easily
be rejected, without furnishing occasion for sentiments he was
unwilling to excite. To the friend who conveyed to him the first
intelligence of this bill, his difficulties were fully expressed.

A correspondence with the Governor on this subject was closed
with a letter in which he said, " whilst I repeat therefore my fervent acknowledgments to the legislature for their very kind sentiments and intentions in my favor, and at the same time beg them
to be persuaded that a remembrance of this singular proof of their
goodness towards me will never cease to cherish returns of the
warmest affection and gratitude, I must pray that their act, so far
as it has for its object my personal emolument, may not have its
effect; but if it should please the General Assembly to permit me
to turn the destination of the fund vested in me, from my private
emolument to objects of a public nature, it will be my study, in
selecting these, to prove the sincerity of my gratitude for the honor
conferred upon me, by preferring such as may appear most subservient to the enlightened and patriotic views of the legislature."

The wish suggested in this letter was gratified: and, at a subsequent time, the trust was executed by conveying the shares respectively, to the use of a seminary of learning established in the
vicinity of each river.

General Washington felt too strong an interest in the success
of these works, to refuse the presidency of the companies instituted
for their completion.

These were not the only institutions which occasionally drew
the farmer of Mount Vernon from his retreat.

In what manner did the legislature of Virginia endeavor to enrich General Washington? Upon what grounds did he decline accepting the bounty,
which they were anxious to bestow?

The sentiments with which the officers of the American army contemplated a final separation from each other will be comprehended by all who are conversant with the feelings of the human heart. Companions in virtuous suffering, in danger, and in glory—attached to each other by common exertions made in a severe struggle for the attainment of a common object—they felt that to part forever was a calamity too afflicting to be supported. The means of perpetuating those friendships which had been formed, and of renewing that endearing social intercourse which had taken place in camp, were universally desired. Some expedient was sought which might preserve the memory of the army, while it cheered the officers who were on the point of separating with the hope that the separation would not be eternal; that the bonds by which they were connected would not be totally dissolved; and that for many beneficial purposes, they would still form one great society.

This idea was suggested by General Knox, and matured in a meeting at which the Baron Steuben presided. An agreement was then entered into by which the officers were to constitute themselves into one society of friends, to be denominated the society of the Cincinnati, to endure as long as they should endure, or any of their eldest male posterity; and, in failure thereof, any collateral branches judged worthy of becoming members were to be admitted into it. Distinguished individuals of the respective states might be admitted as honorary members for life.

The society was to be designated by a medal of gold representing the American eagle. The insignia of the order were to be presented to the ministers who had represented his Most Christian Majesty at Philadelphia, and to the French officers who had served in the United States, and they were to be invited to consider themselves as members of the society, at the head of which the commander-in-chief was respectfully solicited to place his name.

An incessant attention to the preservation of the exalted rights and privileges of human nature, and an unalterable determination to promote and cherish union and national honor between the respective states, were declared to be the immutable principles of the society. Its objects were to perpetuate the remembrance of the American revolution, as well as cordial affection and the spirit of brotherly kindness among the officers, and to extend acts of beneficence to those officers and their families who might require assistance. For this purpose a common fund was to be created by the contribution of one month's pay on the part of each officer becoming a member.

The military gentlemen of each state were to constitute a dis-

What considerations gave rise to the society of the Cincinnati? What were the principles and regulations of this association? Who were to constitute its members?

tinct society, deputies from which were to assemble triennially in order to form a general meeting.

Soon after the organization of this institution, those jealousies which had in its first moments been concealed, burst forth into open view. In October 1783, a pamphlet was published by Mr. Burk of South Carolina, pourtraying in the fervid and impetuous language of passion the dangers to equal rights with which it was supposed to be replete. The alarm was spread through every state and a high degree of jealousy pervaded the mass of the people.

It was impossible for General Washington to view this state of the public feeling with indifference. Bound to the officers of the army by the strictest ties of esteem and affection, he was alive to every thing which might affect their reputation or their interest. However ill-founded the public prejudices might be, he thought this a case in which they ought to be respected; and if it should be found impracticable to convince the people that their fears were misplaced, he was disposed " to yield to them in a degree, and not to suffer that which was intended for the best of purposes, to produce a bad one."

A general meeting was to be held in Philadelphia in May 1784, and, in the meantime, he had been appointed temporary president. The most exact enquiries assiduously made into the true state of the public mind, resulted in a conviction that opinions unfriendly to the institution, in its actual form, were extensively entertained; and that those opinions were founded in real apprehensions for equal liberty.

A wise and necessary policy required, he thought, the removal of these apprehensions; and at the general meeting in May, the hereditary principle, and the power of adopting honorary members, were relinquished. The result demonstrated the propriety of this alteration.

While General Washington thus devoted his time to rural pursuits, to the duties of friendship, and to institutions of public utility, the political state of his country, becoming daily more embarrassed, attracted more and more deeply the anxious solicitude of every enlightened and virtuous patriot. From peace, from independence, and from governments of their own choice, the United States had confidently anticipated every blessing. The glorious termination of their contest with one of the most powerful nations of the earth; the steady and persevering courage with which that contest had been maintained, and the unyielding firmness with which the privations attending it had been supported, had surrounded the infant republics with a great degree of splendor, and

Did this society become the subject of popular disfavor? What alterations were made, to remove this hostile feeling? Were these changes acceptable to the people?

had bestowed upon them a character which could be preserved only by a national and dignified system of conduct. A very short time was sufficient to demonstrate that something not yet possessed was requisite, to ensure the public and private prosperity expected to flow from self-government. After a short struggle so to administer the existing system as to make it competent to the great objects for which it was instituted, the effort became apparently desperate; and American affairs were impelled rapidly to a crisis, on which the continuance of the United States as a nation appeared to depend.

A government authorized to declare war, but relying on independent states for the means of prosecuting it, capable of contracting debts, but depending on thirteen distinct sovereignties for the means of payment, could not be rescued from ignominy and contempt but by finding those sovereignties administered by men exempt from the passions incident to human nature.

It has been already stated that the continent was divided into two great political parties, the one of which contemplated America as a nation, and labored incessantly to invest Congress with powers competent to the preservation of the Union. The other attached itself to the state governments, viewed all the powers of Congress with jealousy, and assented reluctantly to measures, however indispensable, which would enable the head to act, in any respect independently of the members. Men of enlarged and liberal minds who, in the imbecility of the General Government could discern the imbecility of the nation itself, who felt the full value of national character, and the full obligation of national faith, arranged themselves in the first party. The officers of the army, whose local prejudices had been weakened by associating with each other, and whose experience had furnished lessons on the inefficacy of requisitions not soon to be forgotten, threw their weight into the same scale.

The other party, if not more intelligent, was more numerous and more powerful. It was nourished by prejudices and feelings which grew without effort, and gained strength from the intimate connexion between a state and its citizens. It required a concurrence of extrinsic circumstances to force on minds unwilling to receive the demonstration, a conviction of the necessity of an effective national government, and to give even a temporary ascendency to that party which had long foreseen and deplored the crisis to which the affairs of the United States were hastening.

Sensible that the character of the government would be decided by the measures which should immediately follow the treaty of

---

Did the people of the United States derive from their new political condition the advantages that were anticipated? To what causes must we attribute the inefficiency of the national government?

peace, patriots of the first ability sought a place in the Congress of 1783. Combining their efforts for the establishment of principles which might maintain the honor and promote the interests of the nation, they exerted all their talents to impress on the states the necessity of conferring powers on the government which might be competent to its preservation. With unwearied perseverance, they obtained the assent of Congress to a system which, though unequal to what their judgments would have approved, was believed to be the best that was attainable.

The committee to whom this interesting subject was referred, reported sundry resolutions recommending it to the several states to vest in Congress permanent funds, adequate to the immediate payment of the interest on the national debt, and to the gradual extinction of the principal.

After a tedious debate, the report was adopted; and a committee, consisting of Mr. Madison, Mr. Hamilton, and Mr. Ellsworth, was appointed to prepare an address, which should accompany the recommendation to the several states.

This able state paper will excite, even at this day, emotions of admiration for its authors, and of astonishment at its failure. In the refusal of the states to comply with the measures it recommended, we find a complete demonstration of the impracticability of preserving union without investing its government with adequate powers.

No person felt more anxious solicitude for the complete success of the plan recommended by Congress, than General Washington.

Availing himself of the usage of communicating on national subjects with the state governments, and of the opportunity given by his approaching resignation of the command of the army, to convey to them his sentiments impressively, he had determined to employ all the influence which the circumstances of his life had created, in earnest recommendation of measures on which the happiness and prosperity of his country were believed to depend. On the 8th of June, 1783, he addressed a paternal and affectionate letter to the Governors of the respective states, in which his congratulations on the successful termination of their revolutionary struggle, and on the high destinies in prospect, were mingled with solemn admonitions warning them of the perils with which their new situation was environed. With impressive earnestness he urged upon them " four things," as essential " to the existence of the United States as an independent power."

" 1st. An indissoluble union of the states under one federal head.

What was recommended by a committee of Congress, with a view to the procurement of funds for national purposes? State the substance of a letter of Washington to the Governors of the states.

" 2d. A sacred regard to public justice.

" 3d. The adoption of a proper peace establishment.

" 4th. The prevalence of that pacific and friendly disposition among the people of the United States, which will induce them to forget their local prejudices and politics, to make those mutual concessions which are requisite to the general prosperity, and, in some instances, to sacrifice their individual advantages to the interest of the community."

The letter enlarged upon these topics, and pressed them on the consideration of those to whom it was addressed, with that anxious earnestness which grew out of a most devoted love of country, and a deep-felt conviction that the prosperity of that country would be determined by the measures it was about to adopt.

This solemn and affecting admonition was laid by the Governors of the several states before their respective assemblies. Its impression could not be surpassed. Like the counsel of a parent, on whom the grave is about to close forever, it sunk deep into the hearts of all. But, like the counsels of a parent withdrawn from view, the advice was too soon forgotten.

The recommendations of Congress did not receive that prompt consideration which the exigence demanded, nor did they meet that universal assent which was necessary to give them effect.

Not immediately perceiving that the error lay in a system which was unfit for use, the distinguished patriots of the revolution contemplated with increasing anxiety, the anti-American temper which displayed itself in almost every part of the Union.

That the imbecility of the federal government, and the impotence of its requisitions, would abase the American character in the estimation of the world, was no longer a prediction. That course of national degradation had already commenced.

While the system recommended on the 18th of April, 1783, was depending before the states, requisitions for the intermediate supply of the national demands were annually repeated by Congress, and were annually neglected. Happily, a loan had been negotiated in Holland by Mr. Adams, out of which the interest of the foreign debt had been partly paid; but that fund was exhausted, and the United States had no means of replacing it. Unable to pay the interest, they would, in the succeeding year, be liable for the firs instalment of the principal; and the humiliating circumstance was to be encountered of a total failure to comply with the most solemn engagements, unaccompanied with the prospect of being enabled to give assurances that, at any future time, their situation would be more eligible. If the condition of the domestic creditors was not

Were the necessities of the general government attended to by the states? What circumstances of discredit and humiliation were consequent upon this neglect?

22

absolutely desperate, their prospect of obtaining payment was so distant and uncertain, that their evidences of debt were transferred at an eighth, and even at a tenth of their nominal value.

In 1786, the revenue system of April, 1783, was again solemnly recommended to the consideration of the several states, and again failed to receive their unanimous assent; and thus was finally defeated the laborious and persevering effort made by Congress to obtain the means of preserving the faith of the nation.

General Washington's letters of that period abound with passages showing the solicitude with which he watched the progress of this recommendation. In a letter of October, 1785, he said— "The war has terminated most advantageously for America, and a fair field is presented to our view; but I confess to you freely, my dear sir, that I do not think we possess wisdom or justice enough to cultivate it properly. Illiberality, jealousy, and local policy, mix too much in our public counsels for the good government of the Union. In a word, the confederation appears to me to be little more than a shadow without the substance; and Congress a nugatory body, their ordinances being little attended to. To me, it is a solecism in politics;—indeed, it one of the most extraordinary things in nature, that we should confederate as a nation; and yet be afraid to give the rulers of that nation, who are the creatures of our own making, appointed for a limited and short duration, and who are amenable for every action, recallable at any moment, and subject to all the evils they may be instrumental in producing—sufficient powers to order and direct the affairs of the same. By such policy as this the wheels of government are clogged; and our brightest prospects, and that high expectation which was entertained of us by the wondering world, are turned into astonishment."

CHAPTER XXVI.

Differences between the United States and Great Britain.—Mr. Adams appointed Minister to Great Britain.—Discontents excited by the commercial regulations of that power.—Parties in the United States.—Convention at Annapolis—Virginia appoints deputies to a convention at Philadelphia.—General Washington chosen one of them.—Insurrection in Massachusetts.—Convention at Philadelphia.—Form of government submitted to the several states.—Ratified by eleven of them.—General Washington elected President.—Meeting of the first Congress.

WHILE the friends of the national government were making these unavailing efforts to invest it with a revenue which might enable it to preserve the national faith, many causes concurred

---

Was the revenue system again submitted to the several states, without securing their concurrence? State the substance of Washington's letter in reference to this important subject.

to prepare the public mind for some great and radical change in the political system of America.

Scarcely had the war of the revolution terminated, when the United States and Great Britain reciprocally charged each other with violations of the treaty of peace. A serious difference of opinion prevailed, on the construction of that part of the seventh article which stipulates against the "destruction or carrying away of any negroes, or other property of the American inhabitants." In addition to this circumstance, the troops of his Britannic majesty still retained possession of the posts on the American side of the great lakes; which gave them a decided influence over the warlike tribes of Indians in their neighborhood.

On the other hand, the United States were charged with infringing the fourth, fifth, and sixth articles, which contain agreements respecting the payment of debts, the confiscation of property, and prosecution of individuals, for the part taken by them during the war.

These causes of mutual complaint, being permitted to rankle for some time in the bosoms of both nations, produced a considerable degree of irritation.

But the cause of most extensive disquiet was, the vigorous commercial system pursued by Great Britain. While colonists, the Americans had carried on a free and gainful trade with the British West Indies. These ports were closed against them, as citizens of an independent state; and their accustomed intercourse with other parts of the empire, was also interrupted by the Navigation Act. To explore new channels of commerce, was opposed by obstacles which almost discouraged the attempt. On every side, they met with rigorous and unexpected restrictions. Their trade with the colonies of other powers, as well as with those of England, was prohibited; and they encountered regulations in all the ports of Europe, which were extremely embarrassing. From the Mediterranean, they were excluded by the Barbary powers; whose hostility they had no force to subdue, and whose friendship they had no money to purchase.

With many, the desire of counteracting this injurious system triumphed over the attachment to state sovereignty; and the converts to the opinion that Congress ought to be empowered to regulate trade, were daily multiplied. Meanwhile, the United States were unremitting in their endeavors to form commercial treaties. Three commissioners had been deputed for that purpose; and at length, Mr. John Adams was appointed minister plenipotentiary to the court of St. James. His endeavors were not suc-

What differences occurred between the United States and Great Britain? Mention the circumstances of restriction which repressed the activity of American commerce,

cessful.   His overtures were declined, because the government of
the United States was unable to secure the observance of any
general commercial regulations.

Many other causes contributed to diffuse such a general dissatisfaction with the existing state of things, as to prepare the way
for some essential change in the American system.   In the course
of the long war which had been carried on in the bosom of their
country, the people of the United States had been greatly impove-
rished.   Their property had been seized for the support of both
armies; much of their labor had been drawn from agriculture for
military service; the naval power of the enemy had almost annihilated their commerce; those consumable articles which habit
had rendered necessary, were exhausted; and peace found the
American people not only destitute of the elegancies, and even of
the conveniences of life, but also without the means of procuring
them, otherwise than by anticipating the proceeds of future industry.   On opening their ports, an immense quantity of foreign
merchandise was introduced into the country; and they were
tempted, by the sudden cheapness of imported goods, and by their
own wants, to purchase beyond their capacities for payment.
Under the impression made by paper-money, many individuals
had made extensive purchases, at high prices, and had thus contributed to prolong the deception imposed upon themselves by
those who supposed that the revolution was a talisman whose
magic powers were capable of changing the nature of things.   The
delusive hopes created by these visionary calculations, were soon
dissipated; and a great proportion of the people found themselves
involved in debts they were unable to discharge.

The consequence of this unprosperous state of things was, a
general dissatisfaction with the course of trade, and a desire to
compel foreign nations, by retaliatory restrictions, to the adoption
of a more liberal and equal system.   These dispositions displayed
themselves in angry publications, animated resolutions, and addresses to the state legislatures and to the general government,
urging the necessity of investing Congress with power to regulate
commerce.

During these transactions, the public attention was called to
another subject, which increased the impression made on every
reflecting mind, of the necessity of enlarging the powers of the
general government.

The uneasiness occasioned by the infractions of the treaty of
peace on the part of Great Britain, has been noticed.   To obtain
its complete execution, constituted one of the objects for which

What causes concurred to distress the American people, and to force upon
them the conviction, that the powers of the national government were inadequate to the purpose for which it was instituted?

Mr. Adams had been deputed to the Court of St. James. A memorial from that minister, pressing for a full compliance with the treaty, was answered by an explicit acknowledgment of the obligations created by the seventh article, to evacuate every post within the United States. But the British minister insisted, that the obligation to remove every lawful impediment to the recovery of bona fide debts, was equally clear;- and concluded his letter with the assurance, "that whenever America should manifest a real determination to fulfil her part of the treaty, Great Britain would not hesitate to prove her sincerity to co-operate in whatever points depended on her for carrying every article of it into real and complete effect."

Copies of both documents were immediately transmitted to Congress, by whom they were referred to Mr. Jay, the Minister of Foreign Affairs. The report of that upright minister did not affect to exculpate his country.

The government of the United States did not possess the power to carry the treaty into execution on their part; and this inability rendered any attempt to obtain its prior execution on the part of Great Britain entirely hopeless.

The discontents arising from the embarrassments of individuals continued to increase. At length, two great parties were formed in every state, which pursued distinct objects with systematic arrangement.

The one struggled for the exact observance of public and private contracts. Those who composed it were the uniform friends of a regular administration of justice, and of a vigorous course of taxation, which would enable the state to comply with its engagements. By a natural association of ideas, they were also in favor of enlarging the powers of the federal government, and of enabling it to protect the dignity and the character of the nation abroad, and its interests at home.

The other party marked out for themselves a more indulgent course. They were uniformly in favor of relaxing the administration of justice, of affording facilities for the payment of debts or of suspending their collection, and of remitting taxes. The same course of opinion led them to resist every attempt to transfer from their own hands into those of Congress, powers which others deemed essential to the preservation of the Union. Wherever this party was predominant, the emission of paper-money, the delay of legal proceedings, and the suspension of taxes, were the fruits of their rule. Even where they failed to carry their measures, their strength was such as to encourage the hope of succeeding in a

What was the reply of Great Britain, when urged by America to fulfil the stipulations of the treaty of 1783? What two parties now arose in the United States, and what were their distinctive characteristics?

22*

future attempt. Throughout the Union the contest between these parties was annually revived, and the public mind was perpetually agitated with hopes and fears on subjects which affected essentially the fortunes of a considerable portion of society. This instability in principles which ought to be rendered immutable, produced a long train of ills ; and is believed to have been among the operating causes of those pecuniary embarrassments which influenced the legislation of almost every state. The wise and thinking part of the community, who could trace evils to their source, laboured unceasingly to inculcate opinions favorable to the incorporation of some principles into the political system, which might correct its obvious vices, without endangering its free spirit.

While the advocates of union were exerting themselves to impress its necessity on the public mind, measures were taken in Virginia which, though originating in different views, terminated in a proposition for a general convention to revive the federal system.

Commissioners were appointed by the legislatures of that state, and of Maryland, to form a compact relative to the navigation of the rivers Potomac and Pocomoke, and part of the bay of Chesapeake, who assembled in Alexandria in March 1785. While at Mount Vernon on a visit, they agreed to propose to their respective governments the appointment of other commissioners, with power to make conjoint arrangements with the assent of Congress, for maintaining a naval force in the Chesapeake ; and to establish a tariff of duties on imports. Virginia also directed that the resolution relative to the duties on imports should be communicated to all the states in the Union, who were invited to send deputies to the meeting.

A few days after the passage of these resolutions, another was adopted appointing commissioners, "who were to meet such as might be appointed by the other states in the Union, at a time and place to be agreed on, to take into consideration the trade of the United States," "and to report to the several states such an act relative to this great object, as, when unanimously ratified by them, will enable the United States in Congress assembled, effectually to provide for the same."

Annapolis in Maryland was proposed as the place, and the ensuing September as the time of meeting. Before the arrival of the time at which these commissioners were to assemble, the idea was carried, by those who saw and deplored the complicated calamities which flowed from the inefficiency of the General Government, much farther than was avowed by the resolutions of Virginia.

To what cause may be justly attributed the embarrassments which prevailed in the United States ? Mention the circumstances which led to a proposition from Virginia, that deputies from all the states should assemble at Annapolis, in March, 1785.

The convention at Annapolis was attended by commissioners from only five states. Perceiving that more ample powers would be required to effect the beneficial purposes which they contemplated, and hoping to procure a representation from a greater number of states, the convention determined to rise without coming to any specific resolutions on the subject referred to them. They agreed, however, on a report to be made to their respective states, in which they represented the necessity of extending the revision of the federal system to all its defects, and recommended that deputies for that purpose be appointed by the several legislatures, to meet in convention in the city of Philadelphia, on the second day of the ensuing May.

A copy of this report was transmitted to Congress, and to the legislatures of the respective states. On receiving it, the legislature of Virginia passed an act for the appointment of deputies to meet such as might be appointed by other states.

In communicating this act to General Washington, Mr. Madison, its most effective advocate, intimated the intention of aiding it by the influence and character of the chief of the revolution.

"Although," said the General in reply, "I have bid a public adieu to the public walks of life, and had resolved never more to tread that theatre; yet, if upon an occasion so interesting to the well-being of the confederacy, it had been the wish of the assembly that I should be an associate in the business of revising the federal system, I should, from a sense of the obligation I am under for repeated proofs of confidence in me, more than from any opinion I could entertain of my usefulness, have obeyed its call; but it is now out of my power to do this with any degree of consistency—the cause I will mention."

The General then proceeded to state, that the triennial general meeting of the Cincinnati was to be held in Philadelphia at the time the convention was to assemble. He had, a few days previously, addressed a circular-letter to each state society and to the Vice-President, informing them of his intention not to be at the meeting, and of his desire not to be re-chosen President. He could not consent to appear at the same time and place, on any other occasion.

Notwithstanding this letter, the name of General Washington was not withdrawn, and he was unanimously chosen a member of the convention. On receiving private information of this appointment, he addressed a second letter to his confidential friend, detailing more at large the motives which induced him to decline a service the importance of which no man felt more sensibly.

What was done by the convention at Annapolis? Was General Washington reluctant to become a member of the proposed convention at Philadelphia? Mention the chief motive which influenced him?

His name, however, was continued in the appointment. The gloomy state of affairs in the North was supposed to render this the more necessary.

The Governor of Virginia, who was himself elected a member of the convention, transmitted to him the act and the vote of the assembly in a letter, pressing most earnestly on him all those motives for yielding to the general wish, which were furnished by the importance of the crisis, and the gloomy state of American affairs. He was urged, at all events, not to decide positively against it, but to leave himself at liberty to be determined by future events.

General Washington, however, still thought that the delicacy of his situation obliged him to decline the appointment. But it was obvious, that he refused himself reluctantly to the anxious wishes of the wisest of his countrymen; and the executive, unwilling to relinquish the advantages which the legislature expected to derive from exhibiting his name at the head of the Virginia delegation, refused to consider him as having declined the appointment. In the meantime those who expected much good from the proposed convention, continued to urge him, with delicacy but with earnestness, not to withhold on this great and particular occasion, those inestimable services which the confidence so justly reposed in his talents and character enabled him alone to render.

Earnestly as General Washington wished success to the experiment about to be made, he could not surrender his objections to the step its friends urged him to take, without the most serious consideration. In addition to that which grew out of his connexion with the Cincinnati, and to his reluctance to be drawn, on any occasion, into a political station, there were others which could not be disregarded. A convention, not originating in a recommendation of Congress, was deemed by many an illegitimate meeting; and, as the New England states had neglected the invitation to appear by their delegates at Annapolis, it was apprehended they might be equally inattentive to the request now made them to assemble at Philadelphia. To appear in a public character for a purpose not generally deemed of the utmost importance, would not only be unpleasant to himself, but diminish his capacity to be useful on occasions which subsequent events might produce. His enquiries therefore into the public sentiment were carefully and assiduously made.

The ultimate decision of the states on this interesting proposition seems to have been influenced, in no inconsiderable degree, by the commotions which at that time agitated all New England, and particularly Massachusetts.

In what way was Washington repeatedly urged to lend the weight of his name to the proposed convention?

Those causes of discontent which existed in every part of the Union, were particularly operative in New England. The great exertions which had been made by those states in support of the war had accumulated a mass of debt, the taxes for the payment of which were the more burdensome, because their fisheries had become unproductive. The restlessness produced by the uneasy situation of individuals, connected with lax notions concerning public and private faith, and erroneous opinions which confound liberty with an exemption from the control of law, produced a state of things which alarmed all reflecting men.

This disorderly spirit was stimulated by unlicensed conventions, which, after voting their own constitutionality, and assuming the name of the people, arrayed themselves against the legislature, and detailed, at great length, the grievances by which they alleged themselves to be oppressed. Its hostility was directed principally against the compensation promised to the officers of the army, against taxes, and against the administration of justice. A depreciated currency was required, as a relief from the pressure of public and private burdens, which had become, it was alleged, too heavy to be longer borne. To such a dangerous extent were these dispositions indulged, that, in many instances, tumultuous assemblages arrested the course of law, and restrained the judges from proceeding in the execution of their duty. The ordinary recourse to the power of the country was found an insufficient protection, and the appeals made to reason were unavailing. The forbearance of the government was attributed to timidity, rather than to moderation, and the spirit of insurrection appeared to be organized into a regular system for the suppression of courts.

In the bosom of Washington, these tumults excited attention and alarm. To a member of Congress, who suggested the idea of resorting to his influence for the purpose of quieting them, he said— 'You talk, my good sir, of employing influence to appease the present tumults of Massachusetts; I know not where that influence is to be found; nor, if attainable, that it would be a proper remedy for these disorders. *Influence* is not *government*. Let us have a *government*, by which our lives, liberties, and properties will be secured; or let us know the worst at once. Under these impressions, my humble opinion is that there is a call for decision. Know precisely what the insurgents aim at. If they have *real* grievances, redress them, if possible; or acknowledge the justice of them, and your inability to do it in the present moment. If they have not, employ the force of the government against them at once."

What were the chief causes of the popular commotions in New England? Was the course of the law arrested? What was the opinion of Washington, as to the proper mode of dealing with the insurgents?

Finding that the lenient measures adopted by the legislature, to reclaim the insurgents, only enlarged their demands; and that they were proceeding systematically to organize a military force for the subversion of the constitution, Governor Bowdoin determined, with the advice of his council, on a vigorous exertion of all the powers he possessed, for the protection and defence of the commonwealth. Upwards of four thousand militia were ordered into service, and were placed under the command of the veteran General Lincoln. The difficulty arising from an empty treasury was removed by the patriotism of individuals. A number of gentlemen in Boston, preceded by the Governor, subscribed a sufficient sum to carry on the proposed expedition.

In the depth of winter, the troops from the eastern part of the state assembled near Boston, and marched towards the scene of action. Those from the western counties, met in arms under General Shepard, and took possession of the arsenal at Springfield. Before the arrival of Lincoln, a party of insurgents attempted to dislodge Shepard, but were repulsed with some loss.

Lincoln urged his march with the utmost celerity, and soon came up. Pressing the insurgent army, he endeavored by a succession of rapid movements, in which the ardor of his troops triumphed over the severity of the season, to disperse, or to bring it to action. Their generals retreated from post to post, with a celerity which, for some time, eluded his designs; and, rejecting every proposition to lay down their arms, used all their address to procure a suspension of hostilities until an accommodation might be negotiated with the legislature. "Applications were also made," says General Lincoln, " by committees and selectmen of the several towns in the counties of Worcester and Hampshire, praying that the effusion of blood might be avoided, while the real design of these applications was supposed to be, to stay our operations until a new court should be elected. They had no doubt, if they could keep up their influence until another choice of the legislature and of the executive, that matters might be moulded in general court to their wishes. To avoid this was the duty of government." In answer to their applications, Lincoln exhorted those towns who sincerely wished to put an end to the rebellion, without the effusion of blood, " to recall their men now in arms, and to aid in apprehending all abettors of those who should persist in their treason, and all who should yield them any comfort or supplies."

The army of the government continued to brave the rigors of the season, and to press the insurgents without intermission. At length, with the loss of a few killed, and several prisoners, the rebels were dispersed, their leaders driven out of the state, and this formidable and wicked rebellion was quelled.

The same love of country which had supported the officers and soldiers of the late army through a perilous war, still glowed in their bosoms; and the patriot veterans of the revolution, uninfected by the wide-spreading contagion of the times, arranged themselves, almost universally, under the banners of the constitution and of the laws.

The most important effect of this unprovoked rebellion, was a deep conviction of the necessity of enlarging the powers of the general government; and the consequent direction of the public mind towards the convention which was to assemble at Philadelphia.

In producing this effect, a resolution of Congress had also considerable influence.

New York, by giving her final *veto* to the impost system, had virtually decreed the dissolution of the existing government. The confederation was apparently expiring from mere debility. Congress was restrained from giving its sanction to the proposed convention, only by the apprehension that taking an interest in the measure would impede rather than promote it. That body was at length relieved from this embarrassment by the legislature of New York. A vote of that state, which passed in the senate by a majority of only one voice, instructed its delegation to move a resolution in Congress, recommending to the several states to appoint deputies to meet in convention, for the purpose of revising and proposing amendments to the federal constitution. On the succeeding day, the 21st of February, 1787, it was declared, " in the opinion of Congress, to be expedient that, on the second Monday in May next, a convention of delegates, who shall have been appointed by the several states, be held at Philadelphia, for the sole and express purpose of revising the articles of confederation, and reporting to Congress, and the several legislatures, such alterations and provisions therein as shall, when agreed to in Congress, and confirmed by the states, render the federal constitution adequate to the exigencies of government, and the preservation of the Union."

This recommendation removed all objections to the regularity of the convention; and co-operated with the impressions made by the licentious and turbulent spirit which had lately endangered the peace and liberty of New England, to incline those states to favor the measure. By giving the proposed meeting a constitutional sanction, and by postponing it to a day subsequent to that on which the Cincinnati were to assemble, it also removed one impediment,

---

Did this insurrection serve to evince still more evidently the necessity of strengthening the hands of the national government?   Did Congress give its sanction to the proposed convention?

and diminished another, to the attendance of General Washington as a member. He persuaded himself, that by repairing to Philadelphia previous to the second Monday in May, in order to attend the meeting of the Cincinnati, he should efface any unfavorable impressions which might be excited in the bosoms of his military friends. On the 28th of March, he addressed a letter to the Governor of Virginia, declaring his purpose to attend the convention, provided the executive had not turned their thoughts to some other person.

At the time and place appointed, the representatives of twelve states convened. Rhode Island alone refused to send deputies. Having unanimously chosen General Washington for their President, the convention proceeded, with closed doors, to discuss the interesting and extensive subject submitted to their consideration.

More than once, there was reason to fear that the rich harvest of national felicity which had been anticipated from the ample stock of worth collected in convention, would be blasted by the rising of that body, without effecting the object for which it was formed. At length, the importance attached to union triumphed over local interests; and, on the 17th of September, that constitution, which has been alike the theme of panegyric and invective, was presented to the American public.

The instrument, with its accompanying resolutions, was, by the unanimous order of the convention, transmitted to Congress, in a letter subscribed by the President, in which it was said to be "the result of a spirit of amity, and of that mutual deference and concession, which the peculiarity of their political situation rendered indispensable."

Congress resolved, unanimously, that the report, with the letter accompanying it, be transmitted to the several legislatures, in order to be submitted to a convention of delegates chosen in each state, by the people thereof.

Neither the intrinsic merits of the constitution, nor the imposing weight of character by which it was supported, gave assurance that it would be adopted. Its friends and its enemies were stimulated to exertion by motives equally powerful; and, during the interval between its publication and adoption, every faculty of the mind was strained to secure its reception or rejection. The press teemed with the productions of genius, of temperate reason, and of passion.

To decide the interesting question which agitated a continent, the best talents of the several states were assembled in their seve-

When the convention met, who was appointed their President? When was the constitution presented to the nation? Did the subject give rise to much debate and controversy?

ral conventions. So balanced were parties in some of them, that even after the subject had been discussed for a considerable time, the fate of the constitution could scarcely be conjectured; and so small, in many instances, was the majority in its favor, as to afford strong ground for the opinion, that had the influence of character been removed, the intrinsic merits of the instrument would not have secured its adoption.

At length, the convention of eleven states assented to, and ratified the constitution; and the preparatory measures were taken for carrying it into operation.

The attention of all was directed to General Washington, as the first President of the United States. He alone possessed so entirely the confidence of the people, that under his auspices, the friends of the government might hope to see it introduced, with a degree of firmness which would enable it to resist the open assaults and secret plots of its numerous adversaries. Fears were entertained, by all who knew him, that his fondness for private life would prevail over the wishes of the public; and, soon after the adoption of the constitution was ascertained, its friends began to press him on a point which was believed to be essential to the great work on which the grandeur and happiness of America was supposed to depend. The interesting correspondence of the time evinces with how much difficulty he yielded to the very earnest representations and arguments of the friends of a government which might preserve the Union.

After the elections had taken place, a general persuasion prevailed, that the public will, respecting the chief magistrate of the Union, had been too unequivocally manifested not to be obeyed; and several applications were made to General Washington for those offices in the respective states which would be in the gift of the President of the United States. The following extract from one of the many letters written to persons whose pretensions he was disposed to favor, speaks the frame of mind with which he came into the government. "Should it become absolutely necessary for me to occupy the station in which your letter presupposes me, I have determined to go into it perfectly free from all engagements, of every nature whatsoever. A conduct in conformity to this resolution, would enable me, in balancing the various pretensions of different candidates for appointments, to act with a sole reference to justice and the public good. This is, in substance, the answer that I have given to all applications (and they are not a few) which have already been made."

The impotence of the late government, added to the dilatori-

Was the new constitution at length adopted? To whom were all eyes turned, as the first American President? What were the principles which guided Washington in selecting the public officers?

23

ness inseparable from its perplexed mode of proceeding, had produced such habitual disregard of punctuality in the attendance of members, that although the new government was to commence its operations on the 4th of March, 1789, a House of Representatives was not formed until the 1st, nor a Senate until the 6th day of April.

At length the votes for President and Vice-President of the United States were opened and counted in the Senate. Neither the animosity of parties, nor the preponderance of the enemies of the new government in some of the states, could deprive General Washington of a single vote. By the unanimous voice of the people, he was called to the chief magistracy of the nation. The second number of votes was given to Mr. John Adams. George Washington and John Adams were therefore declared to be duly elected President and Vice-President of the United States, to serve for four years, from the 4th day of March, 1789.

CHAPTER XXVII.

The election of General Washington officially announced to him.—He proceeds to the seat of government.—Marks of affection shown him on his journey.—His inauguration.—His system of intercourse with the world.—Answers of both houses of Congress to his speech. — Domestic and foreign relations of the United States. — Debates in Congress. — Amendments to the constitution.—Appointments to office.—Adjournment of Congress.—The President visits New England.—North Carolina adopts the constitution.

THE election of General Washington to the office of chief magistrate of the United States, was announced to him at Mount Vernon, on the 14th of April, 1789. Accustomed to respect the wishes of his fellow-citizens, he did not think himself at liberty to decline an appointment conferred upon him by the suffrage of an entire people.

As the public business required the immediate attendance of the President at the seat of government, he hastened his departure; and, on the second day after receiving notice of his appointment, took leave of Mount Vernon.

In an entry made in his diary, the feelings of the occasion are thus described. "About ten o'clock I bade adieu to Mount Vernon, to private life, and to domestic felicity; and, with a mind oppressed with more anxious and painful sensations than I have words to express, set out for New York in company with Mr. Thompson and Colonel Humphries, with the best dispositions to

---

Who was elected chief magistrate of the Union, by an unanimous vote? Did Washington accept the appointment? What were his feelings on leaving Mount Vernon?

render service to my country in obedience to its call, but with less hope of answering its expectations."

Throughout his journey the people continued to manifest the ardent and respectful affection which animated almost every bosom. Crowds flocked around him wherever he stopped; and corps of militia, and companies of the most respectable citizens escorted him through their respective states.

At Philadelphia, and at Trenton, he was received with peculia splendor, and in a manner calculated to excite the deepest interest. At Brunswick, he was joined by the Governor of New Jersey, who accompanied him to Elizabethtown Point. A committee of Congress received him on the road, and conducted him with military parade to the Point, where he took leave of the Governor and other gentlemen of Jersey, and embarked for New York in an elegant barge of thirteen oars, manned by thirteen branch pilots, prepared for the purpose by the citizens of New York.

"The display of boats," says the General in his private journal, "which attended and joined on this occasion, some with vocal and others with instrumental music on board, the decorations of the ships, the roar of cannon, and the loud acclamations of the people which rent the sky as I passed along the wharves, filled my mind with sensations as painful (contemplating the reverse of this scene which may be the case after all my labors to do good) as they were pleasing."

At the stairs on Murray's wharf, he was received by the Governor of New York, and conducted with military honors through an immense concourse of people, to the apartments provided for him. These were attended by all who were in office, and by many private citizens of distinction.

It is no equivocal mark of the worth of Washington, and of the soundness of his judgment, that it could neither be corrupted nor misguided by these flattering testimonials of attachment.

A President of the United States being a new political personage, to a great portion of whose time the public was entitled, it was obviously proper to digest a system of conduct to be observed in his intercourse with the world, which would keep in view the duties of his station, without entirely disregarding his personal accommodation, or the course of public opinion. After consulting those most capable of advising on the subject, some rules were framed by General Washington for his government in these respects. As one of them, the allotment of a particular hour for receiving visits not on business, became the subject of much animadversion, and has constituted not the least important of the

At what places was Washington received, with enthusiastic applause? How was he honored, on approaching and entering the city of New York? Did he frame rules for his conduct as President?

charges made against his administration, the motives assigned by himself for the rule, may not be unworthy of attention.

Not long after the government came into operation, a gentleman nearly connected with the President, addressed to him a letter stating the accusations which were commonly circulating in Virginia on various subjects; and especially on the regal manners of those who administered the affairs of the nation.

In answer to this letter, the President observed, "while the eyes of America, perhaps of the world, are turned to this government, and many are watching the movements of all those who are concerned in its administration, I should like to be informed through so good a medium, of the public opinion of both men and measures, and of none more than myself;—not so much of what may be thought commendable parts, if any, of my conduct, as of those which are conceived to be of a different complexion."

After some other general observations, the letter adds, "this leads me to think that a system which I found it indispensably necessary to adopt upon my first coming to this city might have undergone severe strictures, and have had motives very foreign from those that governed me, assigned as causes thereof. I mean first, returning no visits; second, appointing certain days to receive them generally, not to the exclusion however of visits on any other days under particular circumstances." After stating a third rule, he added "a few days evinced the necessity of the two first in so clear a point of view that, had I not adopted it, I should have been unable to attend to any sort of business, unless I had applied the hours allotted to rest and refreshment, to this purpose; for, by the time I had done breakfast, and thence until dinner, and afterwards until bed-time, I could not get relieved from the ceremony of one visit before I had to attend to another. In a word, I had no leisure to read or to answer the dispatches that were pouring in upon me from all quarters."

The ceremonies of the inauguration having been adjusted by Congress, the President attended in the Senate chamber, on the 30th of April, in order to take the oath prescribed by the constitution, in the presence of both houses.

To gratify the public curiosity, an open gallery adjoining the Senate chamber had been selected as the place in which the oath should be administered. Having taken it in the view of an immense concourse of people, whose loud and repeated acclamations attested the joy with which the occasion inspired them, he returned to the Senate chamber, where he delivered the first address ever made by a President to a Congress of the United States.

In their answer to his speech the Senate say, "the unanimous suffrage of the elective body in your favor is peculiarly expressive of the gratitude, confidence and affection of the citizens of America, and is the highest testimonial at once of your merit and their esteem. We are sensible, sir, that nothing but the voice of your fellow-citizens could have called you from a retreat; chosen with the fondest predilection, endeared by habit, and consecrated to the repose of declining years. We rejoice, and with us all America, that, in obedience to the call of our common country, you have returned once more to public life. In you, all parties confide; in you, all interests unite, and we have no doubt that your past services, great as they have been, will be equalled by your future exertions; and that your prudence and sagacity as a statesman will tend to avert the dangers to which we were exposed, to give stability to the present government, and dignity and splendor to that country, which your skill and valor as a soldier, so eminently contributed to raise to independence and to empire."

The answer of the House of Representatives glowed with equal affection for the person and character of the President.

"The representatives of the people of the United States," says this address, "present their congratulations on the event by which your fellow-citizens have attested the pre-eminence of your merit. You have long held the first place in their esteem. You have often received tokens of their affection. You now possess the only proof that remained of their gratitude for your services, of their reverence for your wisdom, and of their confidence in your virtues. You enjoy the highest—because the truest honor, of being the first magistrate, by the unanimous choice of the freest people on the face of the earth."

A perfect knowledge of the antecedent state of things being essential to a due administration of the executive department, its attainment engaged the immediate attention of the President; and he required the temporary heads of departments to prepare and lay before him such statements and documents as would give this information.

His attention was attracted to the West, by discontents which were expressed with some violence, and which originated in circumstances and interests peculiar to that country.

Spain, in possession of the mouth of the Mississippi, had refused to permit the citizens of the United States to follow its waters into the ocean; and had occasionally tolerated or interdicted their commerce to New Orleans, as had been suggested by interest or caprice. The eyes of the inhabitants adjacent to the waters of that

State the substance of the address of the two houses to General Washington. What were the feelings of the people in the West, respecting the free navigation of the Mississippi river ?

23*

river, were turned down it, as the only channel through which the surplus produce of their luxurious soil could be conveyed to the markets of the world; and they had given some evidence of a disposition to drop from the confederacy, if this valuable acquisition could not be otherwise made.

The President had received intelligence, previous to his departure from Mount Vernon, of private machinations, by real or pretende agents, both of Spain and Great Britain.

Spain had intimated that the navigation of the Mississippi coul never be conceded, while the inhabitants of the western country remained connected with the Atlantic states, but might be freely granted to them, if they should form an independent empire.

On the other hand, a gentleman from Canada, whose ostensible business was the recovery of some lands formerly granted to him on the Ohio, frequently discussed the vital importance of the navigation of the Mississippi, and privately assured several individuals of great influence that, if they were disposed to assert their rights, he was authorized by the Governor of Canada to assure them that they might rely confidently on his assistance.

In contemplating the situation of the United States, no subject demanded more immediate attention than the hostility of the Indian tribes. The nations between the lakes, the Mississippi and the Ohio, could bring five thousand men into the field. Of these, about fifteen hundred were at war with the United States. Treaties had been concluded with the residue; but there was cause for the apprehension that these treaties would soon be broken.

In the South, the Creeks, whose force amounted to six thousand fighting men, were at war with Georgia. The subject of contest was a tract of land on the Oconee, which Georgia claimed under a purchase, the validity of which was denied by the Indians.

The army of the United States was less than six hundred men. Not only the policy of accommodating differences by negotiation, which the government was in no condition to terminate by the sword, but a real respect for the rights of the natives, disposed the President to endeavor, in the first instance, to remove every cause of quarrel by treaty.

The United States had formed a treaty with the Emperor of Morocco, but had been unable to purchase peace from Algiers, Tunis, or Tripoli; and those regencies considered all as enemies to whom they had not sold their friendship. The unprotected vessels of America presented a tempting object to their rapacity; and their hostility was the more terrible, because, by their public law, prisoners become slaves.

What were the numbers and dispositions of the Indians? What was the entire force of the American army? What were the relations of the United States with the piratical powers in the Mediterranean?

The United States were at peace with all the powers of Europe; but controversies of a delicate nature existed with some of them. The attempt to form a treaty with Spain had been ineffectual. His Catholic Majesty adhered inflexibly to the exclusion of the citizens of the United States from the navigation of the Mississippi below their southern boundary. The violence with which the discontents of the western people were expressed, furnished Spain with additional motives for perpetuating the evil of which they complained. A contest respecting boundary also existed with the same power. The treaty of peace had extended the limits of the United States down the Mississippi to the thirty-first degree of north latitude; but the pretensions of the Catholic King were carried north of that line to an undefined extent. He claimed as far as he had conquered from Britain; but the precise limits of his conquest were not ascertained.

The difference with Great Britain was still more serious, because a temper unfavorable to accommodation had been uniformly displayed. The resentments growing out of the war were not terminated with their cause. The idea that Great Britain was the natural enemy of America had become habitual.

The general restrictions on commerce, by which every maritime power sought to promote its own navigation, and that part of the European system, in particular, by which each aimed at a monopoly of the trade of its colonies, were felt with peculiar keenness when enforced by England. The people of America were the more sensible to the British regulations on this subject, because, having composed a part of that empire, they had grown up in the habit of a free intercourse with all its ports.

The failure of an attempt to form a commercial treaty with Portugal, was attributed to the influence of the cabinet of London. The depredations of the Barbary corsairs, and the bloody incursions of the Indians, were also ascribed to the machinations of the same power.

With France, the most perfect harmony subsisted. Those attachments which originated in the signal services received from his Most Christian Majesty during the war of the revolution, had sustained no diminution; and a disposition was felt extensively to enable the merchants of that nation, by legislative encouragements, to compete with those of Britain in the American market.

A great revolution had commenced in that country, the first stage of which was completed by limiting the powers of the monarch, and by establishing a popular assembly. In no part of the globe was this revolution hailed with more joy than in America.

What difficulties occurred with Spain, and with Great Britain? What was the feeling of America towards France? Mention the first stage of the great revolution which was commencing in the latter nation.

Its ulterior effects were not distinctly foreseen, and but one senti-ment existed respecting it.

The relations of the United States with the other powers of Eu-rope, were rather friendly than otherwise.

The subjects which pressed for immediate attention on the first legislature, were numerous and important. Much was to be cre-ated, and much to be reformed.

The qualification of the members was succeeded by a motion for the House to resolve itself into a committee of the whole on the state of the Union, in which Mr. Madison moved a resolution, de-claring that certain duties ought to be levied on goods, wares, and merchandise imported into the United States; and on the tonnage of vessels. He presented a scheme of impost, by which specific duties were imposed on certain enumerated articles; and an *ad valorem* duty on those not enumerated; to which he added a gen-eral proposition for a duty on tonnage. In proceeding to fill up the blanks with the sum taxable on each article, great contrariety of opinion prevailed. The taxes proposed were believed to press unequally on the states; and apprehensions were expressed that, in the form of protecting duties, the industry of one part of the Union would be encouraged by premiums charged on the labor of another part. On the discrimination between the duty on the ton-nage on foreign and American bottoms, a great degree of sensi-bility was discovered. It was said that the increased tonnage on foreign bottoms operated as a tax on agriculture, and a premium to navigation. This discrimination, therefore, ought to be very small. These arguments were answered with great ability by Mr. Madison.

No part of the system was discussed with more animation than that which proposed to favor those nations with whom the United States had formed commercial treaties. In the debate on this subject, opinions and feelings were disclosed, which, strengthening with circumstances, afterwards agitated every part of the Union.

At length, the bills passed the House of Representatives, and were carried to the senate, where they were amended, by expung-ing the discrimination made in favor of the tonnage and distilled spirits of those nations with which commercial treaties had been formed. These amendments were disagreed to; and each house insisting on its opinion, a conference took place; after which, the point was reluctantly yielded by the House of Representatives.

This debate was succeeded by one on the question in what manner the high officers who filled the executive departments should be removable. In a committee of the whole House, on the

What was the first business of Congress? What argument was used against discriminating duties on American and foreign vessels? Did the two Houses differ, and at last concur?

bill " to establish an executive department, to be denominated the department of foreign affairs," Mr. White moved to strike out the clause which declared the secretary to be removable by the President. The power of removal, where no express provision existed, was, he said, in the nature of things, incidental to that of appointment; and, as the Senate was associated with the President in making appointments, that body must, in the same degree, participate in removing from office.

The amendment was opposed by arguments drawn from the constitution, and from general convenience. The friends of the original bill relied especially on that part of the constitution which vests the executive power in the President. No power, it was said, could be more completely executive in its nature, than that of removal from office.

After an ardent discussion, which consumed several days, the committee divided; and the amendment was negatived. But the express grant of the power rather implied a right in the legislature to give or to withhold it at discretion. To obviate any misunderstanding of the principle, a motion was made in the House to amend the clause, so as to imply clearly that the power of removal resided solely in the President; after which, the whole was stricken out; thus leaving the President to exercise the power as a constitutional privilege. As the bill became a law, it has ever been considered as a full expression of the sense of the legislature, on this important part of the American constitution.

The bill to establish the treasury department contained a clause making it the duty of the secretary, " to digest and report plans for the improvement and management of the revenue, and for the support of public credit." This clause encountered serious opposition. After a very animated discussion, the motion to strike it out was rejected.

Among the interesting points which were settled in the first Congress, was the question by what style the President and Vice-President should be addressed. Mr. Benson, from a committee appointed to confer with a committee of the Senate on the subject, reported, " that it is not proper to annex any style or title to the respective styles or titles of office expressed in the constitution;" and this report was agreed to in the House of Representatives. In the senate, it was disapproved. A committee of conference not being able to agree, the subject was permitted to rest; and the Senate, conforming to the precedent given by the House of Representatives, addressed the President, in their answer to his speech, by the terms used in the constitution.

What arguments were used in relation to the power of the President to dismiss from office ? What was decided on this point ? What other matters were discussed in Congress ?

While the representatives were preparing bills for organizing the great executive departments, the senate was occupied with digesting the system of a national judiciary. This complex and extensive subject was taken up in the commencement of the session, and was completed towards its close.

In the course of the session, Mr. Madison brought forward a proposition for recommending to the consideration and adoption of the states, several articles to be added to the constitution.

To conciliate the affection of their brethren to the government was an object greatly desired by its friends. Disposed to respect what they deemed the errors of their opponents, when that respect could be manifested without a sacrifice of essential principles, they were anxious to annex to the constitution, those explanations and barriers against the possible encroachments of rulers on the liberties of the people, which had been loudly demanded, however unfounded, in their judgments, the fears by which those demands were suggested might be. Among the most zealous friends of the constitution, were found the first and warmest advocates for amendments.

The government being completely organized, and a system of revenue established, the important duty of filling the offices which had been created, remained to be performed. In the execution of this delicate trust, the purest virtue and the most impartial judgment were exercised in selecting the best talents, and the greatest weight of character, which the United States could furnish.

At the head of the department of foreign affairs, since denominated the Department of State, the President placed Mr. Jefferson.

This gentleman had been a distinguished member of the second Congress, and had been offered a diplomatic appointment, which he declined. On withdrawing from the administration of continental affairs, he had been elected Governor of Virginia, which office he filled for two years. He afterwards again represented his native state in the government of the Union; and, in the year 1784, was appointed to succeed Dr. Franklin at the court of Versailles. In that situation, he had acquitted himself much to the public satisfaction. His Notes on Virginia, which were read with applause, were believed to evince sound political opinions; and the declaration of independence was universally ascribed to his pen. He had been long placed by America among the most eminent of her citizens, and had long been classed by the President with those who were most capable of serving the nation. Having obtained permission to return for a short time to the United States, he was, while on his passage, nominated to this important office;

After the organization of the government and a system of revenue, what duty remained to be performed? What is said respecting Mr. Jefferson? What office was conferred upon him by Washington?

and, on his arrival in Virginia, found a letter from the President, giving him the option of becoming the Secretary of Foreign Affairs, or of retaining his station at the court of Versailles. In changing his situation, he appears to have consulted the wishes of the Chief Magistrate, more than the preference of his own mind.

The task of restoring public credit, of drawing order and arrangement from the chaotic confusion in which the finances of America were involved, and of devising means which should produce revenue in a manner least burdensome to the people, was justly classed among the most arduous of the duties which were devolved on the new government. In discharging it, much aid was expected from the head of the treasury. This important, and at that time intricate department, was assigned to Colonel Hamilton.

This gentleman, with all the enthusiasm of youth, engaged first his pen, and afterwards his sword, in the stern contest between the American colonies and their parent state. Among the first troops raised by New York, was a corps of artillery, in which he was appointed a captain. Soon after the war was transferred to the Hudson, his superior endowments recommended him to the commander-in-chief, into whose family, before completing his twenty-first year, he was invited to enter. Equally brave and intelligent, he continued to display, in this situation, a degree of firmness and capacity, which commanded the confidence and esteem of his general, and of the principal officers of the army.

After the capitulation of Yorktown, the war languished throughout America; and the probability that its termination was approaching, daily increased.

The critical circumstances of the existing government gave a deep interest to the events of the civil government; and Colonel Hamilton accepted a seat in the Congress of the United States. He was greatly distinguished amongst those eminent men whom the crisis had attracted to the councils of their country. He had afterwards been active in promoting those measures which led to the convention in Philadelphia, of which he was a member, and had contributed greatly to the adoption of the constitution by the state of New York. In the pre-eminent part he had performed, both in the military and civil transactions of his country, he had acquired a great degree of well-merited fame; and the frankness of his manners, the openness of his temper, the warmth of his feelings, and the sincerity of his heart, had secured him many valuable friends.

The department of war was already filled by General Knox, and he was again nominated to it.

Who was stationed at the head of the Treasury? Sketch the previous career of Hamilton. To whom was assigned the War Department?

Throughout the contest of the revolution, this officer had continued at the head of the American artillery. In this important station, he had maintained a high military character; and, on the resignation of General Lincoln, had been appointed secretary of war. To his past services, and to unquestionable integrity, he was admitted to unite a sound understanding; and the public judgment, as well as that of the chief magistrate, pronounced him to be competent in all respects to the station he occupied.

The office of attorney-general was filled by Mr. Edmund Randolph. To a distinguished reputation in his profession, this gentleman added a considerable degree of political eminence. After having been for several years the attorney-general of Virginia, he had been elected its Governor. While in this office, he was chosen a member of the convention which framed the constitution, and also of that by which it was adopted. After having served the term permitted by the constitution in the executive of the state, he entered into its legislature, where he preserved a great share of influence.

Such was the first cabinet council. In its composition, public opinion as well as intrinsic worth had been consulted, and a high degree of character had been combined with real talent.

In the selection of persons for high judicial offices, the President was guided by the same principles. At the head of this department he placed Mr. John Jay.

From the commencement of the revolution, this gentleman had filled a large space in the public mind. Remaining without intermission in the service of his country, he had passed through a succession of high offices, and, in all of them had merited the approbation of his fellow-citizens. To his pen, while in Congress, America was indebted for some of those masterly addresses which reflected most honor upon the government; and to his firmness and penetration, the happy issue of those intricate negotiations which terminated the war was, in no small degree, to be ascribed. On returning to the United States, he had been appointed secretary of foreign affairs, in which station he had displayed his accustomed ability. A sound judgment improved by extensive reading and great knowledge of public affairs, unyielding firmness, and inflexible integrity, were qualities of which Mr. Jay had given frequent and signal proofs. Although withdrawn for some years from that profession to which he was bred, the acquisitions of his early life had not been lost, and the subjects on which his mind had been exercised were not entirely foreign from those which would, in the first instance, employ the courts in which he was to preside.

Who was made attorney-general? Mention his previous services? What station was occupied by Mr. Jay? Mention his merits?

John Rutledge of South Carolina, John Wilson of Pennsylvania, William Cushing of Massachusetts, Robert Harrison of Maryland, and John Blair of Virginia, were appointed associate justices. Some of those gentlemen had filled the highest law offices in their respective states; and all of them had received distinguished marks of the public confidence.

In the systems of the several states, offices corresponding to those created by the revenue laws of Congress, had been established. Uninfluenced by considerations of personal regard, the President could not be induced to change men whom he found in place, if worthy of being employed. In deciding between candidates for vacant offices, if an equality of fitness existed, former merits and sufferings in the service of the public, gave claims to preference which could not be overlooked.

In the legislature as well as the executive and judicial departments, great respectability of character was also associated with an eminent degree of talent. Impelled by an anxious solicitude respecting the first measures of the government, its zealous friends had pressed into its service; and men were found in both branches of the legislature, who possessed the fairest claims to public confidence.

The Vice-President of the United States, though not a member of the legislature, was classed, in the public estimation, with that department. Mr. John Adams was one of the earliest and most ardent friends of the revolution. Bred to the bar, he had necessarily studied the constitution of his country, and was among the most determined asserters of its rights. Active in guiding that high spirit which animated all New England, he became a member of the Congress of 1774, and was among the first who dared to avow sentiments in favor of independence. He soon attained eminence in that body, and was chosen one of the commissioners to whom the interests of the United States in Europe were confided. In his diplomatic character, he had contributed greatly to those measures which drew Holland into the war; had negotiated the treaty with the Dutch republic, and had, at critical points of time, obtained loans which were of great advantage to his country. In the negotiations which terminated the war, he had also rendered important services; and, after the ratification of the treaty of peace, had been deputed to Great Britain for the purpose of effecting commercial arrangements with that nation.

As a statesman, this gentleman had always ranked high in the estimation of his countrymen. He had improved a sound understanding by extensive political and historical reading; and perhaps

Mention the names of the associate judges. In making a selection from applicants for office, what considerations guided the President? Narrate briefly the character and services of John Adams.

no American had reflected more profoundly on the science of government. The exalted opinion he entertained of his own country was flattering to his fellow-citizens; and the purity of his mind, the unblemished integrity of a life spent in the public service, had gained their confidence.

A government supported in all its departments by so much character and talent, at the head of which was placed a man whose capacity was undoubted, whose life had given one great and continued lesson of patriotism, and for whom almost every bosom glowed with an attachment bordering on enthusiasm, could not fail to make a rapid progress in conciliating the affection of the people.

Towards the close of the session, a petition which had been presented by the creditors of the public residing in Pennsylvania was taken up by the House of Representatives, and two resolutions were passed; the one declaring "that the house considered an adequate provision for the support of the public credit, as a matter of high importance to the national honor and prosperity;" and the other directing "the secretary of the treasury to prepare a plan for that purpose, and to report the same to the house at its next meeting."

On the 29th of September, Congress adjourned to the first Monday in the succeeding January.

Anxious to visit New England, to observe in person the condition of the country, and the dispositions of the people towards the government and its measures, the President determined to avail himself of the short respite from official duties afforded by the recess of Congress, to make a tour through the eastern states. He left New York on the 15th of October; and, passing through Connecticut and Massachusetts, proceeded as far as Portsmouth in New Hampshire. From that place he returned by a different route to the seat of government, where he arrived on the 13th of November.

The reappearance of their General in the high station he now filled, renewed the recollection of the perilous transactions of the war; and the reception universally given to him attested the unabated love which was felt for his person and character, and indicated unequivocally the growing popularity, at least in that part of the Union, of the government he administered.

Soon after his return to New York, the President was informed of the failure of his first attempt to negotiate a treaty with the Creeks. Some difficulties arose on the subject of boundary; but the principal obstacles to a peace were supposed to grow out of the

What resolutions, touching the public debt, were passed by Congress? Mention a tour made by Washington. Was he well received by the people? Mention the failure in treating with the Creeks.

personal interests of Mr. Gillivray, their chief, and his connexions with Spain. —

This information was more than counterbalanced by the intelligence from North Carolina. A second convention had met under the authority of the legislature of that state, in the month of November, and had adopted the constitution by a great majority.

CHAPTER XXVIII.

Meeting of Congress —President's speech —Report of the Secretary of the Treasury.— Debate thereon —Bill for fixing the seat of government —Adjournment of Congress.— —Treaty with the Creek Indians —Relations of the United States with Great Britain and Spain —Constitution adopted by Rhode Island —Congress meets at Philadelphia.—Speech of the President —Debates on the excise.—On the bank.—Division in the cabinet on the law.—Defeat of Harmer.—Adjournment of Congress.

On the 8th of January, 1790, the President met both Houses of Congress in the Senate chamber.

In his speech, which was delivered from the chair of the Vice-President, after congratulating Congress on the adoption of the constitution by the important state of North Carolina, and on the prosperous aspect of American affairs, he proceeded to recommend certain great objects of legislation to their more especial consideration. A provision for the common defence merited, he said, their particular regard. "To be prepared for war," he added, "is one of the most effectual means of preserving peace.

"A free people ought not only to be armed, but disciplined; to which end a uniform and well-digested plan is requisite; and their safety and interest require that they should promote such manufactories as tend to render them independent on others for essential, particularly for military supplies."

He suggested the propriety of providing the means of keeping up their intercourse with foreign nations, and the expediency of establishing a uniform rule of naturalization.

After expressing his confidence in their attention to many improvements essential to the prosperity of the interior, he recommended the promotion of science and literature to their patronage. "Knowledge," he added, "is, in every country, the surest basis of public happiness. In one in which the measures of government receive their impression so immediately from the sense of the community, as in ours, it is proportionably essential."

"Whether this desirable object will be best promoted by affording aids to seminaries of learning already established, by the in-

stitution of a national university, or by other expedients, will be
well worthy of a place in the deliberations of the legislature."

The answers of both Houses indicated the harmony which existed between the executive and legislative departments.

Early in January, the report of the Secretary of the Treasury,
containing a plan for the support of public credit, prepared in obedience to the resolution of the 21st of September, 1789, was laid
before Congress.

" It was agreed," he said, " by all, that the foreign debt should
be provided for, according to the precise terms of the contract. It
was to be regretted that, with respect to the domestic debt, the
same unanimity of sentiment did not prevail."

The first point on which the public appeared to be divided, was
the question " whether a discrimination ought to be made between
original holders of the public securities, and present possessors by
purchase." He supported, with great strength of argument, the
opinion against this discrimination.

He next proceeded to the question, whether any difference ought
to remain between the creditors of the Union and those of individual states. He was earnestly opposed to this difference. " Both
descriptions of debt were contracted for the same objects, and were
in the main the same." Equity required " the same measure of
retribution for all. There were many reasons," some of which
were stated, " for believing this would not be the case, unless the
state debts should be assumed by the nation."

After an elaborate discussion of these and some other points
connected with the subject, the secretary proposed that a loan
should be opened to the full amount of the debt, as well of the particular states as of the Union.

To enable the treasury to support this increased demand upon
it, an augmentation of the duties on imported wines, spirits, tea,
and coffee, was proposed; and a duty on home-made spirits was
also recommended.

This celebrated report, which has been alike the theme of extravagant praise and bitter censure, merits the more attention, because the first systematic opposition to the principles on which the
government was administered, originated in the measures which
were founded on it.

On the 8th of February, Mr. Fitzsimmons moved several resolutions affirmative of the principles contained in the report. To
the first, which respected a provision for the foreign debt, the
House agreed without a dissenting voice. The second, in favor of
appropriating permanent funds for the payment of the interest on

What was recommended by the Secretary of the Treasury, in relation to
the foreign and domestic debt of the nation and the states? What did he
propose, to provide the necessary funds?

the domestic debt, and for the gradual redemption of the principal, gave rise to a very animated debate.

Mr. Scott avowed the opinion that the United States were not bound to pay their domestic creditors the sums specified in their certificates of debt, because the original holders had parted with them at two shillings and six-pence in the pound. He therefore moved an amendment, requiring a resettlement of the debt.

After this proposition had been negatived, Mr. Madison rose and, in an eloquent speech, proposed an amendment to the reso lution, the effect of which was to pay the present holder of assign able paper the highest price it had borne in the market, and to give the residue to the original creditor. The debate was long, argumentative, and interesting. At length the question was put, and the amendment was rejected by a great majority.

The succeeding resolution, affecting political interests and powers which are never to be approached without danger, seemed to un chain all those fierce passions which a high respect for the go vernment, and for those who administered it, had in a great mea sure restrained.

The debt incurred in support of the war, had been contracted partly by the continent and partly by the states. When the mea sure of compensating the army for the depreciation of their pay became necessary, this burden, under the recommendation of Con gress, was assumed by the respective states. Some of them had funded this debt, and paid the interest upon it. Others had made no provision for the interest; but all, by taxes, paper-money, or purchase, had reduced the principal.

The Secretary of the Treasury proposed to assume these debts; and to fund them in common with that which continued to be the debt of the Union.

The resolution which comprehended this principle of the report, was vigorously opposed. Even its constitutionality was questioned. But the argument which seemed to have most weight, was that which maintained that the general government would acquire an undue influence, and that the state governments would be annihi lated by the measure.

After a very animated discussion of several days, the resolution was carried by a small majority. Soon after this decision, while the subject was pending before the House, the delegates from North Carolina took their seats, and changed the strength of parties. The resolution was recommitted by a majority of two voices; and, after a long and ardent debate, was negatived by the same majority.

What was argued against the nation redeeming the debt in full? What modification of Mr. Madison was rejected? Mention the debate, and the decision, upon the question of funding the state debts.

24*

This proposition continued to be supported with a degree of earnestness which its opponents termed pertinacious, but not a single opinion was changed. It was brought forward in the less exceptionable form of assuming specific sums from each state. But this alteration produced no change of sentiment; and the bill was sent to the Senate, with a provision for those creditors only, whose certificates of debt purported to be payable by the United States.

In this state of things, the measure is understood to have derived aid from another, which was of a character strongly to interest particular parts of the Union.

From June, 1783, when Congress was driven from Philadelphia, by the mutiny of a part of the Pennsylvania line, the necessity of selecting some place for the permanent residence of the government, in which it might protect itself from insult, had been generally acknowledged.

In September 1784, an ordinance had been passed for appointing commissioners to purchase land on the Delaware in the neighborhood of the falls, and to erect the necessary buildings thereon; but the southern interest had been sufficiently strong to arrest the execution of this ordinance by preventing an appropriation of funds, which required the assent of nine states. Under the existing government, many different places from the Delaware to the Potomac inclusive, had been earnestly supported; but a majority of both houses had not concurred in favor of any one place. Attempts had been made with as little success to change the temporary residence of Congress. At length a compact respecting the temporary and permanent seat of government was entered into between the friends of Philadelphia and the Potomac, stipulating that Congress should hold its sessions in Philadelphia for ten years, during which time buildings for the accommodation of government should be erected at some place on the Potomac to which the government should remove on the expiration of that time. This compact having united the representatives of Pennsylvania and Delaware with the friends of the Potomac, a majority was produced in favor of both situations; and a bill brought into the Senate in conformity with this arrangement, passed both Houses by small majorities. This act was immediately followed by an amendment to the bill for funding the public debt, similar to that which had been proposed unsuccessfully in the House of Representatives.

When the question was taken in the House of Representatives on this amendment, two members representing districts on the Po-

---

Did the majority of Congress incline against adopting the debt of the states? What other question operated to change the vote, so as to procure the passage of a bill assuming the state obligations?

tomac, who had voted against the assumption, declared themselves in its favor, and thus the majority was changed.

This measure has constituted one of the great grounds of accusation against the administration of Washington. It is fair to acknowledge that, though, in its progress, it derived no aid from the President, it received the full approbation of his judgment. A bill at length passed both houses, funding the debt on principles which lessened the weight of the public burden, and was entirely satisfactory to the public creditors.

The effects produced by giving the debt a permanent value justified the predictions of the most sanguine. The sudden increase of moneyed capital derived from it, invigorated commerce, and gave a new stimulus to agriculture.

About this time a great and visible improvement took place in the circumstances of the people. Although the funding system was not inoperative in producing this improvement, it cannot be ascribed to any single cause. Progressive industry had gradually repaired the losses sustained by the war; and the influence of the constitution on habits of thinking and acting, though silent, was considerable.

On the 12th of August, Congress adjourned, to meet in Philadelphia on the first Monday in the following December.

While the discussions in the national legislature related to subjects, and were conducted in a temper well calculated to rouse the active spirit of party, the external relations of the United States wore an aspect not perfectly serene. An increased degree of importance was given to the hostile temper of the Indians, by the apprehension that their discontents were fomented by the intrigues of Britain and Spain. It was feared that the latter power might take a part in the open hostilities threatened by the irritable dispositions of individuals both in Georgia and the Creek nation. From the intimate connexion subsisting between the members of the house of Bourbon, this event was peculiarly deprecated; and the means of avoiding it were sought with solicitude. These considerations induced the President to make another effort at negotiation; but to preserve the respect of these savages for the United States, it was resolved that the agent employed should visit their country under other pretexts. Colonel Willett was selected for this service; and he acquitted himself so well of the duty as to induce the chiefs of the nation with M'Gillivray at their head, to repair to New York, where negotiations were opened which terminated in a treaty of peace.

The pacific overtures made to the Indians of the Wabash and

Did salutary consequences flow from funding the debt? What was the general condition of the country? What were the apprehensions respecting the savages? Was a treaty at length made with them?

Miamis not having been successful, the inhabitants of the western frontiers were still exposed to their destructive incursions, and still retained the hostility they had originally manifested to the constitution.

No progress had been made in adjusting the points of controversy with Spain and Britain.

The cabinet of St. James having never appointed a minister to the United States, the President felt some difficulty in repeating advances which had been treated with neglect. Yet there was much reason to desire full explanations with the British government. The subjects for discussion were of peculiar delicacy, and could not be permitted to remain unadjusted without hazarding the most serious consequences. In October 1789, the President had resolved on taking informal measures to sound the British cabinet, and to ascertain its views respecting the points of controversy between the two nations. This negotiation was entrusted to Mr. Gouverneur Morris, who had been carried to Europe by private business. In his conferences with the Duke of Leeds and with Mr. Pitt, those ministers expressed a wish to be on the best terms with America; but repeated the complaints which had been made by Lord Carmaerthen of the non-execution of the treaty of peace on the part of the United States. In a subsequent note, the Duke of Leeds avowed the intention, if the delay on the part of the American government to fulfil its engagements should have rendered its final completion impossible, to retard the fulfilment of those which depended entirely on Great Britain, until redress should be granted to the subjects of his majesty on the specific points of the treaty itself, or a fair and just compensation should be obtained for their non-performance.

Whilst these negotiations were depending, intelligence was received at London, of the attack made on the British settlement at Nootka Sound. The vigor with which the government armed in support of its pretensions, furnished strong reasons for the opinion that a war with Spain, and probably with France, would soon be commenced.

This was considered in America as a favorable juncture for urging the claims of the United States to the free navigation of the Mississippi. Mr. Carmichael, their charge d'affaires at the court of Madrid, was instructed not only to press this point with earnestness, but to use his utmost endeavours to secure the unmolested use of that river in future, by obtaining a cession of the island of New Orleans, and of the Floridas.

The opinion was seriously entertained by the American govern-

By what medium did the American government communicate with that of Great Britain? What views, upon the controverted points between the two nations, were expressed by the Duke of Leeds?

ment that, in the event of a war between Great Britain and Spain, Louisiana would be invaded from Canada; and the attention of the executive was turned to the measures which it would be proper to take, should application be made for permission to march a body of troops through the unsettled territories of the United States into the dominions of Spain. Lord Dorchester, the Governor of that province, had intimated a wish to visit New York on his return to England; but the prospect of a rupture with Spain had determined him to remain in Canada. Under the pretext of making his acknowledgments for the readiness with which his desire to pass through New York had been acceded to, his lordship dispatched Major Beckwith, a member of his family, to sound the American government, and, if possible, to ascertain its dispositions towards the two nations.

The communications of this gentleman were entirely amicable. He was instructed to express the conviction of Lord Dorchester that the British cabinet was inclined not only towards a friendly intercourse, but towards an alliance with the United States. After expressing the concern with which that nobleman had heard of the depredations of the savages, he declared that his lordship, so far from countenancing the depredations, had taken every proper opportunity to impress pacific dispositions on the Indians; and, on hearing of the outrages lately committed, had sent a messenger to endeavour to prevent them. Major Beckwith intimated farther, that the perpetrators of the late murders were banditti, composed chiefly of Creeks and Cherokees in the Spanish interest, over whom the Governor of Canada possessed no influence.

The President directed that the further communications of Major Beckwith should be heard civilly, and that their want of official authenticity should be hinted delicately, without urging any expressions which might in the remotest degree impair the freedom of the United States to pursue without reproach the line of conduct which the honor or the interest of the nation might dictate.

In the opinion that it would be equally useless and dishonorable further to press a commercial treaty, the powers given to Mr. Morris were withdrawn. About the same time, the dispute between Great Britain and Spain was adjusted.

In the preceding May, Rhode Island had adopted the constitution; and the union of the states was completed.

On the 6th day of December, 1790, Congress assembled at Philadelphia.

The speech delivered at the commencement of the session, after taking a comprehensive view of the external and internal interests of the nation, concluded with the following impressive sentiment. "It will be happy for us both, and our best reward, if, by a successful administration of our respective trusts, we can make the established government more and more instrumental in promoting the good of our fellow-citizens, and more and more the object of their attachment and confidence."

In the short debate which took place in the House of Representatives, on the address in answer to the speech, a direct disapprobation of one of the measures of the executive was, for the first time, openly expressed.

In the treaty lately concluded with the Creeks, an extensive country claimed by Georgia under treaties the validity of which was contested by Indian chiefs, had been relinquished. This relinquishment excited serious discontents in that state; and was censured by Mr. Jackson with considerable warmth.

Scarcely were the debates on the address concluded, when several reports were received from the Secretary of the Treasury, suggesting such further measures as was deemed necessary for the establishment of public credit.

The assumption of the state debts not having been adopted until late in the preceding session, the discussion on the revenue for this portion of the public debt did not commence until the House had become impatient for an adjournment. As much contrariety of opinion was disclosed, and the subject did not press, it was deferred to the ensuing session; and the Secretary of the Treasury was required to report such further provision as might, in his opinion, be necessary for establishing the public credit. In obedience to this resolution, several reports had been prepared, the first of which repeated the recommendation of an additional impost on foreign distilled spirits, and of a duty on spirits distilled within the United States.

A new tax is the certain rallying point to all those who are unfriendly to the minister by whom it is proposed. The bill introduced in pursuance of the report was opposed with great vehemence and bitterness by a majority of the southern and western members. When required to produce a system in lieu of that which they so much execrated, the opponents of the bill alternately mentioned an increased duty on imported articles generally, a particular duty on molasses, a direct tax, a tax on salaries, pensions, and lawyers, a duty on newspapers, and stamp act.

After a very angry debate, a motion made by Mr. Jackson to strike out the section which imposed a duty on domestic distilled spirits, was negatived by thirty-six to sixteen; and the bill was carried by thirty-five to twenty-one.

What measure of taxation occasioned vehement debate in Congress? By what majority was the bill passed?

Some days after the passage of this bill, another question was brought forward, which was supposed to involve principles deeply interesting to the government.

The Secretary of the Treasury had been the uniform advocate of a national bank. A bill conforming to the plan he had suggested, was sent down from the Senate, and was permitted to proceed, in the House of Representatives, to a third reading. On the final question, an unexpected opposition was made to its passage. The great strength of the argument was directed against the constitutional authority of Congress to pass the act.

After a debate of great length and ability, the bill was carried in the affirmative by a majority of nineteen votes.

The cabinet also was divided on the measure. The Secretary of State and the Attorney-General conceived that Congress had transcended their constitutional powers; while the Secretary of the Treasury maintained the opposite opinion. The advice of each minister, with his reasoning in support of it, was required in writing; and their arguments were considered by the President with that attention which the magnitude of the question, and the interest it had excited, so eminently required. This deliberate investigation terminated in a conviction that the constitution of the United States authorised the measure; and the sanction of the executive was given to the act.

The division of opinion on this constitutional question ought not to excite surprise. It must be recollected, that the conflict between the powers of a general and state government was coeval with those governments. Even during the war, the preponderance of the states was obvious; and, in a very short time after the peace, the struggle ended in the abandonment of the general government. Many causes concurred to produce a constitution more competent to the preservation of the Union; but the old line of division was still as strongly marked as ever.

To this great and radical division of opinion, which would necessarily affect every question on the authority of the national legislature, other motives were added, which were believed to possess considerable influence on all measures connected with the finances.

As an inevitable effect of the state of society, the public debt had greatly accumulated in the middle and northern states. This circumstance could not fail to contribute to the complacency with which the plans of the secretary were viewed by those who had felt their benefit, nor to the irritation with which they were contemplated by others who had parted with their claims on the na-

Upon the subject of a National Bank, what was the action of Congress, and what the opinions of the cabinet? Mention the decision of General Washington upon this question, after mature examination.

tion. It is not impossible that personal considerations also mingled themselves with those which were of a public nature.

This measure made a deep impression on many members of the legislature, and contributed not inconsiderably to the complete organization of those distinct and visible parties which, in their long and dubious conflict for power, have since shaken the United States to their centre.

Among the last acts of the present Congress, was one to augment the military establishment of the United States.

The earnest endeavors of the President to give security to the north-western frontier, by pacific arrangements, having proved unavailing, he had planned an expedition against the hostile tribes in that quarter.

General Harmer marched from fort Washington on the 30th of September, with three hundred and twenty regulars. The army, when joined by the militia of Pennsylvania and Kentucky, amounted to fourteen hundred and fifty-three men. About the middle of October, Colonel Harden was advanced with six hundred men, chiefly militia. On his approach, the Indians set fire to the principal village, and fled to the woods. As the object of the expedition could not be accomplished without defeating the savages, Colonel Harden was again detached at the head of two hundred and ten men, thirty of whom were regulars. About ten miles west of Chillicothe, he was attacked by a party of Indians. The militia fled at the first appearance of the enemy. The regulars, commanded by Lieutenant Armstrong, made a brave resistance. After twenty-three of them had fallen in the field, the surviving seven rejoined the army.

Notwithstanding this check, the remaining towns on the Scioto were reduced to ashes, and the provisions laid up for the winter were utterly destroyed.

Being desirous of wiping off the disgrace which his arms had sustained, General Harmer once more detached Colonel Harden, with orders to bring on an engagement. His command consisted of three hundred and sixty men, of whom sixty were regulars, commanded by Major Wyllys. Early next morning, this detachment reached the confluence of the St. Joseph and St. Mary, where it was divided into three columns. The left was commanded by Colonel Harden in person; the centre, consisting of the regular troops, was led by Major Wyllys; and the right was commanded by Major M'Millar. The columns were soon met by a considerable body of Indians, and a severe engagement ensued. The militia retrieved their reputation. The right flank of the centre was

---

Was the army increased? What general marched against the Indians? Mention the movements and actions which ensued. Did the troops receive a check? What other action occurred?

attacked with great fury. Though Major Wyllys was among the first who fell, the battle was maintained by the regulars with spirit. At length, the scanty remnant of this small band was driven off the ground, leaving Major Wyllys, Lieutenant Farthingham, and fifty of their comrades, dead on the field. The loss sustained by the militia was also severe. It amounted to upwards of one hundred men, among whom were nine officers. After an obstinate engagement, the detachment rejoined the main army, which proceeded to fort Washington.

The information respecting this expedition was quickly followed by intelligence stating the deplorable condition of the frontier: The communications made by the President induced the legislature to add a regiment to the permanent military establishment; and to authorise him to raise a body of two thousand men for six months, and to appoint a Major-General and a Brigadier-General, to continue in command so long as he should think their services necessary.

With the 3d of March, 1791, the first Congress elected under the constitution of the United States terminated. The party denominated federal having prevailed at the elections, a majority of the members were steadfast friends of the constitution. To organize a government, to retrieve the national character, to establish a system of revenue, and to create public credit, were among the arduous duties which were imposed upon them, by the situation of their country. With persevering labor, guided by no inconsiderable portion of virtue and intelligence, these objects were, in a great degree, accomplished. Had it even been the happy and singular lot of America to see its national legislature assemble uninfluenced by those prejudices which grew out of the previous divisions of the country, the many delicate points which they were under the necessity of deciding, could not have failed to disturb this enviable state of harmony, and to mingle some share of party spirit with their deliberations. But when the actual state of the public mind was contemplated, and due weight was given to the important consideration that, at no very distant day, a successor to the present chief magistrate must be elected, it was still less to be hoped that the first Congress could pass away, without producing strong and permanent dispositions in parties, to impute to each other designs unfriendly to the public happiness. As yet, however, these imputations did not extend to the President. His character was held sacred, and the purity of his motives was admitted by all.

What was the result of Major Wyllys's engagement with the Indians? Did Congress further augment the military force? What is said respecting the first Congress?

CHAPTER XXIX.

Major-General St. Clair appointed commander-in-chief.—The President makes a tour through the southern states.—Meeting of Congress.—President's speech.—Debate on the bill for apportioning representatives.—Defeat of General St. Clair.—Opposition to the augmentation of the army.—Report of the Secretary of the Treasury.—Debate thereon. — Arrangement respecting the seat of government. — Congress adjourns. — Disagreement between the Secretaries of State and Treasury.—Opposition to the excise law. — Proclamation issued by the President. — Insurrection in St. Domingo. — General Wayne appointed to command the army. — Meeting of Congress. — President's speech.—Resolution implicating the Secretary of the Treasury rejected.—Congress adjourns.—Progress of the French revolution.—The effects on parties.

MORE ample means for the protection of the frontier having been placed under the control of the executive, the immediate attention of the President was directed to this interesting object. Major-General Arthur St. Clair, governor of the territory north-west of the Ohio, a gentleman who had served with reputation through the war of the revolution, was appointed commander-in-chief of the forces to be employed in the meditated expedition.

After making the necessary arrangements for recruiting the army, the President prepared to make his long-contemplated tour through the southern states. Having remained a few days on the Potomac, in order to execute finally the powers vested in him by the legislature for fixing on a place for the permanent seat of government, he proceeded on this tour. He was received universally with the same marks of affectionate attachment with which he had been welcomed in the northern and middle states. To the sensibilities which these demonstrations of regard could not fail to inspire, was added the high gratification produced by observing the improvements of the country, and the advances made by the government in acquiring the confidence of the people. But this progress towards conciliation was perhaps less considerable than was indicated by appearances. The hostility to the government, which originated with it, though diminished, was far from being subdued; and, under this smooth exterior, a mass of discontent was concealed, which, though it did not obtrude itself on the view of the man who united almost all hearts, was active in its exertions to effect its objects.

The difficulties which impeded the recruiting, protracted the completion of the regiments to a late season of the year; but the summer was not permitted to waste in total inaction. The act for the defence of the frontiers had empowered the President to call mounted militia into the field. Under this authority, two expeditions had been conducted against the villages on the Wabash, the

What expedition against the Indians was now contemplated? Mention the tour of the President in the southern states? Was he well received? What was the state of political feeling?

first led by General Scott, in May; the second, by General Wilkinson, in September. These desultory incursions had not much influence on the war.

On the 24th of October, the second Congress assembled in Philadelphia. In his speech, at the opening of the session, the President mentioned the rapidity with which the shares in the Bank of the United States had been subscribed, as " among the striking and pleasing evidences which presented themselves, not only of the confidence in the government, but of resources in the community."

In his review of Indian affairs, he recommended " justice to the savages, and such rational experiments for imparting to them the blessings of civilization, as might, from time to time, suit their condition."

In speaking of the act laying a duty on distilled spirits, he said, " If there are any circumstances in the law which, consistently with its main design, may be so varied as to remove any well-intentioned objections that may happen to exist, it will comport with a wise moderation to make the proper variations."

The answers of the two Houses, though perhaps less warm than those of the preceding Congress, manifested great respect for the executive magistrate.

Among the first subjects which engaged the attention of the legislature, was a bill for apportioning representatives among the people of the several states, according to the first enumeration.

This bill gave to each state one member for every thirty thousand persons. On a motion to strike out the number " thirty thousand," the debate turned chiefly on the policy of a more or less numerous House of Representatives; but, with the general arguments suggested by the subject, strong and pointed allusions to the measures of the preceding Congress were interspersed, which indicated much more serious hostility to the administration than had hitherto been expressed.

After a long and animated discussion, the amendment was rejected, and the bill passed in its original form.

In the Senate, the bill was amended, so as to give one representative for every thirty-three thousand persons. This amendment was disagreed to; and each House adhering to its opinion, the bill fell; but was again introduced in a new form, though without any material variation in its provisions. After a debate, in which the gross injustice of the fractions produced by the ratio it adopted, was strongly pressed, it passed that House. In the Senate, it was again amended, not by reducing, but by enlarging, the number of representatives.

Specify the chief topics of Washington's speech to the second Congress. What debate arose in that body, as to the rate of apportionment?

The Senate applied the number thirty thousand as a *divisor* to the total population, and taking the *quotient*, which was one hundred and twenty, they apportioned that number among the several states by that ratio, until as many representatives as it would give were allotted to each. The residuary members were then distributed among the states having the highest fractions. The result was a more equitable apportionment of representatives to population; but its constitutionality was questioned.

The amendment was disagreed to in the House of Representatives, and a conference took place. The conferees did not agree; but finally, the House of Representatives receded from their disagreement, and the bill passed.

The duty of deciding the solemn question whether an act of the legislature consisted with the constitution, now devolved once more on the President.

In his cabinet, a difference of opinion is understood to have again existed. The Secretary of State and the Attorney-General were of opinion that the act was at variance with the constitution; the Secretary at War was rather undecided; and the Secretary of the Treasury, thinking that neither construction could be absolutely rejected, was in favor of acceding to the interpretation given by the legislature.

After weighing deliberately the arguments on each side of the question, the President was confirmed in the opinion, that the bill was unconstitutional, and returned it to the House in which it originated, with his objections. The question was taken on its passage by ayes and noes, and it was rejected. One of the objections made by the President would seem to be conclusive. It is, that the bill allotted to eight of the states more than one representative for every thirty thousand persons.

An act was soon afterwards passed, which apportioned the representation on the several states at the ratio of one for every thirty-three thousand persons.

In December, intelligence was received that the American army had been totally defeated on the 4th of the preceding month.

Such delays had attended the recruiting service, that the troops were not assembled in the neighborhood of fort Washington until the month of September. On the 7th of that month, they moved northward. After garrisoning forts Hamilton and Jefferson, two intermediate posts, which were constructed as places of deposit, the effective number of the army, including militia, amounted to rather less than two thousand men. Small parties of Indians frequently interrupted their line of march, and some unimportant

What bill upon the subject of apportionment was passed by Congress? Did Washington approve it? What decision was at last made? Mention the unfavorable intelligence from the army.

skirmishes took place. As the army approached the country in which they might expect to meet an enemy, sixty of the militia deserted in a body. Though this diminution of force was not in itself an object of much concern, there was reason to fear that the example might be followed extensively; and it was reported to be the intention of the deserters to plunder convoys of provisions, which were advancing in the rear. To prevent these serious mischiefs, the General detached Major Hamtrank, with the first regiment, in pursuit of the deserters.

The army, consisting of about fourteen hundred rank and file, continued its march; and encamped in two lines, on the 3d of November, fifteen miles south of the Miamis villages, with a creek about twelve yards wide in its front. The militia crossed the creek, and encamped about a quarter of a mile in advance.

Before sunrise next morning, just after the troops had been dismissed from parade, an unexpected attack was made on the militia, who fled in the utmost confusion; and, rushing into the camp through the first line of continental troops, which had been formed on hearing the first fire, threw them too into disorder. The Indians pressed close on the heels of the flying militia, and engaged General Butler with great intrepidity. The action instantly became extremely warm; and the fire of the assailants, passing round both flanks of the first line, was, in a few minutes, poured with equal fury on the rear division. Its greatest weight was directed against the centre of each wing, where the artillery was posted; and the artillerists were mowed down in great numbers. The assailants were scarcely seen but when springing from one covert to another; in which manner they advanced close up to the American lines, and to the very mouths of their field-pieces. They fought with the daring courage of men whose trade is war, and who are stimulated by every passion which can impel the mind to vigorous exertion.

Under circumstances thus arduous, raw troops may be expected to exhibit that inequality which is found in human nature. Some performed their duty with resolution, others were dismayed and terrified. The officers were, as usual, the victims of this conduct. While fearlessly exposing themselves to the most imminent danger, they fell in great numbers. The commander-in-chief, though enfeebled by a severe disease, delivered his orders with judgment and self-possession.

As the American fire could produce no considerable effect on a concealed enemy, Lieutenant-Colonel Darke, at the head of the second regiment, which formed the extreme left, made an impetu-

When and where was the attack made upon General St. Clair by the Indians? State the manner of the assault, and describe the progress of the battle.

25 *

ous charge with the bayonet, forced the assailants from their ground with some loss, and drove them about four hundred yards. But the want of riflemen to press this advantage deprived him of its benefits; and, as soon as the pursuit was discontinued, the Indians renewed their attack. Meanwhile, General Butler was mortally wounded, the left of the right wing was broken, the artillerists killed almost to a man, the guns seized, and the camp penetrated. Darke was ordered again to charge with the bayonet at the head of his own regiment, and of the battalions commanded by Majors Butler and Clarke. The Indians were driven out of the camp, and the artillery recovered. But, while they were pressed on one point, their fire was kept up from every other with fatal effect. Several corps charged them separately, but no universal effort could be made; and, in every charge, a great loss of officers was sustained. To save the remnant of his army, General St. Clair, about half-past nine, ordered Lieutenant-Colonel Darke to charge a body of Indians who had intercepted their retreat, and to gain the road. Major Clarke, with his battalion, was directed to cover the rear. A disorderly flight commenced. The pursuit was kept up for about four miles; when that avidity for plunder, which is a ruling passion among savages, called back the victors to the camp, where the spoils of the vanquished were to be divided.

The routed troops continued their flight to fort Jefferson, where they met Major Hamtrank. A council of war determined against farther offensive operations, and the army continued its retreat to fort Washington.

In this disastrous battle, the loss on the part of the Americans was very great when compared with the numbers engaged. Thirty-eight officers and five hundred and ninety-three non-commissioned officers and privates were killed. Thirty-one officers, several of whom afterwards died of their wounds, and two hundred and forty-two non-commissioned officers and privates were wounded. Among the dead, was the brave and much-lamented General Butler. At the head of the list of the wounded, were Lieutenant-Colonels Gibson and Darke, Major Butler, and Adjutant-General Sergeant.

Nothing could be more unexpected than this severe disaster. The public had confidently anticipated a successful campaign, and could not believe that the General, who had been unfortunate, had not been culpable.

—The commander-in-chief earnestly requested a court-martial on his conduct; but the army did not furnish a sufficient number of officers of a grade to form a court on military principles. Late in the session, a committee of the House of Representatives was ap-

What was the result of the battle? Did it terminate the campaign? What was the number of killed and wounded? Did the public censure fall on the commander?

pointed to inquire into the cause of the failure of the expedition, whose report exculpated the commander-in-chief. This inquiry, however, was instituted for the purpose of examining the conduct of civil rather than of military officers. More satisfactory testimony in favor of St. Clair is furnished by the fact that he still retained the undiminished esteem and good opinion of the President.

The war now assumed a still more serious aspect. There was reason to fear that the hostile tribes would derive a great accession of strength from the impression which their success would make upon their neighbors. The President, therefore, lost no time in causing the estimates for a competent force to be prepared and laid before Congress. In conformity with the report made by the Secretary of War, a bill was brought into the House of Representatives, directing three additional regiments of infantry and a squadron of cavalry to be raised. The whole military establishment, if completed, would amount to five thousand men. The additional regiments were to be disbanded as soon as peace should be concluded, and the President was authorized to discharge, or to forbear to raise, any part of them.

It must excite some surprise, that even this necessary measure encountered the most strenuous opposition. The debate was conducted in a temper which demonstrates the extent to which the spirit of party had been carried. A motion to strike out the section which authorized an augmentation of force was at length lost, and the bill was passed.

The increased expenses of the war requiring additional revenue, a select committee, to whom the subject was referred, brought in a resolution directing the Secretary of the Treasury to report his opinion on the best mode of raising those additional supplies which the public service might require.

This proposition was opposed earnestly, but not successfully. The resolution was carried; thirty-one members voting in its favor, and twenty-seven against it.

The report made in pursuance of this resolution, recommended an augmentation of duties on imports; and was immediately referred to a committee of the whole House, in which resolutions were passed which were to form the basis of a bill.

Before the question was taken on the bill, a motion was made to limit its duration, the vote upon which marked the progress of opinion respecting those systems of finance which were believed to have established the credit of the United States.

The secretary of the treasury had deemed it indispensable to the creation of public credit that the appropriation of funds for the

Did Washington deem it necessary that the army should be increased? Did Congress pass a bill for this purpose? What was proposed, in a report of a committee of Congress, as a means of increasing the revenue?

payment of the interest, and the gradual redemption of the principal of the national debt, should be not only sufficient but permanent. The arguments used against this permanent appropriation appear to have been more successful with the people, than they had been with the legislature.

The bill founded on the last report of the secretary contained the same principle. Thirty-one members were in favor of limiting the duration of the bill, and thirty against it. By the rules of the house, the speaker has a right to vote as a member, and, if the members should then be equal, to decide as speaker. Being opposed to the limitation, the motion was lost by his voice.

On the 8th of May, Congress adjourned to the first Monday in November.

The asperity which on more than one occasion discovered itself in debate, was a certain index of the growing exasperation of parties; and the strength of the opposition on those questions which brought into review the points on which the administration was to be attacked, denoted the impression which the specific charges brought against those who conducted public affairs, had made on the minds of the people in an extensive division of the continent.

The symptoms of irritation in the public mind had assumed appearances of increased malignity during the session of Congress which had just terminated; and, to the President, who believed firmly that the union and the liberty of the states depended on the preservation of the government, they were the more unpleasant, and the more alarming, because they were displayed in full force in his cabinet.

A disagreement existed between the secretaries of the state and treasury departments, which seems to have originated in an early stage of the administration, and to have acquired a regular accession of strength from circumstances which were perpetually occurring, until it grew into open and irreconcileable hostility.

Without tracing this disagreement to those motives which, in elective governments especially, often produce enmities between distinguished personages neither of whom acknowledge the superiority of the other, such radical differences of opinion were supposed to exist between the secretaries as, in a great measure, to account for this inextinguishable enmity. These differences were, perhaps, to be ascribed in some measure to a difference in the original structure of their minds, and in some measure to the different situations in which they had been placed.

Until near the close of the war, Mr. Hamilton had served his country in the field, and, just before its termination, had passed from the camp into Congress, where he remained for some time after the establishment of peace. In the former station, the danger to which the independence of his country was exposed from the imbecility of its government was perpetually before his eyes; and, in the latter, his attention was forcibly directed towards the loss of its reputation, and the sacrifice of its best interests, which were to be ascribed to the same cause. Mr. Hamilton therefore was the friend of a government which should possess, in itself, sufficient powers and resources to maintain the character and defend the integrity of the nation. Having long felt and witnessed the mischiefs produced by the absolute sovereignty of the states, and by the control which they were enabled and disposed separately to exercise over every measure of general concern, he was particularly apprehensive of danger from that quarter; which he believed was to be the more dreaded, because the habits and feelings of the American people were calculated to inspire state, rather than national prepossessions. He openly avowed the opinion that the greatest hazard to which the constitution was exposed arose from its weakness, and that American liberty and happiness had much more to fear from the encroachments of the states than from those of the general government.

Mr. Jefferson had retired from Congress before the depreciation of the currency had produced an entire dependence of the general on the local governments, after which he filled the highest offices in his native state. About the close of the war, he was re-elected to Congress; but was soon afterwards employed on a mission to the court of Versailles, where he remained while the people of France were taking the first steps in that immense revolution which has astonished and agitated two quarters of the world. It is not unreasonable to suppose that, while residing at that court, and associating with those who meditated the great events which have since taken place, his mind might be warmed with the abuses of monarchy which were perpetually in his view, and he might be led to the opinion that liberty incurred its greatest danger from established governments. Mr. Jefferson therefore seems to have entertained no apprehensions from the debility of the government; no jealousy of the state sovereignties; no suspicion of their encroachments. His fears took a different direction; and all his precautions were used to check and limit the exercise of the powers vested in the government of the United States. From that alone could he perceive danger to liberty.

He did not feel the necessity of adopting the constitution so sensibly as they did who had continued in the country; and he had at

---

To what influential circumstances may we attribute the opinion of Hamilton that the general government should be strong? And why did Jefferson incline to the opposite opinion?

one time avowed a wish that it might be rejected by such a number of states as would secure certain alterations which he thought essential. From this opinion, however, he is understood to have receded.

To these causes of division another was superadded, the influence of which was soon felt in all the political transactions of the government.

The war which terminated in 1783, had left in the bosoms of the American people, a strong attachment to France and enmity to Great Britain. These feelings in a greater or less degree, were, perhaps, universal; and were demonstrated by all those means by which public sentiment is usually displayed.

Although affection for France and jealousy of Britain were sentiments common to the people of America, the same unanimity did not exist respecting the influence which ought to be allowed to those sentiments over the political conduct of the nation. While many favored such discriminations as might turn the commerce of the United States into new channels, others maintained that no sufficient motives existed for that sacrifice of national and individual interests which was involved in the discriminations proposed.

The former opinion was taken up with zeal by the secretary of state, and the latter was adopted with equal sincerity by the secretary of the treasury. This contrariety of sentiment respecting commercial regulations was only a part of a general system. It extended itself to all the relations which might exist between America and those two great powers.

In all popular governments, the press is the ready channel through which the opinions and the passions of the few are communicated to the many; and of the press, the two great parties sought to avail themselves. The Gazette of the United States supported the systems of the treasury department, while other papers enlisted themselves under the banners of the opposition. Conspicuous among these, was the National Gazette, a paper edited by a clerk in the department of state. It became the vehicle of calumny against the funding and banking systems, against the duty on home-made spirits, and against the men who had proposed and supported those measures. With perhaps equal asperity, the papers attached to the party which had defended these systems, assailed the motives of the leaders of the opposition.

This schism in his cabinet was a subject of extreme mortification to the President. Entertaining a high respect for the talents and a real esteem for the characters of both gentlemen, he was unwilling to part with either; and exerted all the influence he pos-

What feeling actuated the American people, in regard to Great Britain and France? What difference upon national policy existed between Hamilton and Jefferson? Did Washington endeavor to reconcile them?

sessed to effect a reconciliation between them. His exertions were not successful. Their hostility sustained no diminution, and its consequences became every day more diffusive.

Among the immediate effects of these internal dissensions was the encouragement they afforded to a daring and criminal resistance which was made to the execution of the laws imposing a duty on spirits distilled within the United States.

To the inhabitants of that part of Pennsylvania which lies west of the Allegheny Mountain, this duty was, from local causes, peculiarly odious; nor was their hostility to the measure diminished by any affection for its source. The constitution itself had encountered the most decided opposition from that part of the state, and this early enmity had sustained no abatement. Its measures generally, and the whole system of finance particularly, had been reprobated with extreme bitterness by the most popular men of the district. With these dispositions, a tax law, the operation of which was extended to them, could not be favorably received, however generally it might be supported in other parts of the Union. But when, to this pre-existing temper, were superadded the motives which arose from perceiving that the measure was censured on the floor of Congress as unnecessary and tyrannical; that resistance to its execution was treated as probable; that a powerful and active party pervading the Union, arraigned the whole system of finance as being hostile to liberty; and charged its advocates with designing to subvert the republican institutions of America; we ought not to be surprised that the awful impressions, which usually restrain combinations to resist the laws, were lessened; and that the malcontents were emboldened to hope that those combinations might be successful.

The resistance commenced with the circulation of opinions which might render the law still more odious, and with endeavors to defeat the collection of the duty, by directing the public resentment against those who were inclined either to comply with the act, or to accept offices under it. These indications of ill-temper were succeeded by neighborhood-meetings, in which resolutions of extreme violence were adopted, and by acts of outrage against the persons of revenue officers. At length, in September, 1791, a meeting of delegates from the malcontent counties was held at Pittsburg, in which resolutions, breathing the same spirit with those which had been previously agreed to in county assemblies, were adopted. Prosecutions were directed against those who had committed acts of violence, but the deputy-marshal was too much intimidated to execute the process. There was even reason to fear

Mention the opposition which was manifested in western Pennsylvania to a law of the Union. To what extent did the malcontents go in their resistance?

that the judiciary would be unable to punish them, and the legislature had not empowered the executive to aid that department. Farther proceedings were suspended, in the hope that the execution of the law elsewhere, and such a revision of it by Congress as should remove any real objections to it which might be suggested by experience, would render measures of coercion unnecessary.

An amendatory act was passed in May, 1792; but this conciliatory measure did not produce the desired effect. Offices of inspection in every county were necessary to its execution. The malcontents, for a considerable time, deterred every individual from permitting one to be held at his house, and the few who were prevailed on by the supervisors to grant this permission, were compelled, by personal violence and by threats, to retract the consent they had given.

A meeting was again convened at Pittsburg, by which committees of correspondence were established; and the determination was avowed to persist in every legal measure to obstruct the execution of the law; and to hold no intercourse with those who held offices for the collection of the duty.

The President issued a proclamation exhorting and admonishing all persons to desist from any combinations or proceedings whatsoever, tending to obstruct the execution of the laws; and requiring the interference of the civil magistrate. The proclamation produced no salutary effect.

Still solicitous to avoid extremities, the government adopted the following system:

Prosecutions were instituted against delinquents. The spirits distilled in the non-complying counties were intercepted in their way to market, and seized by the officers of the revenue; and the agents for the army were directed to purchase only those spirits on which the duty had been paid. Could the distillers have obeyed their wishes, these measures would have produced the desired effect. But, impelled by a furious multitude, they found it much more dangerous to obey the laws than to resist them.

During these party struggles, the external affairs of the United States sustained no material change.

A melancholy occasion had presented itself for evincing the alacrity with which the American executive could embrace any proper occasion for manifesting its disposition to promote the interests of France.

Early and bitter fruits of that malignant philosophy which can deliberately pursue through oceans of blood, abstract systems for the attainment of some imaginary good, were gathered in the

French West Indies. Instead of proceeding in the correction of abuses by those cautious steps which gradually introduce reform without ruin, the revolutionists of France formed the mad and wicked project of spreading their doctrines of equality among persons between whom distinctions and prejudices exist, to be subdued only by the grave. The rage excited by the pursuit of this visionary theory, after many threatening symptoms, burst forth on the 23d day of August, 1791, with a fury alike general and destructive. A preconcerted insurrection of the blacks took place, in one night, throughout the colony of St. Domingo; and the white inhabitants of the country, while sleeping in their beds, were involved in one indiscriminate massacre. Only a few females, reserved for a fate more cruel than death, were intentionally spared; and some were fortunate enough to escape into the fortified cities. A bloody war then commenced between the insurgents and the whites inhabiting the towns. The minister of his Most Christian Majesty applied to the executive of the United States for a sum of money which would enable him to preserve this valuable colony, to be deducted out of the debt to his sovereign; and the request was granted in a manner evincing the interest taken by the administration in whatever might concern France.

Spain still persisted in measures calculated to embroil the United States with the southern Indians.

An official diplomatic intercourse had at length been opened with Great Britain. Mr. Hammond, the minister-plenipotentiary of that nation, had arrived at Philadelphia in the autumn of 1791; upon which Mr. Thomas Pinckney had been charged with the interests of his country at the court of London. Soon after the arrival of Mr. Hammond, the non-execution of the treaty of peace became the subject of a correspondence between him and the Secretary of State, in which the complaints of their respective nations were urged in terms manifesting the sense entertained by each of the justice of those complaints, without furnishing solid ground for the hope that they would be immediately removed on either side. The views of the respective parties in relation to some important principles were too wide apart to render any commercial treaty probable.

The preparations for prosecuting the war with the north-western Indians were earnestly pressed. General Wayne was appointed to succeed General St. Clair, who had resigned the command of the army; but the recruiting business advanced too slowly to authorize a hope that the meditated expedition could be prudently undertaken in the course of the present year. Meanwhile, the

What service did the American administration render to France, when the insurrection took place in St. Domingo? Were terms of official intercourse at length arranged with Great Britain? Who succeeded General St. Clair?
26

clamor against the war continued to be loud and violent. From respect for opinions extensively professed, it was thought advisable to make still another effort to procure peace by a direct communication of the views of the executive. The fate of those who were employed in these efforts, was still more to be lamented than their failure. Colonel Harden and Major Truman, two brave officers and estimable men, were severally despatched with propositions of peace, and each was murdered by the savages.

On the 5th of November, Congress again convened. In the speech delivered at the commencement of the session, Indian affairs were treated at considerable length, and apprehensions were expressed that the war would be extended to the southern tribes also.

The subject next adverted to was the impediments which continued to embarrass the collection of duties on spirits distilled within the United States. After observing that symptoms of such increased opposition had manifested themselves lately in certain places as in his judgment to render his special interposition advisable, the President added—"Congress may be assured that nothing within constitutional and legal limits which may depend on me, shall be wanting to assert and maintain the just authority of the laws."

After noticing various other objects, the President addressed himself particularly to the House of Representatives, and said, "I entertain a strong hope that the state of the national finances is now sufficiently matured to enable you to enter into a systematic and effectual arrangement for the regular redemption and discharge of the public debt, according to the right which has been reserved to the government. No measure can be more desirable, whether viewed with an eye to its intrinsic importance, or to the general sentiments and wish of the nation."

The addresses of the two houses in answer to the speech were, as usual, respectful and affectionate. But the subsequent proceedings of the legislature did not fulfil the expectations excited by this auspicious commencement.

At an early day, Mr. Fitzsimmons moved "that measures for the reduction of so much of the public debt as the United States have a right to redeem, ought to be adopted; and that the Secretary of the Treasury be directed to report a plan for that purpose." After a vehement contest, a motion to strike out the proposed reference to the Secretary of the Treasury was overruled, and the resolution was carried.

The report of the Secretary proposed a plan for the redemption

What were the chief topics of Washington's speech to Congress? What measure was brought forward in that body, touching the redemption of the public debt?

of the debt. But the expenses of the Indian war rendering it unsafe in his opinion to rest absolutely on the existing revenue, he also proposed to extend the internal taxes to pleasure horses, or pleasure carriages, as the legislature might deem most eligible.

The consideration of this report was deferred on various pretexts; and a motion was made to reduce the military establishment. The debate on this subject was peculiarly earnest; and it was not until the 4th of January 1793, that the motion was rejected. While that question remained undecided, the report of the Secretary was unavoidably postponed. It would seem not improbable that the opponents of the financial system, who constituted rather a minority of the present Congress, but who expected to become a majority in the next, were desirous of referring every question concerning the treasury department to the succeeding legislature. The measures earnestly pressed by the administration could not be carried. Those who claimed the favor and confidence of the people as a just reward for their attachment to liberty, and especially for their watchfulness to prevent augmentation of debt, were found in opposition to a system for its diminution, which was urged by men who were incessantly charged with entertaining designs for its excessive accumulation, in order to render it the corrupt instrument of executive influence. But when party passions are highly inflamed, reason itself submits to their control, and becomes the instrument of their will.

Soon after the motion for the reduction of the military establishment was disposed of, another subject was introduced, which effectually postponed for the present session, every measure connected with the finances.

An act of Congress which passed on the 4th of August 1790, authorised the President to cause to be borrowed any sum not exceeding twelve millions of dollars, to be applied in payment of the foreign debt. Another act authorised a loan not exceeding two millions, to be applied in aid of the sinking fund, towards the extinguishment of the domestic debt.

A power to make these loans was delegated by the President to the Secretary of the Treasury. The commission was accompanied by written instructions directing the Secretary to pay such parts of the foreign debt as should become due at the end of the year 1791; but leaving him with respect to the residue, to be regulated by the interests of the United States. Two loans were negotiated in 1790, and others at subsequent periods.

Each loan was negotiated under both laws; and, consequently the moneys produced by each were applicable to both objects, in such proportions as the President might direct.

Was the endeavor successful, to reduce the military establishment? What subjects of debate occurred, to interfere with the enactment of any measure of finance?

At this period the domestic debt bore a low price in the market, and foreign capital was pouring into the United States for its purchase. The immediate application of the sinking fund to this object would consequently acquire a large portion of the debt, and would also accelerate its appreciation. Under the influence of these considerations, the Secretary had, with the approbation of the President, directed a part of the first loan to be paid in discharge of the instalments of the foreign debt which were actually due, and had drawn a part of it into the treasury in aid of the sinking fund.

The execution of the instructions given in May 1791, to the agent of the United States in Europe, to apply the proceeds of future loans in payment to France except such sums as should be specially reserved, was delayed partly by a suggestion of the minister of marine as to a plan, to which a decree of the national assembly would be necessary, for converting a large sum into supplies for St. Domingo; and partly to a desire of the American agent, to settle the rule by which the moneys paid should be liquidated, and credited to the United States. Such was the state of this transaction when the calamities which finally overwhelmed St. Domingo, induced the American government, on the application of the French minister, to furnish supplies to that ill-fated colony, in payment of the debt to France. This being a mode of payment which, to a certain extent, was desired by both creditor and debtor, a consequent disposition prevailed to use it so far as might comport with the wishes of the French government; and a part of the money designed for foreign purposes, was drawn into the United States.

On the 23d of January, Mr. Giles moved several resolutions, requiring information, among other things, on the various points growing out of these loans. Observations were made in the speech introducing them which implied charges of a much more serious nature than inattention to the exact letter of an appropriation law. Estimates were made in support of the position that a large balance was unaccounted for.

The resolutions were agreed to without debate; and in a few days the Secretary transmitted a report containing the information that was required.

On the 27th of February, Mr. Giles moved sundry resolutions founded on the information before the house. The idea of a balance unaccounted for was necessarily relinquished; but the Secretary was charged with neglect of duty, with violating the law of the 4th of August 1790; with deviating from the instructions of the

---

In what way did the American executive discharge a part of the debt due to France? What accusation was made in Congress in reference to this transaction, and what action was had thereupon?

President, with negotiating a loan at the bank while public money lay unemployed in its vaults, and with an indecorum to the House in undertaking to judge of its motives in calling for information.

These resolutions were followed by one directing that a copy of them should be transmitted to the President.

The debate was conducted in a spirit of acrimony, demonstrating the soreness of the wounds which had been given and received in the party war which had been previously waged. It terminated in a rejection of all the resolutions. The highest number in favor of any one of them was sixteen.

On the 3d of March, a constitutional period was put to the existence of the present Congress. The members separated with obvious symptoms of extreme irritation. Various causes had combined to organize two distinct parties in the United States, which were rapidly taking the form of a ministerial, and an opposition party. These divisions were beginning to be essentially influenced by the great events of Europe.

That revolution which has been the admiration, the wonder, and the terror of the civilized world, had, from its commencement, been viewed with the deepest interest. In its first stage, but one sentiment respecting it prevailed. When the labors of the convention had terminated in a written constitution, this unanimity of sentiment was in some degree impaired. A very few feared that a system so ill-balanced could not be permanent. A deep impression was made on the same persons by the influence of the galleries over the legislature, and of mobs over the executive. The tumultuous assemblages of the people, and their licentious excesses, during the short and sickly existence of the regal authority, were not, they thought, symptoms of a healthy constitution, or of genuine freedom. Persuaded that the present state of things could not last, they doubted, and they feared for the future.

In total opposition to this sentiment was that of the public. There seems to be something infectious in the example of a powerful and enlightened nation verging towards democracy, which imposes on the human mind, and binds human reason in fetters. The constitution of France, therefore, was generally received with unqualified plaudits. The establishment of a legislature consisting of a single body, was defended, not only as being adapted to the particular condition of that country, but as being right in itself. To question the duration of the present order of things, was thought to evince an attachment to unlimited monarchy, or a blind prejudice in favour of British institutions.

Were the resolutions reflecting upon General Washington, passed in Congress? In what spirit did Congress separate? Mention the great cause which influenced the formation of parties in the United States, and describe the general feeling of the American people.

26 *

In this stage of the revolution, however, the division of sentiment was not marked with sufficient distinctness; nor the passions
of the people agitated with sufficient violence to produce any powerful effect. But when the monarchy was overthrown and a republic decreed, the people of the United States seemed electrified
by the measure. The war in which the several potentates of Europe were engaged against France, although, in almost every instance, commenced by that power, was pronounced to be a war
for the extirpation of human liberty, and for the banishment of
free government from the face of the earth. The preservation of
the independence of the United States was supposed to depend on
its issue, and the coalition against France was treated as a coalition against America also.

A cordial wish that the war might terminate without diminishing the power of France, and so as to leave the people of that
country free to choose their own form of government, was perhaps
universal; but perfect unanimity of opinion did not prevail respecting the probable issue of their internal conflicts. By some few
individuals, the practicability of governing under the republican
form an immense military nation, whose institutions, habits, and
morals were adapted to monarchy, and which was surrounded by
armed neighbours, was deemed a problem which time alone could
solve. The circumstances under which the abolition of royalty
was declared, the massacres which preceded it, the scenes of tur-
bulence and violence which were acted in every part of the nation,
appeared to them to present an awful and doubtful state of things;
and the idea that a republic was to be introduced and supported
by force, was, to them, a paradox in politics. Under the influence of these appearances, the apprehension was entertained that
the ancient monarchy would be restored, or a military despotism
established.

By the many, these unpopular doubts were deemed unpardona-
ble heresies; and the few to whom they were imputed, were pronounced hostile to liberty. The French revolution will be found
to have exercised great influence over the affairs of the United
States.

When France substituted a republic for her ancient monarchy, what effect
was wrought upon the minds of the American people? What sentiment
upon the subject was universal, and what doubts arose with some, respecting
the applicability and permanence of the new system?

CHAPTER XXX.

General Washington again unanimously elected President of the United States.—War between Great Britain and France.—Proclamation of Neutrality.—Arrival of Mr. Genet as minister of France.—His conduct.—Illegal proceedings of French Cruisers. —Opinions of the Cabinet.—State of Parties.—Democratic Societies.—Genet openly insults the Government.—Rules to be observed in the Ports of the United States respecting the Powers at War.—The President requests the recall of Genet.—British order of the 8th of June, 1793.

THE term for which the President and Vice-President were elected being to expire on the third of March, the attention of the public had been directed to the choice of persons who should fill those offices.

General Washington had been prevailed upon to withhold a declaration he had at one time purposed to make, of his determination to retire from political life; and but one opinion existed respecting the President. The public was divided on the Vice-President.

The profound statesman who had been called to that office, had drawn upon himself a great degree of obloquy by some political tracts in which he had labored to maintain the proposition that a balance in government was essential to the preservation of liberty. He was charged by his opponents with having disclosed sentiments in these disquisitions favorable to distinct orders in society. He was also known to be friendly to the system of finance; and was believed to be among the few who questioned the durability of the French republic.

Mr. Jefferson being excluded by a constitutional restriction which must deprive him of the vote of Virginia, Mr. George Clinton was selected as the opponent of Mr. Adams.

Through the war of the revolution, this gentleman had filled the office of Governor of New York, and had performed its duties with courage and energy. A devoted friend of State supremacy, he had contributed greatly to the rejection of the resolutions for investing Congress with the power of collecting duties on imports, was a determined enemy to the adoption of the constitution, and to the system of measures pursued by the general government.

Both parties seemed confident in their strength, and both made the utmost exertions to ensure success. On opening the ballots in the Senate Chamber, it appeared that the unanimous suffrage of his country had been once more conferred on General Washington: and that Mr. Adams had received the next greatest number of votes.

Did Washington consent once more to be a candidate for the station of President? What two competitors were voted for as Vice-President? Upon whom was the office bestowed?

The unceasing endeavors of the executive to terminate the Indian war had at length succeeded with the savages of the Wabash, and a negotiation was pending with those of the Miamis, during which hostilities were forbidden. This prohibition increased the irritation of Georgia against the administration.

The Indian war was becoming an object of secondary magnitude. The critical and irritable state of things in France began to affect the United States so materially, as to require an exertion of all the prudence and all the firmness of government. The 10th of August, 1792, was succeeded by such a state of anarchy, and by scenes of so much blood and horror; and the nation was understood to be so divided, as to afford reason to doubt whether the fallen monarch would be finally deposed or reinstated. The American minister at Paris requested explicit instructions for the regulation of his future conduct; and, in the mean time, pursued a course which should in no respect compromise the United States.

The administration entertained no doubt of the propriety of recognizing the existing authority of France, whatever form it might assume; nor of paying the instalments of the debt as they should fall due, to those who might be authorized to receive it. These instructions were accompanied with assurances that the government would omit no opportunity of convincing the French people of its cordial wish to serve them.

The attachment of the President to the French nation was as strong as consisted with a due regard to the interests of his own, and his wishes for its happiness were as ardent as was compatible with the duties of a Chief Magistrate to the state over which he presided. But he still preserved the fixed purpose of maintaining the neutrality of the United States, however general the war might be in Europe. The firmness of this resolution was soon put to the test.

Early in April, the declaration of war by France against Great Britain and Holland reached the United States. This event restored full vivacity to a flame which a peace of ten years had not been able to extinguish. A great majority of the American people deemed it criminal to remain unconcerned spectators of a conflict between republican France and their ancient enemy. The few who did not embrace this opinion, and they were very few, were held up as objects of popular detestation; and were calumniated as the tools of Britain and the satellites of despotism. Indications were immediately given in some of the seaports, of a disposition to engage in the business of privateering on the commerce of the belligerent powers. As the President was determined to

What is said respecting Indian hostilities? When the French revolution was disgraced by horrible excesses, what was the course of Washington? Did the American people incline to the French cause?

suppress this practice, he requested the attention of the heads of departments to the subject. At that meeting, it was unanimously agreed that a proclamation ought to issue, forbidding the citizens of the United States to take part in any hostilities on the seas, with or against any of the belligerent powers; warning them against carrying to any of those powers articles deemed contraband; and enjoining them from all acts inconsistent with the duties of a friendly nation towards those at war. The proclamation was prepared by the Attorney-General; and, being approved by the cabinet, was signed by the President.

This measure derives importance from the consideration that it was the commencement of that system to which the American government afterwards inflexibly adhered, and to which much of the national prosperity is to be ascribed. It is not less important in another view. Being at variance with the prejudices, the feelings, and the passions of a large portion of society, and being founded on no previous proceedings of the legislature, it presented the first occasion, which was thought a fit one, for openly assaulting a character around which the affections of the people had thrown an armour theretofore deemed sacred, and for directly criminating the conduct of the President himself. It was only by opposing passion to passion, by bringing the feeling in favor of France into conflict with that in favor of the chief magistrate, that the enemies of his administration could hope to obtain the victory.

As soon as the commotions which succeeded the deposition of Louis XVI. had in some degree subsided, the attention of the French government was directed to the United States; and the resolution was taken to replace the minister who had been appointed by the king, with one who might be expected to enter more zealously into the views of the republic.

The citizen Genet, a gentleman of considerable talents and of an ardent temper, was selected for that purpose.

The letters which he brought to the executive, and his instructions, which he occasionally communicated, were highly flattering to the nation, and decently respectful to its government. But he was also furnished with private instructions, which subsequent events tempted him to publish. These indicate that, should the American executive prove to be not sufficiently compliant with the views of France, the resolution was taken to employ with the people of the United States, the same policy which had been so successful with those of Europe.

On the 8th of April, Mr. Genet arrived, not at Philadelphia, but

---

Did Washington forbid all interference of American citizens, in the contest between France and her enemies? Was he censured for this prudent policy? What was the conduct of the new French minister, citizen Genet?

at Charleston; a port whose contiguity to the West Indies gave it peculiar advantages as a resort for privateers. He was received by the Governor of the state, and by its citizens, with an enthusiasm well calculated to dissipate any doubt concerning the dispositions on which he was to operate. During his stay at that place, he undertook to authorize the fitting and arming of vessels, enlisting men, and giving commissions to commit hostilities on nations, with whom the United States were at peace. The captures made by these cruisers were brought into port, and the consuls of France were assuming, under the authority of Mr. Genet, to hold courts of admiralty for their trial, condemnation, and sale.

On the 16th of May, Mr. Genet arrived at the seat of government, preceded by the intelligence of his transactions in South Carolina. Means had been taken to render his entry triumphal; and the opposition papers exultingly stated that he was met at Gray's ferry by "crowds of people, who flocked from every avenue of the city to meet the republican ambassador of an allied nation."

The day succeeding his arrival, he received addresses of congratulation from particular societies, and from the citizens of Philadelphia, who waited on him in a body, in which they expressed their fervent gratitude for the zealous and disinterested aids which the French people had furnished to America, unbounded exultation at the success of their arms, and a positive conviction that the safety of the United States depended on the establishment of the republic. The answers to these addresses were well calculated to preserve the idea of a complete fraternity between the people of the two nations.

The day after being thus accredited by the citizens of Philadelphia, Mr. Genet was presented to the President, by whom he was received with expressions of a sincere and cordial regard for his nation. In the conversation which took place, he gave the most explicit assurances that France did not wish to engage the United States in the war.

Before the ambassador of the republic had reached the seat of government, a long catalogue of complaints, partly founded on his proceedings in Charleston, had been presented by the British Minister to the American executive. These were still farther aggravated by the commission of actual hostilities within the United States. The ship Grange, a British vessel, which had sailed from Philadelphia, was captured by the French frigate L'Ambuscade, within the capes of the Delaware.

The prizes thus unwarrantably made, being brought within the

What was the procedure of Genet at Charleston? Relate the manner of his reception in Philadelphia. What assurance did he make to the President? Mention the matter of complaint by the British minister.

power of the American government, Mr. Hammond demanded their restitution.

On many of the points suggested by the conduct of Mr. Genet, and by the memorials of the British minister, it would seem impossible that a difference of opinion could exist among intelligent men, not under the dominion of blind infatuation. Accordingly, it was agreed, without a dissenting voice, in the cabinet, that the jurisdiction of every independent nation, within its own territory, being of a nature to exclude the exercise of any authority therein by a foreign power, the proceedings complained of, not being warranted by treaty, were usurpations of national sovereignty, and violations of neutral rights, a repetition of which it was the duty of the government to prevent.

The question of restitution, except as to the Grange, was more dubious. The Secretary of State and the Attorney-General were of opinion that vessels which had been captured on the high seas, and brought into the ports of the United States, by vessels fitted out and commissioned in their ports, ought not to be restored. The Secretaries of the Treasury and of War were of a different opinion.

The President took time to deliberate on the point on which his cabinet was divided. Those principles on which they were united being considered as settled, the Secretary of State was desired to communicate them to the ministers of France and Britain; and circular letters were addressed to the executives of the several states, requiring their co-operation, with force if necessary, in the execution of the rules which were established.

The citizen Genet was much dissatisfied with these decisions. He thought them contrary to natural right, and subversive of the treaties by which the two nations were connected. Intoxicated with the sentiments expressed by a great portion of the people, and not appreciating the firm character of the executive, he seems to have expected that the popularity of his nation would enable him to overthrow that department, or to render it subservient to his views. It is difficult otherwise to account for his persisting to disregard its decisions, and for passages with which his letters abound, such as the following.

"Every obstruction by the government of the United States to the arming of French vessels, must be an attempt on the rights of man, upon which repose the independence and laws of the United States—a violation of the ties which unite the people of France and America, and even a manifest contradiction of the system of neutrality of the President; for in fact, if our merchant

What was the decision upon the matters urged by the British minister? When the President had taken his course in upholding neutrality, what feeling was entertained by Genet? State the substance of one of his letters to the executive.

vessels, or others, are not allowed to arm themselves, when the French alone are resisting the league of all the tyrants against the liberty of the people, they will be exposed to inevitable ruin in going out of the ports of the United States; which is certainly not the intention of the people of America. Their fraternal voice has resounded from every quarter around me, and their accents are not equivocal. They are pure as the hearts of those by whom they are expressed; and the more they have touched my sensibility, the more they must interest in the happiness of America the nation I represent; the more I wish, sir, that the federal government would observe, as far as in their power, the public engagements contracted by both nations; and that, by this generous and prudent conduct, they will give at least to the world, the example of a true neutrality, which does not consist in the cowardly abandonment of their friends in the moment when danger menaces them, but in adhering strictly, if they can do no better, to the obligations they have contracted with them. It is by such proceeding that they will render themselves respectable to all the powers—that they will preserve their friends, and deserve to augment their numbers."

A few days previous to the reception of the letter from which the foregoing extract is taken, two citizens of the United States, who had been engaged by Mr. Genet, in Charleston, to cruise in the service of France, were arrested by the civil magistrate, in pursuance of a determination of the executive to prosecute persons having thus offended against the laws. Mr. Genet demanded their release, in the following extraordinary terms:

"I have this moment been informed that two officers in the service of the republic of France, citizen Gideon Henfield and John Singletary, have been arrested on board the privateer of the French republic, the Citizen Genet, and conducted to prison. The crime laid to their charge—the crime which my mind cannot conceive, and which my pen almost refuses to state—is the serving of France, and defending, with her children, the common glorious cause of liberty.

"Being ignorant of any positive law or treaty which deprives Americans of this privilege, and authorizes officers of police arbitrarily to take mariners, in the service of France, from on board their vessels, I call upon your intervention, sir, and that of the President of the United States, in order to obtain the immediate releasement of the above-mentioned officers, who have acquired, by the sentiments animating them, and by the act of their engagement, anterior to every act to the contrary, the right of French citizens, if they have lost that of American citizens."

What was the demand urged in another extraordinary letter from the French ambassador to the American administration?

Though this lofty offensive style could not fail to make a deep impression on a mind penetrated with a just sense of those obligations by which the Chief Magistrate is bound to guard the dignity of his government, and to take care that his nation be not degraded in his person, yet, in no single instance did the administration permit itself to be betrayed into the use of one intemperate expression.

The deliberate perseverance of Mr. Genet in this open defiance of the executive, appears to have been occasioned by a belief that the sentiments of the people were in direct opposition to the measures of their government. So excessive were the demonstrations of enthusiastic devotion to France, so thin was the veil which covered the Chief Magistrate from that stream of malignant opprobrium directed against every measure which thwarted the views of this minister, that a person less sanguine than Mr. Genet might have cherished the hope of being able ultimately to triumph over the opposition to his designs.

The press, too, to a great extent, was enlisted in his cause. In various modes, that important engine contributed its powerful aid to the extension of opinions calculated to vary the situation of the United States. The proclamation of neutrality, which was denominated a royal edict, was not only considered as assuming powers not belonging to the executive, and as proving the monarchical tendencies of that department, but as demonstrating its disposition to break the connexion with France, and to dissolve the friendship which united the people of the two republics.

With infectious enthusiasm, it was contended that there was a natural and inveterate hostility between monarchies and republics; that the combination against France was a combination against liberty in every part of the world; and that the destinies of America were inseparably linked to those of the French republic.

On every point of controversy between the executive and Mr. Genet, this powerful party openly embraced the principles for which that minister contended. He was exhorted not to relax in his endeavors to maintain the just rights of his country; and was assured, that he would find a firm and certain support in the affections of the people.

These principles and opinions derived considerable aid from the labors and intrigues of certain societies who had constituted themselves the guardians of American liberty.

Soon after the arrival of Mr. Genet, a democratic society was formed in Philadelphia, on the model of the Jacobin Club in Paris; and, to give the more extensive operation to their labors, a corres-

To what may we attribute the persuasion under which Genet acted, in his defiance of the American executive? What course was, in general, taken by the public press, regarding France?

27

ponding committee was appointed, through whom they were to communicate with other similar societies throughout the United States.

Faithful to their founder, and true to the real objects of the association, these societies continued to be the resolute champions of all the encroachments attempted by the agents of the French republic on the government of the United States, and the steady defamers of the views and measures of the American executive.

The President was called to Mount Vernon on urgent business; and, in his absence, the heads of departments superintended the execution of the rules which had been previously established. Information being received that a vessel equipped as a privateer in the port of Philadelphia was about to sail on a cruise, Governor Mifflin was requested to inquire into the fact. Understanding that she was to sail the next day, under the name of *Le Petit Democrat*, the Governor, in pursuance of the instructions of the President, sent Mr. Secretary Dallas for the purpose of prevailing on Mr. Genet to relieve him from the employment of force, by detaining the vessel until the arrival of the President. On receiving this communication, the minister gave way to the most extravagant passion. After much grossly unbecoming language, he said the President was not the sovereign of this country. The powers of peace and war being vested in Congress, it belonged to that body to decide questions which might involve peace or war; and the President, therefore, ought to have assembled the national legislature before he ventured to issue his proclamation of neutrality, or to prohibit, by his instructions to the state Governors, the enjoyment of the particular rights which France claimed under the express stipulations of the treaty of commerce. After many intemperate expressions, he peremptorily refused to delay the departure of the privateer, and cautioned Mr. Dallas against any attempt to seize her, as she belonged to the republic, and would unquestionably repel force by force.

Governor Mifflin ordered out one hundred and twenty militia, and communicated the case to the officers of the executive government. Mr. Jefferson waited on Mr. Genet, in the hope of prevailing on him to detain the privateer in port till the arrival of the President. The minister indulged himself in a repetition of nearly the same violent language he had used to Mr. Dallas, and persisted in refusing to detain the vessel. The threat that, should an attempt be made to take possession of the vessel, force would be repelled by force, was renewed.

He afterwards said she would change her position, and fall

In the absence of the President at Mount Vernon, what dispute arose respecting a French privateer, and how did the French minister demean himself on the occasion?

down the river a small distance on that day; but was not yet ready to sail.

Mr. Jefferson stated to Governor Mifflin his conviction that the privateer would remain in the river until the President should decide on her case, in consequence of which the Governor dismissed the militia, and requested the advice of the heads of departments. Both the Governor and Mr. Jefferson stated that Mr. Dallas, in reporting his conversation with Mr. Genet, said that Mr. Genet threatened, in express words, " to appeal to the people."

Thus braved and insulted in the very heart of the empire, the Secretaries of the Treasury and of War were of opinion that, if the vessel should attempt to depart before the decision of the President could be obtained, military coercion should be employed to arrest her progress at Mud island. The Secretary of State dissenting from this opinion, the measure was not adopted; and the vessel fell down to Chester before the arrival of the President, and sailed on her cruise before the power of the government could be interposed.

On the 11th of July, while the Little Democrat lay at Chester, the President reached Philadelphia, and requested a meeting of his cabinet ministers the next morning at nine.

Among the papers placed in his hands by the Secretary of State, who had retired indisposed to his seat in the country, were those relating to the Little Democrat. On reading them, the President addressed a letter to him, in which he asked, " Is the minister of the French republic to set the acts of government at defiance *with impunity*, and threaten the executive with an appeal to the people? What must the world think of such conduct, and of the American government in submitting to it?"

In answer to this letter, the Secretary stated the assurances which had on that day been given him by Mr. Genet, that the vessel would not sail before the President's decision respecting her should be made. Immediate coercive measures were suspended; and, in the council of the next day, it was determined to retain all privateers in port, which had been equipped by any of the belligerents within the United States. In contempt of this determination, the Little Democrat sailed on her cruise.

In this, as in every effort made by the executive to maintain the neutrality of the United States, that great party, which denominated itself " THE PEOPLE," could perceive only a settled hostility to France and to liberty, a tame subserviency to British policy, and a desire to engage America in the war, for the extirpation of republican principles.

Did the French privateer sail on her cruise, notwithstanding the decision of the American government? In what light did the people view the efforts of the President to maintain the duties of neutrality?

The administration received additional evidence of the difficulty of executing its system, in the acquittal of Gideon Henfield, who had been prosecuted in pursuance of the advice of the Attorney-General.

As the trial approached, a great degree of sensibility was displayed, and the verdict of acquittal was celebrated with the most extravagant marks of exultation. It bereaved the government of the strength to be derived from the opinion that punishment might be legally inflicted on those who should openly violate the rules prescribed for the preservation of neutrality.

About this time a question of considerable importance was presented to the consideration of the executive.

The principle that free bottoms make free goods was engrafted into the treaty of commerce with France, but no stipulation on the subject had been made with England. It followed that the belligerent rights of Britain were to be decided by the law of nations. Construing this law to give security to the goods of a friend in the bottoms of an enemy, and to subject the goods of an enemy to capture in the bottoms of a friend, the British cruisers took French property out of American vessels, and their courts condemned it as lawful prize.

Mr. Genet had remonstrated against the acquiescence of the executive in this exposition of the law of nations, in such terms as he was accustomed to employ. On the 9th of July, in the midst of the contest respecting the Little Democrat, he had written a letter demanding an immediate and positive answer to the question, what measures the President had taken or would take to cause the American flag to be respected.

Towards the close of July, Mr. Genet again addressed the Secretary of State on the subject. After complaining of the insults offered to the American flag by seizing the property of Frenchmen confided to its protection, he added, "your political rights are counted for nothing." "In vain does the desire of preserving peace, lead to sacrifice the interest of France to that of the moment, in vain does the thirst of riches preponderate over honor in the political balance of America; all this management, all this condescension, all this humility, end in nothing; our enemies laugh at it; and the French, too confident, are punished for having believed that the American nation had a flag, that they had some respect for their laws, some conviction of their strength, and entertained some sentiment of their dignity." "If our fellow-citizens have been deceived, if you are not in a condition to maintain the sovereignty of your people, speak; we have guarantied it when

Was the executive able to enforce the laws by punishing the violators of neutrality? What question arose respecting the liabilities of goods belonging to belligerents, when shipped in neutral bottoms? State the substance of Genet's letter on this subject?

slaves, we shall be able to render it formidable having become freemen."

On the day preceding the date of this offensive letter, the Secretary of State had answered that of the 9th; and, without noticing the unbecoming style in which the decision of the executive was demanded, had avowed and defended the opinion that by the general law of nations the goods of an enemy found in the vessels of a friend, are lawful prize. This fresh insult might therefore be passed over in silence.

While a hope remained that the forbearance of the executive, and the unceasing manifestations of its friendly dispositions towards the French republic, might induce the minister of that nation to respect the rights of the United States, an anxious desire not to impair the harmony which subsisted between the two republics, had restrained the President from adopting those measures respecting Mr. Genet, which the conduct of that gentleman required. But the full experiment had now been made; and the result was a conviction that moderation would only invite additional injuries.

The judgment of the President was never hastily formed; but, once formed, it was seldom to be shaken. In a cabinet council, it was unanimously agreed that a letter should be written to Mr. Morris, the minister of the United States at Paris, stating the conduct of Mr. Genet, reviewing the points of difference between the government and that gentleman, assigning the reasons for the opinions of the former, and desiring the recall of the latter; directing also that this letter, with those which had passed between the Secretary of State and Mr. Genet, should be laid before the executive of the French government.

An adequate idea of the passion it excited in Mr. Genet, who received the communication in September, at New York, can be produced only by a perusal of his letter addressed, on that occasion, to the Secretary of State. The asperity of his language was not confined to the President, whom he still set at defiance, nor to those " gentlemen who had been painted to him so often as aristocrats and partisans of England." Its bitterness was also extended to the Secretary of State himself, who had, he said, " initiated him into mysteries which had inflamed his hatred against all those who aspire to an absolute power."

During these deliberations, Mr. Genet was received in New York with the same marks of unlimited attachment which had been exhibited in the more southern states. At this place too, he manifested the same desire to encourage discontent at the conduct of the government, and to embark America in the quarrel by impressing

Did the American government request that of France to recall Mr. Genet? What additional insolence was exhibited by that minister, when he became acquainted with this communication?

the opinion that the existence of liberty depended on the success of the French republic.

While these exertions were successfully making to give increased force to opinions which might subvert the system adopted by the executive, Mr. Jay and Mr. King arrived in New York from Philadelphia. They had been preceded by a report that the French minister had avowed a determination to appeal from the President to the people. These gentlemen were asked whether the report was true, and had answered that it was.

On being repeatedly required in the public papers to admit or deny that they had made this assertion, they published a certificate avowing that they had made the declaration imputed to them.

This communication made a serious impression on reflecting men. The recent events in Poland, whose dismemberment and partition were readily traced to the admission of foreign influence, gave additional solemnity to the occurrence, and led to a more intent consideration of the awful causes which would embolden a foreign minister to utter such a threat. In every quarter of the Union the people assembled in their districts, and the strength of parties was tried. The contest was warm and strenuous. But public opinion appeared to preponderate greatly in favor of neutrality, and of the proclamation by which its observance was directed. Yet it was not to be concealed that the arrogance of Mr. Genet, his direct insults to the President, and the attachment which many, who opposed the general measures of the administration, still retained for the person of that approved patriot, contributed greatly to the prevalence of the sentiment which was called forth by the occasion.

Foreseeing the effect which the certificate of Mr. Jay and Mr. King might have, Mr. Genet sought to defeat its influence by questioning its veracity. Although it was well understood that the exceptionable expressions had not been used to the President or in his presence, he addressed a letter to the chief magistrate, which, being written for publication, was itself the act he had threatened. In this letter he subjoined to a detail of his accusations against the executive, the demand of an explicit declaration that he had never intimated to him an intention to appeal to the people.

In answer, the Secretary of State said, " the President does not conceive it to be within the line of propriety or duty, for him to bear evidence against a declaration, which, whether made to him or others, is perhaps immaterial; he therefore declines interfering in the case."

Immense efforts were made to direct the censure merited by

What evidence established the fact that Genet had threatened to appeal from the American government to the people? Did the nation sustain the President in his neutral course? What direct communication was made by Genet to Washington?

these expressions, against those who had communicated them to the public. The darkest motives were assigned for the disclosure, and the reputation of those who made it, has scarcely been rescued by a lapse of years, and by a change of the subjects of controversy, from the peculiar party odium with which they were, at the time, overwhelmed.

Sentiments of a still more extraordinary character were openly avowed. The people alone being in a republic the source of all power, it was asserted that if Mr. Genet dissented from the interpretation given by the President to existing treaties, he might rightfully appeal to the real sovereign whose agent the President was.

While insult was thus added to insult, fresh instances of the attempts of Mr. Genet to violate the neutrality of the United States were perpetually recurring. Among these was an outrage committed in Boston, too flagrant to be overlooked.

A schooner brought as a prize into the port of Boston by a French privateer was claimed by the British owner, who instituted proceedings at law for the purpose of obtaining a decision on the validity of the capture. She was rescued from the possession of the marshal by an armed force acting under the authority of Mr. Duplaine the French Consul, which was detached from a frigate then lying in port. Until the frigate sailed, she was guarded by a part of the crew; and, in contempt of the determination that Consuls should not exercise prize jurisdiction within the United States, Mr. Duplaine declared his purpose to take cognizance of the case.

It was impossible for the President to submit to this act of open defiance. The exequatur which had been granted to Mr. Duplaine was revoked, and he was forbidden further to exercise the consular functions. Even this necessary measure could not escape censure. The self-proclaimed champions of liberty discovered in it a violation of the constitution, and a new indignity to France.

Mr. Genet did not confine his attempts to wield the force of America against the enemies of his country, to maritime enterprises. He planned an expedition against Florida, to be carried on from Georgia; and another against Louisiana, to be carried on from Kentucky. Intelligence was received, that the principal officers were engaged; and the temper of the people inhabiting the western country furnished some grounds for the apprehension, that the restraints which the executive could impose would be found too weak to prevent the execution of these measures. The course of Britain and Spain, by furnishing weapons to the enemies of neutrality, rendered the task of the executive still more arduous.

Mention the new outrage at Boston, against the American authorities. What did Washington determine, in this case? Did Genet proceed still further, and plan military expeditions?

The avidity with which the neutral merchants pressed forward to reap the rich harvest offered to them by the wants of France, presented a harvest not less rich to the cruisers of her enemies. Captures to a great extent were made, and the irritations insep_rable from disappointment in gathering any of the expected fruits of a gainful traffic, were communicated extensively to the agricultural part of society.

The vexations on the ocean to which neutrals are commonly exposed during war, were aggravated by a measure of the British cabinet, which war was not supposed to justify.

The vast military exertions of the French Republic had carried many cultivators of the earth into the field, and the measures of government had discouraged labor, by rendering its profits insecure. These causes, aided perhaps by unfavorable seasons, had produced a scarcity which threatened famine. This state of things suggested to their enemies the policy of increasing the internal distress, by cutting off the external supply. The British cruisers were instructed " to stop all vessels loaded wholly or in part with corn, flour, or meal, bound to any port in France, or any port occupied by the armies of France, and to send them to such port as shall be most convenient, in order that such corn, meal, or flour, may be purchased on behalf of his Majesty's government, and the ships be relieved after such purchase, and after a due allowance for freight; or that the masters of such ships, on giving due security, to be approved by the Court of Admiralty, be permitted to proceed, to dispose of their cargoes of corn, meal, or flour, in the ports of any country in amity with his Majesty."

This attempt to make a principle which was understood to be applicable only to blockaded places, subservient to the impracticable plan of starving an immense agricultural nation, was resisted with great strength of reasoning, by the administration; and added, not inconsiderably, to the resentments felt by the great body of the people.

Hostilities on the ocean disclosed still another source of irritation, which added its copious stream to the impetuous torrent which threatened to sweep America into the war that desolated Europe.

The British government had long been accustomed to man their fleet by impressment. Merchantmen in their ports, and even at sea, were visited, and mariners taken out of them. The profits of trade enabling neutral merchants to give high wages, British sailors entered their service in great numbers; but the neutral ship furnished no protection.

Why did Great Britain endeavor to exclude provisions from the French ports? What was the effect of this course in the United States? What new cause of controversy added to the difficulty?

The Americans were peculiarly exposed to the abuse to which such usages are liable. The distinction between them and the English was not always so visible as to prevent unintentional error; nor were the captains of ships of war at all times very solicitous to avoid mistakes. Native Americans, therefore, were frequently impressed.

The British cabinet disclaimed all pretensions to the impressment of American citizens, and declared their willingness to discharge them, on the establishment of their citizenship; but time was necessary to procure these testimonials. There was, too, one class of citizens, concerning whose rights a difference of opinion prevailed, which has not yet been adjusted. These were British subjects who had been naturalized in the United States.

The continuance of the Indian war added still another item to the catalogue of discontents.

The efforts of the United States to make a treaty with the savages of the Miamis, had been disappointed. The question of boundary could not be adjusted. It was extensively believed, that the treaty was defeated by British influence.

The causes of discontent which were furnished by Spain, though less the theme of public declamation, continued to be considerable. That which related to the Mississippi, was peculiarly embarrassing. The opinion had been industriously circulated, that an opposition of interests existed between the eastern and the western people, and that the endeavors of the executive to open this great river were feeble and insincere. At a meeting of the Democratic Society, in Lexington, Kentucky, this sentiment was unanimously avowed, in terms of extreme disrespect to the government; and a committee was appointed to open a correspondence with the inhabitants of the whole western country, for the purpose of uniting them on this all-important subject, and of preparing a remonstrance to the President and Congress of the United States, to be expressed " in the bold, decent, and determined language, proper to be used by injured freemen, when they address the servants of the people." They claimed much merit for having thus long abstained from using the means they possessed, for the assertion of " a natural and unalienable right;" and indicated the opinion, that this forbearance could not be long continued. The probability that the public expression of these dangerous dispositions would perpetuate the evil, could not moderate them. This restless temper gave additional importance to the project of an expedition against Louisiana, which had been formed by Mr. Genet.

The apprehension of hostilities with Spain, was strengthened by

What is said respecting the impressment of American citizens, by the cruisers of Great Britain? Was the Indian war still continued? Did Spain also furnish cause of discontent to the people of the west?

private communications. The government had received intelligence from their ministers in Europe, that propositions had been made by the cabinet of Madrid to that of London, the object of which was the United States. The precise nature of these propositions was not ascertained; but it was understood generally, that their tendency was hostile.

Thus unfavorable to the pacific views of the executive, were the circumstances under which Congress was to assemble.

CHAPTER XXXI.

Meeting of Congress.—President's speech.—His message on foreign relations.—Report of the Secretary of State. — His resignation. — Is succeeded by Mr. Randolph. — Mr Madison's resolutions, founded on the report of the Secretary of State.—Debate thereon.—Mission of Mr. Jay to Great Britain.—Inquiry into the conduct of the Secretary of the Treasury.—Internal taxes.—Congress adjourns.

A MALIGNANT fever, believed to be infectious, had severely afflicted the city of Philadelphia, and dispersed the officers of government. Although the fear of contagion was not entirely dispelled, such was the expectation that important communications would be made by the executive, and that legislative measures, not less important, would be founded on them, that Congress was full on the first day.

On the 4th of December, at twelve, the President met both Houses in the Senate chamber. His speech commenced with his own re-election, his feelings at which were thus expressed:—

"Since the commencement of the term for which I have been again called into office, no fit occasion has arisen for expressing to my fellow-citizens at large the deep and respectful sense which I feel of the renewed testimony of public approbation. While, on the one hand, it awakened my gratitude for all those instances of affectionate partiality with which I have been honored by my country, on the other, it could not prevent an earnest wish for that retirement from which no private consideration could ever have torn me. But, influenced by the belief that my conduct would be estimated according to its real motives, and that the people, and the authorities derived from them, would support exertions having nothing personal for their object, I have obeyed the suffrage which commanded me to resume the executive power; and I humbly implore that Being on whose will the fate of nations depends, to crown with success our mutual endeavors for the general happiness."

Did Congress assemble as usual in Philadelphia, notwithstanding some apprehension from the sickness which had prevailed there? State the substance of the President's speech to Congress.

Passing to those measures which had been adopted by the executive for the regulation of its conduct towards the belligerent nations, he observed, " as soon as the war in Europe had embraced those powers with whom the United States have the most extensive relations, there was reason to apprehend that our intercourse with them might be interrupted, and our disposition to peace drawn into question by suspicions too often entertained by belligerent nations. It seemed, therefore, to be my duty to admonish our citizens of the consequence of a contraband trade, and of hostile acts to any of the parties; and to obtain, by a declaration of the existing state of things, an easier admission of our rights to the immunities belonging to our situation. Under these impressions, the proclamation, which will be laid before you, was issued.

" In this posture of affairs, both new and delicate, I resolved to adopt general rules, which should conform to the treaties, and assert the privileges of the United States. These were reduced to a system; which shall be communicated to you."

After suggesting those legislative provisions on this subject, the necessity of which had been pointed out by experience, he pressed on Congress the propriety of placing the country in a state of complete defence; and earnestly recommended measures for the regular redemption and discharge of the public debt.

On the succeeding day, a message was sent to both Houses, containing some important communications relative to the connexion of the United States with foreign powers.

After stating the friendly disposition generally manifested by the French government, he added, " A decree, however, of the National Assembly, subjecting vessels laden with provisions to be carried into their ports, and making enemy-goods lawful prize in the vessel of a friend, contrary to our treaty, though revoked at one time as to the United States, has been since extended to their vessels also."

" It is with extreme concern I have to inform you, that the person whom they have unfortunately appointed minister plenipotentiary here, has breathed nothing of the friendly spirit of the nation which sent him. The tendency, on the contrary, has been to involve us in a war abroad, and in discord and anarchy at home."

The order issued by the British government on the 8th of June, and the consequent measures taken by the United States, were noticed. The discussions which had taken place in relation to the non-execution of the treaty of peace were also mentioned; and the message was concluded with a reference to the negotiations with Spain.

What was said by the President, respecting his course towards belligerents? Mention the substance of Washington's message to Congress upon the subject of relations with foreign powers.

This message was accompanied with copies of the correspondence between the Secretary of State and the French minister; and of the letter written by Mr. Jefferson to Mr. Morris.

The strength of parties had been tried in the late elections; and the opposition had derived so much aid from associating the cause of France with its own principles, as to furnish much reason to suspect that, in one branch of the legislature at least, it had become the majority. The first act of the House of Representatives served to strengthen this suspicion. Each party brought forward a candidate for the chair; and Mr. Muhlenberg, who was supported by the opposition, was elected by a majority of ten votes over Mr. Sedgewic, who was supported by the federalists.

The answers, however, to the speech breathed a spirit indicating that the leaders, at least, still venerated their Chief Magistrate; and that no general intention, as yet, existed to involve him in the obloquy directed against his measures.

The neighborhood of the Spanish colonies to the United States, had given rise to various subjects of discussion in addition to those relating to boundary, and the navigation of the Mississippi. One of these had assumed a serious aspect.

Having strong reason to suppose that the hostility of the southern Indians was excited by the agents of Spain, the President had directed the American commissioners at Madrid to make the proper representations on the subject, and to propose that each nation should, with good faith, promote the peace of the other with their savage neighbors.

About the same time, the Spanish government entertained, or affected to entertain, suspicions of like hostile excitements by the agents of the United States, to disturb their peace with the same nations. These representations were accompanied with pretensions to which the American executive could not be inattentive. His Catholic Majesty claimed to be the protector of those Indians. He assumed a right to mediate between them and the United States, and to interfere in the settlement of their boundaries. At length, his representatives, complaining of the aggressions of American citizens on the Indians, declared "that the continuation of the peace, good harmony, and perfect friendship of the two nations was very problematical for the future, unless the United States should take more convenient measures, and of greater energy than those adopted for a long time past."

Though the pretensions of the French republic, as asserted by their minister, were still supported with enthusiastic zeal out of doors, they found no open advocate in the House. An attack on

---

Did the opposition party elect their Speaker in the House of Representatives? Mention the points of contention with Spain, and state what was said to the executive upon that subject.

tne administration could be placed on no ground more disadvantageous than on its controversy with Mr. Genet. The conduct and language of that minister were offensive to reflecting men of all parties. To the various considerations growing out of the discussions themselves, and of the parties engaged in them, one was added which could not be disregarded. The party in France, to which Mr. Genet owed his appointment, had lost its power; and his fall was the inevitable consequence of the fall of his patrons. That he would probably be recalled was known in America; and that his conduct had been disapproved, was generally believed. The future course of the French republic towards the United States could not be foreseen; and it would be committing something to hazard, not to wait events.

These objections did not exist to an indulgence of the national feeling towards the belligerent powers, in measures suggested by its resentment against Great Britain.

In addition to the causes of dissatisfaction with Great Britain, which have already been suggested, others soon occurred. Under her auspices, a truce for one year had been lately negotiated between Portugal and Algiers, which, by withdrawing a small squadron stationed by the former power in the Streights, opened a passage into the Atlantic to the cruisers of the latter. The capture of American vessels, which was the immediate consequence of this measure, was believed in the United States to have been its motive.

This transaction was afterwards ascribed by England to her desire to serve an ally, and to enable that ally to act more efficaciously in a common cause.

Early in the session, a report was made by the Secretary of State on the nature and extent of the privileges and restrictions of the commercial intercourse of the United States with foreign nations.

Its statements and arguments tended to enforce the policy of making discriminations which might favor the commerce of the United States with France, and discourage that with England; and which might promote the increase of American navigation as a branch of industry, and a resource of defence.

This was the last official act of the Secretary of State. He resigned his office on the last day of December, and was succeeded by Mr. Edmund Randolph. The office of Attorney-General was filled by Mr. William Bradford, a gentleman of considerable eminence in Pennsylvania.

On the 4th of January, the House resolved itself into a com-

<hr>

What circumstance of change in France, rendered uncertain her future course? What new difficulty occurred with Great Britain? What changes took place in the American cabinet?

mittee of the whole on the report of the Secretary of State; when Mr. Madison laid on the table a series of resolutions, which imposed additional duties on the manufactures and on the tonnage of vessels of nations not having a commercial treaty with the United States, while they reduced the duties already imposed on the tonnage of vessels belonging to nations having such treaty.

The debate commenced on the 13th of January, and continued until the 3d of February. It was eloquent, animated, and interesting. Party feelings were mingled with commercial policy; and all the strong passions which agitated the country were manifested in the House. Arguments on the general interests of the United States were also advanced, which still merit the attention of every American statesman.

On the 3d of February, the first resolution was carried by a majority of five. The further consideration of the resolutions was then postponed until the first Monday in March.

This animated debate was succeeded by another, on a question which also brought into full view, the systems of the opposite parties, on some of those great national subjects which determine the character of government.

On the 2d of January, a resolution had been agreed to in the House of Representatives, declaring " that a naval force adequate to the protection of the commerce of the United States against the Algerine corsairs, ought to be provided." The force proposed was to consist of six frigates.

This measure was founded on the communications of the President respecting the improbability of being able to negotiate a peace with the Dey of Algiers; and on undoubted information that the corsairs of that regency had, during their first short cruise in the Atlantic, captured eleven American merchantmen, and made upwards of one hundred prisoners; and were preparing to renew their attack on the unprotected vessels of the United States.

In every stage of its progress this bill was most strenuously opposed. On no question had the influence of party feeling been more strongly exhibited. Not even the argument that it would be cheaper to purchase the protection of foreign powers than to afford it by a small naval force, was too humiliating to be urged.

The original resolution was carried by a majority of two voices only; but as the bill advanced, several members who were accustomed to vote in the opposition gave it their support; and, on the final question, a majority of eleven appeared in its favor. The other branch of the legislature concurred, and it received the cordial assent of the President.

Mention the subject of an interesting debate in the House of Representatives. For what purpose was it proposed to increase the naval force? Who opposed the measure? Was it adopted?

Pending these discussions, the irritations in which they commenced were greatly aggravated by accounts that captures of American vessels were made by British cruisers, to an extent altogether unprecedented; and, early in March, an authentic paper was received which proved that these captures were not unauthorized.

On the 6th of November 1793, additional instructions had been issued to the ships of war and privateers of Great Britain, requiring them to stop and detain all ships laden with goods, the produce of any colony belonging to France, or carrying provisions or other supplies to any such colony, and to bring the same, with their cargoes, to legal adjudication in the British courts of admiralty.

These instructions made a serious impression on the most reflecting men in the United States. It was believed that they originated in a spirit of hostility which must lead to war; and that it had become the part of prudence to prepare for that event.

On the 12th of March, Mr. Sedgewic laid on the table several resolutions, the objects of which were, to raise a military force, and to authorize the President to lay an embargo. Two days afterwards, a motion was made to take up that which related to an embargo; but this motion was negatived for the purpose of resuming the consideration of the commercial resolutions offered by Mr. Madison. On the motion of Mr. Nicholas, those resolutions were amended so as to subject the manufactures of Great Britain alone, instead of those of all nations having no commercial treaty with the United States, to the proposed augmentation of duties. They were again debated with great earnestness, but no decision was made on them.

On the 21st of March, the motion authorizing the President to lay an embargo was negatived by a majority of two voices; but in a few days, the consideration of that subject was resumed, and a resolution was passed, prohibiting all trade from the United States to any foreign port or place for thirty days, and empowering the President to carry the resolution into effect. This resolution was accompanied with vigorous provisional measures for defence.

While the measures of Congress indicated the expectation of war, a document made its appearance which seemed to show that Great Britain also was preparing for that event. This was the answer of Lord Dorchester, on the 20th of February, to a speech delivered by the deputies of a great number of Indian tribes assembled at Quebec. In this answer his lordship had openly

---

What further aggressions were made by Great Britain on American commerce? Mention the various propositions connected with this subject, which were debated in Congress. What intimation was given by Lord Dorchester?

avowed the opinion, that a war between Great Britain and the United States was probable, and that a new line between the two nations must then be drawn by the sword.

On the 27th of March, Mr. Dayton moved a resolution for sequestering all debts due to British subjects, and for taking means to secure their payment into the treasury, as a fund out of which to indemnify the citizens of the United States for depredations committed on their commerce by British cruisers.

The debate on this resolution was such as was to be expected from the irritable state of the public mind. Before any question was taken on it, Mr. Clarke moved a resolution to prohibit all intercourse with Great Britain until her government should make full compensation for all injuries done to the citizens of the United States, by armed vessels, or by any person or persons acting under the authority of the British King; and until the western posts should be delivered up.

On the 4th of April, the President laid before Congress a letter just received from Mr. Pinckney, communicating additional instructions to the commanders of British armed ships dated the 8th of January, which revoked those of the 6th of November, and directed British cruisers to bring in those neutral vessels only which were laden with cargoes, the produce of the French islands, and were on a direct voyage from those islands to Europe.

This letter detailed a conversation with Lord Grenville in which his lordship explained the motives which led to the order of the 6th of November. It was intended to answer two purposes;— one, to prevent the abuses which might be the consequence of the whole St. Domingo fleet having gone to the United States; the other, on account of the attack designed upon the French West India islands by the armament under the command of Sir John Jarvis, and Sir Charles Grey; but it was no longer necessary to continue the regulations for those purposes. His lordship added, that the order of the 6th of November did not direct the confiscation of all vessels trading with the French islands, but only that they should be brought in for adjudication.

The influence of this communication on the federal party was considerable. Believing that the differences between the two nations still admitted of adjustment, they opposed all measures which tended to irritate, or which might be construed into a dereliction of the neutral character they were desirous of maintaining; but gave all their weight to those which might prepare the nation for war should negotiation fail.

No change of sentiment or of views was produced on the oppo-

What was proposed by Mr. Dayton? What by Mr. Clarke? State the substance of a letter from Mr. Pinckney. What was the effect of this communication upon the federal party, and on their opponents?

site party. Their system seems to have been matured, and not to have originated in the feelings of the moment. Their propositions were still discussed with great animation; but, notwithstanding an ascertained majority in their favor, were permitted to remain undecided, as if their fate depended on some extrinsic circumstance.

Meanwhile, great exertions were made to increase the public agitation, and to stimulate the resentments which were felt against Great Britain. The artillery of the press was played with unceasing fury, on the minority of the House of Representatives; and the democratic societies brought their whole force into operation. Language will scarcely afford terms of greater outrage than were employed against those who sought to moderate the rage of the moment.

The proceedings of the legislature continued to manifest a fixed purpose to pursue the system which had been commenced. That the nation was advancing rapidly to a state of war was firmly believed by many intelligent men who doubted its necessity, and denied its policy. In addition to the calamities which must in any state of things result from the measure, there were considerations belonging exclusively to the moment which were certainly entitled to great respect.

That war with Britain during the continuance of the passionate and almost idolatrous devotion of a great majority of the people to the French republic, would throw America so completely into the arms of France, as to leave her no longer mistress of her own conduct, was not the only fear which the temper of the day suggested. That the ferocious spirit which triumphed in that nation, and deluged it with the blood of its revolutionary champions, might cross the Atlantic, and desolate the hitherto safe and peaceful dwellings of the American people, was an apprehension not unsupported by appearances. Already had an imitative spirit, captivated with the splendor and copying the errors of a great nation, reared up self-created corresponding societies, who, claiming to be the people, assumed a control over the government, and were loosening its bonds. Already were the Mountain, and a revolutionary tribunal, favorite toasts; and already were principles familiarly proclaimed, which, in France, had been the precursors of that tremendous and savage despotism, which, in the name of the people, and by the instrumentality of affiliated societies, had spread its terrific sway over that fine country, and had threatened to extirpate all that was wise and virtuous. That a great majority of those statesmen who conducted the opposition would deprecate such a result, was no security against it. When the physical

What engine was used to inflame the minds of the people? To what extent did certain societies imitate the French revolutionists? What apprehensions might reasonably be entertained from the progress of such sentiments?

28 *

force of a nation usurps the place of its wisdom, those who have produced such a state of things no longer control it.

These apprehensions produced in those who felt them, an increased solicitude for the preservation of peace. Their aid was not requisite to confirm the judgment of the President. Fixed in his purpose of maintaining the neutrality of the United States until foreign aggression should clearly render neutrality incompatible with honor; and conceiving from the last advices received from England, that the differences between the two nations had not yet attained that point, he determined to make one decisive effort which should either remove the ostensible causes of quarrel, or demonstrate the indisposition of Great Britain to remove them. This determination was executed by the nomination of an Envoy Extraordinary to his Britannic Majesty, which was announced to the Senate on the 16th of April, in the following terms:

"The communications which I have made to you during your present session, from the despatches of our minister in London, contain a serious aspect of our affairs with Great Britain. But as peace ought to be pursued with unremitted zeal, before the last resource which has so often been the scourge of nations, and cannot fail to check the advanced prosperity of the United States, is contemplated, I have thought proper to nominate, and do hereby nominate John Jay, as Envoy Extraordinary of the United States to his Britannic Majesty.

"My confidence in our Minister Plenipotentiary in London, continues undiminished. But a mission like this, while it corresponds with the solemnity of the occasion, will announce to the world a solicitude for the friendly adjustment of our complaints, and a reluctance to hostility. Going immediately from the United States, such an Envoy will carry with him a full knowledge of the existing temper and sensibility of our country; and will thus be taught to vindicate our rights with firmness, and to cultivate peace with sincerity."

No public act of the President has drawn on his administration a greater degree of censure than this. That such would be its effect could not be doubted by any person who had observed the ardor with which the opinions it thwarted had been embraced, or the extremity to which the contests and passions of the moment had carried all orders of men. But it is the province of real patriotism to consult the utility, more than the popularity of a measure; and to pursue the path of duty although it may be rugged.

In the Senate, the nomination was approved by a majority of ten voices; and, in the House of Representatives, it was urged as

Did Washington still determine to preserve peace, if consistent with the national honor? With this view, upon what step did he resolve? Did the measure call forth disapprobation from the opposition?

an argument against persevering in the system which had been commenced. On the 18th of April, however, the resolution for cutting off all commercial intercourse with Great Britain was carried in the affirmative; and a bill conforming to it passed by a considerable majority. It was lost in the Senate by the casting vote of the Vice-President. The system of the House of Representatives was pressed no further.

The altercations between the executive and the minister of the French republic had given birth to many questions on which a great diversity of sentiment prevailed.

The opinion that the relations produced by existing treaties, and indeed by a state of peace independent of treaty, imposed obligations on the United States, an observance of which it was the duty of the executive to enforce, had been reprobated with extreme bitterness. It was contended, certainly by the most active, perhaps by the most numerous part of the community, not only that the treaties had been grossly misconstrued, but also that, under any construction of them, the interference of the executive required the sanction of the legislature. The right of the President to call out the militia for the detention of privateers about to violate the rules he had established, was, in some instances, denied; attempts to punish those who had engaged, within the United States, to carry on expeditions against foreign nations, were unsuccessful; and a grand jury had refused to find a bill against Mr. Duplaine for having rescued a vessel which had been taken into custody by an officer of justice. The propriety of legislative provision was suggested by the President at the commencement of the session, and a bill was brought into the Senate "in addition to the act for punishing certain crimes against the United States."

Necessary as this measure was, the whole strength of the opposition was exerted to defeat it. Motions to strike out the most essential clause were repeated, and each motion was negatived by the casting vote of the Vice-President. It was only by his voice that the bill finally passed. In the House of Representatives also the bill encountered serious opposition, and a section which prohibited the sale of prizes in the United States was struck out.

The preparations for an eventual war, and a heavy appropriation which, under the title of foreign intercourse, was made for the purpose of purchasing peace from Algiers, and liberating the Americans who were in captivity, created demands upon the treasury which the ordinary revenues were insufficient to satisfy.

The Committee of Ways and Means reported several resolutions for extending the internal duties to various objects, for an augmentation of the imposts, and for a direct tax.

Mention the difficulties of the President in enforcing the laws. What act was passed? What revenue measures were now necessary?

Only thirteen members voted for the direct tax. The augmentation of the duty on imports met with no opposition. The internal duties were introduced in separate bills, that each might encounter those objections only which should be made to itself. A resolution in favor of stamps was rejected; the others were carried, after repeated and obstinate debates.

On the 9th of June, this active and stormy session was closed by an adjournment to the first Monday in November.

CHAPTER XXXII.

Genet recalled.—Is succeeded by Mr. Fauchet.—Mr. Morris recalled.—Is succeeded by Mr. Monroe.—Kentucky Remonstrance.—Intemperate Resolutions of the people of that State.—General Wayne Defeats the Indians on the Miamis.—Insurrection in the western part of Pennsylvania.—Quelled.—Meeting of Congress.—President's Speech.—Democratic Societies.—Resignation of Colonel Hamilton.—He is succeeded by Mr. Wolcott.—Resignation of General Knox.—He is succeeded by Colonel Pickering.—Treaty with Great Britain.—Conditionally ratified.—Is unpopular.—Mr. Randolph resigns.—Is succeeded by Colonel Pickering.—Mr. M'Henry appointed Secretary of War.—Charges against the President rejected.—Treaty with the Indians.—With Algiers.—With Spain.—Meeting of Congress.—President's Speech.—Mr. Adet succeeds Mr. Fauchet.—The House of Representatives call on the President for papers.—He declines sending them.—Debates on the treaty-making power.—On the bill for making appropriations to carry the Treaty with Great Britain into effect.—Congress adjourns.—The President endeavours to procure the liberation of Lafayette.

THAT the most material of those measures on which the two great parties in the United States were divided might be presented in one unbroken view, some transactions have been passed over, which will now be noticed.

The resolution of the President to bear with the insults of Mr. Genet until his appeal to the French government should be fairly tried, was shaken by fresh proofs, received in January, of conduct which could not be tolerated. That minister had deliberately planned two expeditions to be carried on against the dominions of Spain, and had granted commissions to citizens of the United States, who were privately recruiting troops for the service. The first was destined against the Floridas, and the second against Louisiana. That against the Floridas, while in progress, was fully developed by the vigilance of the legislature of South Carolina, and some of its principal agents were arrested.

About the same time, intelligence was received that the expedition against Louisiana, which was to be carried on from Kentucky, down the Ohio, was in equal maturity.

Believing further forbearance to be incompatible with the dignity,

---

Were these bills passed? What further proofs of improper conduct on the part of Genet, came to the knowledge of the President? What body suppressed one of the contemplated expeditions?

perhaps with the safety of the United States, the cabinet came to the resolution of superseding his diplomatic functions; and a message was prepared, communicating to Congress the determination to carry this measure into execution, unless it should be disapproved by that body, when the business was arrested by a letter received from Mr. Morris, announcing the recall of this rash minister.

His successor, Mr. Fauchet, arrived in February, and brought with him strong assurances that his government disapproved the conduct of his predecessor.

Not long afterwards, the executive of France requested the recall of Mr. Morris. Mr. Monroe, a senator from Virginia, who had embraced the cause of the French Republic with ardor, and was particularly acceptable to the party in opposition, was appointed to succeed him.

The discontents long fomented in the west, had assumed an alarming appearance.

A remonstrance from the inhabitants of Kentucky, respecting the navigation of the Mississippi, was laid before the executive and each branch of the legislature. In the language of an offended sovereign people, injured by the maladministration of public servants, it demanded the use of the Mississippi as a natural right, which had been unjustly withheld; and charged the government openly with being under the influence of a local policy, which had prevented its making a single real effort for the security of a good which was all-essential to the western people. Several intemperate aspersions on the legislature and executive were accompanied by threats obviously pointing to dismemberment.

Both branches of the legislature expressed their conviction, that the executive was urging the claim of the United States to the navigation of the Mississippi in the manner most likely to prove successful; and the Senate added a resolution, " that the President of the United States be, and he is hereby required, to cause to be communicated to the executive of the state of Kentucky, such part of the existing negotiation between the United States and Spain, relative to this subject, as he may deem advisable, and consistent with the course of the negotiation."

Had the measures pursued in the western country been dictated exclusively by a wish to obtain an important good, these resolutions would have allayed the ferment. But when the real motives for human action are latent, it is vain to demonstrate the unreasonableness of those which are avowed. After they were received, a number of the principal citizens, from various parts of

Who succeeded Mr. Genet as minister to the United States? And who was the successor of Mr. Morris at Paris? What were the declarations and intimations of a memorial from Kentucky?

Kentucky, assembled at Lexington, and passed other resolutions, breathing the same intemperate and dangerous spirit.

These proceedings were intimately connected with the machinations of Mr. Genet.

Authentic information of the measures taken by that minister, for the expedition against New Orleans, had been communicated to the Governor of Kentucky, so early as October, 1793, by Mr. Jefferson, with a request that he would use those means of prevention which the law enabled him to employ. This letter was accompanied with one from the Secretary of War, conveying the desire of the President, that should preventive means fail, he would employ military force to arrest the expedition; and General Wayne was ordered to hold a body of troops at the disposal of the Governor, should he find the militia insufficient for his purpose.

The Governor was apprised of the proposed expedition, but doubted the lawfulness of arresting it; and was unwilling to exercise the power, if he possessed it. On the reception of the very extraordinary letter which announced this determination, the President directed General Wayne to establish a post at fort Massac, on the Ohio, for the purpose of stopping by force, if peaceable means should fail, any body of armed men who should be proceeding down that river.

This precaution appears to have been necessary. The preparations for the expedition were still carried on with considerable activity; and there is reason to believe that it was not absolutely relinquished until Spain ceased to be the enemy of France.

While these turbulent scenes were acting, the loud plaudits of France were re-echoed from every part of the American continent. The friendship of that republic for the United States, her respect for their rights, the ingratitude with which her continuing benefits were repaid, the injustice done her by the executive, and its tameness under British insults, were the inexhaustible themes of loud, angry, and unceasing declamation.

After the total failure of the attempt to treat with the hostile Indians, the campaign was opened with as much vigor as circumstances would permit. It was too late to complete the preparations which would enable General Wayne to enter their country, and to hold it. He therefore contented himself with establishing his troops for the winter about six miles in advance of fort Jefferson, and taking possession of the ground on which the Americans had been defeated in 1791, on which he erected fort Recovery. These positions afforded considerable protection to the frontiers.

Did the Governor of Kentucky decline to interfere with an expedition against New Orleans? What was done towards subduing the Indians? Where was General Wayne posted?

The delays inseparable from the transportation of supplies through an uninhabited country, infested by an active enemy, peculiarly skilled in partisan war, unavoidably protracted the opening of the campaign until near midsummer. Meanwhile, several sharp skirmishes took place, in one of which a few white men were said to be mingled with the Indians.

On the 8th of August, General Wayne reached the confluence of the Au Glaize and the Miamis of the Lakes. The richest settlements of the western Indians lay about this place.

The mouth of the Au Glaize is distant about thirty miles from a post then occupied by the British, on the Miamis of the Lakes; in the vicinity of which, the whole strength of the enemy, amounting, as General Wayne was informed, to rather less than two thousand men, was collected. The legion was not much inferior in number to the Indians; and a reinforcement of eleven hundred mounted militia, commanded by General Scott, had been received from Kentucky.

On the 15th of August, the American army advanced down the Miamis; and on the 18th, arrived at the rapids, where they halted, on the 19th, in order to erect a temporary work for the protection of the baggage, and to reconnoitre the situation of the enemy.

The Indians were advantageously posted behind a thick wood, and behind the British fort.

At eight, in the morning of the 20th, the American army advanced in columns, the right flank of the legion covered by the Miamis. One brigade of mounted volunteers, commanded by General Todd, was on the left; the other, commanded by General Barbee, brought up the rear. A select battalion, commanded by Major Price, moved in front of the legion.

After marching about five miles, Major Price received a heavy fire from a concealed enemy, and was compelled to retreat.

The Indians had chosen their ground with judgment. They had advanced into a thick wood in front of the British works, and had taken a position rendered almost inaccessible to horse by a quantity of fallen timber. They were drawn up in three lines, extending at right angles with the river, about two miles, and their immediate effort was to turn the left flank of the American army.

On the discharge of the first rifle, the legion was formed in two lines, and the front was ordered to advance with trailed arms, and rouse the Indians from their covert at the point of the bayonet; then, and not till then, to deliver a fire, and to press the fugitives

Where did General Wayne halt his troops, and when did he advance on the Indians? How were the savages posted? In what manner did Wayne direct the attack to be commenced?

too closely to allow them time to load after discharging their pieces. Perceiving that the enemy was endeavoring to turn the American left, the general ordered up the second line. The legion cavalry, led by Captain Campbell, was directed to penetrate between the Indians and the river, in order to charge their left flank; and General Scott, at the head of the mounted volunteers, was directed to make a considerable circuit, and to turn their right.

These orders were executed with spirit and promptitude; but so impetuous was the charge made by the first line of infantry, so entirely was the enemy broken by it, and so rapid was the pursuit, that only a small part of the second line, and of the mounted volunteers could get into the action. In the course of one hour, the Indians were driven more than two miles, through thick woods; when the pursuit terminated within gun-shot of the British fort.

General Wayne remained three days on the banks of the Miamis, in front of the field of battle, during which time the houses and corn-fields above and below the fort, some of them within pistol-shot of it, were reduced to ashes. During these operations, a correspondence took place between General Wayne and Major Campbell, the commandant of the fort, which shows that hostilities between them were prevented only by the prudent acquiescence of the latter in this destruction of property within the range of his guns.

On the 28th, the army returned to Auglaize by easy marches, destroying, on its route, all the villages and corn within fifty miles of the river.

In this decisive battle, the loss of the Americans, in killed and wounded, amounted to one hundred and seven. Among the dead, was Captain Campbell of the cavalry, and Lieutenant Towles of the infantry. General Wayne bestowed great and well-merited praise on every part of the army.

The hostility of the Indians still continuing, their whole country was laid waste, and forts were erected in the heart of their settlements, to prevent their return.

This seasonable victory rescued the United States from a general war with the Indians.

About this time, the resistance to the execution of the law imposing duties on spirits distilled within the United States, had advanced, in the western counties of Pennsylvania, to a point which required the decisive interposition of government.

In consequence of a steady adherence to the system of counteraction, adopted by the executive, the law was slowly gaining ground, and several distillers in the disaffected country were in-

Mention the result of the battle, and the loss of the Americans. What was the nature of Wayne's correspondence with a British officer? Did the resistance to the government, in western Pennsylvania, still continue?

duced to comply with its requisites. Congress having at length passed an act containing those provisions which had been suggested by
the chief of the Treasury Department, the malcontents perceived
that the certain loss of a market for the article, added to the penal-
ties to which delinquents were liable, would gradually induce a
compliance on the part of the distillers, unless they could deprive
the government of the means it employed for carrying the law into
execution.

Bills of indictment had been found in a court of the United
States against some of the perpetrators of the outrages which had
been committed, upon which, as well as against several of the
non-complying distillers, process was directed to issue.

On the 15th of July, while the marshal was in the execution of
his duty, he was fired on by a party of armed men; and, at daybreak the ensuing morning, a party attacked the house of General
Nevil the inspector, but were compelled to retreat. Apprehending
that it would be repeated, he applied to the magistrates and militia
officers for protection, but could obtain none.

On the succeeding day, the insurgents reassembled to the number of about five hundred men, to renew the attack. The inspector
had obtained a detachment of eleven men from the garrison at fort
Pitt, who were joined by Major Kirkpatrick. Successful resistance
being hopeless, a parley took place, at which the assailants, after
all their other demands were conceded, required that the party in
the house should march out and ground their arms. This being
refused, the assault commenced. The action continued until the
assailants set fire to several adjacent buildings, which compelled
the party defending the house to surrender.

The marshal was seized on his way to General Nevil's house,
and his life was threatened. He obtained his liberty only by entering into a solemn engagement to serve no more processes on
the western side of the Allegheny Mountains.

The perpetrators of these treasonable practices, desirous of discovering their latent enemies, intercepted the mail from Pittsburg
to Philadelphia, and took out the letters it contained. On acquiring
the intelligence they sought, delegates were deputed to Pittsburg,
to demand the banishment of the offenders. The inhabitants of
Pittsburg complied with this demand, and also agreed to assemble
the next day in Braddock's field, and to elect delegates to a convention which was to meet on the 14th of August at Parkinson's
ferry. The avowed objects of these outrages were to compel the
resignation of all officers engaged in the collection of duties; to
withstand the authority of the United States by force of arms; to

What civil process was employed against the malcontents in western
Pennsylvania? Did they resist? What outrage against the marshal was
perpetrated? And what violation of the mail?

extort the repeal of the law imposing those duties; and to compel an alteration in the conduct of the government.

The opposition had now reached a point which seemed to forbid the continuance of a temporizing system. The alternative of subduing resistance, or of submitting to it, was presented to the government.

The act of Congress, which provided for calling forth the militia, required, as a prerequisite to the exercise of the power, that a judge should certify "that the laws of the United States were opposed, or their execution obstructed, by combinations too powerful to be suppressed by the ordinary course of judicial proceedings, or by the powers vested in the marshals." It also provided, "that if the militia of the state where such combination may happen, shall refuse or be insufficient to suppress the same, the President may employ the militia of other states."

The certificate of the judge having been obtained, the subject was again seriously considered in the cabinet; and the Governor of Pennsylvania was also consulted. All concurred in the appointment of commissioners, who should convey a full pardon for past offences, upon the condition of future submission; but a difference of opinion prevailed respecting ulterior eventual measures. The act made it the duty of the President, previous to the employment of military force, to issue his proclamation commanding the insurgents to disperse within a limited time. The Secretary of State, (and the Governor of Pennsylvania was understood to concur with him,) was of opinion that this conciliatory mission should be unaccompanied by any measure which might wear the appearance of coercion. The Secretaries of the Treasury and of War, and the Attorney General, were of a different opinion. They thought that the occasion required a full trial of the ability of the government to enforce obedience to the laws; and that the employment of a force which would render resistance desperate, was dictated equally by humanity and sound policy. The insurgent counties contained sixteen thousand men capable of bearing arms; and the computation was that they could bring seven thousand into the field. An army of twelve thousand would present an imposing force, which the insurgents could not venture to meet.

It was impossible that the President could hesitate to embrace the latter of these opinions. The proclamation, therefore, was issued, and, on the same day, a requisition was made on the Governors of New Jersey, Pennsylvania, Maryland, and Virginia, for their several quotas of militia, to compose an army of twelve thousand men.

While steps were taking to bring this force into the field, a last essay was made to render its employment unnecessary. Three distinguished and popular citizens of Pennsylvania were deputed as the bearers of a general amnesty on the sole condition of future obedience to the laws.

Meanwhile the insurgents omitted nothing which might enlarge the circle of disaffection. They made incursions into the counties east of the Allegheny, and into the neighboring counties of Virginia, for the purpose of spreading their principles, and suppressing offices of inspection.

The convention at Parkinson's ferry had appointed a committee of safety, consisting of sixty members, who chose fifteen of their body to receive and report the propositions of the commissioners. They expressed themselves unanimously in favor of accepting the terms offered by the government. The committee of safety appeared rather inclined to the same opinion, but determined finally to refer the question to the people.

This reference resulted in demonstrating that, though many were disposed to demean themselves peaceably, a vast mass of opposition remained, determined to obstruct the re-establishment of civil authority.

From some causes, among which was disaffection, the prospect of bringing the Pennsylvania quota into the field was at first unpromising. But the assembly, which was convened by the Governor, expressed its abhorrence of this daring attempt to subvert the government: and a degree of ardor was displayed by the people of other states which exceeded the hopes of the most sanguine friends of the administration. Some feeble and insidious attempts to produce disobedience to the requisition, by declaring, among other things, that the people would never be made the instruments of the Secretary of the Treasury to shed the blood of their fellow-citizens, were silenced by the general sense of the nation, which loudly proclaimed that the government and laws must be supported. From the exertions of her Governor, Pennsylvania was not behind her sister states.

On the 25th of September, the President issued a second proclamation, stating the perverse spirit in which the lenient propositions of government had been received, and declaring his fixed determination, in obedience to the high duty consigned to him by the constitution, to reduce the refractory to obedience.

The troops of New Jersey and Pennsylvania were directed to rendezvous at Bedford, and those of Maryland and Virginia at Cumberland, on the Potomac. The command of the expedition had been conferred on Governor Lee of Virginia.

Did the insurgents accept the overtures of the government? Where did the troops rendezvous? On whom was the command conferred?

From Cumberland and Bedford, the army marched in two divisions into the country of the insurgents. The disaffected did not venture to assemble in arms. Several of the leaders, who had refused to give assurance of future submission to the laws, were seized, and some of them detained for legal prosecution.

But although no direct and open opposition was made, the spirit of insurrection was not subdued. A sour and malignant temper was displayed, which indicated, too plainly, that the disposition to resist had sunk under the great military force brought into the country, but would rise again should that force be withdrawn. It was therefore thought advisable to station a detachment to be commanded by Major-General Morgan, in the centre of the disaffected country, for the winter.

Thus, without shedding a drop of blood, did the prudent vigor of the executive terminate an insurrection which, at one time, threatened to shake the government to its foundation. That so perverse a spirit should have been excited in the bosom of prosperity, without the pressure of a single grievance, is among those political phenomena which occur, not unfrequently, in the course of human affairs, and which the statesman can never safely disregard.

To the intemperate abuse which was cast on the measures of the government, and on all who supported them; to the violence with which the discontents of the opponents of those measures were expressed; and especially to the denunciations which were uttered against them by the democratic societies; the friends of the administration ascribed that criminal attempt which had been made to oppose the will of the nation by force. Had these misguided men believed that the opposition was confined within their own narrow limits, they could not have been so mad or so weak as to engage in it.

The ideas of the President on this subject were freely given to his confidential friends. "The *real people*," he said, "occasionally assembled in order to express their sentiments on political subjects, ought never to be confounded with permanent self-appointed societies usurping the right to control the constituted authorities, and to dictate to public opinion. While the former is entitled to respect, the latter is incompatible with all government, and must either sink into general disesteem, or finally overturn the established order of things."

In his speech at the opening of Congress, the President detailed the progress of opposition, and the measures finally taken to reduce the refractory to submission. After bestowing a high en-

---

When the army arrived in the disaffected district, what was the issue? Was it necessary to station a force there? To what may we attribute this daring attempt to subvert the government?

comium on the alacrity with which persons in every station had come forward to assert the dignity of the laws, he added, " but let them persevere in their affectionate vigilance over that precious deposit of American happiness—the constitution of the United States. And when in the calm moments of reflection, they shall have retraced the origin and progress of the insurrection, let them determine whether it has not been fomented by combinations of men who, careless of consequences, and disregarding the unerring truth that those who rouse cannot always appease a civil convulsion, have disseminated, from an ignorance or perversion of facts, suspicions, jealousies, and accusations of the whole government."

He mentioned the intelligence from the army, the state of Indian affairs, recommended a revisal of the militia system, and urged a definitive plan for the redemption of the public debt.

After referring to subsequent communications respecting the intercourse of the United States with foreign nations, he added, " it may not, however, be unreasonable to announce that my policy in our foreign transactions has been, to cultivate peace with all the world; to observe treaties with pure and inviolate faith; to check every deviation from the line of impartiality; to explain what may have been misapprehended, and correct what may have been injurious to any nation; and having thus acquired the right, to lose no time in acquiring the ability, to insist upon justice being done to ourselves."

An answer was reported in the Senate, containing a direct censure on the disorganizing proceedings of certain self-created societies, and an unequivocal approbation of the policy adopted by the executive with regard to foreign nations. To the latter, no objection was made. The clause respecting democratic societies was seriously opposed; but the address reported by the committee was agreed to without alteration.

The same spirit did not prevail in the House of Representatives. In that branch of the legislature, the opposition party continued to be the most powerful, and the respect of their leaders for the person and character of the Chief Magistrate was visibly diminishing. His interference with a favorite system was not forgotten; and the mission of Mr. Jay still rankled in their bosoms. No direct censure of the democratic societies, or approbation of the conduct of the administration towards foreign powers, could be carried.

This triumph over the administration revived for a moment the drooping energies of these pernicious societies. But it was only for a moment. The agency ascribed to them by the opinion of the

Specify the chief topics in the President's address to Congress. What answer was given by the Senate? Was the House of Representatives equally friendly to the administration?

public as well as of the President, in producing an insurrection which was generally execrated, had essentially affected them; and while languishing under this wound, they received a deadly blow from a quarter whence hostility was least expected.

The remnant of the French convention, rendered desperate by the ferocious despotism of the jacobins, and of the sanguinary tyrant who had become their chief, had at length sought for safety by confronting danger; and, succeeding in a desperate attempt to bring Robespierre to the guillotine, had terminated his reign of terror. The colossal power of the clubs fell with that of their favorite member, and they sunk into long-merited disgrace. Not more certain is it that the boldest streams must disappear if the fountains which fed them be emptied, than was the dissolution of the democratic societies in America, when the jacobin clubs were denounced in France. As if their destinies depended on the same thread, the political death of the former was the unerring signal for that of the latter.

Notwithstanding the disagreement between the President and one branch of the legislature, concerning self-created societies, and the policy observed towards foreign nations, his speech was treated with marked respect; and the several subjects which it recommended engaged the immediate attention of Congress.

He had repeatedly pressed on the legislature the adoption of measures which might effect the gradual redemption of the public debt; but, although that party which had been reproached with a desire to accumulate debt as a means of subverting the republican system, had exerted themselves to accomplish this object, their efforts had hitherto been opposed by obstacles they were unable to surmount. These were intrinsic difficulties in the subject.

The duty on imported articles and on tonnage could not, immediately, be rendered sufficiently productive to meet the various exigencies of the treasury, and yield a surplus for the secure establishment of a fund to redeem the principal of the debt. Additional sources of revenue were to be explored. New taxes are the never-failing sources of discontent. In a government where popularity is power, it requires no small degree of patriotism to encounter the odium which, however necessary, they seldom fail to excite. No clamour could deter the Secretary of the Treasury from continuing to recommend measures which he believed to be essential to the due administration of the finances. While the legislature was engaged in discussing a report made by a select committee on a resolution moved by Mr. Smith, of South Carolina, purporting that farther provision ought to be made for the reduction of the public debt, he addressed a letter to the House of Representatives, through their Speaker, informing them that he had digested and prepared a plan on the basis of the actual revenues, for the farther support of public credit, which he was ready to communicate.

This comprehensive and valuable report presented the result of his laborious and useful investigations, on a subject equally intricate and interesting.

It was the last official act of Colonel Hamilton. The penurious provision made for those who filled high offices in the executive departments, excluded from a long continuance in them, all men of moderate fortune, whose professional talents placed a decent independence within their reach. While slandered as the accumulator of thousands by illicit means, he had wasted in the public service a great part of the property acquired by his previous labors, and had found himself compelled to decide on retiring from political station. The accusations brought against him in the last session of the second Congress, had postponed the execution of this design, and subsequent events of a nature to render the continuance of peace precarious, deferred it still longer. On the first of December, on his return from the western country, the dangers of domestic insurrection or foreign war having subsided, he gave notice that he should, on the last day of January, give in his resignation.

Seldom has any minister excited the opposite passions of love and hate in a higher degree than Colonel Hamilton. His talents were too prominent not to receive the tribute of profound respect from all; and his integrity and honor as a man, not less than his official rectitude, though slandered at a distance, were admitted to be superior to reproach by those enemies who knew him.

But with respect to his political principles and designs, the most contradictory opinions were entertained. While one party sincerely believed his object to be the preservation of the Constitution of the United States in its purity; the other, with perhaps equal sincerity, imputed to him the insidious intention of subverting it. While his friends were persuaded that, as a statesman, he viewed foreign nations with an equal eye, his enemies could perceive in his conduct only hostility to France, and attachment to her rival.

In the good opinion of the President, to whom he was best known, he had always held a high place; and he carried with him out of office the same cordial esteem for his character, and respect for his talents, which had induced his appointment.

The vacant office was filled by Mr. Wolcott, of Connecticut, a gentleman of sound judgment, who was well versed in its duties.

What report was presented to Congress by Colonel Hamilton? Mention the cause which induced him to resign. Sketch his character. Who succeeded him in office?

The report of the select committee recommended additional objects for internal taxation, and that the temporary duties already imposed should be rendered permanent. The opposition was so ardent that the bill did not pass till late in February. At length, by the persevering exertions of the federal party, it was carried, and a system adopted which would discharge all the engagements of the United States.

On the 3d of March, this important session was ended. Although the party in opposition had obtained a small majority in one branch of the legislature, several circumstances had concurred to give great weight to the recommendations of the President. Among these, were the victory obtained by General Wayne, and the suppression of the western insurrection. In some points, however, which he had pressed with earnestness, his sentiments did not prevail. One of these was a plan for preserving peace with the Indians by protecting them from the intrusions of the whites. He had scarcely permitted a Congress to pass without calling their attention to this subject. It had been mentioned in his speech at the commencement of this session, and had been farther enforced by a message accompanying a report made upon it by the Secretary of War. The plan suggested in this report was, to add to those arrangements respecting trade which were indispensable to the preservation of peace, a chain of garrisoned posts within the territory of the Indians, provided their assent could be obtained; and to subject all trespassers on their lands to martial law. A bill founded on this report passed the Senate, but was lost in the House of Representatives.

This report preceded the resignation of the Secretary of War but a few days. This valuable officer, too, was driven from the service of the public by the scantiness of the compensation allowed him.

Colonel Pickering, a gentleman who had filled many important offices through the war of the revolution; who had discharged several trusts of confidence under the present government; and who, at the time, was Post-Master General, was appointed to succeed him.

On the 7th of March, the treaty of amity, commerce, and navigation, between the United States and Great Britain, which had been signed on the 19th of the preceding November, was received at the office of State.

From his arrival in London, Mr. Jay had been assiduously employed on the objects of his mission. By a deportment respectful, yet firm, this minister avoided those little asperities which frequently

Did Congress adopt a system for the extinction of the public debt? What other recommendations of Washington were complied with? Who succeeded the Secretary of War? What treaty was received?

embarrass measures of great concern, and smoothed the way to the adoption of those which were suggested by the real interests of both nations. Many and intricate were the points to be discussed. On some of them an agreement was found to be impracticable; but, at length, a treaty was concluded, which Mr. Jay declared to be the best that was attainable, and which he believed it to be for the interest of the United States to accept. Indeed it was scarcely possible to contemplate the evidence of extreme exasperation which was given in America, and the nature of the differences between the two countries, without feeling a conviction that war was inevitable should this attempt to adjust those differences prove unsuccessful.

On Monday, the 8th of June, the Senate, in conformity with a summons from the President, convened in the Senate chamber, and the treaty, with the documents connected with it, were submitted to their consideration.

On the 24th of the same month, after a minute and laborious investigation, the Senate, by precisely a constitutional majority, advised and consented to its conditional ratification.

In regulating the intercourse between the United States and the British West Indies, the parties intended to admit the direct trade, but not to permit the productions of the latter to be carried to Europe in the vessels of the former. To give effect to this intention, the exportations from the United States of those articles which were the principal productions of the islands, was to be prohibited. Among these was cotton. This article, which a few years before was scarcely raised in sufficient quantity for domestic consumption, was becoming one of the richest staples of the southern states. The Senate, being informed of this fact, which was unknown to Mr. Jay, advised and consented that the treaty should be ratified, on condition that an article be added thereto, suspending that part of the 12th article, which related to the intercourse with the West Indies.

This resolution of the Senate presented difficulties which required consideration. Whether they could advise and consent to an article which had not been laid before them, and whether their resolution was to be considered as the final exercise of their power, were questions not free from difficulty. Nor was it clear that the executive could ratify the treaty, under the advice of the Senate, until the suspending article should be introduced into it. When these doubts were removed, intelligence was received from Europe, which superseded the determination the President had formed.

What was the nature of the conditional ratification which the Senate gave to Jay's treaty with Great Britain? Mention the doubts which arose upon this subject.

The English papers contained an account that the order of the 8th of June, 1793, respecting provisions going to French ports, was renewed. In the apprehension that this order might be intended as a practical construction of the article which seemed to favor the idea that provisions might occasionally become contraband, a construction in which he had determined not to acquiesce, he thought it wise to reconsider his decision. A strong memorial against this objectionable order was directed; and the propositions to withhold the ratification of the treaty, until the same should be repealed—to make the exchange of ratifications dependent on that event, and to connect his ratification with the memorial, he had directed, as explanatory of the sense in which his ratification was made, were severally under consideration. In conformity with his practice of withholding his opinion on controverted points, until it should become necessary to decide them, he suspended his determination until the memorial should be prepared and laid before him. In the mean time, his private affairs required that he should visit Mount Vernon.

Meanwhile, the restless, uneasy temper of parties was active in its operations. That the instrument itself was not communicated to the public even previous to its being laid before the Senate, and that the Senate deliberated upon it with closed doors, were considered as additional evidences of the contempt in which their rulers held the people.

Although the contents of the treaty were unknown, a decisive judgment was extensively formed on any reconciliation between the two countries. The sentiments called forth by the occasion, demonstrated that no possible adjustment with Great Britain could be satisfactory. That a treaty of amity and commerce should have been concluded, whatever might be its principles, was said to be a degrading insult to the American people, a pusillanimous surrender of their honor, and an insidious injury to France.

Such was the state of parties, when the Senate advised the ratification of the treaty. In violation of common usage, and of a positive resolution of the Senate, an abstract of this instrument, not very faithfully taken, was given to the public; and, on the 29th of June, a senator of the United States transmitted a copy of it to the most distinguished editor of the opposition party in Philadelphia, for publication.

If amicable arrangement, whatever might be its character, had been previously condemned, it was not to be expected that the treaty would assuage the irritation. If the people at large enter keenly into the points of controversy with a foreign power, they

What order was renewed in England? What was the general temper of the people, in reference to any arrangement with Great Britain? Was an abstract of the treaty improperly published?

can seldom be satisfied with any equal adjustment of those points : nor will it be difficult, unless there be undue attachment to the adversary nation, to prove to them that they give too much, and receive too little. The operation of this principle was not confined to those whose passions urged them to take part in the war, nor to the open enemies of the executive. The friends of peace and of the administration had generally received impressions unfavorable to the fair exercise of judgment in the case, which it required time and reflection to efface. Even among them, strong prejudices had been imbibed in favor of France, which her open attempts on the sovereignty of the United States had only weakened.

The treaty, therefore, found one party prepared for an intrepid attack ; but the other not ready in its defence.

That an instrument involving many complicated national interests, and adjusting differences of long standing, would require a patient and laborious investigation before even those most conversant in diplomatic transactions could form a just estimate of its merits, would be conceded by all reflecting men. But an immense party in America, not in the habit of considering national compacts, without understanding the instrument, and in most instances without reading it, rushed impetuously to its condemnation ; and, confident that public opinion would be surprised by the suddenness, and stormed by the fury of the assault, expected that the President would be compelled to yield to its violence.

In the populous cities, meetings of the people were immediately summoned to take the instrument into consideration, and express their opinion of it. Those who distrusted their capacity to form intuitively a correct judgment on so complex a subject, and who were disposed to act knowingly, declined attending these meetings. The most intemperate assumed as usual the name of the people, pronounced an unqualified condemnation of every article in the treaty, and, with the utmost confidence, assigned reasons for their opinions which, in many instances, had no real existence, and in some, were obviously founded on their strong prejudices with regard to foreign powers.

The first meeting was held in Boston. The example was soon followed by New York, Philadelphia, Baltimore, and Charleston ; and, their addresses being designed at least as much for their fellow-citizens as for their President, while one copy was transmitted to him, another was committed to the press. The precedent set by these large cities was followed with wonderful rapidity throughout the Union ; and the spirit of violence sustained no diminution in its progress.

Mention the procedure of a large party in the United States, in reference to Jay's treaty. Were they well qualified to judge so difficult a matter ? Were they reasonable and temperate in examining the treaty ?

On the 18th of July, at Baltimore, on his way to Mount Vernon, the President received the resolutions passed at Boston, in a letter from the selectmen of that town. His answer evinced the firmness with which he had resolved to meet the effort that was obviously making to control the exercise of his constitutional functions, by giving promptness and vigor to the expressions of the sentiments of party, which might impose it on the world as the deliberate judgment of the public.

He viewed the opposition which the treaty was receiving in a very serious light:—" not because there was more weight in any of the objections than was foreseen; for in some, there was none; and in others, there were gross misrepresentations: nor as respected himself personally, for that should have no influence on his conduct." But he was alarmed on account of the effect it might have on France, and the advantage which the government of that country might be disposed to make of the spirit which was at work, to cherish a belief that the treaty was calculated to favor Great Britain at her expense. " Whether she believed or disbelieved these tales, their effect," he said, " would be nearly the same.

In the afternoon of the 11th of August, the President returned to Philadelphia; and, on the next day, the question respecting the immediate ratification of the treaty was laid before the cabinet. The Secretary of State maintained, singly, the opinion that, during the existence of the provision order, this step ought not to be taken. His opinion did not prevail. The resolution was adopted to ratify the treaty immediately, and to accompany its ratification with a strong memorial against the provision order, which should convey, in explicit terms, the sense of the American government on that subject. By this course, the views of the executive were happily accomplished. The order was revoked, and the ratifications of the treaty were exchanged.

The President was most probably determined to the immediate adoption of this measure by the extreme violence with which the treaty was opposed, and the rapid progress which this violence was making. It was obvious that, unless this temper could be checked, it would soon become so extensive, as to threaten dangerous consequences. It had become necessary either to attempt a diminution of its action by rendering its exertions hopeless, and by giving to the treaty the weight of his character and influence, or to yield to it.

The soundness of this policy was proved by the event. The confidence which was reposed in the judgment and virtue of the

What did Washington reply to the letter from the selectmen of Boston? Mention the decision of the President and his cabinet, on Jay's treaty? Did the event show that it was a wise one?

Chief Magistrate, induced many, who, swept away by the popular current, had yielded to the common prejudices, to re-examine and discard opinions which had been too hastily embraced; and many were induced to take a more active part in the general contest than they would otherwise have pursued. The consequence was, that more moderate opinions began to prevail.

If the ratification of the treaty increased the number of its open advocates, it also gave increased acrimony to the opposition.

Previous to the mission of Mr. Jay, charges against the Chief Magistrate, though frequently insinuated, had seldom been directly made. That mission visibly affected the decorum which had been usually observed towards him; and the ratification of the treaty brought sensations into open view, which had long been ill-concealed. His military and political character was attacked with equal violence; and it was averred that he was totally destitute of merit, either as a soldier or a statesman. The calumnies with which he was assailed were not confined to his public conduct; even his qualities as a man were the subjects of detraction. That he had violated the constitution in the treaty lately negotiated with Great Britain, was openly maintained, for which an impeachment was publicly suggested; and that he had drawn from the treasury for his private use, more than the salary annexed to his office, was asserted without a blush. This last allegation was said to be supported by extracts from the treasury accounts which had been laid before the legislature, and was maintained with the most persevering effrontery.

Though the Secretary of the Treasury denied officially in the papers, that the appropriations made by the legislature had ever been exceeded, the atrocious charge was still confidently repeated; and the few who could triumph in any spot which might tarnish the lustre of Washington's fame, felicitated themselves on the prospect of obtaining a victory over the reputation of a patriot to whose single influence they ascribed the failure of their political plans.

The confidence felt by the real public in the integrity of their Chief Magistrate, remained unshaken; but so imposing was the appearance of the documents adduced, as to excite an apprehension that the transaction might be placed in a light to show that some indiscretion in which he had not participated, had been inadvertently committed.

This state of anxious suspense was of short duration. The late Secretary of the Treasury, during whose administration of the finances this peculation was alleged to have taken place, came for-

Did Washington's ratification of the treaty increase the hostility of his political adversaries? What charges did they bring against him, and how were they satisfactorily explained?

30

ward with a full explanation of the fact. It appeared that the President himself had never touched any part of the compensation annexed to his office, but that the whole was received and disbursed by the gentleman who superintended the expenses of his household;—that it was the practice of the Treasury, when a sum had been appropriated for the current year, to pay it to that gentleman occasionally, as the situation of the family might require. The expenses at some periods of the year exceeded, and at others fell short of the allowance for the quarter; so that sometimes money was paid in advance for the ensuing quarter, and at others, that which was due at the end of the quarter was not completely drawn out; the Secretary entered into an examination of the constitution and laws to show that this practice was justifiable; and illustrated his arguments by many examples in which an advance on account of money appropriated to a particular object, before the service was completed, would be absolutely necessary. However this might be, it was a transaction in which the President, personally, was unconcerned.

When possessed of the entire fact, the public viewed with just indignation, this attempt to defame a character which was the nation's pride. Americans felt themselves involved in this atrocious calumny on their most illustrious citizen; and its propagators were frowned into silence.

The Secretary of State had resigned on the 19th of August, and, after some time, was succeeded by Colonel Pickering. Mr. M'Henry was appointed to the Department of War. By the death of Mr. Bradford, a vacancy was also produced in the office of Attorney-General, which was filled by Mr. Lee.

Many of those embarrassments in which the government had been involved from its institution, were now ended or approaching their termination.

The opposition to the laws in the western counties of Pennsylvania existed no longer.

A firm peace had been made with the north-western Indians; and an accommodation had taken place with the powerful tribes of the south.

After the failure of several attempts to purchase peace from the regency of Algiers, a treaty was at length negotiated on terms which, though disadvantageous, were the best that could be obtained.

The unwearied exertions of the executive to settle the controversy with Spain had at length been successful. That power, embarrassed by its war with France, had lately discovered symptoms of a temper more inclined to conciliation, and a treaty was concluded on the 20th of October, at Madrid, in which the claims of the United States on the important points of boundary, and the navigation of the Mississippi, were fully conceded.

Although the signature of the treaties with Spain and Algiers had not been officially announced, the intelligence was such as to enable the President, in his speech at the opening of Congress, to assure the legislature that those negotiations were in a train which promised a happy issue.

After expressing his gratification at the prosperous state of American affairs, the various favorable events which have been enumerated were detailed in a succinct statement, at the close of which he mentioned the treaty with Great Britain.

In the Senate, an address was reported which echoed back the sentiments of the speech.

In this House of Representatives, as in the last, the party in opposition to the administration had obtained the majority. This party was unanimously hostile to the treaty with Great Britain. The answer reported by the committee, contained a declaration that the confidence of his fellow-citizens in the Chief Magistrate remained undiminished.

On a motion to strike out this clause, it was averred that it asserted an untruth. It was not true, that the confidence of the people in the President was undiminished.

The friends of the administration opposed the motion with zeal, but were outnumbered; and, to avoid a direct vote, the address was recommitted, and two members were added to the committee, who so modified it as to avoid the exception.

Early in the month of January, the President transmitted a message to both Houses of Congress, accompanying certain communications from the French government, which were well calculated to cherish those ardent feelings that prevailed in the legislature.

It was the fortune of Mr. Monroe to reach Paris soon after the death of Robespierre. On his reception, which was in the convention, he delivered to the President of that body, with his credentials, two letters addressed by the Secretary of State to the committee of public safety.

So fervent were the sentiments expressed on this occasion, that the convention decreed that the flags of the two republics should be united, and suspended in its own hall. To evince the impression made by this act, Mr. Monroe presented to the convention the flag of the United States, which he prayed that body to accept as a proof of the sensibility with which his country received every mark of friendship from its ally.

On what occasion were the friends of the President outnumbered in the House of Representatives? Mention the proceedings of Mr. Monroe at Paris.

The committee of safety again addressed the legislature in terms adapted to that department of government which superintends its foreign intercourse. Mr. Adet, the successor of Mr. Fouchet, was the bearer of this letter, and also brought with him the colors of France, which he was directed to present to the United States. He announced them late in December; and the first day of the new year was named for their reception, when they were delivered to the President, with the letter directed to Congress.

In executing this duty, Mr. Adet addressed a speech to the President, which, in the glowing language of his country, represented France as struggling not only for her own liberty, but for that of the world.

To answer this speech was a task of some delicacy. It was necessary to express feelings adapted to the occasion, without implying sentiments respecting the belligerent powers, which the Chief Magistrate of a neutral country could not properly avow. The President, in his reply, kept both these objects in view.

The address of Mr. Adet, the answer of the President, the colors of France, and the letter from the committee of safety, were transmitted to Congress.

In the House of Representatives, a resolution was passed unanimously, requesting the President to make known to the representatives of the French republic the sincere and lively sensations which were excited by this honorable testimony of the existing sympathy and affection of the two republics.

In the Senate, a resolution passed expressing these sentiments to the President, unaccompanied with a request to communicate them to the government of France.

In February, the treaty with Great Britain was returned, ratified by his Britannic Majesty. The constitution having declared a treaty to be the supreme law of the land, the President announced it officially to the people in a proclamation requiring its observance by all persons; a copy of which was transmitted to each House on the 1st of March.

The party in opposition having openly denied the right of the President to negotiate a treaty of commerce, was not a little dissatisfied at his venturing to issue this proclamation before the sense of the House of Representatives had been declared on the obligation of the instrument.

On the 7th of March, Mr. Livingston moved a resolution requesting the President " to lay before the House a copy of the instructions to the minister of the United States who negotiated the treaty with the King of Great Britain, communicated by his mes-

Specify the communications from the French government, and the replies of the two Houses of Congress. Was Jay's treaty ratified by the British King? What resolution respecting it was moved in the House?

sage of the 1st of March, together with the correspondence and other documents relative to the said treaty.".

The debate on this resolution soon glided into an argument on the nature and extent of the treaty-making power. The opposition contended that the power to make treaties, if applicable to every object, conflicted with powers which were vested exclusively in Congress. That it must be so limited as not to touch these objects, or the assent and co-operation of the House of Representatives must be required to the validity of any compact, so far as it might comprehend them. A treaty, therefore, so far as it required an act of Congress to carry it into effect, had no obligatory force until the House of Representatives had acted on it. They were at liberty to withhold such law without incurring the imputation of violating any existing obligation, or of breaking the faith of the nation.

The debate was protracted until the 24th of March, when the resolution was carried by sixty-two to thirty-seven voices.

The situation in which this vote placed the President was peculiarly delicate. The popularity of a demand for information, the large majority by which that demand was supported, the additional force which a refusal to comply with it would give to suspicions already insinuated, that circumstances had occurred in the negotiation which the administration dared not expose, and that the President was separating himself from the representatives of the people, furnished motives not lightly to be overruled, for yielding to the request which had been made.

But these considerations were opposed by others which possess an irresistible influence over a mind resolved to pursue steadily the path of duty, however it may abound with thorns.

That the future diplomatic transactions of the government might be seriously affected by establishing the principle that the House of Representatives could demand as a right, the instructions given to a foreign minister, and all the papers connected with a negotiation, was too apparent to be unobserved. It was, too, a subject for serious reflection, that the information was asked for the avowed purpose of determining whether the House of Representatives would give effect to a public treaty, and that, in an elaborate debate, that House had claimed a right of interference in the formation of treaties, which, in his judgment, the constitution had denied them. The opinion of the President being completely formed on the course it became him to pursue, he returned an answer to the resolution which had been presented to him, in which, after detailing his reasons in an argument of great strength, he declined making the communications which had been required.

What opinions were declared, in the debate on this resolution? Did it pass the House? Did Washington comply with its requisitions?

30 *

The terms in which this decided, and it would seem unexpected, negative to the call for papers had been conveyed, appeared to break the last cord of that attachment which had theretofore bound some of the active leaders of the opposition to the President personally. Amidst all the irritations of party, a sincere respect and real affection for the Chief Magistrate, the remnant of former friendship, had still lingered in the bosoms of some who had engaged with ardor in the political contests of the day. If the last spark of this affection was not now extinguished, it was concealed under the more active passions of the moment.

A motion to refer the message of the President to a committee of the whole house was carried by a large majority. In committee, resolutions were moved by Mr. Blount of North Carolina, declaring the sense of the House respecting its own power on the subject of treaties. Those resolutions take a position less untenable than had been maintained in argument, and rather inexplicit on an essential part of the question.

In the course of the month of March, the treaties with his Catholic Majesty, and with the Dey of Algiers, were ratified by the President, and were laid before Congress. On the 13th of April, Mr. Sedgewic moved "that provision ought to be made by law for carrying into effect with good faith, the treaties lately concluded with the Dey and Regency of Algiers, the King of Great Britain, the King of Spain, and certain Indian tribes north-west of the Ohio."

This motion produced a warm altercation. After a discussion manifesting great irritation, the resolution was so amended as to declare that it was expedient to make provision by law for carrying into effect the treaty lately concluded with the King of Spain. The resolution, thus amended, was agreed to without a dissenting voice; and then similar resolutions passed respecting the treaties with Algiers, and with the Indians.

This business being dispatched, the treaty with Great Britain was brought before the House. The friends of that instrument urged an immediate decision of the question. They appeared to have entertained the opinion that the majority would not dare to encounter the immense responsibility of breaking that treaty without previously ascertaining that the great body of the people were willing to meet the consequences of the measure. But its opponents, though confident of their power to reject the resolution, called for its discussion.

The minority soon desisted from urging an immediate decision of the question; and the spacious field which was opened by the

Upon receiving the President's negative, what resolutions were passed? What other treaties were laid before Congress? and what resolutions were adopted respecting them? What treaty was now debated in full?

propositions before the House, was entered with equal avidity and confidence by both parties.

At no time have the members of the national legislature been stimulated to great exertions by stronger feelings than impelled them on this occasion. Never has a greater display been made of argument, of eloquence, and of passion, and never has a subject been discussed in which all classes of their fellow-citizens took a deeper interest. Those who supported the resolution, believed firmly that the faith of the nation was pledged, and that its honor, its character, and its constitution, depended on the vote about to be given. They also believed that the best interests of the United States required an observance of the compact as formed.

The opposite party was undoubtedly of opinion that the treaty contained stipulations really injurious to the United States. But no consideration appears to have had more influence than the apprehension that the amicable arrangements made with Great Britain, would seriously affect the future relations of the United States with France.

Might a conjecture be hazarded, it would be that, in the opinion of many intelligent men, the preservation of that real neutrality at which the executive had aimed, was impracticable; that America would probably be forced into the war; and that the possibility of a rupture with France, was a calamity too tremendous not to be avoided at every hazard.

As had been foreseen, this animated debate drew forth the real sentiments of the people. The whole country was agitated; meetings were again held throughout the United States; and the strength of parties was once more tried.

The fallacy of many objections to the treaty had been exposed, the odium originally excited against it had been diminished, and the belief that its violation must precipitate the nation into a war was almost universal. These considerations brought reflecting men into action; and the voice of the nation was pronounced unequivocally with the minority in the House of Representatives.

This manifestation of the public sentiment was decisive with Congress. On the 29th of April, the question was taken in committee of the whole, and was determined by the casting vote of the chairman in favor of making the necessary laws. The resolution was finally carried, fifty-one voting in the affirmative, and forty eight in the negative.

That necessity to which a part of the majority had reluctantly yielded, operated on no other subject.

So excessive had been the hostility of the opposition to a mari-

---

Was the debate vehement? What persuasions seemed to actuate each party? What was found to be the will of the people on the subject? What was the influence of this upon the House?

time force, that, even under the pressure of the Algerine war, the
bill providing a naval armament could not be carried through the
House without the insertion of a section suspending all proceedings
under the act, should that war be terminated. That event having
occurred, not a single frigate could be completed without further
authority from the legislature. Although no peace had been concluded with Tunis or Tripoli, it was with the utmost difficulty,
that a bill for the completion of three, instead of six frigates could
be carried.

To secure the complete execution of the system for the gradual
redemption of the public debt, it was believed that some additional
aid to the treasury would be required. The friends of the administration were in favor of extending the system of indirect internal
taxation. But those who wished power to change hands had
generally manifested a disposition to oblige those who exercised it
to resort to a system of revenue by which a greater degree of sensibility will always be excited. The indirect taxes proposed were
strongly resisted; and only that for augmenting the duty on carriages for pleasure was passed into a law.

On the 1st day of June, this long and interesting session was
terminated.

It may not be unacceptable to turn aside for a moment from this
view of the angry conflicts of party, and to look back to a transaction in which the movements of a feeling heart were disclosed.

No one of those foreigners who, during the war of the revolution, had engaged in the service of the United States, had embraced
their cause with so much enthusiasm, or had held so distinguished
a place in the affections of General Washington, as the Marquis
de Lafayette. For his friend while guiding the course of a revolution which fixed the anxious attention of the world, or while a
prisoner in Prussia, or in the dungeon of Olmutz, the President
manifested the same esteem, and felt the same solicitude. The
extreme jealousy however with which those who administered the
government of France as well as a large party in America,
watched his deportment towards all whom the ferocious despotism
of the jacobins had banished from their country, imposed upon
him the painful necessity of observing great circumspection in his
official conduct, on this delicate subject. A formal interposition in
favor of the virtuous and unfortunate victim of their fury would
have been unavailing. But the American ministers at foreign courts
were instructed to seize every fair occasion to express, unofficially,
the interest taken by the President in the fate of Lafayette. A
confidential person had been sent to Berlin to solicit his liberation;

Was the opposition party averse to a naval force? and to indirect taxation? Mention the manner in which Washington continued to manifest his
esteem and friendship towards Lafayette?

but before this message had reached his destination, the King of Prussia had delivered over his illustrious prisoner to the Emperor of Austria. Mr. Pinckney had been instructed not only to indicate the wishes of the President to the Austrian minister at London, but to endeavor unofficially to obtain the powerful mediation of Britain.

After being disappointed in these attempts, he addressed a private letter to the Emperor of Germany. How far it operated in mitigating immediately the rigor of Lafayette's confinement, or in obtaining his liberation, is unknown.

CHAPTER XXXIII.

Hostile measures of France.—Mr. Monroe recalled, and General Pinckney appointed to succeed him.—General Washington's valedictory address.—The minister of France endeavors to influence the election of President.—The President's speech to Congress. —He denies the authenticity of certain spurious letters, republished as his.— John Adams elected President, and Thomas Jefferson Vice-President.—General Washington retires to Mount Vernon.—Political situation of the United States.—The French government refuses to receive General Pinckney.—Congress convened.—President's speech.— Three envoys extraordinary deputed to France.— Their treatment.— The United States prepare for war.—General Washington appointed commander-in-chief. —His death—And character.

THE confidential friends of the President had long known his fixed purpose to retire from office at the end of his second term, and the people generally suspected it. Those who dreaded a change of system in changing the person of the chief magistrate, manifested an earnest desire to avoid this hazard. But his resolution was to be shaken only by the obvious approach of a perilous crisis, which, endangering the safety of the nation, would make it unworthy of his character, and incompatible with his principles, to retreat from its service. In the apprehension that the co-operation of external and internal causes might bring about such a crisis, he had yielded to the representations of those who urged him to leave himself master of his conduct, by withholding a public declaration of his intention, until the propriety of affording a reasonable time to fix on a successor should require its disclosure. "If," said Colonel Hamilton, in a letter of the 5th of July, "a storm gather, how can you retreat? This is a serious question."

The suspense produced by this silence seemed to redouble the efforts of those who laboured to rob the Chief Magistrate of the affection of the people, and to attach odium to his political system.

With what purpose did Washington write to the emperor of Germany? What was known as to the intentions of the President respecting his official station? Why did he refrain from a public declaration of his purpose?

As passion alone can contend successfully with passion, they still sought, in the hate which America bore to Britain, and in her love of France, for the most powerful means with which to eradicate her love of Washington. Amongst the numerous artifices employed to effect this object, was the publication of those queries which had been submitted by the President to his cabinet, previous to the arrival of Mr. Genet. This publication was intended to demonstrate the existence of a disposition in the Chief Magistrate, unfriendly to the French Republic. Some idea of the intemperance of the day may be formed from the conclusion of that number of a series of virulent essays in which these queries were inserted.

It is in these words :—" The foregoing queries were transmitted for consideration to the heads of departments, previously to a meeting to be held at the President's house. The text needs no commentary. It has stamped upon its front, in characters brazen enough for idolatry to comprehend, perfidy and ingratitude. To doubt, in such a case, was dishonorable, to proclaim those doubts, treachery. For the honor of the American character and of human nature, it is to be lamented that the records of the United States exhibit such a stupendous monument of degeneracy. It will almost require the authenticity of holy writ to persuade posterity that it is not a libel ingeniously contrived to injure the reputation of the savior of his country."

Of the numerous misrepresentations which were pressed upon the public, no one marked more strongly the depravity of that principle which justifies the means by the end, than the republication of forged letters, purporting to have been written by General Washington, in 1776.

They were originally published in 1777 ; and in them were interspersed, with domestic occurrences which might give them the semblance of verity, certain political sentiments favorable to Britain in the then existing contest.

But the fabricator of these papers missed his aims. In assigning the manner in which the possession of them was acquired, circumstances so notoriously untrue were stated, that at the time the meditated imposition deceived no person.

In the indefatigable search for testimony which might countenance the charge that the executive was hostile to France, and friendly to Britain, these letters were drawn from the oblivion into which they had sunk, and were republished as genuine. The silence with which the President treated this, as well as every other calumny, was construed into an acknowledgment of its

What remarks were made by the enemies of Washington, upon certain queries to his cabinet ? Mention another project to injure his reputation ? What was the general course of the President, in reference to such accusations ?

ιruth; and the malignant commentators on this spurious text
would not admit the possibility of its being apocryphal.

Those who labored incessantly to establish the favorite position
that the executive was under other than French influence, re-
viewed every act of the administration connected with its foreign
relations, and continued to censure every part of the system, with
extreme bitterness. No opinion which had been advanced by Mr.
Genet was too extravagant to be approved. The ardent patriot
cannot maintain the choicest rights of his country with more zeal
than was manifested in supporting all the claims of the French
Republic on the American government.

Whatever might be the real opinion of the Directory of France
on the validity of its charges against the United States, they were
too vehemently urged, and too powerfully espoused in America, to
be abandoned at Paris. If at any time they were in part relinquished, they were soon resumed.

In the anxiety which was felt by the President to come to full
and immediate explanation with the French Directory on the
treaty with Great Britain, the American minister at Paris had
been furnished, even before its ratification, and still more fully
afterwards, with ample materials for the justification of his government. But, misconceiving the views of the administration,
he reserved these representations until complaints should be made,
and omitted to urge them while the Directory was deliberating on
the course it should pursue. Meanwhile, his letters kept up the
alarm with regard to the dispositions of France; and intelligence
from the West Indies served to confirm it. The President received information that the special agents of the Directory in the
islands were about to issue orders for the capture of all American
vessels laden in whole or in part with provisions, and bound for
any port within the dominions of the British crown.

Knowing well that the intentions of the executive had been at
all times friendly to the French Republic, the President had relied
with confidence on early and candid communications for the removal of any prejudices or misconceptions. That the Directory
would be disappointed at the adjustment of those differences which
threatened to embroil the United States with Great Britain, could
not be doubted; but, as neither this adjustment, nor the arrangements connected with it, had furnished any real cause of complaint, he had cherished the hope that it would produce no serious
consequences, if the proper means of prevention should be applied
in time. He was therefore dissatisfied with delays which he had
not expected; and seems to have believed that they originated in

Was the President anxious to prevent any collision with the Directory of
France? What documents were forwarded to Mr. Monroe? Did he delay
presenting them? What was the purport of his letters?

a want of zeal to justify a measure which neither the minister himself, nor his political friends, had ever approved. To ensure an earnest and active representation of the true sentiments of the executive, the President was inclined to depute an envoy extraordinary for the particular purpose, who should be united with the actual minister; but an objection, drawn from the constitution, was suggested to the measure. It was doubted whether the President could, in the recess of the Senate, appoint a minister when no vacancy existed. From respect to this construction of the constitution, the resolution was taken to appoint a successor to Colonel Monroe. The choice of a person calculated for this mission, was not without its difficulty. While a disposition friendly to the administration was indispensable, it was desirable that the person employed should have given no umbrage to the French government.

After some deliberation, the President selected General Charles Cotesworth Pinckney, of South Carolina, for this critical and important service. In the early part of the French revolution, he had felt and expressed all the enthusiasm of his countrymen for the establishment of the republic; but, after the commencement of its contests with the United States, he stood aloof from both those political parties which divided America.

He was recommended to the President by an intimate knowledge of his worth; by a confidence in the sincerity of his personal attachment to the Chief Magistrate; by a conviction that his exertions to effect the objects of his mission would be ardent and sincere; and that, whatever might be his partialities for France, he possessed a high and delicate sense of national as well as individual honor, was jealous for the reputation of his country, and tenacious of its rights.

In July, immediately after the appointment of General Pinckney, letters were received from Colonel Monroe communicating the official complaints which had been made against the American government, in March, by Mr. de La Croix, the minister of exterior relations, with his answer to those complaints. He had effectually refuted the criminations of Mr. de La Croix; and the executive was satisfied with his answer. But the Directory had decided on their system; and it was not by reasoning that their decision was to be changed.

As the time for electing the Chief Magistrate approached, the anxiety of the public respecting the person in office seemed to increase. In states where the electors are chosen by the people, names of great political influence were offered for their approba-

Did the President resolve to recall Mr. Monroe from Paris? Who was appointed his successor? What communication was subsequently received from Mr. Monroe?

tion. The strong hold which Washington had taken of the affections of his countrymen, was, on this occasion, fully evinced. In districts where the opposition to his administration was most powerful, where all his measures were most loudly condemned, where those who approved his system possessed least influence, the men who appeared to control public opinion on every other subject, found themselves unable to move it on this. Even the most popular among the leaders of the opposition found themselves reduced to the necessity of surrendering their pretensions to a place in the electoral body, or of pledging themselves to vote for the actual President. The determination of his fellow-citizens had been unequivocally manifested, and it was believed to be apparent that the election would again be unanimous, when he announced his resolution to withdraw from the honors and the toils of office.

Having long contemplated this event, and having wished to terminate his political course with an act which might be, at the same time, suitable to his own character, and permanently useful to his country, he had prepared a valedictory address for the occasion, in which, with the solicitude of a person, who, in bidding a final adieu to his friends, leaves his affections and his anxieties for their welfare behind him, he had made a last effort to impress upon his countrymen those great political truths which had been the guides of his administration, and could alone, in his opinion, form a sure and solid basis, for the happiness, the independence, and the liberty of the United States. This interesting paper contains precepts to which the American statesman cannot too frequently recur.

The sentiments of veneration with which it was received were manifested in almost every part of the Union. Some of the state legislatures directed it to be inserted at large in their journals; and nearly all of them passed resolutions expressing their respect for the person of the President, their high sense of his exalted services, and the emotions with which they contemplated his retirement from office. Although the leaders of party might rejoice at this event, it produced solemn and anxious reflections in the great body even of those who belonged to the opposition.

The person in whom alone the voice of the people could be united, having declined a re-election, the two great parties brought forward their respective chiefs. Mr. John Adams and Mr. Thomas Pinckney were supported as President and Vice-President by the federalists; the whole force of the opposite party was exerted in favor of Mr. Jefferson.

Motives of vast influence were added, on this occasion, to those which usually impel men to a struggle to retain or acquire power.

Was it manifest that Washington would once more have been elected President, if he had been a candidate? Did he decline? What is said respecting his Farewell Address? Who were the candidates?

The continuance, or the change, not only of those principles on which the internal affairs of the United States had been administered, but of the conduct which had been observed towards foreign nations, was believed to depend on the choice of a Chief Magistrate.

In such a struggle, it was not to be expected that foreign powers could feel no concern. In November, on the eve of the election, while the parties were so balanced that neither scale could be perceived to preponderate, Mr. Adet addressed a letter to the Secretary of State, in which he recapitulated the numerous complaints which had been urged against the government, and reproached it, in terms of great asperity, with violating those treaties which had secured its independence, with ingratitude to France, and with partiality to England. These wrongs, which commenced with the "*insidious*" proclamation of neutrality, were said to be so aggravated by the treaty with Great Britain, that Mr. Adet announced the orders of the Directory to suspend his ministerial functions with the federal government. "But the cause," he added, "which has so long restrained the just resentment of the Executive Directory from bursting forth, now tempered its effects. The name of America, notwithstanding the wrongs of its government, still excited sweet sensations in the hearts of Frenchmen; and the Executive Directory wished not to break with a people whom they loved to salute with the appellation of friend." This suspension of his functions, therefore, was not to be regarded "as a rupture between France and the United States, but as a mark of just discontent which was to last until the government of the United States returned to sentiments and to measures more conformable to the interests of the alliance, and to the sworn friendship between the two nations." "Let your government return to itself," concluded Mr. Adet, "and you will still find in Frenchmen faithful friends, and generous allies."

As if to remove any possible doubt respecting the purpose for which this extraordinary letter was written, a copy was transmitted, on the day of its date, to a printer for publication.

This open and direct appeal of a foreign minister to the American people, in the critical moment of their election of a Chief Magistrate, did not effect its object. Reflecting men, even among those who had condemned the course of the administration, could not approve this interference in the internal affairs of the United States; and the opposite party resented it as an attempt to control the operations of the American people in the exercise of one of the highest acts of sovereignty, and to poison the fountain of their lib-

---

What extraordinary letter was addressed by the French minister to the American government? Quote some of its expressions. Did its publication answer the intended purpose?

erty and independence by mingling foreign intrigue with their elections.

On the 7th of December, the President, for the last time, met the national legislature in the Senate chamber. His address was comprehensive, temperate, and dignified. No personal consideration could restrain him from recommending those great national measures which he believed would be useful to his country, although open and extensive hostility had been avowed to them.

After presenting a full view of the situation of the United States, and the late transactions of the executive, he added, "To an active external commerce, the protection of a naval force is indispensable—this is manifest with regard to wars in which a state is itself a party—but besides this, it is in our own experience that the most sincere neutrality is not a sufficient guard against the depredations of nations at war. To secure respect to a neutral flag requires a naval force, organized and ready to vindicate it from insult or aggression—this may even prevent the necessity of going to war, by discouraging belligerent powers from committing such violations of the rights of the neutral party as may, first or last, leave no other option. From the best information I have been able to obtain, it would seem as if our trade to the Mediterranean, without a protecting force, will always be insecure, and our citizens exposed to the calamities from which numbers of them have but just been relieved."

The speech next proceeded earnestly to recommend the establishment of national works for manufacturing such articles as were necessary for the defence of the country; and also for an institution which should grow up under the patronage of the public, and be devoted to the improvement of agriculture. The advantages of a military academy, and of a national university, were also urged; and the necessity of augmenting the compensation to the officers of the United States, in various instances, was explicitly stated.

Adverting to the dissatisfaction which had been expressed by one of the great powers of Europe, the President said, "It is with much pain and deep regret I mention that circumstances of a very unwelcome nature have lately occurred. Our trade has suffered, and is suffering, extensive injuries in the West Indies, from the cruisers and agents of the French republic; and communications have been received from its minister here, which indicate the danger of a farther disturbance of our commerce by its authority."

After stating his constant and earnest endeavors to maintain cordial harmony, and a perfectly friendly understanding with that republic, and that his wish to maintain them remained unabated;

Mention the several recommendations of Washington in his last address to Congress; and specify, in particular, his remarks in regard to French aggression.

he added, "In pursuing this course, however, I cannot forget what is due to the character of our government, and nation; or to a full and entire confidence in the good sense, patriotism, self-respect, and fortitude of my countrymen."

After some other communications, the speech was concluded in the following terms:

"The situation in which I now stand, for the last time, in the midst of the representatives of the people of the United States, naturally recalls the period when the administration of the present form of government commenced; and I cannot omit the occasion to congratulate you and my country on the success of the experiment; nor to repeat my fervent supplications to the Supreme Ruler of the universe, and Sovereign Arbiter of nations, that his providential care may still be extended to the United States;—that the virtue and happiness of the people may be preserved; and that the government which they have instituted for their protection may be perpetual."

The answer of the Senate embraced the various topics of the speech, and approved all the sentiments it contained.

It expressed the ardent attachment of that body to their Chief Magistrate, and its conviction that much of the public prosperity was to be ascribed to the virtue, firmness, and talents of his administration. After expressing the deep and sincere regret with which the official ratification of his intention to retire from the public employments of his country was received, the address proceeds to say, "The most effectual consolation that can offer for the loss we are about to sustain, arises from the animating reflection that the influence of your example will extend to your successors, and the United States thus continue to enjoy an able, upright, and energetic administration."

In the House of Representatives, a committee of five had been appointed to prepare a respectful answer to the speech, three of whom were friends to the administration. Hoping that the disposition would be general to avow, in strong terms, their attachment to the person and character of the President, the committee united in reporting an answer which promised, in general terms, due attention to the various subjects recommended to their consideration, but was full and explicit in the expression of attachment to himself, and of approbation of his administration.

The unanimity which prevailed in the committee did not extend to the House.

After amplifying and strengthening the expressions of the report, which stated regret that any interruption should have taken

What was the nature of the Senate's answer to the President's speech? Mention the circumstances attending the reply of the House of Representatives.

place in the harmony which had subsisted between the United States and France, and modifying those which declared their hope for the restoration of that harmony, so as to avoid any implication that its rupture was exclusively ascribable to France, a motion was made by Mr. Giles to expunge all those paragraphs which expressed attachment to the person and character of the President, approbation of his administration, or regret at his retiring from office.

After a very animated debate, the motion to strike out was lost, and the answer was carried by a great majority.

Early in the session, the President communicated to Congress the copy of a letter addressed by the Secretary of State to General Pinckney, containing a minute and comprehensive detail of all the points of controversy which had arisen between the United States and France, and defending the measures which had been adopted by America, with a clearness and a strength of argument believed to be irresistible. The letter was intended to enable General Pinckney to remove from the government of France all impressions unfavorable to the fairness of intention which had influenced the conduct of the United States; and to efface from the bosoms of the great body of the American people, all those unjust and injurious suspicions which had been entertained against their own administration. Should its immediate operation on the executive of France disappoint his hopes, the President persuaded himself that he could not mistake its influence in America; and he felt the most entire conviction, that the accusations made by the French Directory against the United States would cease, with the evidence that these accusations were supported by a great portion of the American people.

The letter and its accompanying documents were communicated to the public; but, unfortunately, their effect at home was not such as had been expected, and they were, consequently, inoperative abroad.

The measures recommended by the President in his speech at the opening of the session were not adopted; and neither the debates in Congress, nor the party publications with which the nation continued to be agitated, furnished reasonable ground for hope that the political intemperance which had prevailed from the establishment of the republican form of government in France, was about to be succeeded by a more conciliatory spirit.

It was impossible for the President to be absolutely insensible to the bitter invectives and malignant calumnies of which he had long been the object. Yet in one instance only did he depart from the

What communication was prepared for the French government, and published in the United States? Was the design of it accomplished? Did the executive still experience much opposition?

31 *

rule he had prescribed for his conduct regarding them.   Appre
hending permanent injury from the republication of certain spurious letters which have been already noticed, he, on the day which
terminated his official character, addressed a letter to the Secretary
of State, declaring them to be forgeries, and stating the circumstances under which they were published.

In February the votes for the first and second magistrate were
opened and counted in the presence of both Houses; and the
highest number appearing in favor of Mr. Adams, and the second
in favor of Mr. Jefferson, the first was declared to be the President,
and the second the Vice-President of the United States, for four
years, to commence on the fourth day of the ensuing March.

After the solemnities of the occasion had been concluded, and
General Washington had paid those respectful compliments to his
successor which he believed to be equally due to the man and to
the office, he hastened to that real felicity which awaited him at
Mount Vernon.

The same marks of respect and affection which had on all great
occasions been manifested by his fellow-citizens, still attended him.
His endeavors to render his journey private were unavailing; and
the gentlemen of the country through which he passed, were still
ambitious of testifying their sentiments for the man who had, from
the birth of the republic, been deemed the first of the American
citizens.   Long after his retirement, he continued to receive addresses from legislative bodies, and various classes of citizens,
expressive of the high sense entertained of his services.

Notwithstanding the extraordinary popularity of the first President of the United States, scarcely has any important act of his
administration escaped the most bitter invective.

On the real wisdom of the system which he pursued, every
reader will decide for himself. Time will, in some measure, dissipate the prejudices and passions of the moment, and enable us to
view objects through a medium which represents them truly.

Without taking a full view of measures which were reprobated
by one party and applauded by the other, the reader may be requested to glance his eye at the situation of the United States in
1797, and to contrast it with their condition in 1788.

At home, a sound credit had been created; an immense floating
debt had been funded in a manner perfectly satisfactory to the creditors; an ample revenue had been provided; those difficulties
which a system of internal taxation, on its first introduction, is
doomed to encounter, were completely removed; and the authority
of government was firmly established. Funds for the gradual

Who were elected to the offices of President and Vice-President ? Whither
did Washington retire ?   Did the public affection attend and follow him in
his retirement.   What were the results of his administration ?

payment of the debt had been provided ; a considerable part of it had been actually discharged ; and that system which has operated its entire extinction, had been matured and adopted. The agricultural and commercial wealth of the nation had increased beyond all former example. The numerous tribes of warlike Indians, inhabiting those immense tracts which lie between the then cultivated country and the Mississippi, had been taught, by arms and by justice, to respect the United States, and to continue in peace. This desirable object having been accomplished, that humane system was established, for civilizing and furnishing them with those conveniences of life which improve their condition, and secure their attachment.

Abroad, the differences with Spain had been accommodated, and the free navigation of the Mississippi had been acquired, with the use of New Orleans as a place of deposit for three years, and afterwards, until some other equivalent place should be designated. Those causes of mutual exasperation which had threatened to involve the United States in war with the greatest maritime and commercial power in the world, had been removed ; and the military posts which had been occupied within their territory from their existence as a nation, had been evacuated. Treaties had been formed with Algiers and with Tripoli, and no captures appear to have been made by Tunis ; so that the Mediterranean was opened to American vessels.

This bright prospect was indeed shaded by the discontents of France. Those who have attended to the points of difference between the two nations, will assign the causes to which these discontents are to be ascribed, and will judge whether it was in the power of the President to have avoided them without surrendering the real independence of the nation, and the most invaluable of all rights,—the right of self-government.

Such was the situation of the United States at the close of Washington's administration. Their condition at its commencement will be recollected ; and the contrast is too striking not to be observed.

That this beneficial change in the affairs of America is to be ascribed exclusively to the wisdom which guided the national councils, will not be pretended. That many of the causes which produced it originated with the government, and that their successful operation was facilitated, if not secured by the system which was adopted, can scarcely be denied. To estimate that system correctly, their real influence must be allowed to those strong prejudices and turbulent passions with which it was assailed.

What was our condition, with reference to the Indian nations ? with respect to Spain, and the Barbary powers? Mention the drawback in the case of France. To what extent may the government have credit for the national prosperity ?

Accustomed in the early part of his life to agricultural pursuits, and possessing a real taste for them, General Washington was particularly well qualified to enjoy, in retirement, that tranquil felicity which he had anticipated. A large estate in the management and improvement of which he engaged with ardor, an extensive correspondence, and the society of men and books, gave employment to every hour, and furnished ground for the hope that the evening of a life which had been devoted to the service of the public, would be as serene as its midday had been brilliant.

But the designs of France were soon manifested in a form too unequivocal and too dangerous to admit of even seeming indifference to them.

The Executive Directory, after inspecting the letters of credence delivered by General Pinckney, announced to him their haughty determination "not to receive another minister from the United States, until after the redress of grievances demanded of the American government, which the French Republic had a right to expect from it." This message was succeeded first by indecorous verbal communications, and afterwards by a written mandate to quit the territories of the republic:

This act of hostility was accompanied with another equally unequivocal. On giving to the recalled minister his audience of leave, the President of the Directory addressed a speech to him, in which terms of outrage to the government were mingled with expressions of affection for the people, so as to demonstrate the expectation of ruling the former by their influence over the latter, too clearly to be misunderstood. To complete this system of hostility, American vessels were captured wherever found, and condemned as prizes.

On receiving the despatches which communicated this serious state of things, the President issued his proclamation, requiring Congress to meet on the 15th day of May. The firm and dignified speech delivered by the chief magistrate at the commencement of the session, exhibited that sensibility which a high-minded and real American might be expected to feel, when representing to the national legislature the great and unprovoked outrages of a foreign government. He declared, however, his purpose to institute a fresh attempt at negotiation, and to continue his utmost endeavors to promote an accommodation on terms compatible with the "rights, duties, interests, and honor of the nation." But, while he should be making these endeavors to adjust all differences with the French Republic, he earnestly recommended it to Congress to provide effectual measures of defence.

In what manner did France indicate hostile intentions towards the United States? On receiving intelligence of these insults, what measure was adopted by Mr. Adams?

To carry into effect the pacific dispositions avowed in the speech, three envoys extraordinary were appointed, at the head of whom General Pinckney was placed. Their instructions conformed to the public language of the President.

For a considerable time, no certain intelligence reached the United States respecting the negotiation at Paris. At length, in the winter of 1798, letters were received from the American envoys, indicating an unfavorable state of things; and in the spring, despatches arrived, announcing the total failure of the mission.

History will scarcely furnish the example of a nation, not absolutely degraded, which has received from a foreign power such open insult and undisguised contumely, as were, on this occasion, suffered by the United States, in the persons of their ministers.

It was insinuated that the American executive, by taking two of the three from that party which had supported the measures of their own government, had furnished just cause of umbrage. While the Directory, under slight pretexts, delayed to accredit them, they were assailed by persons exhibiting sufficient evidence of the source from which their powers were derived, who, in explicit terms, demanded money from the United States, as the condition which must precede, not only the reconciliation of America with France, but any negotiation on the differences between the two countries.

Though a decided negative was given to the demand made by these unofficial agents, they returned to the charge with wonderful perseverance, and used unwearied art to work upon the fears of the American ministers, for their country and for themselves. The immense power of France was painted in glowing colors; the humiliation of the house of Austria was stated, and the conquest of Britain was confidently anticipated. In the friendship of France alone, could America look for safety; and the fate of Venice was held up to warn her of the danger which awaited those who incurred the displeasure of the great republic. The ministers were assured that, if they believed their conduct would be approved in the United States, they were mistaken. The means which the Directory possessed in that country to excite odium against them were great, and would unquestionably be employed.

This degrading intercourse was at length terminated by the positive refusal of the envoys to hold any further communication with the persons employed in it.

Meanwhile, the Directory still refused to acknowledge the Ameri-

---

What mission was sent to France? Mention the particulars of their treatment by the Directory, and the humiliating conditions which were intimated as the price of friendship.

can ministers in their public character; and the Secretary of Exterior Relations, at unofficial visits, which they made him, renewed the demand for money which his agents had pressed unsuccessfully.

Finding the objections to their reception in an official character insurmountable, the envoys addressed a letter to the Minister of Exterior Relations, in which they entered at large into the explanations committed to them by their government, and illustrated, by a variety of facts, the uniform friendliness of its conduct to France. But the Directory counted too confidently on its influence in America, to desist from its course. Notwithstanding the failure of this effort, the envoys continued, with a passiveness which must search for its apology in their solicitude to demonstrate the real views of the French Republic—to employ the only means in their power to avert the rupture which was threatened.

During these transactions, occasion was repeatedly taken to insult the American government. Open war was waged by the cruisers of France on American commerce; and the flag of the United States was a sufficient justification for the capture and condemnation of any vessel over which it waved.

At length, when the demonstration had become complete, that the resolution of the American envoys was not less fixed than their conduct had been guarded and temperate, various attempts were made to induce two of them voluntarily to relinquish their station; on the failure of which, they were ordered to quit the territory of the republic. As if to aggravate this national insult, the third, who had been selected from the party friendly to France, was permitted to remain, and was invited to resume the discussions which had been interrupted.

The despatches communicating these events, were laid before Congress, and were ordered to be published. The indignation which they excited was warm and extensive. The attempt to degrade the United States into a tributary nation, was too obvious to be concealed; and the resentment produced, as well by this attempt as by the threats which accompanied it, was not confined to the federalists.

The disposition still existed, among the leaders of party, to justify France; but their efforts were, for the moment, unsuccessful; and it required the co-operation of other causes to re-establish the influence of those who made them.

Vigorous measures were adopted in Congress for retaliating the injuries which had been sustained, and for repelling those which were threatened. Among these was a regular army.

No sooner had a war become probable, than the eyes of all were directed to General Washington as the commander-in-chief. He alone could be seen at the head of a great military force without exciting jealousy; he alone could draw into public service, and arrange properly, the best military talents of the nation; and he more than any other could induce the utmost exertion of its physical strength.

Indignant at the unprovoked injuries which had been heaped upon the United States, and convinced that the conflict, should a war be really prosecuted by France with a view to conquest, would be extremely severe, and would require, on the part of America, a persevering exertion of all her force, he could not determine, should such a crisis arrive, to withhold those services which his country might demand.

In a letter of the 22d of June, respecting military preparations, the President said, "we must have your name, if you will in any case permit us to use it. There will be more efficacy in it than in many an army."

A letter from the Secretary of War concludes with asking, "May we flatter ourselves that in a crisis so awful and important, you will accept the command of all our armies? I hope you will, because you alone can unite all hearts and all hands, if it is possible that they can be united."

In his letter to the President, after stating his views of the crisis, and the reluctance with which he should once more appear in any public station, General Washington said, "In case of actual invasion by a formidable force, I should not intrench myself under the cover of age and retirement, if my services should be required by my country to assist in repelling it. And if there be good cause to expect such an event, which certainly must be better known to the government than to private citizens, delay in preparing for it may be dangerous, improper, and not to be justified by prudence." He could not, however, believe that France, when undeceived respecting the support she expected from the American people, would be so mad as to persist in waging unprovoked war against the United States.

To the Secretary of War he said, "the principle by which my conduct has been actuated through life would not suffer me, in any great emergency, to withhold any services I could render when required by my country;—especially in a case where its dearest rights are assailed by lawless ambition and intoxicated power, in contempt of every principle of justice, and in violation of solemn compact, and of laws which govern all civilized nations:—and

In the crisis with France, who was looked to as the fittest commander of our armies? What sentiments did Washington express, in a letter to the Secretary of War?

this, too, with the obvious intent to sow thick the seeds of dissension for the purpose of subjugating our government, and destroying our independence and happiness."

He proceeded to state the points on which his consent to take the command of the army must depend.

Before the reception of these letters, the President had nominated him to the chief command of all the armies raised or to be raised in the United States; and the Senate had unanimously advised and consented to his appointment.

In the letter announcing this appointment, of which the Secretary of War was the bearer, the President said, " My reasons for this measure will be too well known to need any explanation to the public. Every friend and every enemy of America will comprehend them at first blush. To you, sir, I owe all the apology I can make. The urgent necessity I am in of your advice and assistance, indeed of your conduct and direction of the war, is all I can urge, and that is sufficient justification to myself and the world I hope it will be so considered by yourself."

The communications of General Washington with the Secretary of War were unreserved. They resulted in his acceptance of the command of the army, on condition that he should be permitted to select those in whom he could place confidence for the highest places in it—especially for the military staff; and that he should not be called into service until the country should be actually invaded.

From this period General Washington intermingled the cares and attentions of office with his agricultural pursuits. His solicitude respecting the organization of an army which he might possibly be required to lead against the most formidable enemy in the world, was too strong to admit of his being inattentive to its arrangements. Yet he never did believe that an invasion of the United States would actually take place. His conviction that the hostile measures adopted by the Directory, originated in the opinion that those measures would overthrow the administration, and place power in the hands of those who had uniformly supported all the pretensions of the French republic, remained unshaken. As a necessary consequence of this conviction, he was persuaded that the indignation which these aggressions had excited would effect a change of system.

Events soon demonstrated the correctness of this opinion. Although America, supplicating peace, had been spurned with contempt; although the Executive Directory had rejected with insult her repeated prayers to be permitted to make explanations, and

On what conditions did Washington accept the command of the army ? Did he assist in its arrangement ? What was his opinion respecting the views of the French government, in its arrogant treatment of the United States ?

had haughtily demanded a concession of their arrogant and unfounded claims, or large pecuniary advances, as a preliminary to negotiation, America in arms was treated with some respect. Indirect-pacific overtures were made, and a willingness on the part of France to accommodate existing differences on reasonable terms, was communicated.

The President, truly solicitous to restore harmony between the two nations, caught at the overtures thus indirectly made, and again appointed three Envoys Extraordinary and Ministers Plenipotentiary to the French republic. These gentlemen found the government in the hands of a man who entered into negotiations with them which terminated in the amicable adjustment of differences.

General Washington did not live to witness the restoration of peace. On Friday, the 13th of December, while attending to some improvements on his estate, he was exposed to a light rain, by which his neck and hair became wet. Not apprehending danger from this circumstance, he passed the afternoon in the usual manner; but in the night was seized with an inflammatory affection of the wind-pipe. The disease commenced with a violent ague, accompanied with some pain in the upper and fore part of the throat, a sense of stricture in the same part, a cough, and a difficult deglutition, which were soon succeeded by fever, and a quick and laborious respiration.

Twelve or fourteen ounces of blood were taken from his arm, but he would not permit a messenger to be despatched for his family physician until the appearance of day. About eleven in the morning, Doctor Craik arrived; and, perceiving the extreme danger of the case, requested that two consulting physicians should be immediately sent for. The utmost exertions of medical skill were applied in vain. The powers of life were manifestly yielding to the force of the disorder; speaking became almost impracticable, respiration became more and more contracted and imperfect, until half-past eleven on Saturday night, when, retaining the full possession of his intellect, he expired without a struggle.

During the short period of his illness, he economised his time in arranging those few concerns which required his attention; and anticipated his approaching dissolution with every demonstration of that equanimity for which his life was so uniformly and singularly conspicuous.

The deep and wide-spreading grief occasioned by this melancholy event, assembled a great concourse of people for the purpose of paying the last tribute of respect to the first of Americans. His

What mission was sent to France? Were the difficulties adjusted? Mention the particulars of General Washington's last sickness, and death. What was the public feeling, upon this melancholy event?

body, attended by military honors, and the ceremonies of religion, was deposited in the family vault at Mount Vernon, on Wednesday the 28th of December.

At the seat of government, the intelligence of his death preceded that of his indisposition. On receiving it, both Houses of Congress adjourned. On the succeeding day, as soon as the orders were read, the House of Representatives passed several resolutions expressive of their deep feeling for the illustrious deceased, the last of which directed, "that a committee in conjunction with one from the Senate, be appointed to consider on the most suitable manner of paying honor to the memory of the MAN, first in war, first in peace, and first in the hearts of his fellow-citizens."

Immediately after the passage of these resolutions, a written message was received from the President accompanying a letter from Mr. Lear, which he said, "will inform you that it had pleased divine providence to remove from this life, our illustrious fellow-citizen GEORGE WASHINGTON, by the purity of his life, and a long series of services to his country, rendered illustrious through the world. It remains for an affectionate and grateful people, in whose hearts he can never die, to pay suitable honor to his memory."

The members of the House of Representatives waited on the President in pursuance of a resolution which had been passed, and the Senate addressed a letter to him condoling with him on the loss the nation had sustained, in terms expressing their deep sense of the worth of the deceased. The President reciprocated, in his communications to each House, the same deep-felt and affectionate respect "for the most illustrious and beloved personage America had ever produced."

The halls of both Houses were shrouded in black; and the members wore mourning for the residue of the session.

The joint committee which had been appointed to devise the mode by which the nation should express its feelings on this melancholy occasion, reported the following resolutions:

"That a marble monument be erected by the United States at the city of Washington, and that the family of General Washington be requested to permit his body to be deposited under it; and that the monument be so designed as to commemorate the great events of his military and political life.

"That there be a funeral procession from Congress Hall to the German Lutheran Church, in memory of General Washington, on Thursday the 26th instant, and that an oration be prepared at the request of Congress, to be delivered before both Houses on that day; and that the President of the Senate, and Speaker of the

---

Mention the proceedings of both Houses of Congress, upon receiving intelligence of Washington's death? Repeat the resolutions by which it was designed to honor his memory.

House of Representatives, be desired to request one of the members of Congress to prepare and deliver the same.

"That it be recommended to the people of the United States to wear crape on the left arm as a mourning for thirty days.

"That the President of the United States be requested to direct a copy of these resolutions to be transmitted to Mrs. Washington, assuring her of the profound respect Congress will ever bear to her person and character, of their condolence on the late affecting dispensation of Providence, and entreating her assent to the interment of the remains of General Washington in the manner expressed in the first resolution.

"That the President be requested to issue his proclamation, notifying to the people throughout the United States the recommendation contained in the third resolution."

These resolutions passed both Houses unanimously; and those which would admit of immediate execution were carried into effect. The whole nation appeared in mourning. The funeral procession was grand and solemn; and the eloquent oration, which was delivered by General Lee, was heard with profound attention and with deep interest.

Similar marks of affliction were exhibited throughout the United States. In every part of the continent funeral orations were delivered, and the best talents of the nation were devoted to an expression of its grief.

To the letter of the President which transmitted to Mrs. Washington the resolutions of Congress, that lady answered —"Taught by the great example which I have so long had before me, never to oppose my private wishes to the public will, I must consent to the request made by Congress, which you have had the goodness to transmit to me;—and in doing this, I need not, I cannot say what a sacrifice of individual feeling I make to a sense of public duty."

The monument, however, has not been erected. That the great events of the political as well as military life of General Washington should be commemorated, could not be pleasing to those who had condemned, and who continued to condemn, the whole course of his administration. This resolution, although it passed unanimously, had many enemies. That party which had long constituted the opposition, and which, though the minority for the moment, nearly divided the House of Representatives, declared its preference for the Equestrian statue which had been voted by Congress at the close of the war. The division between a statue and a monument was so nearly equal, that the session passed away without appropriation for either. The public feeling soon subsided, and those who quickly recovered their ascendency over the public sentiment, employed their influence to draw odium on the men who favored a monument; to represent that measure as a part of a general system to waste the public money; and to impress the idea that the only proper monument to the memory of a meritorious citizen was that which the people would erect in their affections: A man who professed an opinion in favor of the monument was soon branded with the mark of an anti-republican.

General Washington was rather above the common size. His frame was robust, and his constitution vigorous. His figure created in the beholder the idea of strength united with manly gracefulness.

His manners were rather reserved than free; though on all proper occasions he could relax sufficiently to show how highly he was gratified by the charms of conversation, and the pleasures of society. His person and whole deportment exhibited an unaffected and indescribable dignity, unmingled with haughtiness, of which all who approached him were sensible; and the attachment of those who possessed his friendship and enjoyed his intimacy, though ardent, was always respectful.

His temper was humane, benevolent, and conciliatory; but there was a quickness in his sensibility to any thing apparently offensive, which experience had taught him to watch and to correct.

In the management of his private affairs, he exhibited an exact yet liberal economy. His funds were not wasted on capricious and ill-examined schemes, nor refused to beneficial, though costly improvements. They remained, therefore, competent to that expensive establishment which his reputation, added to a hospitable temper, had, in some measure, imposed upon him; and to those donations which real distress has a right to claim from opulence.

He had no pretensions to that vivacity which fascinates, or to that wit which dazzles, and frequently imposes on the understanding. More solid than brilliant, judgment rather than genius constituted the prominent feature of his character.

Without making ostentatious professions of religion, he was a sincere believer in the Christian faith, and a truly devout man.

As a soldier, he was brave, enterprising, and cautious. That malignity which has sought to strip him of the higher qualities of a general, has conceded to him personal courage, and a firmness of resolution which danger could not appal, nor difficulties shake. But candor must allow him greater and higher endowments. If

Describe the person of General Washington,—his manners, deportment, and temper. How did he manage his private affairs? What were the characteristics of his mind? Was he a devout Christian? For what qualities did even his enemies award him credit? Had he higher endowments than these?

his military course does not abound with splendid achievements, it exhibits a series of judicious measures adapted to circumstances, which probably saved his country.

Placed, without having studied the theory, or being taught in the school of experience the practice of war, at the head of an undisciplined, ill-organized multitude, which was impatient of the restraints, and unacquainted with the ordinary duties of a camp, without the aid of officers possessing those lights which the commander-in-chief was yet to acquire, it would have been a miracle, indeed, had his conduct been absolutely faultless. But, possessing an energetic and distinguishing mind, on which the lessons of experience were never lost, his errors, if he committed any, were quickly repaired; and those measures which the state of things rendered advisable were seldom, if ever, neglected. Inferior to his adversary in the numbers, the equipment, and in the discipline of his troops, it is evidence of real merit that no decisive advantages were ever obtained over him, and that the opportunity to strike an important blow never passed away unused. He has been termed the American Fabius; but those who compare his actions with his means, will perceive as much of Marcellus as of Fabius in his character.

In his civil administration as in his military career, ample and repeated proofs were exhibited of that practical good sense, and of that sound judgment, which is perhaps the most rare, and is certainly the most valuable quality of the human mind. Devoting himself to the duties of his station, and pursuing no object distinct from the public good, he was accustomed to contemplate at a distance those situations in which the United States might probably be placed; and to digest, before the occasion required action, the line of conduct which it would be proper to observe. Taught to distrust first impressions, he sought all the information which was attainable, and heard, without prejudice, all the reasons which could be urged for or against particular measures. His judgment was suspended until it became necessary to determine; and his decisions, thus maturely made, were seldom, if ever, to be shaken. His conduct, therefore, was systematic, and the great objects of his administration were steadily pursued.

Respecting, as the first magistrate in a free government must ever do, the real and deliberate sentiments of the people, their gusts of passion passed over without ruffling the smooth surface of his mind. *Trusting to the reflecting good sense of the nation, he had the magnanimity to pursue its real interests in opposition

Under the disadvantages with which Washington had to contend in the war of the Revolution, what may fairly be considered as the true estimate of his military merit? Specify the principles on which he conducted his civil administration, and the system to which he uniformly adhered.

to its temporary prejudices; and, in more instances than one, we find him committing his whole popularity to hazard, and pursuing steadily the course dictated by a sense of duty, in opposition to a torrent which would have overwhelmed a man of ordinary firmness.

In speculation, he was a real republican, devoted to the constitution of his country, and to that system of equal political rights on which it is founded. But, between a balanced republic and democracy, the difference is like that between order and chaos. Real liberty, he thought, was to be preserved only by upholding the authority of the laws, and maintaining the energy of government. Scarcely did society present two characters which, in his opinion, less resembled each other than a patriot and a demagogue.

No man has ever appeared upon the theatre of human action whose integrity was more incorruptible, or whose principles were more perfectly free from the contamination of those selfish and unworthy passions which find their nourishment in the conflicts of party. His ends were always upright, and his means always pure. He exhibits the rare example of a politician to whom wiles were absolutely unknown. In him was fully exemplified the real distinction between wisdom and cunning, and the truth of the maxim that "honesty is the best policy."

Neither the extraordinary partiality of the American people, the extravagant praises which were bestowed upon him, nor the inveterate opposition and malignant calumnies which he encountered, had any visible influence on his conduct. The cause is to be looked for in the texture of his mind.

In him, that innate and unassuming modesty which adulation would have offended, which the voluntary plaudits of millions could not betray into indiscretion, and which never obtruded upon others his claims to superior consideration, was happily blended with a high and correct sense of personal dignity, and with a just consciousness of that respect which is due to station. Without exertion, he could maintain the happy medium between that arrogance which wounds, and that facility which allows the office to be degraded in the person who fills it.

It is impossible to contemplate the great events which have occurred in the United States, under the auspices of Washington, without ascribing them, in some measure, to him. If we ask the causes of the prosperous issue of a war against the successful termination of which there were so many probabilities,—of the good

---

Mention the requisite, in Washington's opinion, to the possession of true liberty. Repeat the lofty encomium upon the stainless integrity of Washington. What rendered him so self-poised and collected, in every circumstance? May not the successful issue of the contest for independence, be attributed in a measure to Washington?

which was produced, and the ill which was avoided during an administration fated to contend with the strongest prejudices that a combination of circumstances and of passions could produce? of the constant favor of the great mass of his fellow-citizens, and of the confidence which to the last moment of his life they reposed in him?—the answer will furnish a lesson well meriting the attention of those who are candidates for political fame.

Endowed by nature with a sound judgment, and an accurate discriminating mind, he feared not that laborious attention which made him perfectly master of those subjects on which he was to decide; and this essential quality was guided by an unvarying sense of moral right which would tolerate the employment of those means only that would bear the most rigid examination; by a fairness of intention which neither sought nor required diguise; and by a purity of virtue which was not only untainted, but unsuspected.

Mention the qualifications which enabled Washington fully to understand the questions submitted for his consideration. And by what principles was this perception guided?

THE END.